Labor in American Politics

LABOR
in AMERICAN
POLITICS

J. David Greenstone
University of Chicago

ALFRED · A · KNOPF

New York

THIS IS A BORZOI BOOK
PUBLISHED BY ALFRED A. KNOPF, INC.

First Printing

© *Copyright, 1969 by Alfred A. Knopf, Inc.*
All rights reserved under International and Pan-American
Copyright Conventions. Published in the United States by
Alfred A. Knopf, Inc., New York, and simultaneously in Canada

by Random House of Canada Limited, Toronto.
Distributed by Random House, Inc., New York.

Library of Congress Catalog Card Number: 68–24675

Manufactured in the United States of America

Epigraph from "The United States: The Functional Approach to Party
Government," by E. E. Schattschneider, in *Modern Political Parties,*
edited by Sigmund Neuman, is reprinted by permission of
The University of Chicago Press. Copyright © 1956 by The University
of Chicago.

Epigraph from *Class and Class Conflict in Industrial Society*
by Ralf Dahrendorf is reprinted by permission of Stanford University
Press, Stanford, California, 1959.

To My Parents

. . . a shift in the locus of power or a revision of party functions may leave the formal structure untouched, or new structures may arise without being recognized as parts of the party system. Thus pressure groups may become so partisan that they might properly be described as ancillary organizations of one or the other of the major parties.

E. E. SCHATTSCHNEIDER, "The United States: The Functional Approach to Party Government," in Sigmund Neuman (ed.), *Modern Political Parties,* p. 213.

Wherever Marx used the concept [of class] in a sociological sense, he was not concerned with describing an existing state of society. He was concerned, rather, with the analysis of certain laws of social development and of the forces involved in this development. To use the misleading terms of modern sociology, the heuristic purpose of the concept of class was for Marx not "static" but "dynamic," not "descriptive" but "analytical." . . . The theory of class was not a theory of a cross-section of society arrested in time, in particular not a theory of social stratification, but a tool for the explanation of changes in total societies.

RALF DAHRENDORF, *Class and Class Conflict in Industrial Society,* p. 19.

Preface

My greatest debt in this study of labor political action is to the men and women of organized labor in Detroit, Chicago, Los Angeles, and union headquarters in Washington, D.C. Their willingness to discuss their political activities and aspirations made this research possible. I owe a debt almost as great to other participants in the congressional process in Washington, D.C., and in the political life of Detroit, Chicago, and Los Angeles; principally, but not exclusively, to leaders in the Democratic party who discussed their relations to labor activities. Because all my informants were assured that they would not be identified in any way, I can now only express my gratitude for their cooperation.

It is a pleasure to record the many other individuals and organizations without whom this volume would have been impossible, although none bears the responsibility for the book's errors. Beginning in 1962, several sources provided indispensable financial support, including the Falk Foundation through its fellowship program in American politics at the University of Chicago, the Brookings Institution where I held a dissertation fellowship in 1962–1963, and the Social Science Research Committee of the University of Chicago. In addition I received Ford Foundation funds for faculty research in industrial relations, which were made available by the Graduate School of Business of the University of Chicago.

I am indebted to Derek Bok, John Dunlop, Fred Hoehler, Fred Jaher, Kent Jennings, John Laslett, Duncan MacRae, John Moore, Robert Packenham, Paul Peterson, Nelson W. Polsby, H. Douglas Price, C. Herman Pritchett, Randall B. Ripley, Lawrence Rogin, Donald Rothchild, Alan Seltzer, Leo Snowiss, and James Q. Wilson for their comments on portions of earlier drafts of the manuscript. I have profited from useful and stimulating conversations with Henry Bienen, Richard Flathman, Nathan Leites, and Theodore J. Lowi. Two of my students, Isaac Balbus and Ronald Kahn, provided the searching criticisms typical of graduate students. Mrs. Margaret Boies, Mrs. Millicent Markson, and Mrs. Billie Paige have been extraordinarily patient and helpful in the preparation of the manuscript. I should also like to thank Judith Brachman, Erika Fromm, Tina Lo Proto, and Vera Sky.

Two colleagues, Grant McConnell and Michael Rogin, have directly and continuously shaped the entire perspective and argument of the manuscript for the last five years. Their specific contributions were legion. Finally, I wish to thank my wife not only for her patience and understanding but also for her perceptive criticisms, which led me to remove countless confusions and obscurities from the manuscript.

J. D. G.

Contents

Contents

Introduction

Formal organizations, in particular their "active minorities,"[1] have increasingly dominated national politics in the United States for at least three generations. This study focuses on the activities and origins of one such organizational elite, the officers and leaders of the American Federation of Labor–Congress of Industrial Organizations (AFL-CIO), its constituent local and state federations, and its national and international union affiliates. Thus the title "labor in American politics" primarily refers to the activity of American trade union organizations in national electoral politics. This study, then, does not concentrate on the voting behavior of rank and file union members and their families, but on how their unions have attempted to organize election campaign work, how labor officials recruit their most politicized rank and file members into that activity, and what these members do. The most relevant survey data do indicate that where union campaign organizations have been strongest, specifically in Detroit, union members operating within the Democratic party have favorably affected the turnout rates of Democratically inclined voters.[2] Limited resources, however, unfortunately made it impractical to undertake the extensive survey research necessary to determine the effectiveness of this activity in terms of changing specific voter decisions. My primary concern is instead to describe the organizational patterns such activity took, to explain these patterns in terms of relevant economic, social, and political variables, and to indicate the organizational consequences which these patterns have had through the mid-1960s for the unions and the party system. This organizational analysis, however, corroborates Harry Scoble's systematic review of labor's financial role in political campaigns and of the voting behavior of union members.[3]

Scoble's review and my own findings indicate that the emergence of organized labor as a major, nationwide electoral organization of the national Democratic party represents the most important change in the *structure* of the American party system during the last quarter century. The consequences of this change for the usual distinction between political parties and pressure groups and for the common pluralist interpretation of American politics are considered at length in the chapters that follow. These chapters also emphasize that labor's relationship with the Democratic party is more significant for industrial unions and labor union federations (including the AFL-CIO itself) than for nonfactory unions; that the alliance has more appeal for unions formerly in the CIO than unions once affiliated with the AFL; and that it is more important in urban than in rural areas, particularly in the South. Trade unions are also more Democratically oriented in national politics than in state politics and are least Democratically inclined at the local level. AFL-CIO unions have endorsed a few Republicans in congressional and gubernatorial elections, more in state legislative contests, and still more in elections for local office. Finally, this description of labor's entry into the national party system as a Democratic campaign organization is most fully applicable to the first half of the 1960s. Despite important historical precursors, it was during the first six years of the Kennedy-Johnson administrations that this working relationship reached a peak. At this writing (1968), the alliance appears likely to continue for some time. But it faces both short- and long-run difficulties (e.g., the break between the United Automobile Workers and the AFL-CIO, the relative decline of the number of industrial workers caused by automation, and the racial divisions emphasized by the 1968 Presidential campaign of George Wallace). On the other hand, the substantial influence of union leaders in securing the nomination of Hubert Humphrey and persuading so many potential Wallaceites among their members to vote Democratic in November indicates that as of 1968 the union-party alliance retained much of its importance.

But whatever its historical durability, the largest economic interest group's assumption of many vital activities ordinarily undertaken by or attributed to our largest political party raises important analytic questions concerning the relationship between economic, social, and political life. These questions, in turn, form the most persistent analytic theme of the entire study.

The focus on organized labor's place in the national party

system also determined the shape and scope of the research reported here. I have concentrated on the actions of those unions that work through the AFL-CIO's Committee on Political Education (COPE); the campaign work of individual AFL-CIO affiliates, which often work independently of COPE; and some activities of COPE's predecessor organizations before the AFL-CIO merger. Other groups, for example, the Teamsters, the railroad unions, and the Postal Clerks, and other phases of labor political activity, notably the entire area of lobbying in local politics, have been largely excluded. This older and still very important pluralist phase of union political activity in which unions seek specific goals for their organizations and members on all government levels is only discussed (as it is in Chapters I, III, and X) where it is relevant to the analysis of political national campaign activities.[4]

The central portion of this study, Chapters III through IX, is based on intensive field research during 1962 with two to three months spent in each of three of our largest cities, Detroit, Chicago, and Los Angeles, including the suburban areas of Wayne, Cook, and Los Angeles counties respectively. As already suggested, I focused on such campaign activities as door-to-door contacts, mailings, and telephone and newspaper publicity.[5] The bulk of the field research consisted of interviews that covered all the relevant major events for a two- to four-year period before 1962. Supplementary data was later obtained on the most important developments from 1962 to 1965.

The over 300 informants who provided the data for this analysis were mainly labor officials, rank and file members active in politics, and their Democratic allies. The informants were selected to cover every major type of union in the AFL-CIO and all congressional districts in the three counties where labor was active or where Democrats were not hopelessly outnumbered by Republicans. Each interview was directed toward questions of process and structure, i.e., the interaction between union members and other Democrats, over a period of from two to four years, long enough to reveal characteristic patterns of behavior. The goal was not primarily to investigate the political consciousness or Democratic partisanship of any given proportion of union members—questions already covered by survey research. In any case this political orientation could not be directly attributed to labor's political action programs. As a member of an active, internally differentiated organizational elite, each respondent was instead questioned about his unique perspective on the stream of behavior encompassed by political action, and few, if any, interviews were identical. Although this technique made any significant quantification difficult, as a practical matter, the variation in labor activities between cities was so great that the description of each appears to represent intercity differences accurately. Replication, verification, or disconfirmation of these findings should, therefore, be possible as labor activities are studied in other cities.

Obviously, three metropolitan areas cannot provide a wholly comprehensive or representative picture of labor's campaign efforts, particularly in smaller cities and towns, especially in the South. The patterns analyzed here, particularly those discovered in Los Angeles, may begin to emerge in the South, but only if the Democratic party continues its present effort toward building a liberal coalition of blacks and lower-income whites. The metropolitanization of the United States continues unabated, however, and labor's own strength is concentrated in these urban centers. And, as Nicholas Masters puts it, labor's "support is desired [by Democratic candidates and leaders] not because union political activists control a large block of votes which they can swing one way or another—they have never had this kind of control—but rather because they may be able to affect the *size of the urban majorities* for the Democratic Party."[6]

Fortunately, the three areas studied ran the gamut of most labor–Democratic party relationships in metropolitan areas. As Chapters III, IV, and V show, Chicago represents a polar case. Severe limitations are placed on labor activity and influence by strong and suspicious regular party organizations. Detroit represents the opposite case—extensive labor activity and influence. In several respects, the level of Los Angeles union activity is at a midpoint between Chicago and Detroit levels. These differences may be explained by the fact that the three cities vary widely along several critical dimensions that affect political action. In terms of labor history, Los Angeles is the largest American city with a vigorous and tenacious open-shop tradition. Detroit has the strongest current tradition of political participation by a powerful industrial union. Chicago has one of the most firmly entrenched groups of politically conservative and cautious unionists in the country. In terms of economic structure, Detroit is dominated by the automobile industy; Chicago has a variety of manufacturing industries; whereas Los Angeles has a relatively smaller concentration of heavy industry. The relative strength of the industrial unions formerly associated with the CIO varies accordingly. In terms of party structure, whereas Detroit and especially Los Angeles have very weak party organizations, the regular Democratic party in Chicago has been the strongest in any large city for at least a generation. Finally, in terms of political demography, Detroit and Chicago typify the ethnic minority-group politics of relatively stable industrial centers in the East and Midwest. Los Angeles, on the other hand, has the relatively high population growth, low density, high residential mobility, and lack of ethnic consciousness typical of Southern and Western cities.

In Chapters VI through IX, labor's activities in these three cities are analyzed on a systematic comparative basis. Chapters VI and VII specify the conditions that encourage or limit political action. These factors include the structures and political incentives in the unions themselves and the economic, social, and political environments in different congressional districts. The next two chapters examine the consequences of these campaign activities. In Chapter VIII labor is viewed as a factional group carrying out activities (or functions) normally undertaken by the Democratic party and influencing party decisions. Chapter IX explicitly suggests some consequences that labor's alliance with the Democratic party has had for relations between the party and pressure groups and the ways political scientists conceptualize these relations.

The seven chapters on the Chicago, Detroit, and Los Angeles areas are preceded by two chapters that attempt to place contemporary labor political action in its historical context. In these chapters, I have relied largely on secondary sources because my major goal is to reinterpret labor political history by linking it explicitly with the most important changes in American voting behavior and party alignments during this century. Given the AFL-CIO's reformist rather than radical orientation, the historical review focuses on such conventional, or at least nonradical, organizations as the Knights of Labor, the AFL, and the CIO.

Chapter X, which is based on interviews in May 1965, examines labor's coalition with the party in an explicitly national setting, Congress, where the payoff from labor's efforts in the congressional districts can be most clearly examined. The final chapter summarizes my findings concerning labor's campaign activities. It then turns to the broader question of class cleavage and ongoing political change in a highly industrialized democracy such as the United States. Since World War II, class conflict between American workers and employers has evidently given way to a new class cleavage—between producers and consumers. Producers seek greater economic efficiency, profitability, and growth through the rationalization of production. Consumers, on occasion led by organized labor, insist on protecting the quality of life—as expressed by individual and collective patterns of consumption—against the dislocations that this economic rationalization can impose. Consistent with my continuing focus on economy and polity, the chapter concludes by suggesting that, as a class, consumers are particularly dependent on political organizations such as parties for their initiative, unity, and program. Given the unions' at least potentially prominent place in consumer class politics, this observation reinforces my basic interpretation of American labor politics: However much it primarily appeals to economic interests in recruiting its members, the American labor movement has increasingly come to act in national politics less as an economic interest group than as an integral part of one of our two major political parties.

Labor in American Politics

I

The Pluralist Period:
The AFL Until the New Deal

Marx developed so forceful and penetrating an interpretation of working-class politics under capitalism that his categories continue to affect our political and scholarly discourse. Even in the 1960s, such terms as "proletariat," "consciousness," "ideology," and even "working class" retain ideological, radical, anticapitalist connotations. The Marxist impact on our political vocabulary has had unfortunate consequences for the analysis of union political behavior in the United States. Most American unions have always vigorously rejected even the most moderate socialist doctrines. Many American scholars have reacted to this distaste for socialism by maintaining a pluralist group-politics interpretation of American labor politics. But in the 1960s pluralism explains the behavior of American organized labor with respect to either national elections or to the important welfare-state issue no better than Marxism. The increasing moderation of most contemporary European trade unions hardly confirms Marx's socialist prophecies, of course, even in those countries from which he drew the evidence for his analysis. But it is equally true that, as many European unions lose their socialist militancy, American unions have increasingly, though still far from completely, come to resemble them on at least two counts. In the policy process, the American labor movement supports the continuous expansion of welfare-state measures. In national electoral politics, the unions have assumed many of the functions of the political campaign apparatus for the Democrats, the dominant party in the United States since 1930.

A decline in industrial employment together with the emergence of more liberal Republican candidates may someday reduce labor's partisan activity on behalf of the Democrats. Nevertheless, the American labor movement's political development through the mid-1960s remains important if we are to gain a theoretical understanding of the range of possible relationships between American parties and pressure groups and of the connection between political and social change. Significantly, labor's partisan campaign role emerged in conjunction with a political revolution that produced a class or at least an income-group partisan alignment resembling that of many Western European nations.[1] As a result, although this study focuses on an organizational elite of paid union officials, elected local union officers, and the small proportion of politically active union members, the efforts of these groups to elect mainly Democratic candidates have been paralleled in the voting behavior of union members. V. O. Key's reanalysis of 1936 to 1948 survey data, for example, showed a high correlation between prounion issue attitudes and Democratic partisanship.[2] The authors of *The American Voter* confirmed earlier findings of Democratic leanings among AFL union members and suggested that there was (by a relatively constant margin of about 10 percent) a still stronger Democratic preference in the industrial unions formerly in the CIO. Their analysis showed that these party affiliations reflected the intensity of the union's own efforts to activate their rank and file politically.[3]

The Group Interpretation of Labor
in American Politics

These facts may conform to Marx's prophecy but they hardly validate it. His analysis did not primarily concern worker and union support in a capitalist system for welfare programs that constituted only "immediate demands" short of socialism. For Marx, the decisive questions were instead the workers' passions, beliefs, and self-consciousness as manifested by their loyalty to their own specifically socialist and working-class organizations. American and European labor politics have always differed from the Marxist expectation. American unions have only infrequently represented class-conscious workers loyal to their own at least formally socialist party. Instead, they have traditionally acted as much more narrowly based economic interest groups that displayed no recognition of a historical mission to end capitalism. Given these inadequacies of the Marxist analysis, pluralism has seemed to many a highly attractive alternative explanation.

As a social theory, pluralism refers to the overlapping social-group memberships that supposedly prevent any one group from pursuing extremist goals that would threaten the entire regime. In this discussion, however, the term "pluralism" will primarily refer to a *political* pattern of behavior in which the major actors are self-interested groups, representing relatively narrow and usually homogeneous constituencies. Because these groups' political demands are relatively limited, the major parties try to build alliances on particular issues with as many interests as possible, rather than make broad programmatic commitments that might alienate possible supporters. The pressure groups tend to move between the parties, bargaining for the best arrangement.

As we shall see, this pluralist pattern did dominate trade-union politics until the New Deal, and it cannot be too strongly emphasized that it persists in most local communities and in many state political systems. A number of traditional unions with highly skilled members have adhered to this pluralist tradition even in national politics with considerable success, although their activities are not the main concern of this study. The central thesis of this book concerns instead the emergence particularly at the state and national levels of the American Federation of Labor–Congress of Industrial Organizations (AFL-CIO) as a Democratic party campaign organization. This partisan involvement cannot be reconciled with pluralism because it has taken from the labor movement much of its freedom to bargain with each of the major parties. In addition, the union's effective *political* constituency in national politics has been widened far beyond that anticipated by pluralist theory and now includes most of the welfare-state oriented supporters of the Northern Democratic party.

A pluralist interpretation has, nevertheless, proved so persuasive that it is accepted by radical and even Marxist critics who are dissatisfied with American labor's political activities. Marc Karson points out organized labor's Democratic party and welfare-state inclinations, but concludes, "The top men running America's unions are called labor leaders, but . . . politically they follow the methods of the pressure groups."[4] According to Paul Jacobs:

> In Israel, in the Scandanavian countries, in England and in many other foreign lands unions are an integral part of the political system, not onlookers as they are in America, where the simplistic AFL tradition of rewarding friends and punishing enemies in the political arena is still dominant.[5]

In the late 1940s, C. Wright Mills described the CIO's Political Action Committee (PAC) as "an appendage of the Democrats," but still argued that the New Deal "left no durable instrument for liberal, much less radical activity . . . its effect on the political development of labor in America was essentially to put it aside."[6] American labor leaders viewed politics "as a pluralist system of interests which balanced each other in shifting compromise."[7]

As this study will attempt to demonstrate, however, the radical critique of American unions since the New Deal as simply pluralist is fatally overstated despite the AFL's and CIO's undeniable opposition to socialism. In their support of the Democrats as a mass pro-welfare-state party, American trade unions have forged a political coalition with important—although hardly complete—structural and behavioral similarities to the socialist party–trade union alliances in

Western Europe. The radical critics have made the valid point that the New Deal, which forged the contemporary alliance of the Democratic party and the American unions, advocated modest reforms rather than spurred the working class on to social revolution. These reforms were significant enough to help the working class adjust to, rather than overthrow, the existing system of corporate capitalism, as much of the data and interpretations offered here will show. I would only add that the social democratic parties of Western Europe have been similarly—although not identically—conservative in function. They have left undisturbed a very large proportion of their countries' capitalist economies.

The validity of their insight, in other words, does not obscure the fact that at another level these radical writers share the empirical view of avowed pluralists. Without excepting organized labor, Donald Blaisdell argues, for example, that group leaders operate inside parties, but he believes that the groups themselves "work autonomously, but in cooperation with [parties] . . . throwing their weight first to one party then to the other depending on which party seems to offer more."[8] Two other analysts of interest-group behavior, Harmon Zeigler and Abraham Holtzman, both point out organized labor's affinity for the Democrats. Zeigler, however, concludes that labor "is not a unified and reliable basis of support for the Democratic Party," basing the statement on the voting behavior of individual union members. Holtzman observes that

> there is nothing [in the United States] comparable to the ideological ties between interest groups and parties which exist in Italy. Groups forge temporary alliances with other interest groups in the absence of ideological inhibitors, and groups cooperate with members and leaders of both parties.[9]

Significantly, although the ostensible focus of these writers is pluralist, that is, they emphasize the behavior of organized interest groups, they assert the pluralist character of American labor by citing attitudinal factors. In Zeigler's analysis it is the presumably uncertain partisan preferences of union members as voters and, in Holtzman's, the weak ideological affinity between parties and such groups as trade unions.

This view of labor as "basically" nonpartisan has been bolstered by some of labor's own spokesmen, partly to minimize the break with earlier nonpartisan doctrines, partly to placate Republican union members, and partly to avoid embarrassing the Democrats. Mary Goddard Zon, research director for the AFL-CIO's Committee on Political Education (COPE), explicitly denied and then implicitly conceded labor's partisan involvement in two consecutive sentences.

> While COPE is non-partisan, and supports liberal candidates of both parties, it is a simple fact that many more Democrats than Republicans qualify for COPE support. The success of liberal legislation in the immediate future will depend on the ability of the Democrats to hold the seats they have and, if possible, to increase their margin.[10]

A Democratic bias is conceded, but the unions are also depicted as operating independently of either party. When they endorse candidates, the unions are thought to be "as free as before" they made their alliance with the Democrats. V. O. Key makes the same assumption with his characteristic caution.

> Those critics who deplore [labor's apparently recent Democratic allegiance] . . . make too much of the new practice of the formal endorsement of presidential candidates. . . . In 1916, Sam Gompers, in his "private" capacity, asserted "If the men of labor have to depend on what is promised by the Republican Party in this campaign, God save them. That is all." The non-partisan policy makes of labor, as one of its leaders has remarked, "non-partisan Democrats."[11]

An Alternative Partisan Interpretation

Even as revised by Key, this pluralist interpretation views the largest of our economic interest groups as pro-Democratic but still outside the party in terms of political organization and activity. Key was entirely right in stressing the continuity of Democratic partisan preference and the steadfast rejection of the rhetoric and emotion of European socialism. As a result of the New Deal, however, a distinct break did occur when American unions emerged as a *party* campaign organization. And organized labor's formal endorsements of Democratic Presidential candidates accurately symbolized this major alteration in its political *behavior* rather than any change in partisan *attitudes*. The difference of interpretation is qualitative. In my view, labor is not simply at one end of a continuum of organizations distributed according to their Democratic versus Republican partisanship, but in many cases is a valued and integral part of the Democrats' normal campaign apparatus.

This thesis is supported by an impressive number of observers who have focused on the specific content of the labor–Democratic party alliance rather than uncritically invoking pluralism as a universally valid explanation for the political behavior of all American economic interest groups. As early as 1945, Richard Rovere, in an article on the Democrats' 1944 victory, described the CIO's Political Action Committee, as

> a national machine, and although it will use local issues to advantage where that can be done, its principle concern is with national policy.
> This has never been true of our regular party machines. Neither major party is really a national organization.[12]

Labor's activity, of course, is not tantamount to effectiveness in winning elections. In fact, the assessment of such effectiveness requires extensive survey techniques beyond the scope of this research. The unions' contributions, however, are valued by experienced politicians. Rovere, for example, questioned labor's actual assistance to the Democrats in 1944. "But all this scarcely matters now," he wrote a year later. "PAC today has the prestige of association with victory. Most of the men it marked for defeat were defeated; most of those it sought to elect were elected."[13] Four years later, Max Kampelman, counsel to Senator Hubert Humphrey, asserted, "The labor movement was unmistakably, though perhaps unofficially, considered an essential arm of the Democratic Party." By 1948, he noted, labor had come to realize the "importance of local Party organization."[14] In periods of Democratic success (e.g., 1960) this was a common verdict.[15]

Political scientists studying party and electoral politics have also tended to recognize labor's partisan role. Ralph Goldman observes, "Union officials and members found that they could perform many of the activities—registering voters, helping candidates campaign, raising funds, getting voters to the polls—ordinarily left to the parties.

. . . Often, union locals served the Democratic cause in the absence of party locals."[16] "In many parts of the country," adds Clinton Rossiter, "it is more correct than misleading to describe the Democrats as a 'labor party.' "[17] E. E. Schattschneider, writing in 1955 with the labor-Democratic alliance explicitly in mind, provided an epigraph for this volume:

> . . . a shift in the locus of power or a revision of party functions may leave the formal structure untouched, or new structures may arise without being recognized as parts of the party system. Thus pressure groups may become so partisan that they might properly be described as ancillary organizations of one or the other of the major parties.[18]

This view has been further substantiated by several writers who have focused on organized labor in national politics. In his suggestively titled article "The Organized Labor Bureaucracy as a Base of Support for the Democratic Party," Nicholas Masters argues:

> The AFL-CIO has been able to provide for the Democratic Party one thing business interests have been unable to supply for the Republicans . . . namely organization. The most fundamental point to emphasize is the sheer muscle union workers can provide in a campaign.[19]

Fay Calkins concluded the first comparative study of unions and the Democratic party in several locales by describing industrial unions as "party pressure groups" that "give life and direction to the party mechanism."[20]

The most comprehensive evidence supporting the thesis of labor's organizational integration into the Democratic party has been assembled by Harry Scoble. "The most fundamental post-war change in the structure and process of political parties," he writes, "has been the entrance of organized labor into electoral activity at the precinct level and on up."[21] Scoble not only rejects Schattschneider's low estimate of labor's contribution to the Democratic vote but also calculates that labor accounted for a fourth of the party's total financial support and contributed almost nothing to the Republicans.[22] In addition, labor used this money to support Democrats from rural areas with few unions and concentrated its contributions in close races so that "labor's electoral efficiency—measured solely by percentage of victories [of candidates it has supported]—has closely paralleled the ebb and flow of the Democratic Party fortunes in the past fifteen years.[23] Scoble concludes, "Organized labor acts a party-within-a-party," although he admits that "the descriptions available [on which to base this judgment] are fragmentary and discontinuous."[24]

If these views are accurate, they force us at least to qualify the pluralist notion that both American parties, save for the vestiges of urban machines, have elite or "cadre" structures. Except perhaps in Detroit, American unions did not provide the Democrats with the branch structures comparable to those of some European working-class parties in which rank and file party activists are organized on a permanent basis to mobilze the party's supporters.[25] Organized labor's campaign organizations in the United States, however, have provided a significantly closer equivalent to the monetary support and electoral work of European branch organizations than is usually recognized.[26] The behavioral equivalence of American union campaign organizations and the European party branches is suggested by the fact that unions have been less important for the party in the United States where branch electoral activities are still performed by regular patronage organizations.

British trade unionists, to take just one example, have, of course, been tied to the Labour party by much stronger class feelings than those that bind American workers to the Democrats, although both groups are committed to welfare-state programs. British unions also have had a much more important role in the Labour party with respect to holding formal party offices, informal influence, financial contributions, and campaign work than the AFL-CIO has enjoyed in the Democratic party.[27] But if the Democrats regularly seek but much less regularly follow the advice of AFL-CIO leaders, the Labour party's increasingly middle-class, moderate leaders had by the 1960s also begun to disregard some important union demands. In sum, this partial approximation of party branch structures increasingly permits meaningful comparisons and contrasts between European and American party systems.

It is possible, of course, that a sufficiently broad pluralist interpretation could account for these developments within a group-politics framework. As Schattschneider suggests, however, a definition of pluralism broad enough to cover almost every conceivable relationship between parties and pressure groups and to explain all possible outcomes in general explains nothing in particular. Propositions built on such an interpretation of pluralism are almost impossible either to refute or to verify empirically.[28] Scoble and Calkins, for example, seem inclined to interpret party behavior as the consequence of the interests and activities of its constituent groups. As this study will show, however, the labor movement lost much of its independent bargaining position vis-à-vis the party when it began to function as a party campaign organization. It actually became subject to many of the external constraints that limit the party itself.[29] A broad definition of pluralism, then, prevents us from making relevant theoretical distinctions between the clearly pluralist behavior of the early AFL described in this chapter and its present role as a Democratic electoral organization and finally as a potential bulwark of consumer class politics described in the chapters that follow. Such a definition also makes it more difficult to compare—and contrast—the American party system with those in Western Europe and deprives us of the opportunity to treat American politics as a standard subject for comparative political analysis rather than as a unique area to be studied by area specialists.

Toward a Partial Theory of Group Politics

If American free-enterprise rhetoric has tended to disguise, as well as to retard, our acceptance of collectivist welfare-state programs, the pluralist rhetoric of group politics has disguised the nonpluralist alliance between our largest party and our largest economic interest group. The admittedly real differences between American and European politics have thus been exaggerated and the considerable differences between the contemporary situation and our own political past have been understated. Pluralism thus obstructs development of a new partial theory that distinguishes politics in the 1920s from politics in the 1960s. Such a theory should account not only for the remaining important differences between American and European poli-

s. The emergence of labor as a Democratic party electoral
ation is likely to alter the political balance among social
This change will rarely mean that the union pressures or
the party. The complex labor-party coalition instead often
on the basis of shared decisions and a division of labor and
bilities in the political struggle. But simply because labor
s as a vital element in the Democrats' entire campaign opera-
ty leaders are likely to anticipate the reaction of their labor
workers and thus to cater to some of their wishes. For
n, class as a political category must refer not only to ob-
onomic position or to subjective awareness of social status
o organizational structures through which collective inter-
erspectives are expressed.

the importance of interest groups and parties, this labor-
n has equally important consequences for the analysis of
stems and roles. Labor's position within the party enables
in and to strengthen the process of aggregating the many
nonlabor interests by which the party builds its majority
turn, this concern for successfully assembling a majority
elect Democratic candidates has transformed labor's own
e. As the arm of a political party, the unions' behavior is
mply a reflex of their own economic position and constitu-
also consider the entire political constituency that the
to mobilize. In Easton's terms, the pattern of labor's
he political system includes relatively more support and
ds than a typical interest group's inputs and is thus far
pattern of a major party.[38] This process moderates
ds and broadens labor's political constituency to include
rived groups who do not happen to belong to trade

terms of size-of-political-unit analysis, the incorpora-
ed labor as a functioning partner in a partisan coalition
rease the prevailing size of constituency and scope of
same time it is likely to reduce the relative importance
particularistic (as opposed to public-regarding or class-
ies and incentives. In general, the party will be in-

tics, especially in the legislative and administrative processes, but also for the growing similarities, especially in the party system. It should indicate not only the effect of group behavior on parties but also the effect that the AFL-CIO's alliance with the Democrats has had on labor's own political goals and activity. This partial theory would thus avoid reducing political behavior either to the pluralist politics of largely economic interest groups or to a Marxist conflict among classes generated entirely out of economic relationships. It would expect that when two political organizations cooperate intimately for a long period of time, their patterns of activities begin to fuse. It would prepare us, in other words, to find that the large formal organizations that have dominated pressure politics for most of this century have begun to operate inside at least one of the major American parties.[30]

Three Analytical Approaches to Labor Politics

In order to contribute toward such a partial theory, this book draws on three overlapping dimensions of analysis. The first, the social stratification approach, which is derived from European sociology, looks at politics in terms of the interaction of particular social strata, like that between the industrial working class and their employers. This view can be directly traced to Marx, who viewed politics as a struggle between social classes, regulated by the values and world view of the ruling class. But it is also related to that part of Aristotle's analysis in which he empirically classified different regimes according to the social groups and values that controlled them. The social stratification approach has the merit of concentrating on the substantive character of the political regime. It examines the distribution of influence and power among social and economic groups and the prevailing system of philosophical values, standards of excellence, and patterns of prestige or deference. This orientation then considers the differential policy outputs of the system to various social groups.

A second approach, the analysis of political systems and roles, tends to emphasize the causal importance, or autonomy, of the polity. It must be stressed that this view is not logically incompatible with predominantly economic and social explanations. Nevertheless, this approach turns our attention to the differentiation and variation among political roles such as citizen ruler, statesman and broker of interests, and institutions such as parties, legislatures, and administrative bureaucracies. In one version of this approach politics is conceptualized as a differentiated system of behavior with its own complex inputs and outputs handled by political actors in ways that contribute to or detract from system maintenance.[31]

A related concept sees politics as a constellation of actors and interests that the system creates, combines, controls, and serves through a basic set of functions.[32] Behind this concentration on political systems and roles appears to be a basic assumption, powerfully formulated by Max Weber, that since the Middle Ages the Western polity has become increasingly independent of social relationships, and is therefore capable of the creative alleviation of societal strain.[33]

The third analytic dimension, perhaps the most fruitful yet employed in the interpretation of American political behavior, focuses on the size of the relevant political unit. This unit can be the *constituency* of the particular group or political leader or the *scope* of political conflict (the ratio of active participants to the uninvolved audience). We can also consider the *type of government policy,* conceptualized as the size and number of benefits distributed, ranging from a few large disbursements to social classes to more numerous smaller ones intended for individuals and small groups. Finally, the analyst may also focus on the political *incentives* that organizational leaders dispense to induce political activity. These vary from such small and divisible incentives as patronage jobs and monetary payments appealing to individual self-interest to larger and collective incentives, that is, ideal benefactions appealing to a wider group loyalty.[34] Like the mode of analysis that focuses on political systems and roles, the size-of-political-unit approach stresses patterns of political behavior and political structures. Both approaches, for example, treat the different methods that politicians use to build coalitions as significant research questions in their own right. But the size-of-political-unit focus is less directly concerned with the consequences for the American political system as a whole than for

the particular individuals and groups w and even relief of societal strain have s questions for the highly stable Ameri tions of alternative methods of alloca public and private interests. This con actors is obviously shared by the s size of a political unit like a constit logically or necessarily connected t groups. It is not directly and overtly can workers or to unions. The urb both business groups and poor in small divisible material payoffs. Pe also explain this characteristic of for the predominance of middle-cl little stimulation to focus on s aristocrats, bourgeoisie, and pr

Each of these three analytic interpretation of American poli litical systems and roles, the itself securely through reliance semble different interests throu strain and avoid deep politica compact, relatively homogene centives, individualist and gr rather than broad conflict a and thus be appropriate subj Unions themselves play this theorists can also pluralist dominated by business an class and collectivist value and inheritance taxes ap tempt at redistributing w

A Nonpluralist Interp

The interpretation c
a substantial modificat

analysi
organiz
classes.
controls
operates
responsi
function
tion, pa
campaig
this reas
jective ed
but also
ests and
Given
party fusi
political s
it to share
labor and
coalition. I
coalition to
political rol
no longer si
ency; they
party seeks
inputs into t
fewer deman
closer to th
labor's dema
relatively de
unions.
Finally, i
tion of organi
is likely to in
conflict. At th
of narrow and
oriented) poli

fluenced to favor class legislation whereas labor will have to pay greater attention to interests larger than its own.

Measured on all three dimensions of analysis, then, European and American politics have, by the 1960s, appreciably converged in the area of party and interest group behavior as well as in the more widely recognized areas of welfare policies and voter alignment. Indeed, Chapter XI suggests a common focus on consumer-producer conflict. This interpretation of the American labor movement in national politics therefore includes an explicitly historical component. As the rest of this chapter will show, before the New Deal the politics of most American trade unions were genuinely pluralist. Under the leadership of Samuel Gompers, the AFL was first nonpartisan and then pro-Democratic in national politics. But its political operations remained independent of the party, and, under less aggressive leadership in the 1920s, the federation returned to a more nearly neutral position without seriously disrupting its limited political activities. Chapter II will contrast this pluralism with the intimate relationship between organized labor, the New Deal, and the party realignment of 1928–1936.

The first two chapters and this entire study are thus intended to help us formulate tentative solutions to two of the most important theoretical debates that have emerged out of Marx's analysis of working-class political behavior under industrial capitalism. The first debate, which, for purposes of abbreviation only, can be associated with the names of Marx and Max Weber, involves the competing claims of the stratification and political system–role analyses discussed here. Is working-class politics simply a reflex of the proletarians' economic position or does it reflect political and social variables that cannot be reduced to economic factors? The second debate, which for purposes of abbreviation can be associated with the names of Robert Michels and V. I. Lenin, grew out of the recognition by many late nineteenth-century Marxists that the industrial proletariat could not be relied upon to stage anticapitalist revolutions. Michels blamed the bureaucratic nature of working-class organizations for this failure and depicted their officials with their middle-class life styles as a conservative check on the rank and file. Lenin, on the other hand, blamed the conservatism of the workers themselves and called for a highly organized revolutionary party prominently staffed with middle-class intellectuals. Chapter II concludes with an effort to resolve both arguments with respect to the American labor movement. But these two subjects are also an implicit theme of both the historical analysis in Chapters I and II and the analysis of field research data that follows.

The Disorganization of the American Working Class

The American labor movement in the nineteenth century adhered to pluralist principles primarily because the extraordinary barriers to forming any union organizations created an overriding preoccupation with organizational security. The greatest of these obstacles was the absence of a European class-consciousness or solidarity as nineteenth-century American society lacked inherited feudal institutions and class distinctions.[39] Union organizers could not exploit deep-seated social antagonisms to recruit members and to build the members' solidarity. In addition, the rapid exploitation of the continent's natural resources produced recurrent labor shortages and generally rising levels of real income. As a result, relatively few Americans believed that they or their children were permanent members of the working class.

The dominance of these liberal-democratic attitudes and the wide diffusion of real property also led to universal white male suffrage long before it was instituted in most of Europe. Not only did American workers share no common grievance because they were excluded from full citizenship, but they also developed strong loyalties toward both of the two major capitalist parties, a development that further reduced their sense of class unity. Equally important, the ethnic and racial heterogeneity of American workers in the nineteenth and early twentieth centuries often overshadowed their common status as wage earners, a fact that worked to the advantage of many employers.[40] Ethnic and partisan divisions, economic opportunity, and social and political equality created an individualist, materialist ethic that often prevailed over trade-union, let alone class, solidarity.[41]

Employer hostility toward unions also inhibited their development. As a leading historian observed before the New Deal:

> Employers in no other country, with the possible exception of those in the metal and machine trades of France, have so persistently, so vigorously, at such costs, and with such a conviction of serving a cause opposed and fought trade unions as the American employing class. In no other Western country have employers been so much aided in their opposition to unions by the civil authorities, the armed forces of government and their courts.[42]

This antiunion hostility may have reflected the relatively late emergence of American capitalism and the repressiveness typically associated with the first years of heavy capital accumulation. But the righteous antiunionism of the almost entirely Protestant entrepreneurial class may have also reflected the unchallenged Protestant individualism that had earlier produced the peculiar harshness of American slavery.[43] The intensity of employer opposition was symbolized by the giant steel industry whose overwhelming resources were fully committed to the antiunion struggle.[44] Although comparatively well paid, some steel workers worked twelve strenuous hours, 363 days a year, as late as 1920.* In order to keep the workers out of unions the employers used physical violence and company informers who infiltrated union organizations, spread antistrike propaganda, stimulated ethnic quarrels, and stole secret union documents.[45] As Blankenhorn observed, "Industrial espionage is confined to America; what espionage there is in Europe is a government monopoly; no other civilized country tolerates large scale, privately owned labor-spying."[46]

Because American capitalists after the Civil War did not have to compete with an older elite of birth and rank, workers could not ally with either antibusiness tory radicals or antiaristocratic liberal businessmen. In fact, employers often enjoyed broad support from other groups. In the 1919 steel strike the Pittsburgh-area newspapers functioned as employer propaganda sheets.[47] The workers also

---

* By modern standards, and those of some contemporary Europeans, workers also had an appallingly high accident rate and little provision for death or injury benefits. Wolfe, *op. cit.*, pp. 31–39, 255.

faced physical repression by state, federal, and local authorities. In 1892 alone, state militia helped break the Homestead Steel Strike and the Buffalo Switchmen's Strike, and federal troops played a similar role at the Coeur d'Alene, Idaho, silver mines.[48] The use of troops was supplemented, late in the nineteenth century, by the actions of state and federal courts. The courts regularly broke strikes with sweeping antiunion injunctions.[49] Apart from the Presidency of Woodrow Wilson, occasional governmental support like President Theodore Roosevelt's actions in the 1902 coal strike proved dramatic exceptions. Even the strongly antisocialist leaders of the American Federation of Labor (AFL) accepted Marx's judgment that in America the state was indeed the creature of the bourgeoisie. In the face of these frustrations, worker discontent took violent and often poorly organized and illicit forms. Both the Molly Maguires, who flourished among Irish coal miners during the 1860s and 1870s, and the later more explicitly class-conscious Industrial Workers of the World, profited from the weakness of less violent, more moderate unions. But neither group created large, stable organizations.[50]

Just as characteristic but still more transient were the spontaneous, uncoordinated, but violent mass strikes of the late nineteenth century that "bore in every way the aspect of a social war."[51] In the 1877 railroad strike a Pittsburgh mob destroyed $5 million worth of railroad property after troops killed twenty-six persons. The strike began spontaneously after the workers failed to organize a union to resist the Pennsylvania Railroad's wage reduction. The occasional victories that this spontaneity won by sheer surprise provided only temporary success against the far better organized large corporations.[52]

These obstacles to organization so weakened American unions that until the 1880s most of them were unable to survive economic depressions. Motivated far more by economic individualism than proletarian consciousness, workers joined unions when labor shortages made their jobs secure. When a depression produced a labor surplus, however, the risks of discharge for union membership outweighed the benefits of affiliation with a union.[53] One response of union leaders was a preoccupation with the most effective techniques for organizational survival. But, as the Knights of Labor showed, it was not the only attitude that emerged.

The Knights of Labor:
A Nonpluralist Alternative

Repression and violence did stimulate at least temporarily the workers' hostility against their employers. But, given American conditions, it did not provide sufficient long-term worker solidarity to produce large stable unions or the class consciousness needed for a widely based socialist movement. To be sure, the first large-scale American labor organization, the Noble Order of the Knights of Labor, attempted to survive on precisely such an appeal to the fraternity of working men. The Order was actually "not a business but a religion, not a doctrinal religion like socialism, but a vague, primitive embryonic sentiment" that united workers from extremely diverse social backgrounds.[54] But the Knights failed because they never seriously faced, let alone solved, the problem of organizing the divided and self-interested American working class. There was a fatal disjunction between the Order's ambitious goal of uniting all workers in a single organization and the vagueness with which it defined its specific constituency and its strategy and tactics.

The leaders of the Order not only moved in and out of the working class into business and politics but welcomed almost everyone except "bankers, stockbrokers, gamblers, and liquor dealers."[55] This mixed constituency was in turn "in sympathy with everything and involved in nothing."[56] The Knights endorsed programs of economic cooperation in which groups of workers became their own employers largely to satisfy the middle-class desire to escape from the wage system rather than to solve the problems of wage earners.[57] The Order embraced middle-class solutions like currency reform and land reform, but its interest in independent politics was itself undercut by a strong strain of disillusionment.[58] The Knights used the boycott more effectively than any other American union, but they were effective largely because "they were as much a consumer as a producer body."

Their most basic failure was thus their general ineffectiveness in strikes, the essential union technique. The Order had several important craft units, but its predominantly industrial or, more precisely, mixed-district form of organization that grouped together workers from different trades and industries had some disadvantages as an organizational basis for fighting strikes.[59] In particular, heterogeneous local units had difficulty coordinating their activities against any one employer or group of employers engaged in a crucial strike. The mixed-district form, on the other hand, enabled one organizer to recruit all the workers in a single town and gave the Knights so many local assemblies that a company could not evade unionization by moving to another city.[60]

The real difficulty was the Order's own ambivalent, hostile attitude to strikes. Relying on strikes as a major weapon was viewed by some members as acceptance of a more or less permanent place in the wage system.[61] As a result, the Order's most successful strikes were almost always the result of spontaneous rank and file revolt, not leadership planning.[62]

Given the economic individualism of American workers, this failure to devise an adequate strategy for winning economic gains produced a highly unstable membership. Many joined, withdrew, and came back after the spectacular victories of 1885.* But they left as defeats mounted, and the Order declined in membership and finally drifted into a middle-class reformism and an alliance with agrarian populism.† The Knights, then, dramatized rather than solved the American workers' problem of organization. The failure of their appeal to a broad constituency only strengthened the determination of AFL leaders to adhere to their pluralist principles.

---

* In particular, many immigrants saw America as "the land of individual enterprise and opportunity." They joined the Order between 1884 and 1886 as a reaction to "their first contact with industrialism in general and its ugly harshness in the America of the 1880's. But after their first shock and violent reaction they . . . [returned to the pursuit of individual gain and] left the Order to its own fate." Lorwin, *op. cit.*, p. 26.

† On the reformist period see Ware, *op. cit.*, pp. 364ff. The Order suffered from other handicaps including Gompers' implacable hostility, association with the notorious Haymarket bombing, attacks by business, the suspicion of the Roman Catholic Church, and Powderly's incompetent leadership. See *ibid.*, p. 85.

The AFL: Organization and Homogeneity

Far more preoccupied than the Knights with finding effective techniques of organizational maintenance, the AFL set for itself much more limited aspirations and realized them far more successfully. Because American workers were so individualistic, the AFL systematically encouraged the growth of trade unions whose members were so similar to one another that they could easily perceive their common interest. Not only were nonworkers excluded from the beginning, but these unions also often brought together skilled tradesmen from a single craft or set of allied crafts, in contrast to the Knights' policy of mixing together men of different trades and skills. In order to exploit their members' economic individualism still more, many AFL unions adopted a system of high dues and high benefits that gave individual members a strong material stake in their organization. At least as important, they also sought to make the union a fighting organization that could defend its members on the job. By establishing the supremacy of the national organization over its locals, the leaders of the AFL enabled it to conserve resources by preventing ill-conceived strikes and to transfer funds from strong locals to weaker ones under attack.[63]

Samuel Gompers was symbol, spokesman, and architect of this stress on organizational survival. A gifted organizational executive, Gompers took pains to strengthen his own position by invariably allying with the leaders of those affiliates who controlled the federation.[64] He fought the Knights implacably, partly because they competed with the crucial affiliates for skilled workers. Under Gompers' leadership, the federation also brought together scattered locals of unorganized trades to form new international unions and refused to recognize locals that did not join existing national unions in their trade. At the same time, Gompers would tolerate any conflict or theoretical inconsistency if such flexibility would allow the federation to retain a strong affiliate. Despite his general adherence to craft unionism, Gompers explicitly recognized an industrial union's (Mineworkers) jurisdiction over craftsmen working near the mines and he opposed ousting another industrial union, the Brewery Workers.[65]

This preoccupation with organizational maintenance and strength helped the AFL unions persist through the 1893–1897 depression whereas other national federations had succumbed during previous economic declines. By 1898, the AFL had 278,016 members, a little more than a third of the Knights' peak membership. In the next six years it grew six-fold to over 1 million and almost doubled again by 1914.[66]

This growth, however, did not produce much social or economic diversity. As Perlman observed in 1918, "the Federation remains, with the striking exceptions of the miners' and garment workers' organizations, mainly the organizations of the upper and medium strata among the native wage earners."[67] The AFL did little to organize other industrial workers, and most of its unskilled members were relegated to isolated federal locals which were not affiliated with international unions and thus had little voting power.[68] Powerful craft unions often covertly undercut organizing drives in such manufacturing industries as auto making.[69] Craft unions that claimed jurisdiction over an entire industry, for example, the carpenters, often admitted only the skilled workers. As Rogin put it:

> Here is what is known in Constitutional law as a deficit of power. The American Federation of Labor has been thought of as a limited function organization, but it would be more accurate to say that while it acted only in certain areas, it claimed universal jurisdiction in an attempt to shut out competition of rival organizations.[70]

In these cases the narrow-constituency principle prevented rather than protected union organization.

As Perlman's 1918 observation implies, the exclusion of the unskilled simultaneously excluded most of the newer, less skilled immigrants from eastern and southern Europe. By the 1920s, the dominant and by then assimilated German and Irish groups in the federation generally favored a restriction of immigration from Europe and Asia.[71] The AFL consequently had little attraction for these newer groups, nor did it appeal to blacks, who were formally excluded by many affiliates.[72]

Voluntarism: Continuity and Change

The AFL defended its concern with building durable organizations based on narrow constituencies by invoking the thoroughly
pluralist ideology of voluntarism. As Gompers' associate Adolph
Strasser put it, "We have no ultimate ends, we are going on from
day to day. . . . We are all practical men."[73] Obviously, this principle
was entirely at odds with socialism. The federation did have a sizable
socialist minority among its trade-union members until at least
World War I, and in 1893 it circulated a political program that included the collective ownership of the major means of production.
But the 1894 convention explicitly defeated this plank.[74] Indeed, the
central voluntarist tenet was a principled opposition to all compul-
sion and paternalism either by government in economic life or by
the federation with regard to the affairs of its affiliates. This doctrine
meant almost invariably cooperating with the most powerful entrenched officials of the labor movement against dissident local
leaders. As a sympathetic scholar admitted:

> The American Federation of Labor was occasionally forced, despite
> the reluctance of its active officers, to intervene on the side of an
> affiliate engaged in controversy with some of its members or with
> their locals, even when the heads of the Federation believed that the
> members or locals . . . had right on their side.[75]

The narrowing of organized labor's effective constituency to its own
officers, sometimes produced anomalous results. "In employing
[against rebels] special deputies, scabs, and the law, the labor movement was utilizing perhaps its three worst enemies."[76]

Borrowing the Marxist tenet of the state as the creature of the
bourgeoisie, voluntarists saw governmental interference in the economy as necessarily antiunion. Gompers thus justified opposing most
social-insurance programs that were designed to assist both organized
and unorganized workers because they coercively subjected workers
to "a special bureaucratic administration . . . not contemplated under
a government made up of free and equal citizens."[77] But, as Rogin
argues, this doctrine served what the AFL leaders thought were the
interests of the AFL's affiliates and their officials. These unions usu-

ally had sufficient control of the market to bargain successfully on behalf of their members without government assistance. Such assistance was much more important for the less-skilled industrial and service-trades workers outside the federation.

AFL officials were particularly opposed to programs that might have allowed the government to compete for their members' loyalties such as protection for collective bargaining, medical insurance, minimum-wage and maximum-hour laws (at least for privately-employed adult males), and unemployment insurance. This last program, for example, threatened to make union activities like collective bargaining seem less vital.*

By the late 1920s voluntarism became so reified that some AFL leaders adhered to it by opposing unemployment insurance in the middle of the 1929 Depression, even though they may well have reduced the very member loyalty they sought. Certainly the persistence of voluntarism as an ideology for over forty years indicates the ability of the federation's limited constituency to sustain continuity of attitude and ethos.[78]

Nevertheless, within a generally pluralist framework, the AFL's political attitudes and roles went through at least two distinct changes of emphasis before the New Deal. During its first two decades, faced with the same hostile environment that defeated the Knights of Labor, the federation and its affiliates pursued a narrow organizational self-interest. But the AFL's membership was so small, and its position so precarious, that it pursued its self-interest with considerable militancy, fighting spirit, and even violence. AFL officials were content with low wages, and they articulated through their voluntarist ideology a hostility to the capitalist system that had at least vague overtones of socialist rhetoric.[79]

---

* Gompers' opposition to maximum-hours legislation actually contributed to the defeat of eight-hour referenda in the three Pacific Coast states. Rogin, *op. cit.*, p. 174. On this particular question of hours and wages, Gompers faced considerable opposition within the federation and his opponents included his successor William Green. And he won in the 1915 convention by an unusually close margin. See Karson, *op. cit.*, pp. 128–130. Gompers' admirer Philip Taft saw this position as "largely doctrinaire." Taft found "no proof that the enactment of general wage and hour laws would either injure the morale of the workers or endanger the [organized labor] movement." Taft, *op. cit.*, p. 148.

By 1906 the AFL had grown to over 1.5 million members, and the federation's leaders, like their European counterparts analyzed by Robert Michels, had a substantial organization to protect for their own sake as well as for their members'. Their rhetoric lost its sometimes mildly socialist flavor and the AFL convention explicitly approved Gompers' participation in the National Civic Federation (NCF), a group of business and professional men devoted to industrial peace. Gompers and his associates saw the NCF as a weapon against antiunion employers, and it was attacked by some businessmen. According to Lorwin, however, "The Civic Federation proceeded with . . . sophisticated or enlightened methods, but it was bent on pulling the teeth of aggressive unionism. . . . It was concerned with settling strikes—and often settlements it applauded were disastrous to unionism.[80]

Greater caution in collective bargaining, however, was accompanied after 1906 by more political activism, particularly for programs that did not appear to threaten its organizational efforts. Voluntarist theory approved hours legislation for women, wage and hour legislation for government workers, and child-labor laws because they would not diminish the liberty of groups that had always lacked the effective freedom to bargain collectively. Few such groups, however, except some government workers (who usually could not strike), were in the AFL. Similarly, the federation approved of old-age pensions, even if unenthusiastically, because retaining the loyalty of retirees was not a serious worry.[81] The federation also favored women's suffrage, direct election of U.S. Senators, an expanded program of public works, nationalization of telephone and telegraph systems, and municipal ownership of public works and utilities.[82] Urged on by its socialist minority, which reached its peak by 1912, the federation became, in Lorwin's words, "a part of the progressive forces of the nation . . . an ally of the farmers and liberal middle class."[83] As Michael Rogin has suggested, this turn to politics can be seen as an adaptation to middle-class progressive political goals and as an abandonment of an earlier militant syndicalist reliance on union organization alone. It reflected in part the AFL's significantly altered organizational environment. The same growth in union membership that led the AFL to seek industrial stability also meant that after 1904 the federation represented a substantial block of voters. These moderate rather than radical reforms were also sanctioned by important, often prestigious, middle-class progressive allies. At the same time, government harrassment, particularly the antistrike injunction, made politics seem relevant to efficient organizational operations. In sum, as the problem of sheer organizational *survival* receded, the federation turned to politics to protect and expand its organizational *influence*.

In the period immediately following World War I, a progressive group forced through the federation's convention a resolution endorsing government control of the railways over Gompers' opposition.[84] As the 1920s wore on, however, concern with organizational survival mounted and the AFL's behavior revealed an unmistakably cautious and defensive conservatism, both economically and politically. Significantly, federation membership had declined to about 2.5 million by 1932 under the pressure of employers' opposition and the Great Depression, after reaching a high of over 4 million in 1920.[85] Equally serious, the political and economic environment had turned more threatening. A resurgent Republican-business coalition triumphed in national politics. Employers launched bitter and highly effective antiunion drives. The courts renewed their onslaught, invalidating child-labor legislation, awarding damages in suits against unions, granting antiunion injunctions, and enforcing new state antipicketing laws.[86] Later in the decade management began to compete for worker loyalty through welfare capitalist plans like grievance procedures, health and safety programs, employees' stock purchases, and company unions. Trying to placate its enemies, the 1926 federation convention asserted that "the union is essentially an agency for cooperation, for service to the union members and to the industry in which its members are employed."[87] During the 1929 textile strikes, AFL President Green toured the South preaching conciliation, cooperation, and efficient production rather than worker militancy. Rogin concludes that "voluntarism, which grew up out of a distrust of capital and its power to control the state led finally to a belief in the harmony of interests of capital and labor."[88] After 1925, the federation dropped all its demands for nationalization of industry.

This more extreme form of pluralist voluntarism also reflected changes within the AFL itself. Industrial unions like the Mineworkers and Brewers had declined in membership. By 1930 the skilled building and printing trades, whose workers made up less than 10 percent of the labor force, by themselves composed almost two-fifths of the entire AFL membership. Industrial unionism made progress only among the garment trades. As Lorwin put it, "The Federation became more homogeneous in spirit than ever before. . . . At the conventions of 1923–24 there were no contests for office. . . . [At] the 1924 convention . . . there were no extended debates and not a single roll call."[89]

In retrospect, it appears that the AFL's broadened political goals were related internally to increased size and heterogeneity in membership and externally to a friendly political climate, conditions that had both disappeared in the 1920s. When these two conditions reemerged far more strongly during the New Deal, they ended organized labor's pluralist period in national politics and a Democratic partnership replaced a Democratic partisanship.

The AFL and the Democratic Party, 1906–1928

Section 8, Article III of the AFL's constitution under Gompers decreed in strict pluralist terms, "Party politics, whether they be Democratic, Republican, Socialistic, populistic, prohibition, or any other, should have no place in the conventions of the American Federation of Labor."[90] Even nonsocialist parties might compete with trade unions for the workers' loyalty by involving them in middle-class reform movements or entangling the unions in a hostile political system. Any party seeking an electoral majority would also have to try to assemble a constituency of the unorganized and unskilled workers that was much broader than that of the AFL. Even in voluntarist terms, however, bargaining impartially with both major parties could work only if the parties did not differ decisively on the anti-strike injunction and other issues that directly affected the organizational interests that voluntarism defended. But the parties' attitudes toward these issues in turn depended on the Republicans' relations to the business community and on the broader quest of the Democratic party to forge a majority political constituency to oppose the influence of the new corporate giants. Gompers recognized this problem in part in an often paraphrased but misunderstood statement of nonpartisanship which did not in fact entirely rule out partisan preferences. "We will stand by our friends and administer a stinging rebuke to men or *parties* who are either indifferent, negligent or hostile . . ."[91]

The AFL remained entirely nonpartisan in fact as well as in theory only from its founding in 1886 to 1906. In the Presidential election of 1896, when Gompers was accused of Democratic leanings, the federation took the trouble to exonerate him officially.[92] After that election a Democratic preference became evident. A contributing factor was undoubtedly the affinity of many AFL union leaders for their fellow Irish Catholics who led the Democrats in many Northern cities. But the primary reason was the Republicans' increasingly anti-union posture, which made the AFL's protestations to strict nonpartisanship increasingly untenable. In 1902, the pro-Republican National Association of Manufacturers (NAM) changed "from a group to promote trade expansion to one openly dedicated to opposing organized labor."[93]

In 1906 the AFL ended its political passivity at the national level by presenting to President Roosevelt, the Speaker of the House, and the President of the Senate a "Bill of Grievances" emphasizing opposition to the strike-breaking injunctions and to antitrust prosecutions. The bill also proposed eight-hour legislation for government workers, improvement of seamen's working conditions, and regulation of convict labor and immigration. After publishing the reactions of the three Republican leaders (Speaker Cannon was notably hostile), the federation sent the bill to all senators and representatives. At this point the AFL's partisan role was still somewhat equivocal. Forty-seven of fifty Democrats and only twenty-three of seventy-two Republicans who replied were friendly, but party affiliation was not mentioned in the AFL's comments. After the Republican Congress ignored the bill, however, the federation resolved to take the political offensive. The new program began with an attack on a conservative Republican, Representative Charles E. Littlefield, in Maine's September general election. Gompers himself made a series of speeches, often preceded by parades. In the November elections elsewhere, the federation's efforts were uneven, but it again used speakers and parades and printed evaluations of incumbent congressmen, which were requested by many affiliates.[94]

The 1906 election set a pattern that, with variations from election to election, continued until at least 1922. Its Democratic preference was not officially expressed by a formal convention resolution, but it was unmistakable nevertheless, because a Republican victory was equated with an AFL defeat. The federation tried to educate its members to vote for prolabor and usually Democratic congressmen regardless of the members' traditional partisan loyalties. Indeed, with respect to election campaign work, Gompers' goal of changing his members' partisan loyalty was more ambitious than the AFL-CIO's later efforts. He could not adopt the more recent and less taxing strategy of mobilizing a Democratic majority because the Democrats were a minority party in his time and his own membership included many Republicans.[95]

The AFL's Democratic leaning in 1906 was modified by its friendliness toward a number of progressive Republican congressmen. In 1908, however, the Presidential contest forced a choice between the two parties as national units. As alarm over hostile court decisions mounted, Gompers felt pressured to respond with "something new, something extraordinary, something spectacular."[96] But like the CIO leaders in the 1930s and 1940s, he believed a third-party campaign would only help antilabor Republicans.[97] The federation therefore drew up "Labor's Protest to Congress" and "Address to the Workers" and formally presented its demands to both major party conventions, a procedure that was followed in subsequent elections. These maneuvers were a successful "tactical stroke planned by Gompers . . . to justify to the AFL membership an endorsement of the Democratic presidential candidates."[98] The Republicans, who were about to nominate the "injunction judge" William Howard Taft, showed their inclination to cooperate with Gompers by hearing labor's representatives in front of the NAM president, whom Gompers felt had helped draft the entirely unsatisfactory Republican platform. After the Democrats included many federation demands in their platform, the executive council voted to support Democrat

William Jennings Bryan. From August to November *The American Federationist* became an "almost continuous unit of political propaganda."[99]

During the election about 1,100 unions contributed approximately $8,500 for printed matter and speaking tours by Gompers and others. Equally significant, the AFL established a pattern of cooperation with the Democrats. The executive council met with Democratic National Chairman Norman Mack and Gompers met several times with Bryan. The federation also placed representatives in party headquarters in four states, recommended speakers, and agreed that the party should print large quantities of AFL campaign material to distribute to its members.[100]

The 1908 election marked the evolution of the AFL's involvement in national politics on two distinct dimensions, its partisan orientation and its campaign techniques. In terms of partisanship, organized labor was probably more openly and emotionally Democratic in 1908 than at any time until at least 1936. The federation's top leadership achieved a remarkable consensus (there were only three or four dissenters) in the face of its formal commitment to nonpartisan politics and the socialist or Republican leanings of many of its rank and file.[101] Despite Taft's election, Gompers boasted that the AFL had helped to reduce the Republican House majority in 1906 and still more in 1908.[102]

In terms of campaign techniques, the AFL established patterns of campaigning in 1906 and 1908 that were elaborated but not basically altered during the generation that followed, although Gompers himself thought these early efforts were crude.[103] Particularly in Presidential election years, the AFL continued to print political editorials in its publications, organized campaign speaking tours, distributed campaign literature, including the records of individual congressmen, and sometimes closely collaborated with party leaders.

The federation's Democratic loyalties were further reinforced in 1912 by the highly prolabor record of the Democratic House of Representatives elected in 1910 as well as by President Taft's veto of a bill exempting labor from antitrust prosecutions.[104] By 1912, the AFL's participation as a Democratic ally was so well established that it was undeterred by either its original lack of enthusiasm for Woodrow Wilson as a Presidential candidate or by the prolabor platforms of Theodore Roosevelt's Progressive party.[105] The AFL actually wrote the Democratic convention's labor plank in that year. Although Gompers and his organ, *The American Federationist,* were less outspoken than in 1908 in order to avoid the public criticism he received in that election year, the AFL's campaign organization, the Labor Representation Committee, introduced a pro-Wilson weekly newsletter.[106]

Taken together, the 1908 and 1912 campaigns demonstrated that organization was more important than personalities in the Democratic-AFL alliance. In 1908, the contrast between Presidential candidates reinforced labor's preference for Democratic congressmen as well. In 1912, when Roosevelt's candidacy complicated the Presidential contest, the federation accepted Wilson in part because of the Democratic record in the House. Wilson and the Democrats strengthened the alliance still further in 1913 and in 1914 particularly because Congress passed the Clayton Act, which, Gompers thought, exempted labor from antitrust prosecutions, and other prolabor measures like the La Follette Seaman's Act.[107] President Wilson's selection of Mineworker William B. Wilson as Secretary of Labor symbolized his administration's friendship for the labor movement. Equally impressive, the federal troops sent to Colorado after the Ludlow massacre displayed an unprecedented concern for the strikers' rights.

In 1916, Gompers wrote a preface to a Democratic pamphlet, "Wilson and Labor," and the official federation campaign group, the Labor Representation Committee, in effect endorsed him for reelection, using AFL Executive Council stationery. Some scholars credit the AFL with carrying Ohio and California for the Democrats, thus providing Wilson with his winning margin.[108]

Beginning in the late nineteenth century, formal organizations representing particular economic interests became increasingly important in national politics. The AFL's campaign activity was part of this larger process. The federation's work for Wilson seems all the more significant in view of the fact that by 1916 it had already begun to lose its interest in social reforms. But the AFL's Democratic preferences could be interpreted as consistent with its voluntarist concern

with organizational maintenance and with its cautious conservatism
in other fields. In a two-party system, the Republicans' indifference
to labor's complaints continued to make the Democrats seem obvious
allies.

The federation's campaign activity was, therefore, an effort to
use in politics the effective organizational techniques that AFL affiliates had employed to become the first stable American unions. In
the 1920 election, for example, the AFL expanded the bureaucratic
structure of its campaign apparatus. The Nonpartisan Campaign
Committee, successor to the Labor Representation Committee, created separate bureaus for speakers, publicity, and information as
part of its now standard campaign operations. The federation continued its extensive distribution of campaign literature throughout the
1920s.[109] The general conservatism of the 1920s, however, eventually
affected labor's partisan orientation. Under President William Green,
Gompers' successor, *The American Federationist* dropped most of
its strong political tone. By 1926, the compilation of congressional
voting records no longer included critical evaluations and overtly
partisan commentary.[110] But the federation's ties to the Democrats
had begun to weaken even under Gompers because the *party* rather
than the AFL had become increasingly conservative. Although Gompers in 1920 strongly opposed Harding as being too reactionary and
favored his more progressive and prolabor opponent James M. Cox,
the AFL's enthusiasm for the Democrats seemed to decline. According to Harris, the Democratic platform merely appeared to be "more
friendly or rather less hostile and indifferent than the Republicans'."[111] Another scholar concluded, "both [candidates] were
businessmen . . . the Wall Street reaction to Cox's nomination was
almost placid. Neither his record nor his reputation seemed to cause
alarm in business circles." Cox was so preoccupied with the League of
Nations issue and reform questions so quickly receded that "by
the end of September all the issues for the Democrats led to the
League. It became a one-way, one-street campaign thereafter."[112]

In 1922, two federation leaders, one of whom was William Green,
participated in the Conference for Progressive Political Action, which
was sponsored by the railroad unions, included Socialist party representatives, and led the movement for La Follette in 1924. The AFL's

own support for La Follette's independent Progressive candidacy
was an obvious reaction to the conservatism of the Democrats' candidate John W. Davis. In contrast to La Follette's prolabor position
on most issues including the antistrike injunction, the Democratic
convention had been little more receptive to the AFL's demands than
the Republicans. On the other hand, the federation's own growing
conservatism led it to oppose the labor and independent progressive
parties that emerged in Indiana, Chicago, Seattle, the North Central
states, and elsewhere.[113] Neither Gompers nor La Follette himself
encouraged a third-party movement.

This entire period after World War I reflected increasingly acute
ideological tensions. Voluntarism, as a guide to action, was torn between the pressures generated by AFL's own narrow constituency and
the broader social conflict that unavoidably affected these organizational interests. To some extent, this tension involved the different
effects of government policies on the AFL and its local affiliates. The
injunction did not threaten all AFL affiliates equally, but it threatened
the labor movement as a whole, and the federation felt justified in
backing the Democrats on the national level. However, local licensing, inspection, and strike policies directly affected the craft union's
ability to control local labor markets. Many local unions allied with
those local machines of either party that were dominant even though
such machines were often close to local business groups. These affiliates were therefore opposed to the La Follette endorsement, which
strained their local alliances, and their protests largely immobilized
the federation in the 1924 election.[114]

As the 1928 election demonstrated, these local, partisan alliances
were mainly Democratic, for the federation's own neutrality on the
Presidency in 1928 obscured a widespread informal commitment.
According to *The Literary Digest,* the AFL Executive Council's decision not to endorse Smith was made "not by friends of Herbert
Hoover but by friends of Smith."[115] Bornet, in his exhaustive study
of labor and the 1928 election, observes that "the important thing
is that so many and so varied a group of AFL union organizations did
support the Democratic candidate in 1928 and so few endorsed the
Republican."[116] In fact, Bornet concluded, "There proved to be
much outright favoritism toward the Democratic Party in the non-

partisan policies of [the] American Federation of Labor . . ."[117] This Democratic partisanship in 1928 reflected the appeal of the first major-party Catholic Presidential candidate to Catholic AFL leaders, the prolabor reputation that the Democrats acquired under Wilson, and the system of mutual favors between local union officials and Democratic politicians. In any case, substantial Hoover support among trade-union officials was limited to the Mineworkers, led by Republican John L. Lewis, and to other labor groups in the Pittsburgh and Chicago areas, Ohio, and Indiana.[118]

The Labor-Democratic Alliance: Precursor of Party Realignment

As Schattschneider has so well observed, the very words we use to describe organized labor's activities "imply a tremendous socialization of conflict which was once regarded as a purely private matter . . ."[119] The AFL's strictly pluralist strategy of nonpartisan bargaining with each party proved untenable. Gompers and the federation leadership concluded that the emphasis on homogeneity to make organization possible had to be supplemented by an alliance with a party seeking a majority constituency in order to make organization secure. Nevertheless, the AFL's third-party endorsement in 1924 and its refusal to openly support the Democrats in 1928 and 1932 demonstrated that—before the New Deal—the federation continued to conform to many of the current pluralist formulations of labor's political role. It was pro-Democratic in attitude but its campaign activities had not yet been integrated into Democratic party operations. The federation primarily attempted to influence its own membership to vote Democratic whereas the AFL-CIO's Committee on Political Education (COPE) now seeks to mobilize the party's entire constituency. As Bornet describes the situation in 1928, "The labor group seems to have visualized itself chiefly as a negotiator with the parties," and it did little to enter any party structure.[120]

The 1928 election itself, however, marked a portentous political revolution. Until 1928, the Democratic party shared with the AFL a failure to reach the new immigrant stock and the Negroes in large urban industrial centers. In 1920, for example, Harding successfully cultivated Greek, Syrian, Italian, and black groups that were uninfluential in the AFL.[121] Al Smith's unsuccessful candidacy marked the first time such minority groups, as well as urban residents and wage earners generally, made a switch to the Democratic party, a process that the appeal of Franklin Roosevelt completed in 1936.[122] In the 1930s the newly victorious Democrats came to depend increasingly on these voting groups for victory, and then pursued a labor policy that helped the many workers among these groups organize into durable industrial unions. American labor history thus stood Marx on his head. The economic organization of industrial workers took place only after they had achieved political unity as overwhelming supporters of the Democratic party. Detailed studies of partisan voting in the 1920s and 1930s revealed, however, that this realignment of voter loyalties actually began before 1928.[123] The La Follette campaign in 1924, which the AFL had explicitly supported, contributed significantly to the erosion of Republican support. More significant perhaps, the AFL's unofficial and fluctuating support for the Democrats from 1906 onward appears to have anticipated at the institutional or organizational level a parallel development in the electorate, that is, the massive reorientation of partisan attitudes, which had begun at least in 1922.[124] In other words, trade unions as organizations began to shift to the Democrats in 1906 much as individual workers began to shift in the early 1920s. In itself, this union behavior was consistent with voluntarism. Labor officials had a stronger personal interest in union survival than the rank and file did, and the union leaders more quickly perceived the relevance of the party conflict to working-class interests. Nevertheless, just as the AFL's shift to the Democrats was not in itself motivated by a comprehensive working-class ideology, the shift of some urban workers to the Democrats in 1928 may well have been a result of ethnic and religious as well as class motives. Yet both the voter shifts of the 1920s and the AFL's earlier turn to partisanship were the precursors of the crucial organizational and voter reorientations that took definite shape under the New Deal. Similarly, whereas the voter shifts before 1928 were too small to prevent massive Republican victories, the AFL's campaign efforts under Gompers were both small in scale and technically primitive by comparison with later political action.

These organizational and voter aspects of the New Deal realignment were also causally related. Given the Northern Democrats' need for a somewhat harmonious political constituency, it was not sheer accident that the party more favorable to unions also proved more favorable to the broader welfare-state issues that were designed to benefit wage earners as a whole. If the AFL's support for the Democrats anticipated the electoral realignment, the realignment itself helped produce the far-reaching changes in the labor movement that resulted in the creation of the CIO. Indeed, because many of the less-skilled workers also desired to join unions, the New Deal helped create a far larger American labor movement, with a constituency that resembled the still larger constituency of the Democratic party in spirit, class composition, and ethnic heterogeneity. As Chapter II shows, organized labor's far more intimate alliance with the Democrats followed. Viewed in retrospect, however, the Democrats' pro-labor policies early in the century were undoubtedly encouraged by the AFL's support for Wilson and Bryan. For all his sincere and fervid pluralism, Gompers' own Democratic partisanship thus pointed the way to the demise of the voluntarist laissez-faire politics that he had so strongly supported.

II

Labor as a Party Organization:

The New Deal and After

The transition of the American labor movement during the New Deal period from a pluralist, if often pro-Democratic, voluntarism to an intimate partisan alliance illuminates the organizational link between electoral mandates and political decision making. As V. O. Key, Jr. has written, "Retrospective judgments by the electorate seem far more explicit than do its instructions for future action." Even "the most acute ear," he adds, "can sense only the vaguest guidance for innovation."[1] By forming its alliance with the Democratic party, organized labor vitally affected the translation of these general electoral mandates into specific policies. Indeed, this chapter depicts labor's national campaign apparatus as the primary organizational consequence of the New Deal realignment in the electorate.

Even though Gompers' campaign efforts as early as 1906 had anticipated these developments, the 1930s were a turning point in labor political history because they marked an increase in the rate and magnitude of the unions' entry into national party politics. The

AFL-CIO's role as a Democratic party electoral organization also continued to affect American politics—by helping to preserve the effects
of the electoral revolution into the 1960s—more than a generation
after the voter reorientation was itself completed.

Labor and the New Deal Critical Elections

In short, the 1930s were almost as critical a period for labor as
for the Democratic party *and in very much the same ways.* In his
classic analysis, Key listed three attributes of critical elections: (1) a
durable realignment of party support among the electorate; (2) an
unusually intense interest among the voters; and (3) a redistribution
of power.[2] First, as a result of the realignment, the Democrats dramatically expanded their constituency to include the same groups of
urban industrial workers and ethnic minorities that the CIO brought
into organized labor. Second, labor and the party profited from an
intense, if transient, political and social awareness. These feelings,
temporarily approaching class consciousness, destroyed traditional
partisan allegiances often acquired in childhood, as well as the deep-
seated ethnic hostilities that had inhibited unionization among industrial workers.[3] Third, both the Democratic party, which had a
regular electoral majority for the first time since the Civil War, and
labor, which had gained unprecedented access to the councils of
the dominant partisan coalition, far surpassed the influence they had
enjoyed in the time of Gompers.

The same union political activities and organizations that developed during the New Deal realignment of the party system became,
by the 1950s, the focal points of an effort to preserve this alignment's political consequences. To be sure, as many critics have
charged, the unions' alliance with a procapitalist party ended any
prospects for socialist or even radical working-class politics among
industrial workers. The once militant industrial unions that founded
the CIO suffered after World War II from a "crisis" of spirit and
aspirations, reflecting, it was charged, the bureaucratization of their
officialdom. Like the AFL in 1906, however, moderation in rhetoric,
militancy, and economic tactics completed, rather than subverted,

the unions' increased organizational commitment to partisan politics. In fact, the crisis and the growth of political action were two aspects of the same process, the emergence of the American industrial working class during the 1930s as an influential and recognized participant in the national political community.

Durable Realignment: The CIO Widens Labor's Constituency

The most obvious change in organized labor's constituency during the 1930s was its numerical growth from less than 3 million members in 1933 to over 8 million in 1939. By 1937 almost 4 million of these workers belonged to the newly formed Committee (later Congress) of Industrial Organizations.[4] The new industrial unions in the CIO, and even some industrial units in AFL unions, substantially increased the heterogeneity of the labor movement. These industrial unionists could only share a consciousness of their common position as wage earners in a particular factory, rather than the awareness of similar skills and ethnicity of the traditional AFL craft unions.

As a result, the new unions also lowered the barriers that, until the 1930s, had divided the organized Yankee, Irish, German, Scandinavian, and Jewish workers in the AFL from the unorganized blacks and southern and eastern Europeans.[5] The new industrial unions were also concentrated in the urban areas of the Northeast, Midwest, and, to some extent, the Pacific Coast, rather than in the more socially homogeneous small towns and cities where the AFL remained stronger than the CIO.[6] The Democrats made their largest gains in both 1928 and 1938 in just these urban areas and among just these predominantly working-class ethnic groups. These similarities in constituency are so great that it is not surprising to find that, in some areas, for example, in Wisconsin, labor played an important role in bringing urban progressives into the Democratic party.[7]

So radical a departure from the AFL's voluntarist, narrow-constituency tradition provoked a bitter response. In 1933 and 1934, powerful craft unions insisted on raiding members from the industrial locals directly affiliated with the AFL that had been successfully organizing factory workers.[8] In 1936, only a year after the CIO was explicitly founded to foster industrial unionism, its constituent unions were expelled from the AFL. Philip Taft, a generally sympathetic historian of the federation, concluded, "There is no evidence that the members of the CIO wanted to secede from the A.F. of L. . . . [but President] Green [of the AFL] instead of seeking some method for solving the crisis, sought the advice of his lawyer, Charlton Ogburn, on how the CIO unions might be legally suspended." This was "a failure of leadership that has no equal in the history of American labor."[9] Despite all this resistance, however, the voluntarist labor movement of Gompers' era was now profoundly and, it seems, permanently altered.

Intense Interest: Class Consciousness During the 1930s

The CIO induced so many factory workers to risk employer reprisals and to ignore their own racial and ethnic animosities because the workers were moved by a powerful, if temporary, class solidarity and outrage at the failure of American capitalism. The extent of this failure is difficult to grasp in an era of prosperity. In 1932, one-quarter of the entire work force could not find jobs. Among those who were employed, steel workers, many still working a seven-day week, earned only $13.20 a week in 1932 as opposed to $32.60 in 1929.[10] Hunger marches took place across the country, mobs enforced moratoria on mortgage sales, and some observers seriously feared a revolution.[11] Both private and municipal programs for the relief of the destitute had collapsed; the mayor of Chicago repeatedly warned that the federal government would either have to send money for relief or call out the militia. These conditions produced a nearly complete general strike in San Francisco, another under Trotskyite leadership in Minneapolis, and organized looting elsewhere.[12] In 1932, the Bonus Expeditionary Force, a spontaneously organized collection of jobless war veterans, traveled to Washington in a futile and pathetic effort to secure immediate payment of the bonus due them in 1945.[13] Meanwhile, political radicals established large organizations of unemployed workers that stimulated "the militancy of the employed" and pointed "out to the unemployed their responsibilities [to support strikes of employed workers] and to prevent the unemployed from acting as strike breakers."[14]

Economic discontent led to political protest. Politicians, from Huey Long and Father Coughlin to Floyd Olson and Upton Sinclair, attracted impressive, if transitory, followings by varying combinations of personal magnetism and radical political appeals. This lower-class political consciousness was still more widely and durably expressed in the massive popular support for Franklin Roosevelt. Both his rhetoric and his relief and recovery programs to alleviate the misery of the Depression, identified his administration and party with "the forgotten man" against "the economic royalists." As a symbol of the capacity of the government to serve the common interests of the poor and dispossessed, Roosevelt encountered massive outpourings of popular emotion throughout the country, bolstered no doubt by the intense public hatred he aroused among the wealthy.[15]

These strong feelings of devotion to the President paralleled a widespread, often spontaneous, desire among countless wage earners to join unions. Just as enthusiasm for the bonus army caught even the communists unaware, "the unprecedented enthusiasm with which workers responded to union organizers" in 1934, once the National Industrial Recovery Act asserted the right to organize, "startled many of the leaders of labor unions."[16] Two years later, the intense and often violent opposition of large corporations elevated the infant CIO's struggle to establish industrial unions into a central symbol of revolt against the existing economic order. Management not only infiltrated union locals with spies, but resorted to systematic violence, including the murder and injury of workers in the Little Steel Strike.[17] In 1937, in one of the most carefully documented cases of employer violence, Walter Reuther and other Autoworker leaders were brutally beaten by former criminals and prize fighters employed by the Ford Motor Company.[18]

The CIO's own most militant and dramatic weapon was the sit-down strike in which the workers took physical possession of the factories. These strikes, including the first sit-down in a rubber factory in 1936 and the decisive victory over General Motors in Flint in early 1937, often began and spread spontaneously without the direction of union leadership[19] and were sustained by a notable dedication and enthusiasm. In some instances, the strikers evidently achieved a sense of community or comradeship and even moral exultation one sometimes finds during battle, or in "an armed camp in a war zone."[20] Class solidarity was so strong that during such important conflicts as the Youngstown Steel Strike and the recurrent sit-downs against the automobile companies, workers from other cities, states, and industries would arrive to provide moral and, if necessary, physical support. The Flint Chevrolet workers articulated this determination and commitment, probably unmatched since the 1890s, in a telegram to Michigan's Governor Frank Murphy.

> We have decided to stay in the plant. We have no delusions about the sacrifices which this decision will entail. We fully expect that if a violent effort is made to oust us, many of us will be killed. Unarmed as we are, the introduction of the militia, sheriffs, or police with murderous weapons will mean a blood bath of unarmed workers.[21]

For some the very name CIO symbolized militant, indeed radical, social protest. "So great was its force, so powerful its impetus that the shouts of C.I.O.! C.I.O.! C.I.O.! sounding like the beat of giant machinery and greeting John L. Lewis at the I.L.G.W.U. convention, only echoed the shout of C.I.O.! throbbing through the whole country."[22] Despite his own political conservatism, Lewis, the CIO's first president, contributed to this image with a combination of intelligence, rhetoric, and ruthlessness unmatched in American labor history.[23] In addition, he hired all types of radicals as CIO organizers in order to profit from their commitment, courage, and experience. In 1937, J. Raymond Walsh, later CIO research and education director, voiced what appeared at that time to be the radicalism of the movement. "America has entered upon a revolutionary period . . . the basic modification required is the progressive socialization of private property in industry . . ."[24] According to Mary Vorse, "this new unionism does not stop at the formal lodge meeting. It sees the union as a way of life which involves the whole community."[25] Pluralism or voluntarism hardly described the CIO of the 1930s.

The Redistribution of Power

Rank and file militancy, however, was no more intense and was much less violent in the 1930s than in the late nineteenth century. Yet, during the New Deal, the balance of power in industrial relations shifted appreciably. The CIO finally built durable industrial unions by successfully combining this rank and file enthusiasm with organizational skill. Unlike the AFL, it sought out industrial workers; unlike the Knights of Labor, it devised successful organizational techniques for factory unions, including strikes. CIO unions were tactically shrewd enough to ally with, rather than alienate, such important allies as the AFL's Amalgamated Association of Iron, Steel, and Tin Workers and the company union leaders in the automobile industry. The Steelworkers won recognition at United States Steel, long the antiunion bulwark of the industry, through Lewis' flair for negotiation—his talks were so secret that his own organizers did not learn of them—which dwarfed that of any of the Knights' leaders.

Other CIO unions won most of their important victories through carefully planned campaigns explicitly designed to fit the particular circumstances involved. In many of the sit-down strikes, the plant was organized on a military basis with guards and sentries frisking those entering to discover liquor and arms. Other workers maintained transportation, picketing, and lookout operations and issued a plant newspaper, often on complicated schedules. As a technique, the sit-down strike offered a number of important tactical advantages. As Walsh pointed out, the sit-down was nonviolent in itself, and the employer or the police would have to initiate violence to oust the strikers, thus risking damage to company property and possibly alienating the public. The sit-down also gave the strikers an advantageous position from which to repel police attacks. Walsh estimated in 1937 that only 25 out of over 1,000 such strikes were defeated by police action.[26]

In the single most important strike of the era, the defeat of General Motors in Flint, the Autoworkers skillfully outmaneuvered company strategists and seized the most important plant in the Chevrolet division, entirely immobilizing operations.[27] A level of cohesion that the Knights of Labor had never even approached was common. Of particular importance were the often highly disciplined flying squadrons that assisted the men in the plants. When this discipline was absent, as in the Little Steel Strike, the CIO was less successful.[28] Overall, however, as *Barrons Magazine* put it, "For the first time in the history of the United States, industrial management is faced with a labor movement which is smart and courageous, wealthy and successful—a movement moreover, which is winning its battle by applying a shrewd imitation of big business organization and techniques."[29]

The substantial change in power relations extended beyond industrial relations to politics. Of course, the New Deal legislative regulation of particular economic groups or sectors benefited established economic interests in agriculture, coal, securities, banking, and even utilities. In general, the New Deal may have functioned to forestall radical change by eliminating the most unpopular features of American capitalism. By grouping most lower-class voters in one party, however, the 1928–1936 realignment radically altered the agenda of national politics. And, as E. E. Schattschneider remarks, *"the definition of the alternatives is the supreme instrument of power . . . He who determines what politics is about runs the country . . ."*[30]

The new agenda included assistance for lower-income groups in general and protections for wage earners in particular. Such measures for recovery, relief, and employment as Works Progress Administration (WPA), Public Works Administration (PWA), the Civil Conservation Corps (CCC), and the National Youth Administration (NYA) attacked immediate deprivation. As more permanent structural changes, the New Deal introduced a more progressive income-tax structure; a system of social insurance including federal welfare assistance, old-age pensions, and unemployment compensation; low-income public housing; low-cost public power; the insurance of small saving and checking accounts; and mortgage protection for homeowners. However uncertainly, the Roosevelt administration also groped toward a policy of public spending as a cure for periodic depressions and unemployment.

With respect to wages, hours, working conditions, and child and convict labor, the New Deal provided a series of regulations, first through the National Industrial Recovery Act (NIRA) industry codes, then through the Walsh-Healey Act, which covered work done under federal government contract, and finally through the Fair Labor Standards Act of 1938. Unions benefited directly from Section 7(a) of the NIRA under which every industrial code recognized the employees' right to organize, to bargain collectively, and to choose their own representatives without management interference. Even though these provisions were not vigorously enforced, they enabled union leaders to claim that President Roosevelt had personally endorsed unionism. By 1934, the AFL membership increased to over 4 million from less than 3 million in 1933, with industrial unions making the greatest gains.[31]

In 1935, the Wagner Act not only sought the same goals more explicitly but provided the National Labor Relations Board (NLRB) as effective enforcement machinery. Besides guaranteeing the right to join a union and requiring bona fide collective bargaining by employers, the act provided that a majority of any bargaining unit could choose a union to bargain collectively for all workers in the unit. This procedure seemed wholly at odds with the voluntarist view of an inevitably antiunion government, for it put the coercive power of government to extort union recognition from their employers at the disposal of employees. As Edelman observes, the NLRB had a vested organizational interest in preserving the labor movement, because without unions to generate cases the agency would have no function.[32]

At the end of Hoover's administration in 1932, the AFL had secured passage of the Norris-La Guardia Act, which provided sweeping protection against antilabor injunctions. But the Wagner Act, together with the CIO's successful organizational techniques, represented much more completely the culmination of the long and often frustrating search for organizational security that Gompers had begun in the 1880s. The influence of the federal government on the stability and growth of many unions, particularly the newer organizations of industrial workers, created a continuing organizational interest on their part in partisan national politics.[33] To that extent, the union-party alliance remained consistent with voluntarist theory. But such a pluralist view could not account so easily for the labor movement's subsequent political behavior. Even apart from the CIO's rather transient radicalism of the 1930s, organized labor felt itself indebted to the Democratic party, and it took the party's interest in winning national elections as its own. As a result, it began to maximize the party's broad political following or constituency, rather than exclusively considering the interests of its own somewhat smaller membership. In this way, the redistribution of economic power to the labor movement partially merged with the redistribution of political power to the Democrats.

Most directly, the many CIO victories in the auto and steel industries in early 1937 have been attributed in part to the Roosevelt landslide of 1936, which, for example, dispelled fear of employer coercion among many steelworkers.[34] Roosevelt himself was, of course, not primarily concerned with union organizational security, but with the welfare of individual workers, and he did little to help pass the Wagner Act. In fact, "he invariably failed to support labor legislation actively until he was convinced it had adequate political support, and he sometimes sabotaged pro-labor policies already declared to be the law because of strong business pressures."[35] But the same process that forced labor to help maximize the party's constituency forced Roosevelt in his role as party leader to consider the interests of one of the most important organized groups in the Democrats' constituency. After the President's break with the business community became explicit in 1935, for example, his overt friendliness to unions increased; he consistently appointed prolabor members to the NLRB.[36] Indeed, the Roosevelt administration was more unqualifiedly and effectively behind such legislation as the Walsh-Healey and Fair Labor Standards acts than the AFL or even the CIO.[37] Roosevelt was not the exclusive architect of the Democrats' alliance with the labor movement, however. Although the President did not involve himself directly in the crucial Flint strike, Michigan's liberal Democratic governor, Frank Murphy, played a vital and sympathetic role. And, despite the influence and seniority of Southern Democrats, Edelman concludes that, from 1931 to at least 1935, organized labor's interests were better served by a predominantly Democratic Congress than by the White House.[38]

The Emergence of Labor's Partisan Campaign Role

By 1936, as a result, a large part of the labor movement went far beyond Gompers' endorsements and exhortations on behalf of the Democrats and began to assume the role of a party electoral organization. The passive official neutrality that the AFL had assumed in 1928 and 1932 could not obscure the federation's commitment to Roosevelt's reelection in 1936, if only because it wanted to have the Wagner Act vigorously enforced. The fledgling CIO, however, made the basic innovations in organized labor's electoral role both in financial contributions and in campaign work. For one thing, as a contemporary scholar observed, until 1936, "the dependence of both Republicans and Democrats upon much the same economic groups for the bulk of their campaign funds [was] one of the factors (although not the only one) which has prevented either of them from becoming outspokenly 'liberal.' "[39] Although John L. Lewis had traditionally been a Republican, his United Mineworkers (UMW) contributed almost $.5 million to the Democrats and other industrial unions contributed lesser sums, permitting the party to make an extensive campaign in the face of a boycott by its former business contributors.[40] Meanwhile, with the cooperation of a number of AFL leaders, including George Berry of the Printing Pressmen as chairman, several CIO unions established Labor's Nonpartisan League as a union campaign organization.[41]

Although the league's efforts were less comprehensive and openly partisan than those of later labor campaign organizations, its workers in heavily industrial states like New York, Pennsylvania, Illinois, and Ohio began to contact voters generally rather than specifically concentrating on union members as Gompers had done.[42] Furthermore, widespread straight-ticket party voting meant that efforts to arouse Roosevelt supporters amounted to campaigning for the entire Democratic slate. This concern with campaign operation increased after 1936. In 1938, the CIO distributed a bulletin called "How to Organize and Conduct a Local Political Campaign," and it supported Roosevelt's efforts to purge Democratic conservatives, claiming several victories.[43] At that point, Joel Seidman suggested that the Democrats, at least under Roosevelt, were a functional substitute for, and were performing many functions of, a labor party. In his view "should [Roosevelt] . . . be succeeded by a conservative in the leadership of the Democratic Party, however, a National Labor or Farmer-Labor Party might be the outcome."[44]

These developments, however, were arrested by the 1940 campaign. As the conflict between the AFL and CIO intensified, President Green denounced the Labor's Nonpartisan League as a CIO puppet and indicated that league support would be a mark against an otherwise prolabor candidate.[45] Although he and other AFL leaders made their personal support for Roosevelt unmistakable in 1940 and 1944, the federation itself remained officially neutral.[46] In 1944, the AFL promised "the most ambitious political drive in the American Federation of Labor's history."[47] But a resolution calling for "permanent, complete and concise plans for getting out the vote," and increasing registration was merely referred to the Executive Council for study.[48]

Meanwhile, the CIO's efforts in 1940 were hindered by John L. Lewis' personal opposition to Roosevelt, which led the executive vice-president of Labor's Nonpartisan League to resign in protest.[49] But the CIO's officers and members remained overwhelmingly Democratic. Many CIO leaders participated as delegates to the Democratic national convention that drafted Roosevelt for a third term and, after the election, they punished Lewis by deposing him as CIO president. Samuel Lubell also found that most CIO workers thought Lewis had betrayed them by opposing Roosevelt.[50] By comparison with 1936, Roosevelt's percentage of the vote actually declined less sharply in industrial areas and among the CIO members than in other parts of the country and among other groups of workers.[51]

Just as Gompers had first entered national party politics in 1906 in reaction to the antistrike injunctions, the Political Action Committee (PAC) was the CIO's response in 1943 to the Smith-Connally Act's curbs on wartime strikes and union contributions to political campaigns.[52] The CIO blamed passage of the law on the defeat of many liberal Democrats in the wartime 1942 elections in which many Democratic voters stayed home. In its efforts to increase the pro-Democratic vote, PAC won the cooperation of some Teamsters' locals, the Hotel and Restaurant Workers, Garment Workers, Trainmen, and many Pacific Coast unions in the AFL.[53] In any case, PAC represented a further significant development in the labor movement's organizational commitment to the Democratic party.

Particularly on the national level, PAC developed a highly bureaucratized operation. PAC not only issued sophisticated campaign manuals like "What Every Canvasser Should Know," but its campaign pamphlets, which evoked the admiration of Richard Rovere, were recognized by *Time* magazine as "far and away the slickest political propaganda in a generation."[54] In this initial effort, PAC was not equally active or thorough everywhere. But in some places it sought to canvass the entire community through "elaborate organization work along the lines of political machines from the bottom up."[55] The CIO's partisan commitment had by now become so explicit, even by comparison with 1936, that it demanded from Congress not just a good labor record but support of the whole New Deal. It carried this battle into Democratic primaries. For example, its opposition helped dissuade militantly conservative Congressman Martin Dies, of Texas, Democratic chairman of the House Un-American Activities Committee, from seeking renomination. For the first time since the AFL's far less extensive campaign for Woodrow Wilson in 1916, a number of knowledgeable observers could credit labor with an indispensable role in a Democratic Presidential victory in 1944, as they would again in 1948 and in 1960.

Samuel Huntington suggested in 1950 that the emergence of the welfare state meant that both major parties would "strive to win, not by converting their opponents, but by effectively mobilizing their own supporters, not by extending their appeal but by intensifying it."[56] But outside the strongholds of their urban machines, the Democrats lacked the organizations that the mobilization of their new urban supporters required, especially in the many states where the Republicans had long been effectively unchallenged. With Roosevelt as a candidate, this process of mobilization through precinct work was less important. But the party's need increased after his death, and it was this need that labor attempted to fill.

The 1944 campaign thus marked organized labor's emergence as a major national campaign organization. It influenced major party decisions as well as partially offsetting one of the Democrats' major organizational deficiencies. Typically, almost everyone was ready to concede organized labor's influence in selecting the Democratic candidate for Vice-President who, only a few months later, became Roosevelt's successor. The AFL had joined the successful coalition that blocked the CIO's first choice, incumbent Henry Wallace. But the CIO was instrumental in vetoing the leading conservative contender, James Byrnes, whereas Sidney Hillman of the CIO quietly but openly supported the eventual willing candidate, Harry S Truman.[57]

Labor After Roosevelt: Political Action, Decline of Militancy, Merger

The CIO retained some of the radical rhetoric and aura of the 1930s in the following decade. Samuel Lubell attributed Roosevelt's victory in 1940 to "a class conscious vote for the first time in American history" on the part of urban workers.[58] In the 1944 campaign, PAC made national governmental planning for reconversion its primary issue, claiming that "some big business-men already have a plan . . . [which] would mean less education for our children, no medical or dental care for millions . . . housing unfit for habitation for a third of the nation."[59]

By the late 1950s, however, articulate critics detected a "crisis" that threatened the American labor movement's vitality and influence.[60] These critics pointed out that union membership had begun to decline in the late 1950s, especially as a percentage of the nonfarm work force, in the face of automation in heavy industry and the increase in hard-to-organize white-collar workers. Meanwhile, the industrial unions that formed the heart of the now-merged AFL-CIO's political campaign apparatus also faced the gradual erosion of the viability of the strike as a weapon in the face of public hostility. The AFL-CIO was so large that even an erosion in size, if it were limited by prosperity and a steady reduction in hours worked per year, would not substantially reduce its potential as a base for a campaign structure in national politics for some time. But the real point of the critique turned on labor's, more precisely the CIO unions', stagnation and loss of militancy.

The critics emphasized changes in both union leaders and members. In 1948, Samuel Lubell observed that, instead of agents of protest, "unions have become a disciplining and stabilizing force upon their own membership." In 1940, one United Autoworkers (UAW) local he visited had reminded him of "the street barricades and sit-down strikes; eight years later it was almost like a lodge hall."[61] Critics like Paul Jacobs complained that even industrial unions, which, unlike the craft unions, had many Negro members, did little to bring Negroes into the top leadership. Older and often complacent bureaucratic union leaders were convinced "that fundamentally the world in which they have achieved leadership is the best of all possible worlds." Yet this complacency, Jacobs implied, "reflects a general satisfaction among their members." Indeed the radicals of the 1930s helped "to create a new middle class of placid workers."[62]

The potential for this accommodationist, nonradical orientation had always been present in the 1930s, but it had been obscured by the bitterness of the CIO's struggle for survival. That struggle was only for recognition by employers in economic life and for the corollary, entry into the political community. It did not really seek basic social change. For all their militancy in trade-union matters, the CIO leaders of the 1930s had no coherent intellectual system that could have stabilized and radicalized their demands for reform. Rather, they conformed to Hoxie's observation a generation earlier that American labor leaders "have been prone to act first and to formulate theories afterwards, and that they have acted habitually to meet the problems thrust upon them by immediate circumstances."[63] Despite his desire to nationalize industry, Walsh saw the CIO "as a group of workaday unions, not a labor movement built on theory. The leaders are workers up from the ranks, not 'intellectuals' . . . [they] can be expected to map its course more by yesterday's experience than by tomorrow's vision."[64] As practical men, CIO leaders were powerfully attracted to the New Deal's moderate social reforms, to the governmentally sanctioned security for unions that the Wagner Act promised, and finally to the status as valued allies of the dominant political party. In its early formative period, therefore, the CIO could never feel excluded from political life, let alone persecuted by a hostile state, as did the AFL in its important formative years. By 1944, the CIO had rejected any third party, either socialist or radical, in favor of more immediate gains. According to President Philip Murray, "we have no desire to organize another political party. As a matter of fact, we are opposed to the organization of a third party, surely at this time, because it would divide the forces of the Progressives throughout the nation."[65]

Murray did not mention another highly practical consideration militating against any radical third party venture: From the CIO's first secession, the more conservative AFL had remained the larger union federation. Even though the NLRB at first favored the CIO, AFL craft unions that had some members in most smaller towns supported AFL competitors including the Electrical Workers and Machinists against CIO unions. In addition, many anti-CIO employers agreed to recognize AFL unions as the lesser of two evils.[66] As a result, the CIO was limited generally to the populous and heavily industrialized East and Midwest. With the larger part of the labor movement opposed, an independent labor party seemed a dubious undertaking.

But while the CIO was abandoning its radical rhetoric, the AFL gradually abandoned nonpartisan voluntarism in national politics. To be sure, the federation was not entirely enthusiastic about either the Social Security Act of 1935 or the Fair Labor Standards Act of 1938 at the time of their passage. But the AFL entirely reversed its earlier opposition to government intervention in union-management relations when it supported both section 7(a) of the National Industrial Recovery Act in 1933 and the Wagner Act in 1935.[67] By the end of World War II, voluntarism as a laissez-faire political doctrine was entirely dead. The federation not only backed the Keynesian fiscal policy of the Employment Act of 1946, but joined the CIO in working for expanded social-insurance programs, including the inauguration of national health insurance and the periodic strengthening of minimum-wage legislation.[68] As early as 1946, Kreps concluded that "the most significant difference" in the political attitudes of the AFL and the CIO "seems to be a difference in scope." Each had moved toward what Father George C. Higgins called a tertium quid between voluntarism and socialism, which happened to correspond closely to the social philosophy of the Catholic Church.[69] Given their common support of essentially all of the Democrats' domestic programs, party leaders, including President Roosevelt, from time to time pressured the two for a merger.

By 1948, the two organizations had also adopted similar formal structures for their national campaign activities. In 1947, the Republican Eightieth Congress had passed the Taft-Hartley Act, which outlawed several important union practices. As in 1942, both the AFL and the CIO attributed the Democrats' defeat in 1946 to a low turnout and relatively little union campaign work.[70] And just as the CIO reacted to the Smith-Connally Act by forming PAC, the AFL formed Labor's League for Political Education (LLPE), with similar campaign goals and congressional-district structure.[71]

In practice, the more conservative traditions of the AFL meant that few AFL affiliates have matched the efforts of CIO unions. In 1948, LLPE's proposal to endorse Truman was deleted from its official report, despite its unofficial Democratic preference. But LLPE functioned within the federation nationally as an organizational pressure group that provided the more politically aggressive AFL leaders such as David Dubinsky, George G. Harrison, and George Meany with a new lever to expand political activities in cooperation with both the CIO and the party. From the beginning, PAC and LLPE found it easy to cooperate on campaign activities in such industrial states as Pennsylvania, Massachusetts, Illinois, and New York. By 1950, united labor committees had begun to coordinate AFL and CIO activities in over a score of states.[72]

In 1949, for example, the AFL agreed to participate in two Democratic party regional conferences.[73] The federation scheduled its 1952 convention before the election so that it could make an official convention endorsement of the Democratic Presidential candidate, Adlai Stevenson. Significantly, the federation cited broader issues like health insurance, Social Security, and public housing, as well as the Taft-Hartley Act, in order to justify so complete a break with voluntarist tradition, and the badly outnumbered pro-Eisenhower contingent did not even protest.[74]

After the AFL-CIO merger in 1955, harmonious cooperation in

electoral campaigns for the national Democratic party contrasted sharply with the bitter quarrels over matters like union jurisdiction. Indeed, the AFL-CIO's organizational ties to the Democratic party and its enthusiasm for the Committee on Political Education (COPE), the successor to PAC and LLPE, steadily increased in the decade that followed. National COPE officials not only cited financial support, but also indicated that COPE reports, which at first had only aroused perfunctory interest within the national executive board, were provoking animated discussion by the mid-1960s.

The AFL-CIO's first president, George Meany, whose own Plumbers adhered to voluntarism, asserted relatively conservative positions on some foreign-policy questions, for example, on the advisability of a United States-Russian detente. Nevertheless, on domestic policies, Meany generally shared the perspective of COPE leaders. As early as 1961, Meany indicated his partisan feelings by endorsing Democrat Richard Hughes for governor of New Jersey against a personal friend, James Mitchell, Secretary of Labor under Eisenhower. Meany feared that even a liberal Republican like Mitchell would be forced by party loyalty to support conservatives opposed to labor. Selecting a successor for COPE director James McDevitt, who died in 1963, presented a different problem. Many CIO officials felt that the logical successor was Alexander Barkan, an articulate and energetic former CIO Textile Workers official. But in the tacit division of offices accompanying the merger, the sensitive COPE directorship had been allotted to the AFL. Still, Meany feared disturbing COPE's operations by appointing an AFL official who had no recent personal experience in the national office. Instead, he postponed the decision, allowing Barkan to serve as acting director, while support for Barkan's promotion mounted among the presidents of the state federations of labor. These officials had worked closely with Barkan on political campaigns and preferred him to an unfamiliar COPE director. Because almost all these officials had AFL backgrounds, their support enabled Meany to make Barkan's promotion permanent.

Under both Barkan and McDevitt, COPE continued LLPE's efforts within the AFL to increase the extent and sophistication of labor's political money-raising, publicity, and campaign activities with apparent success. In 1950, PAC's opposition to Republican Senator

Robert Taft, Sr., of Ohio actually helped to reelect him. But the elder Taft's son, Robert Taft, Jr., a Republican senatorial candidate in 1964, attributed his own unexpected defeat to COPE, which had worked quietly and effectively behind the scenes.[75]

Since its founding, COPE's interrelated goals have consistently been to maximize the alliance with the Northern Democrat party and to rely on issue-oriented welfare-state criteria, in endorsing and working for candidates. COPE's importance as the political bureau of the labor movement with regard to both these goals was illustrated in 1962 by the race for United States Senator for California. The leadership of the California State Federation of Labor, in which AFL unions were overwhelmingly dominant, desired to remain officially neutral rather than to openly endorse Richard Richards, the Democratic challenger. The liberal Republican incumbent, Senator Thomas Kuchel, a good friend of the building trades, appeared likely to win overwhelmingly and had recently pleased many union members by supporting the Kennedy administration's compromise Medicare bill. But COPE had endorsed Richards against Kuchel in 1956, and the Democrat had a nearly perfect labor record as a state senator. By contrast, Kuchel, on COPE's own tally, voted correctly only 55 percent of the time in 1962, or less often than 43 Democrats.[76]

COPE leaders at the national level for this reason and because of their general Democratic partisanship, privately but strongly supported Richards. And the state COPE convention supported them over the objection of several service and craft unions by officially endorsing Richards. The victorious coalition of CIO unions, Building Service, the printing trades, Carpenters, Painters, Laborers, Machinists, and a powerful Los Angeles Electrical Workers local generally shared COPE's welfare-state ideology. But the coalition invoked organized labor's Democratic loyalties as well as the issue criteria set forth by the AFL-CIO bureaucracy. Endorsing Kuchel, these pro-COPE unionists argued, would undercut labor's opposition to the rest of the Republican ticket.

Richards' supporters among the craft unions won an equally significant concession by forcing the California Building Trades Convention to send Kuchel only a letter of commendation, which was obviously somewhat less useful than an outright endorsement. They argued that it would be improper to dissent publicly from the position of the state COPE, to which many building-trades unions belonged. In addition, they threatened to force a vote for or against all the incumbent Democratic state officials running in 1962, many of whom were highly popular with building-trades leaders. Of course, these considerations of partisanship and of the legitimacy of COPE status in the AFL-CIO were important partly because they were articulated by a powerful minority, some of whom threatened to walk out of the convention to protest any official vote for Kuchel. But the importance of COPE's formally legitimate status deserves attention. Many of Kuchel's warmest supporters were secretaries of the state and city building-trades councils who dealt with legislative matters and felt indebted to him. But for many of the local union leaders who were less personally committed to either candidate, the most appropriate course was not to openly disagree with the official endorsing body for AFL-CIO unions.

This organizational commitment of the AFL-CIO to the national Democratic party makes it inappropriate to compare or contrast the labor politics of the 1960s solely with either the militancy of the CIO in the 1930s or with the AFL's political passivity in the 1920s. We must instead distinguish among labor's *political orientation* toward welfare-state issues, the *intensity* of its members' involvement in politics, and the extent of *organizational commitment* to political action. Two decades after World War II, a "crisis" was most evident with regard to a decline in political interest among the rank and file and in the radicalism of union officials. By contrast, the commitment of organizational resources dramatically increased. Perhaps most interesting of all, as the old CIO unions moved toward the Right, abandoning any tendency toward radical political goals, they converged with the AFL unions, which moved toward the Left by abandoning their laissez-faire voluntarism.

Bureaucratization and Working-Class Politics

In terms of empirical political theory these considerations suggest a somewhat peculiar and unexpected association between the development of labor's political organization and the evolution of its political goals. The AFL's movement to the Left in political orientation, and the CIO's movement to the Right were *both* accompanied by the development of formal, permanent, and bureaucratized political action organizations. This development raises in concrete empirical terms an issue that has vexed theoretical analysts of industrial proletarian behavior; the connection between the bureaucratization of working-class organizations and the degree of acquiescence that industrial workers display toward an existing and entrenched capitalist order.

This issue drew the attention of Marxist writers when it appeared at the end of the nineteenth century that the industrial proletariat in Western countries was unlikely to stage a successful socialist revolution. But this debate about bureaucratization paralleled a second dispute that derived from Marx's own teachings, which concerned the importance of economic as opposed to social and political factors in explaining proletarian behavior. The concluding sections of this chapter will attempt to show that, however important the undeniable consequences of bureaucratization on union behavior, they have been too mixed and contradictory to explain satisfactorily the AFL-CIO's role in partisan politics. This conclusion emerges most clearly from the juxtaposition of data about contemporary labor politics in America with the observations of Robert Michels and of V. I. Lenin, who among all of Marx's students had perhaps the most penetrating insights about organizational behavior.

Lenin and Michels on Bureaucratization

For Marx, the proletariat's "vocation in history" was "the overthrow of the capitalist mode of production."[77] Perhaps the most influential explanation for the failure of the proletariat to fulfill the mission Marx set for it has been Robert Michels' analysis of the bureaucratic character of socialist parties and, secondarily, socialist trade unions. As these organizations became large, secure, and bureaucratized, their ruling officials lost their desire to upset their existing way of life and work by seeking basic social change. Michels himself recognized that this bureaucratic conservatism partly reflected the membership's own often conservative distrust of, or simply apathy toward, political change.[78] Nevertheless, these officials were even less willing to embark on risky political ventures that might endanger the organizations that provided them with their middle-class, white-collar positions and styles of life than was their membership. In Michels own words, the former proletarian, turned official,

> accommodates himself to the existing order, and ultimately, weary of the struggle, becomes even reconciled to that order. What interest for . . . [the officials] has now the dogma of the social revolution? Their own social revolution has already been effected. At bottom, all the thoughts of these leaders are concentrated upon the single hope that there shall long continue to exist a proletariat to . . . provide them with a livelihood.[80]

Michels thus emphasizes the political aspects of what Merton calls "the occupational psychosis of the bureaucrat" in which ritualistic repetitive behavior to assure routine and predictable outcomes overshadows other motives and in which change is sacrificed for stability.[80]

Of course, Michels was primarily concerned with overtly socialist parties and unions in Europe rather than with the much more moderate American labor movement. Nevertheless, the AFL's preoccupation with organizational survival and its mainly laissez-faire conservatism in politics before the New Deal seems to fit his interpretation. The CIO's radical posture in the 1930s decisively modified this pattern, yet its abandonment of even verbal interest in the rapid and substantial transformation of American society also seems consistent with a Michelian view. Certainly this view has gained wide currency.[81]

In any case, the specific issue that these Michelian interpretations pose is the greater disposition of the membership than the leadership to insist on and to work for collectivist, welfare-state reforms of American society. Two variables can be identified here: First, the change in the labor bureaucrats' own attitudes because of their middle-class occupations; second, a sense of insufficient political power, or, as Michels put it, "a continued increase in the prudence, the timidity which inspires its policy. The party, continually threatened by the state . . . carefully avoids (once it has attained to maturity) everything which might irritate the state to excess."[82]

An almost directly opposite view, also based on the Marxist tradition, emerged in V. I. Lenin's celebrated early treatise, "What Is To Be Done?" Here, too, several caveats are in order. First, this tract by no means constitutes a final statement of Lenin's own theories. Second, he discusses revolutionary socialist parties in czarist Russia, which are hardly equivalent to American unions after World War II. Indeed, Lenin would probably dismiss the AFL-CIO's efforts as mere "bourgeois social reformism."[83] He contrasts the work of the revolutionaries with "the economic struggle the workers carry on [even through socialist unions] against the employers *and the government.*"[84] Lenin even recognized that the workers' lack of revolutionary zeal could be encouraged, in some cases, by trade-union conservatism, including a preoccupation with "details which positively reek of red tape and bureaucracy."[85] Like Michels, however, Lenin specifies the intervening causal variables by which bureaucratization affects the political activism of working-class organizations. And these variables resemble those in Michels' analysis, including both the officials' superior organizational skills and their middle-class traits of thought and behavior.

Lenin makes a central distinction between the antipolitical spontaneity of the rank and file and the truly political consciousness of the revolutionaries who staff the party organization. The decisive first step from spontaneity to at least embryonic consciousness occurred when "definite demands were put forward, the time to strike was carefully chosen, known cases and examples in other places were discussed, etc."[86] Nevertheless, Lenin insisted, "The history of all countries shows that the working class exclusively by its own efforts is able to develop only trade union consciousness . . . the theory of socialism, however, . . . [was] elaborated [only] by educated representatives of the propertied classes, the intellectuals."[87]

The connection between the Leninist working-class organization and bureaucratization deserves emphasis. Lenin called for a working-class version of precisely those qualities that Max Weber asserts to be the rational asceticism essential to the spirit of capitalism and modern bureaucracy. Rather than going on strike at the moment of greatest passion, Lenin insists on instrumental efficiency, that is, the methodical consideration of the most effective techniques. To quote a descriptive proposition from Nathan Leites, "The Bolshevik must have his feelings under complete control, as does the bourgeois enemy."[88] For both bourgeoisie and Bolsheviks the nemesis was spontaneity. "This ascetism [of the early Calvinists] turned with all its force against one thing: the spontaneous enjoyment of life."[89] Both rejected any desire for economic gain as such. Lenin, for his part, scorned "the spontaneity of those workers who were carried away by the argument that a kopek added to a ruble was worth more than socialism and politics." The Puritans constantly steeled themselves against the temptations of wealth.[90] On the other hand, Lenin aspired to an "organization [that] must consist chiefly of persons engaged in revolutionary activity as a profession," a view remarkably similar to the Puritan ethic of a calling or vocation.[91]

The contrast with Michels could hardly be more decisive. In fact, Lenin goes so far as to advocate explicitly the _embourgeoisement_ of proletarian revolutionaries by taking them out of the factory and training them for middle-class political activity—precisely the process Michels sees as producing conservatism.[92] Equally to the point, Weber specifically relates this ascetic rationality to the development of bureaucracy, whereas Lenin fills "What Is To Be Done?" with a litany on the need for organization and specialization of activity as opposed to the fumbling of a "wretched amateur."[93] In fact, "What Is To Be Done?" emphasizes that this kind of organization is necessarily centralized and authoritarian rather than one that encourages democracy and dissent, thus dovetailing with Michels' analysis.[94]

Effects of Bureaucratization among American Unions

When we apply these Michelian and Leninist propositions to the very different conditions of the American labor movement, we find a clear disagreement as to which strata—the rank and file or the unions' bureaucratic officialdom—has been relatively more "conscious." Which group, in other words, has been relatively more disposed to secure collectivist reforms by partisan political activity than by almost exclusive emphasis on union economic activities?

Significantly, the present study provides abundant evidence that could support both views. Chapters III, IV, and V, which discuss labor's campaign operations in specific urban contexts, indicate a common tendency of union leaders to accommodate themselves to, rather than try to change, the existing pattern of political power. For example, each leadership group found itself at one point supporting an incumbent mayor who had appointed labor officials to prestigious and sometimes well-paying positions but who had not been strongly committed to the social causes of CIO unions. The most striking case involved the most liberal and effective union group examined in this study, the Detroit UAW. Although the UAW and the Wayne County AFL-CIO that it controlled usually supported liberals for mayor and city councilmen, they moved well to the right of their rank and file in 1961 by endorsing incumbent Louis Miriani. They joined conservative businessmen, newspapers, and civic associations, all of whom were humiliated by the upset victory of a liberal Democrat, Jerome Cavanaugh. Labor's endorsement of Miriani thus conformed to much of Michels' analysis. Despite some reservations about Miriani, top UAW leaders as well as the UAW leaders of the county organization had been personally gratified by Miriani's inclusion in his circle of intimates of some of Detroit's most important leaders or their representatives. Union leadership in the county clearly lost touch with their members' sentiments, because the mayor had alienated many white workers who thought him too inactive in the face of the city's massive unemployment. Still more important, he had outraged Negroes of all income groups by failing either to stop a police crackdown in Negro neighborhoods or to support a civil-rights ordinance sponsored by the city's only Negro councilman.

At the same time, the unions' endorsement of Miriani also reflected their leaders' perception of their limited power, another factor Michels perceived. After the repeated defeats of liberal mayoral candidates throughout the 1940s and 1950s, these union officials reconciled themselves to striking the best bargain they could with a moderate candidate who seemed the almost certain winner. With respect to both *embourgeoisement* and timidity because of weakness, the Detroit UAW thus reflected something of the cautious definition of their unions' organizational self-interest that motivated both Gompers and his European contemporaries whom Michels analyzed.

Despite the relevance of Michels' analysis, this study also provides considerable evidence for Lenin's apparently contradictory view, because COPE itself is a bureau of the AFL-CIO devoted to securing a wide number of collectivist welfare-state reforms. Indeed, Chapters VI through IX, which discuss the actual operations of COPE and similar organizations at the precinct level, depict a bureaucratic elite diverting the membership from a primary concern with union economic activity, which Lenin would call spontaneity, to at least an embryonic political consciousness.

Equally important, as the case of Los Angeles COPE shows, this effort is assisted by COPE's recognized status in the labor movement's bureaucratic organization. Weber, of course, may have overestimated the effect of officially prescribed rules in securing uniform behavior in formally monocratic, hierarchical organizations.[95] But in organizations like the AFL-CIO that have few coercive sanctions, the legitimation of an explicitly political bureaucratic structure may be the most powerful agent for coordinating the political behavior of constituent units and for making it more uniform. In 1944, for example, the AFL's Los Angeles Central Labor Council anticipated the federation's commitment to national campaign activities through LLPE by organizing the United AFL Voters League, but some conservative and still voluntarist building-trades unions successfully undermined its activities.[96] Yet by 1962 COPE was functioning without serious challenge as the main political arm for Los Angeles unions. During the intervening period, the area's CIO unions that supported COPE had entered the central council and the still voluntarist Teamsters had left. But AFL unions remained such a large majority (about 80 percent) that COPE could not have won this acceptance unless it retained its status as the bureaucratically designated political organization of the national AFL-CIO. Of course, unions whose feelings or interests were directly involved in particular electoral races freely ignored COPE endorsements. In most races, however, such unions were a minority, and, as in the case of the Kuchel endorsement, unions without a direct involvement tended to follow the course of least resistance and accept the COPE endorsement as authoritative.

The political consciousness of the 1930s was thus "routinized" into organized bureaucratic behavior. For Weber, routinization designated the adoption of a more stable pattern of behavior by an administrative staff previously united by strong personal loyalty to a charismatic leader who had personally assigned duties as he pleased. This more regularized pattern of responsibilities signals the decline of community and spontaneity based on intimate personal communication among disciples who make no distinctions of office, status, or function among themselves. In her report on the sit-down strikes, Mary Vorse found an analogous sense of community and spontaneous enthusiasm generated by the struggle for union recognition. Responsibilities were assigned and accepted on a temporary basis to meet the crisis. Even then, however, this spontaneity was subordinated to the organizational skills and discipline that proved vital for victory. And once recognition was won, CIO unions did bureaucratize as rapidly as their critics charge. In politics, this routinization and functioning specialization through COPE paralleled Joseph Schumpeter's model of bureaucratic corporate innovation in economic affairs.[97]

To be sure, this chapter, among others, shows that on some occasions rank and file workers display considerable militancy. During the Depression, their disaffection was strong enough to override widespread Republican loyalties and ethnic hostility. But such intense class feeling largely succumbed to the general patriotic involvement in World War II. If the successes of the 1930s were to have any longterm effect, they required both economic and political organization (i.e., rationalization) through the bureaucratic development of specialized skills that rank and file spontaneity alone could not provide. At any rate, observers of organized labor's political campaign efforts as early as the 1940s saw labor's campaign organizations as *the substitution of bureaucracy, that is, organizational activity, resources, and expertise, for the rank and file political militancy of the 1930s.* In 1944, Helen Fuller interpreted the formation of PAC as an effort to offset the tendency of labor members to vote only when they were aroused by economic collapse.[98] After the 1948 election, Samuel Lubell suggested that an equivalent for labor's political militancy was "being sought in terms of intensive organization and the expenditure of huge sums of money."[99] In other words, given the decline of class consciousness and especially of interclass hostility, subjective awareness of the differences in political interest among occupational groups was supplemented as the source of class or income cleavage by the emergence of formal political organizations.

In sum, the bureaucratic characteristics that both Lenin and Michels consider cannot by themselves account for either acquiescence in, or a desire to, change the existing social and political order. In linguistic terms, organizational "discipline" signifies a trait that can either enhance the efficiency and thus the fighting quality of a union or enable a bureaucratic elite to control and resist rank and file militancy. The same discipline that united the CIO members so effectively in the sit-down strikes made it possible subsequently for union leaders to enforce their contracts with employers in the face of rank and file dissatisfaction. By differentiating leaders and followers, bureaucratization usually enables union officials to play the most prominent role when they seek either stability or change.

The essential difficulty is that both neo-Michelian and neo-Leninist analyses rely on such organizational or personality attributes as rationality, hierarchy, specialization, and ideological facility to account for substantive goal orientations. Such attributes refer to the technical means that individual or collective actors use to achieve their goals, rather than to the goals themselves. As Weber observed, "bureaucracy as such is a precision instrument which can put itself at the disposal of quite varied—purely political as well as purely economic, or any other sort of—interests . . ."[100] Indeed, the ascetic rationality Weber describes not only characterized Lenin's anticapitalist and antidemocratic aspirations but also those of religious and often theocratic Puritans and those of the secular, purely capitalistic but democratic Benjamin Franklin.[101] Bureaucratization magnifies, clarifies, and rationalizes whatever goals the organization or individual bureaucrat seeks, but it does not determine their substantive content.

Conditions Favoring Union Activity in
National Politics

Our problem, therefore, is to specify the conditions that pre-
dispose union officials toward aggregating class-oriented activities in
national political campaigns and those that encourage them to adopt
a cautious pluralist posture. The first two chapters have suggested
a variety of such factors. The composition of the unions' constituencies directly reflects the impact of industrialization. The growth
of union membership during the New Deal in itself promoted
bureaucratization, but it also meant that only broad welfare programs
of the federal government could comprehend the new diversity in
the political interests of union members. This tendency was particularly strengthened by a change in the movement's class composition
through the addition of many unskilled and semiskilled industrial
workers. Their relatively weaker economic-bargaining position made
these workers more dependent on governmental assistance than were
the highly skilled AFL craftsmen, whose unions accordingly proved
less enthusiastic COPE supporters. In addition, these factory workers
produced for national markets affected by federal government
policies, unlike the service and construction workers in the AFL. For
several reasons, then, industrial-union officials could justify an active
role in national politics as directly benefiting their members with
regard to social insurance, rate of pay, and working conditions. As a
service to the membership, political action thus served the union
officials' organizational maintenance objectives.[102]

The process of industrialization also contributed to the activism
of union officials in a less direct way. Broad government regulation
of the economy is not the inevitable result of the growth of heavy
industry, as attested by the wide differences among countries in the
extent of this government intervention and in the promptness with
which it appeared. Nevertheless, the stresses and dislocations imposed by the heavily industrialized but disastrously deranged American economy in the 1930s was an indisputable motive for the spate
of New Deal regulatory legislation. As this economic regulation increased, the national government came to affect not only the wages,

hours, working conditions, and employment of the rank and file as well as their overall income but also the regulation of collective bargaining itself and thus the union organizations that provided labor officials with their jobs. Given the differences of the two major parties on just such issues, even AFL officials acquired a strong incentive to influence party politics. Of course, Gompers himself, the architect of voluntarism, favored the Democrats in national politics to the degree that he found them more friendly than the Republicans. Once the New Deal began extensive regulation of the economy, however, this contrast was sharply increased, and a stress on actual campaign work rather than mere endorsements developed. One reason for this shift may have been that a major danger to union survival—the restrictive provisions of the Taft-Hartley Act— were attributed by the AFL as well as by the CIO officials to too little union involvement in national politics rather than too much. The obstacles to the additional growth of union membership, and thus to greater organizational power, in the South and among white-collar workers made political campaign activity an inviting arena in which union officials could seek to increase their influence.[103]

Among officials from nonfactory unions this consideration proved most important to the officers and staff of the AFL-CIO and many local and state federations of labor. Because these officials do not perform many economic functions, they need other activities to justify their organizations, and thus their own positions, to their immediate constituency, the officialdom of their affiliates. Because national government actions have begun to affect so directly the activities of these affiliates and thus of union officials, the function of coordinating political activities through COPE provides union federations with a justification that their constituents increasingly recognize.[104] By 1962, President Meany could say that political action is "labor's important activity at this time."[105] In sum, as the national and regional "peak" association of employee organizations, the AFL-CIO and its local and state federation affiliates began to represent wage earners as a class in the increasing number of cases in which the government undertook to regulate industrial capitalism. The conjunction of these direct and indirect consequences of industrialization on labor officialdom was reflected in the alignment within the AFL-CIO. In the face of still vigorous voluntarist opposition from some nonfactory AFL leaders, industrial-union officials of largely CIO background joined with these largely AFL union federation officials to form a pro-COPE coalition.

A third condition affecting the activism of union officials has been the very different relationships the AFL and the CIO each had with the political authorities during their first formative years. From the very beginning, CIO unions were so much a product of the entire New Deal period that their own organizational security became associated in the minds of many of their leaders with the larger struggle for welfare legislation. By contrast, the trade unions that founded the AFL faced a hostile state, but one much less repressive than, say, the czarist government in Lenin's time. As a result, neither reformist nor revolutionary politics attracted the early AFL. Even in the 1960s, Amalgamated Meat Cutters and Butcher Workmen (formerly AFL) followed a less aggressive role in national politics than the Packing House Workers (formerly CIO), another industrial union in the same industry.*

The impact of historical experience has been mediated and modified by still another factor, the unions' subsequent relation to the party system. From the 1930s on, the opportunity to ally so closely with a major party slowly but visibly undermined the AFL's traditional political caution. As Michels expected, union officials did associate increasingly with other members of the middle class, but, given the American party system, their associates in national politics were often liberal Democrats as favorable or more favorable to welfare-state programs than many union officers themselves. Still, these politicians, almost without exception, shared the AFL's satisfaction with capitalism. In the case of CIO officials, however, this association with middle-class liberal Democrats had an opposite effect. The CIO leaders' inclusion as valued participants in the majority-party coalition that accepted capitalism from the unions' very first years almost inevitably sapped these industrial-union leaders' political militancy, sense of outrage, and desire for radical change.

This last condition affecting union officials' political posture thus brings us back to the basic descriptive thesis of this study: Organized

---

* This point was suggested to me by John Dunlop of Harvard University.

labor functioned throughout the 1960s as the most important nation-wide electoral organization for the Democratic party. Indeed, this alliance with the party helped produce the convergence of AFL and CIO unions with respect to both political goals and the formation of political campaign units. In order to help the party assemble the electoral majority necessary to win power, CIO unions had to abandon their radical rhetoric and aspirations just as the AFL had to abandon their exclusive political concern with the specifically organizational goals associated with voluntarism.

Labor, the Lower Classes, and the Party System: A Comparative Analysis

A list of factors such as those just considered does not tell us their relative importance or which part of the variance (in this case the union officials' behavior) each factor explains. The first two factors, however, involve industrialization, and the other two involve the historical and contemporary impact of the political environ-ment. Our analysis of the effects of bureaucratization thus raises the still older debate concerning the importance of economic, rather than political, variables in explaining working-class political behavior. In order to pursue this issue we shall make use, in different ways, of each of the three analytic approaches considered in Chapter I, that is, social stratification, political system and role, and size of political unit. It must be emphasized, however, that this analysis is designed to explain primarily the period *from the New Deal through World War II,* when the American labor movement was unusually animated by the working-class loyalties aroused during the Great Depression. To be sure, these activities, which have been described earlier in this chapter, decisively shaped the development of labor politics in the generation that followed the war. Nevertheless, as the following chapters make clear, the later period of union political activity was characterized by a *partisan* rather than an overwhelm-ingly *working*-class orientation. In Chapter XI we shall propose an interpretation of American labor politics in the 1960s that looks beyond working-class issues to the consumer-class politics now emerging. What follows may be considered an interpretation of the working-class interlude in American labor history.

Political Conditions: Suffrage and the Party System

The argument for weighting political factors heavily in explaining working-class political activity, presumably including trade-union campaign activities, has been powerfully stated in Reinhard Bendix's analysis of nineteenth-century Europe.

> Marx looks upon social movements of the 19th century as protests against psychic and material deprivations that cumulate as a result of the capitalist process. . . . I interpret these movements as *political* and define their character in terms of the contrast between a premodern and modern political community.[106]

Rather than alienation from the work process, Bendix therefore emphasizes *"political alienation,* that is, a sense of not having a recognized position in the political community or of not having a civic community in which to participate."[107] One among several sources of this sense of deprivation was the suffrage issue. Specifically, having come to believe in civic equality, lower-class citizens view their exclusion from the suffrage as a "denial of respectability . . . tantamount to the right of existence."[108] It would seem to follow, therefore, that the political activity of American union members during the New Deal reflects a desire for the right to vote less as an instrument to alleviate economic inequality than as a good in itself.* The early formal extension of suffrage in America—even though it seems related to the absence of feudal class distinctions—creates a difficulty, since workers during the New Deal did not resent the symbolic

---

* Conceivably Bendix might consider the protests of the 1930s as a demand for another civic right, that of association in trade unions. (*Ibid.,* pp. 80ff.) But this right was long held by American workers and even the crippling effect of injunctions had been reduced by the Norris-La Guardia Act *before* Roosevelt took office. Rather than the political right to organize, the real issue in the 1930s was the unions' economic power to survive. This power against a hostile management was materially increased by the Wagner Act, but the effectiveness and strength of unions are basically economic phenomena, and the workers' support for the CIO appears to have been directly the result of the economic grievances in the plant. See Vorse, *op. cit.,* and Walsh, *op. cit.*

indignity of legal exclusion from the electorate. If, however, we consider actual electoral participation rather than formal qualifications to vote, the situation appears analogous, if not identical, to those Bendix studied. This step has been made possible by Walter Dean Burnham's brilliant study of the American electorate's changing participation rates.[109] Burnham argues that by driving the Democrats back to their Southern and Border State strongholds and by making the rest of the country overwhelmingly Republican, the 1896 voter realignment caused by the nomination of Bryan reduced voting turnout.[110] By depriving the voters of a meaningful opportunity to defeat one party and to elect another, the electoral system produced "a devolution, a dissociation from politics as such among a growing segment of the eligible electorate and an apparent deterioration in the bonds of party linkage between electorate and government."[111] For example, turnout nationally was lowest in 1920–1924, when relatively conservative Democratic candidates provided the least contrast with Republicans on domestic issues since 1904. The highest turnout levels, both nationally and in the five states that Burnham studies in detail, occurred between 1876 and 1896, a period of extremely close partisan competition.[112]

Unfortunately, Burnham's voting data do not provide specific evidence that the decline in turnout was disproportionately heavy among the urban lower classes. Indeed, the absence of survey data and the limitations of the 1890 census make statistical testing of this proposition difficult. As V. O. Key has pointed out, however, one-party systems generally discourage lower-class voting. And Burnham adds that in the North, the Republican party, which from the first attracted the support of the most economically privileged elements in American society,[113] was the chief beneficiary of the 1896 realignment. It became the dominant party nationally, losing the Presidency only twice until 1932, once by an extremely narrow margin and once because of its own internal divisions. Its almost unprecedented landslide victories occurred in elections at which turnout declined. Furthermore, once in control of federal and state governments, the Republicans pursued probusiness policies that alienated the AFL. A similar conservative predominance was even more dramatic in the one-party Democratic South where the entire low-

income caste of black ex-slaves and many poor whites were dis-
enfranchised during much of this same period.[114]

Burnham's analysis intersects with the argument of this chapter
because the decline in turnout was at least moderately reversed by
the 1928–1936 critical election that strengthened the Democrats
throughout the country (as he emphasizes, however, participation
remained well below nineteenth-century levels). Once again, the
rapidity of the increase made it unlikely that assimilation of immigrants was the sole cause. Bendix's analysis, therefore, enables us
to attribute the lower-class upheavals of the 1930s, especially the
outbursts of industrial workers and the CIO's alliance with the Democratic party, not to economic alienation but to effective exclusion
from the political community. This view is strengthened by the often
explicitly political form many of the protests in the 1930s took. The
period not only saw massive changes in party loyalty but unusually
strong affection—and hatred—toward the chief political figure, the
President, as well as the more diffuse, short-lived but still impressive,
popular support for various radical politicians. The CIO itself demonstrated a concern for politics unprecedented among well-established
major American unions. Bendix's explanation of the decline of
radicalism among European socialists in terms of political factors
appears to work equally well in explaining the CIO's loss of militancy
since the 1930s, provided we equate political equality with actual
voting as well as with formal extension of suffrage.

> Rather than engage in a millenarian quest for a new social order, the
> recently politicized masses protest against their second-class citizen-
> ship, demanding the right of participation on terms of equality in the
> political community of the nation-state . . . we [thus] have a clue
> to the decline of Socialism. For the civic position of these classes is
> no longer a pre-eminent issue in societies in which the equality of
> citizenship has been institutionalized successfully.[115]

In Bendix's terms the labor-Democratic alliance would thus represent
an informal arrangement by which "participation on terms of equality
in the political community of the nation-state" is "institutionalized."

The correspondence between the informal character of this institutionalization—in contrast to the formally working-class socialist
parties of Europe—and the informal exclusion of workers from the

vote up to 1932 provides the most persuasive argument of all for accepting Bendix's approach. In the case of the United States in the 1930s, precisely because the exclusion from suffrage was not formal (except for Southern blacks) it had less symbolic impact and was much less explicitly "a denial of respectability." In turn, these weaker feelings of political alienation appear to explain the moderate, welfare-state rather than socialist, orientation of the labor movement under Roosevelt and the essentially "practical" rather than ideological character of the CIO *even in the 1930s*. Similarly, at an organizational level, mass suffrage meant the Democrats already enjoyed the allegiance of some urban workers and were ready to seek the allegiance of others as the Depression deepened. This procapitalist party thus had a relatively easy time co-opting the leaders of industrial unions as they appeared. This amalgam of Bendix's and Burnham's analyses is a powerful argument for heavily weighting the influence of political factors on the behavior of union officials.

Economic Conditions: Industrialization

At best, however, this approach cannot account for the predominance of industrial unions, including those which were founded long before the CIO itself, in organized labor's national campaign activities. The classic counterargument for the impact of industrialization on working-class political behavior appears in the *Communist Manifesto*:

> . . . with the development of industry the proletariat not only increases in number; it becomes concentrated in greater masses, its strength grows, and it feels that strength more. . . . Thereupon the workers begin to form combinations (trade unions) against the bourgeois; they club together in order to keep up the rate of wages; they found permanent associations. . . . This union is helped on by the improved means of communication that are created by modern industry and that place the workers of different localities in contact with one another [and] . . . centralize the numerous local struggles . . . into one national struggle between classes. But every class struggle is a political struggle.[116]

To an impressive degree this formulation accurately identifies the important factors that enabled CIO unions to organize in the face of both employer opposition and the ethnic and racial divisions among factory workers. Many welfare-state reforms sought by American unions also seem specifically designed to alleviate the problems posed for industrial wage earners by an impersonal urban society.

Significantly, Burnham's own historical account is more favorably disposed toward Marx's concern with economic causation than is Bendix's. In his view, the "system of 1896" meant "the conversion of a fairly Democratic regime into a rather broadly based oligarchy."[117] During the "take-off phase of industrialization," this oligarchical system with its reduced voting functioned "to provide adequate insulation of the industrializing elite from mass pressures and to prevent their displacement by a coalition of those . . . damaged by the process of capital accumulation."[118] By contrast, the 1928 realignment—which increased the electoral participation of the lower classes—provided, in Burnham's words, "at least partial orientation toward the broader ends of an urban industrialized society."[119] The history of nineteenth-century strikes reviewed in Chapter I reinforces this stress on the economic component in lower-class discontent. American workers used far more violence in their spectacular strikes half a century after they acquired the vote and while voting rates were at their peak than the CIO strikers used during the New Deal. Certainly the economic alienation of industrial workers subjected to the particularly hard working conditions of the period seems far more important than a sense of exclusion from political life. If anything, the political repression of trade unions in this period indicates a reduction in the autonomy of the American political system from political and social pressures. Industrialization made the nineteenth-century capitalists so powerful that judicial and legislative policies came to reflect, almost directly, the wishes and interests of a single privileged economic stratum.

Just as obviously, the timing of these lower-class protests of the 1930s can only be explained by the collapse of American capitalism after 1929. The hostility that many industrial workers revealed toward their employers suggests that whatever the undeniable sense of political exclusion, economic grievances played their role in both the founding of the CIO and the construction of the Roosevelt coalition. Indeed, Burnham's own published data indicate that voter participation—as distinct from strength of partisan identification—actually continued to increase.[120] For example, national turnout in Presidential elections, which grew from 51.1 percent in 1920–1928 to 59.1 percent in 1932–1946, rose to 60.3 percent in 1948–1960. Off-year turnout rose from 35 percent in 1922–1930 to 41 percent in 1934–1946 to 44.1 percent in 1950–1962. It was the rate of increase rather than the increase in participation itself that declined.

Stated in terms of rate of increase, Burnham's data conform to our interpretation of the AFL-CIO's campaign activities as an effort to maintain the effects of the New Deal realignment, after the decline of rank and file militancy during the 1930s threatened to weaken the Democrats. This organizational analysis in this volume, however, is hardly consistent with Burnham's assumption that a "political organization more advanced than the 19th century middle class cadre party [failed] to develop in this country."[121] Important details of Burnham's own analysis actually suggest that industrialization had a vital impact on the labor movement's role within the party system. Out of the five states he studied in detail, the two where the New Deal had the most dramatic impact in increasing voter participation were Michigan and Pennsylvania, the centers of the auto and steel industries and the domains of two strongest CIO unions, the UAW and the Steelworkers. And, as Burnham himself adds, one reason Ohio had so limited a resurgence in voting since the 1930s was the weakness of organized labor.* At least indirectly, these considerations indicate the continued importance of the economic factors that

---

* *Ibid.*, p. 19. Burnham's entire analysis represents an insightful instance of the size-of-analytic-unit approach. Among other things, it contrasts the larger, presumably more diverse electorate and larger, more diverse constituency of the Democrats after 1930 with the smaller electorate and Democratic constituency earlier. Through employing party system, urbanization, and industrialization as explanations for these shifts, Burnham's findings illustrate the partial overlap of the size-of-analytic-unit approach with both the social stratification and political system role analysis. This overlap reflects the concentration of size-of-unit-analysis on empirically characterizing the policy outputs and other behaviors of the political system. In turn, this characterization facilitates the moral evaluation of the system as distinct from the comparison of the causal importance of political and economic variables. Perhaps for this reason, Burnham does not specify what part of the political change he discusses can be traced to political causes and what part can be traced to economic factors.

stimulated the political activism of labor officials, notably those from industrial unions.

Polity, Economy, and Lower-Class Protest

In the case of the United States, the lower-class protests involved resentment both at exclusion from the political community and at the rigors of industrial capitalism. The American case is revealing because each type of grievance first appeared by itself before they appeared together in the 1930s. When economic resentment operated alone in the late nineteenth century, such protest often took the violent but disorganized and transient form of riots. When the political motive operated alone, it stimulated the democratic nationalism of the Jacksonian era.[122] Both motives operated jointly in the United States in the 1930s, as they did in parts of late nineteenth-century Europe.

Examined in detail, these American revolts compared with the protests of European socialism reveal a pattern of similarities and differences. With Marx, we can say that the similarities reflect the common experience of industrialization and the workers' common grievances against it. In all countries, these feelings encouraged political activism on the part of union leaders. With Bendix, we can say that the differences reflect the widely varied problems that the lower classes encountered as they sought entry into the life of their political communities. The degree of disaffection caused by political exclusion and the resulting militancy varied from country to country depending on each country's particular political traditions. In sum, we would explain the common impact of industrialization in terms of that cluster of attributes of American labor politics (prominently including the behavior of union officials) that at least partially approximated the collectivist and still nominally socialist unions of Europe. On the output or policy side these attributes include similar government functions, that is, welfare-state programs designed to improve the working and living conditions generated by industrial capitalism and the bureaucracies charged with administering these programs. On the input or demand side they include somewhat similar alignments based on class or income among party supporters and the emergence of parties oriented toward the working class that have trade-union allies and somewhat similar campaign structures for mobilizing supporters.

On the other hand, if these lower-class movements have similar welfare-policy contents and similar party *structures,* they are animated by very different ideologies and emotions. Furthermore, as Burnham emphasizes, the New Deal realignment did not raise turnout rates to the pre-1896 levels, which were comparable to those in contemporary Western Europe. Even after Roosevelt, the American party system failed to involve the "lowest income strata" of the potential electorate.[123] The lower levels of turnout (in comparison with Western Europe) parallel the less impressive unions and the smaller welfare-state programs and the weakness of American socialism. We would agree with Bendix that this cluster of attributes, which highlight the conservatism of American politics, can be explained in terms of the idiosyncratic political norms, traditions, and structures of the American polity. And it is precisely these conservative factors that have encouraged the voluntarist tendencies and general political caution of American trade-union officials.

However paradoxical the outcome seems, the net effect of the economic process of industrialization has been to increase organized labor's political activism. At the same time, the political conditions that have contributed to American labor's unique conservatism encouraged concentration on the immediate economic interests of the unions. At least for a decade beginning in the 1950s, however, most union activities in national partisan politics centered around —though they were far from encompassed by—the organizational complex of the AFL-CIO and its affiliates. This fact, as well as conceptual parsimony, makes it desirable to characterize organized labor's politics not in terms of these two contradictory aspects, but as a single subsystem of activity specifically linked with other parts of the American political order.

As this chapter has shown, the labor union-Democratic party alliance was part of a larger change in the entire structural pattern of the American party system. In turn this different structural pattern qualitatively changed the "mix" of welfare issues that reached the American political agenda, reflecting the impact of industrialization.[124] By contrast, the important differences that have continued to exist between American and European working-class politics tend to be behavioral and quantitative—consistent with the size-of-political-unit approach—rather than qualitative and structural. They include, in comparison with Western European countries, the lower turnout rates in American politics, the smaller size (as a percentage of the work force) of the trade-union movement, and the less collectivist ideology of labor and the Democratic party. This situation suggests the analytic utility of Easton's concept of flow channels of demands, the pattern by which citizen demands reach the authorities, provided it includes organizational structures.[125]

The union-Democratic party alliance, as part of the larger welfare-state pattern of flow channels that emerged after 1928, qualitatively resembles the equivalent flow channels elsewhere. Both patterns of channels reduce (i.e., collect and combine) the demands of similar economic strata, chiefly lower-class wage earners, into roughly similar issues that relate to welfare-state programs.[126] All these flow channels direct such demands and issues to roughly comparable authorities including the welfare-state bureaucracies and the political appointees who supervise them. On the other hand, the flow-channels notion is equally suited to characterizing the quantitative differences we have attributed, with Bendix, to political factors. First, the flow channels in European political systems have greater capacity to process and handle working-class demands, say, for national health insurance, than the comparable channels in the United States. Second, the persistence of pluralist politics in the United States, including many trade-union political activities, indicate that this pattern of welfare-state flow channels in America constitutes a relatively smaller fraction of the entire network of channels in the political system as a whole than those in Europe.

The origin of these quantitative differences in channel capacity and extent are clear enough. In most Western European countries, traditional class antagonisms had already made the working class so cohesive that, after enfranchisement, its Socialist parties, often allied with unions, could quickly place proletarian demands high on the national political agenda. In the United States, a working-class partisan coalition emerged much more slowly, partly because it depended on realigning many long-enfranchised workers into one political party, itself traditionally capitalist, which then through the New Deal helped create a friendly industrial-union movement. Clearly, this re-alignment of existing channels rather than forming new ones left a residue of norms, loyalties, and habits that reduced the impact of the change. Even apart from the question of accepting socialist ideology, many AFL unions retained their pluralist conception of politics, whereas the Democrats remained a largely rural, conservative party in the South and some other areas. Necessarily, the resulting pattern of welfare-state flow channels had less capacity and made up a smaller part of the whole system than in Europe. This pattern continued in the generation after World War II. Nevertheless, the pattern of union participation underwent a subtle change in which a partisan orientation toward the Democratic party gradually replaced the *working*-class orientation of the 1930s. In the chapters that follow, I will explore and interpret the sources and character of this shift, which reached particular prominence during the Democratic party's national dominance from 1961 to 1966.

III

Chicago:

The Dilemmas of Patronage Politics

A study of union campaign activities in the cities of Chicago, Detroit, and Los Angeles from the AFL-CIO merger in 1955 through the mid-1960s, both confirms and elaborates the propositions that concluded our historical review of trade unions in national party politics. In all three areas a substantial group of unions that campaigned for liberal Democrats in national elections found over time that they had to come to terms with—and were thus restrained by—the local political and social environment. Yet the political activism of union leaders in the three cities and their capacity to serve as structural flow channels for certain welfare-state demands varied with both the economic and the political context. The power of a patronage-oriented Democratic party organization encouraged the unions' cautious pluralist attitudes toward national party politics. On the other hand, a concentration of heavy industry and thus a strong industrial-union movement encouraged vigorous partisan activity.

Fortunately for comparative analysis, the three cities differed so much on these economic and political variables that the Chicago, Detroit, and Los Angeles labor movements actually covered much of the voluntarist welfare-state dimension. Because of the United Automobile Workers' unusual political militancy and activism, Detroit COPE's political style reflected the relatively class-conscious ideological labor politics of the 1930s. Detroit thus ranked at the upper end of a continuum among large American cities that measures the scope and influence of labor political action organizations. Los Angeles COPE confronted the fragmented suburbanized politics of the 1960s, characterized by weak party organizations and shifting individual and group alliances. The resulting situation (the Los Angeles unions became one of several active party groups) best exemplified the influential, but clearly not dominant, relationship of the entire American labor movement to the national Democratic party. Certainly, the position of the Los Angeles unions fell between the positions of Detroit and Chicago unions. In fact, organized labor's role in Chicago, even after the AFL-CIO merger, was in many ways closer to the voluntarist politics of the 1920s than to the political ethos of either the 1960s or the 1930s, with a relatively low level of influence within the party on behalf of welfare-state issues.

Machine Politics and Organized Pluralism

During the 1960s, corruption in Chicago government was sometimes proved and much more frequently alleged, but, as one of its better-known aldermen put it, "Chicago ain't ready for reform yet." The city's political life was an anachronism, bemoaned by many, savored by others, and still more or less effectively imitated by many cities in the Northeast. The difficulties of Chicago COPE paralleled those of "good government" reformers who were limited by the strength of the last survivor of the great political machines. Indeed, this regular Democratic party organization operated on pluralist principles that valued politics as a source of specific discrete, often material, benefits for particular small groups or individuals. The system was hostile not only to reform, but also to any primary concern with welfare-state issues. Political loyalties were based on a network of personal friendships and alliances that were far more important than one's position on issues affecting large classes of people. Equally important, through its own effective electoral organization in the lower-income areas of the city, the regular Democratic party organization substantially, although not completely, preempted the campaign function that COPE and its allies have sought to assume elsewhere. Political activists in the Chicago labor movement thus found themselves frustrated by their inability to conform to national COPE policy.

Of course, Chicago in this period was neither antiunion nor politically conservative. The city had a large labor movement with a substantial group of former CIO unions and a benevolent official attitude toward strikers and pickets. The Chicago area was also a Democratic stronghold and the party's cohesive congressional delegation regularly compiled, in COPE's eyes, an unblemished voting record. Nevertheless, the limits on labor's role within the Democratic party were set by the strength, following, and ambivalent attitude of the regular Democratic organization rather than by Republican hostility. This ambivalence did not grow out of the principled objection to labor goals that unions still find among many conservative Southern Democratic leaders. The real difficulty was a subtle and often unacknowledged indifference among party leaders to any general social principles whatever—and a determined refusal to see such principles become the central criteria in making party decisions.[1] COPE's predicament was magnified because ambivalence, and thus an instinctive desire to curb the entire political-action enterprise, also characterized the party's basically voluntarist labor allies who include many of Chicago's most powerful union leaders.

COPE only gradually accepted its subordinate position in this system of highly organized pluralism. Relations between the Chicago party organization and industrial unions oriented toward political action began with great bitterness in 1937 when the CIO was just emerging. In the celebrated Memorial Day massacre the city's police shot and killed ten strikers and wounded others in front of the Republic Steel plant. The CIO's attitude is revealed by the account of one of its partisans. "The testimony [before the La Follette Civil Liberties Committee of the U.S. Senate] goes on to show that this was a planned attack, that the police came out with the intention of shooting down the workers and then arresting them wholesale."[2] Public reaction was so outraged and the new industrial unions already so large that the party organization agreed to alter drastically the police department's attitude toward strikes.[3] Tension continued, however, and in the late 1940s and early 1950s those union leaders who were trying to conform to labor's ideological orientation in national politics at times openly opposed some of the Chicago party's nominees as too conservative. When Fay Calkins surveyed the relationship of the party organization to COPE's CIO predecessor, the Political Action Committee (PAC), in several states, Chicago provided her one illustration of overt conflict between the CIO and a regular party organization.[4]

Yet the party and the anti-COPE labor groups who were relatively inactive in campaigns for national office—working together and separately—effectively curtailed COPE's operations so that by the 1960s it no longer attempted to place its campaign workers throughout the city. Nor did it usually contest party nominations— even when it had qualms about the organization's candidate. Fifteen years after the Calkins' study, the once rebellious labor political-action movement accepted its status as one of the relatively junior partners in the party's coalition. It concentrated on activities and areas important to labor but not threatening to the Democratic organization.

Even in the 1960s, however, an underlying tension remained. COPE's most faithful supporters, the city's large industrial unions, continued to rely heavily, though not exclusively, on a welfare-state reformist ideology to recruit their campaign organization. The use of such ideological incentives encouraged political alliances with like-minded politicians who inspired campaign workers to undertake often tedious election work. In other words, COPE sought to "rationalize" its selection of political goals or ends by basing its endorsements on the impersonal criteria of the candidates' adherence to liberal social issues. It thus invoked such formal standards as voting records on government policies that benefitted entire classes of citizens rather than specific persons, and it relied on abstract appeals designed to motivate entire groups of union members.

By contrast, the party and non-COPE unions preferred a relatively narrow politics of group and individual interest. Both appealed to the material self-interest of their members. Similarly, both relied on a network of personal contacts and friendships in making political alliances, and within these networks positions on issues were not decisive in themselves. It was only in terms of selecting goals for campaign work, however, that COPE can be said to have sought a more "rationalized" politics than the party and the party's powerful labor allies. In terms of political means, these groups used patronage and the motive of personal gain to achieve an organizational effectiveness that rivalled and partly resembled that of successful business corporations, and that far outstripped COPE's.[5]

Chicago thus exemplified the pluralist tendency in American politics since the late nineteenth century—successful interests attempt to magnify their power by creating strong formal organizations.[6] In Chicago, the power of the party organization stimulated individualism, concern for specific economic-group interests, and loyalty to individual political allies. Such considerations can powerfully motivate lower-class and lower-middle-class wage earners, as well as the more economically prosperous. We have already seen that, with some variation, these motives fostered pluralist union politics from the demise of the Knights of Labor to the rise of the CIO, and hindered the voluntarist AFL's acceptance of the welfare state. Although a similar problem also confronted COPE in Los Angeles and Detroit, the organizational strength of the Chicago party leaders and their labor allies enabled them to elevate these tendencies into a widespread if not pervasive pattern of behavior. In other words, they built a local political culture that rendered Chicago COPE an alien organization.

Chicago COPE retained some vitality in the face of these obstacles primarily because its political goals formed part of a larger set of mutually compatible developments produced at least indirectly by industrialization. These trends include not only the emergence of the welfare state but also a nationwide evolution in urban politics that eroded even some of the Chicago organization's strength and made union efforts for Democratic candidates welcome. To be sure, the party's continued power, including its control over the offices of local government, has made its co-optation of most industrial unions quite visible. But in a simultaneous if less obvious process, while COPE accepted its organizationally marginal position within the party, it found an area where its activity was accepted. It did so by operating in precisely those politically marginal areas where Democrats and Republicans were nearly equal in numbers and where the party electoral organization had faltered.

Pluralist Constraints on COPE Within the Party Organization

Even though patronage-based party organizations have been greatly weakened since the 1930s, a generation later they still influenced or controlled the politics of such major American cities as Buffalo, Philadelphia, Cleveland, Pittsburgh, St. Louis, Kansas City, Albany, Newark, Gary, and parts of New York.[7] In the case of Chicago, the party's unusually effective system of jobs and favors that still motivated its formidable corps of precinct workers in the 1960s has been accurately and repeatedly described.[8] This persisting strength may reflect the fact that patronage-oriented Chicago Democrats acquired full control of local politics later than their counterparts elsewhere. As a newly secure organization inhibited by few outdated patterns inherited from an earlier era, it appears to have had far greater flexibility than other machines in adapting to changed conditions of urban political life after 1930.[9]

Fundamentally, such adaptability meant blending those elements essential to the survival of machine politics with more general elements of political pluralism that made Chicago's Democratic city administration acceptable to influential upper-income groups in the community. This blending meant that in its entire range of transactions as a "business organization"[10] with its employees, customers, and suppliers, the machine preferred to deal pluralistically with small rather than large aggregations of people.

In the case of the precinct captains, the machine's employees, the predominant motive was individual material rewards, often including full-time employment. As a result, a pluralist principle of catering to narrow, specific group and individual interests pervaded the party's own internal operations. The otherwise substantial discretion of its top leadership was limited by a set of internal norms that governed the relationships among the ethnic, economic, and political interests in the party. Labor leaders, for example, suggested to Mayor Daley that the party might reduce the suburban Republican majorities and thus help elect county and statewide Democratic candidates by strengthening the undermanned suburban-township organizations with more patronage.[11] This suggestion was not widely adopted partly because allocating large numbers of jobs to the suburban organizations would violate the party tradition of rewarding the most successful constituent organizations, that is, the Democratic city wards. Redistributing patronage would take jobs away from these ward organizations, and thus conflict with the immediate self-interest of their workers, who depend on such jobs for their livelihood. As a result, the party sacrificed the opportunity to increase its capacity for winning certain crucial elections, because its precinct workers, who collectively influenced party policy, valued jobs even more than they valued maximizing political power.[12]

In making payments to the electorate, the group that supplies the party with votes, the precinct captains, traditionally employed positive inducements like personal friendships with individual voters, assistance in finding jobs, and help in dealing with public law enforcement and service agencies. As welfare-state bureaucracies took over these functions, the captains increasingly offered to help secure welfare payments and, it is alleged, began to threaten uncooperative voters with such sanctions as eviction from public housing or cessation of welfare payments. Party workers have also been reported to dispense whiskey or a Christmas basket and to pay as much as $10 for theoretically passing out campaign literature on election day, as well as making smaller outright payments to secure a vote.[13] The precinct captain also looked after the physical condition of the precinct and handled voters' complaints about traffic lights, garbage collection, and street cleaning. The party's continued success in both primary and general elections in the inner-city wards suggests that these divisible incentives to individuals or particular neighborhoods primarily appeal to the lower-income and lower–middle-income voters. These groups presumably assigned so low a value to their vote and so high a utility to the precinct captain's specific material inducements and friendship that they were willing to sell him their franchise. More generally, these voters expected relatively concrete and divisible benefits from politics—precisely the attitude of such voluntarist ideologies as pluralism.[14] Indeed, the party workers' own view of politics as the means of earning a living reflected their usually, though not invariably, lower-class background.[15]

In dealing with its customers, from whom it receives substantial financial contributions, the party also favored widely distributed disbursements to specific groups or individuals in the form of contracts or purchases. Indeed, the essence of the party's technique was to reduce conflict among important groups in the city by allowing each to influence the policies that most directly affected it. In this way it built as large a constituency as possible, thus securing its own tenure in office. The narrower each group's demands, the less likely that they would conflict with the goals of other important groups in the party's diverse constituency. During the 1950s and the early 1960s, for example, the party cooperated in the *Chicago Tribune*'s successful campaign to build the McCormick Place exhibition hall; the University of Chicago obtained both an ambitious urban renewal project and increased police protection in its neighborhood; and each Democratic ethnic group received a share of places on party tickets. Meanwhile, the Chicago business community got "new lights on bustling State Street; an all out city campaign to attract new industry; urban renewal; . . . labor peace with few crippling strikes; [and] some five hundred million dollars in super-highways to lure suburbanites downtown to shop."[16] All these groups supported Mayor Daley for re-election in 1959, 1963, and 1967.

The Chicago Democratic party, in other words, acquired a formidable expertise, or professional competence, in the practice of organized political pluralism. When two important groups did clash, the party thus tended to act as a neutral broker to reduce the conflict without committing itself to the substance of the issues. Black civil-rights leaders charge that because of white pressure, Chicago lagged behind other big Northern cities on civil-rights issues, especially education, well into the 1960s. On the other hand, the Daley administration has gradually increased police protection for blacks moving into white areas adjacent to the ghetto and for those wading off formerly white public beaches. The party organization also supported an Illinois Fair Employment Practices Act and a Chicago city ordinance that required that blacks be admitted to all hospitals and forbade discrimination in housing by real-estate brokers. Again, despite Chicago's international reputation for organized crime and graft, the city tried to pacify "good government" reformist opinion by cleaning up its contract-awarding procedures and dramatically revitalizing a scandal-racked police department. In each case, however, it made concessions that it thought would arouse the minimum adverse reaction among those who were opposed to the change.

The extent to which this pluralist organization differs not only from COPE but also from other professional politicians deserves some emphasis. Members of the Chicago party organization did not entirely conform to a Schumpeterian or Downsian model of political behavior, in which issues are viewed instrumentally as a means to specific material payoffs, especially jobs. It is in precisely this respect that the party was "apolitical."[17] As Chapter VIII indicates, labor unions in COPE were more willing than some middle-class liberal groups to condone material payoffs for the party if they helped elect liberal Democratic legislators. Even so, however, COPE's causal priorities were the reverse of the party's. Such jobs were valued as a means to power, and power in turn was valued as a means for effecting labor's social policy.

This reversal of priorities as to jobs, power, and issues illuminates a critical difference between labor's relations with professional Democratic politicians in the Chicago party organization and its relations with Democratic professionals in other cities that did not have a powerful machine. Although Democratic officeholders elected in Detroit and Los Angeles were generally more commmitted to pressing welfare-state issues than those chosen by the Chicago organization, they too were obviously concerned with gaining and holding power, that is, elective office (for example, consider the analysis in Chapter

IX). But patronage jobs, at least on a scale large enough to support a significant campaign organization, were simply unavailable in both cities. As a result, even where professional politicians treated power as their primary concern, issues became a major secondary consideration and, indeed, an immediately available instrument for obtaining their primary goal of winning elections. In sum, labor could deal with these politicians more easily because they treated issues as a second-order rather than as a third-order consideration. In the case of the Chicago party leaders, jobs and power (in that order) had to be considered before issues. The result was not simply nor even primarily the relatively conservative records that Democratic officials compiled in Illinois. This downgrading of issues also created a difference in style and temperament that continuously interfered with communication between the party organization and COPE workers.

A centrally organized pluralism of this sort differed from equally pluralist systems in which entry to the political marketplace depended almost entirely on the group's own organizational strength. The resistance of Chicago's pluralist political system to nonpluralist politics was intensified by the organizational power with which suspicious and often openly hostile party leaders could oppose all organized ideological groups, notably middle-class reformers.[18] As an independent political organization seeking to mobilize the same Democratic voters as the party, COPE posed a potential threat. First, union members could convince undependable Democrats who might vote against the organization to register, and such registrations would upset the captains' calculations. Second, COPE's issue-oriented appeals to the electorate could have weakened the loyalty of those voters on whom party precinct captains already rely. Theoretically, the party's ultimate sanction was to support governmental policies relatively unfavorable to labor. Such punishment was difficult to employ on major issues, because the Democrats also had a lower-class constituency, both in national and in local politics. But the sheer professional skills of the organization's precinct captains enabled them to freeze COPE workers out of particular precincts, wards, and even whole congressional districts, for example, the south- and west-side black ghettos and the nineteenth ward. As a result many unions simply refused to support any COPE activity in areas where the party objected.

Many congressional-district COPE organizations were not so directly subject to the party leader's orders. For one thing, neither the party nor the COPE structures were sufficiently monolithic to enforce central commands in every case. For another, many COPE organizations and leaders perceived themselves as essentially free agents. They did not operate as if they were under party orders continually but justified very limited COPE activity in the poorest areas of the city by pointing to the normal large Democratic majority, which suggested that COPE workers could add little to the party effort. Of course, ward committeemen had other ways of effectively obstructing COPE. By not telling COPE leaders where the ward organization was weak, top party leaders let COPE workers waste their time in precincts that the party workers had already effectively covered, thus preventing them from reaching more fruitful areas. In some cases, inexperienced COPE workers were discouraged from covering a precinct simply by the assertion of a party leader that the district was already well covered.

When an individual precinct captain protested the arrival of a COPE worker in his precinct, his ward leaders sometimes called the congressional-district COPE headquarters to demand withdrawal of the COPE member. The response varied from district to district but, if COPE was satisfied with the precinct's voting record, it usually agreed lest the member do more harm than good. If the COPE organization did not agree, the captain could tell his loyal core of voters in the precinct that the COPE worker was a fool or a carpetbagger meddling in the neighborhood. When the COPE worker called on these voters, he faced many hostile morale-sapping receptions. If the COPE worker replied in kind, the resulting quarrel could lead the voter to oppose COPE's congressional candidates, who were less important to the organization and its precinct captains than local candidates who dispense patronage. When the COPE worker was unfamiliar with the voters in the precinct, a common occurrence, the precinct captain could imitate his ward leader by not revealing which homes were Republican, Democratic, or independent. The COPE worker thus had to spend most of his time speaking to hostile

Republican partisans and Democrats who had already been covered by party workers, and would have little time for undecided or apathetic voters.

Apart from sabotaging COPE efforts in the precincts, the party could also threaten to withdraw or reduce the substantial benefits it made available to organized labor as a whole. The party controlled the reception that the disciplined Democratic delegations in Congress and the Illinois legislature gave labor's demands. Although the party was necessarily prolabor on well-publicized issues, it had more latitude on bills of interest to particular unions and still greater discretion on the material incentives that it offered union leaders and members. Broadly speaking, the party could: (1) offer material incentives to individual COPE rank and file precinct workers and thus merge them into the party organizations; (2) offer incentives for cooperation from individual union leaders in the form of public appointments and other perquisites from the party; (3) induce particular union organizations to follow the party's line on major political issues. As Chapter VII shows, each of these tactics in varying degree affected every major union in Chicago. Together they substantially limited COPE operations. In a city where politics was most fundamentally not a contest for power and therefore control over public policy, but a primary source of livelihood and only secondarily a contest for power, COPE continues to be a suspect and relatively weak alien.

Pluralist Constraints on COPE Within the Labor Movement

The leadership of the powerful Chicago Federation of Labor (CFL) strengthened the obstacles the party leadership presented to COPE's political action objectives. After an excursion outside the two-party system into militant independent labor party politics in the 1920s, when the Democrats were weaker,[19] the CFL consistently followed the formula and philosophy of "business unionism," little changed from Gompers' voluntarism. The most significant political action activities were therefore undertaken by the CIO unions affiliated with the Cook County Industrial Union Council (CCIUC). In 1962, the CFL and the much smaller CCIUC merged to form the Chicago

Federation of Labor-Cook County Industrial Union Council (CFL-CCIUC). In the discussion that follows, CFL refers both to the Chicago Federation of Labor before merger and the voluntarist business-union leaders who retained control of the merged CFL-CCIUC.[20]

As business unionists, these CFL leaders found the pluralist political style of the Chicago party much more congenial than COPE's ideological goals. Their voluntarist view that unions should concentrate on securing the best possible wages, hours, and working conditions for their members squared with the party's preference for pluralist group allies with limited aims. And because wages in many of these unions, particularly the building trades, ranged above $5 per hour, the leaders felt little need to tinker with the existing system. The nature of the work of the building trades enabled the leaders to do favors for the many small employers with whom the unions bargained—facilitating work and assigning good workmen, for example. As good businessmen, many leaders profited from this situation.

Such leaders were no more antipolitical than the Democratic party organization. Rather, both groups subordinate national political issues to local ones; policies benefiting a few broad groups, to pluralist policies benefiting many smaller groups. Craft unions in particular have traditionally been vitally concerned with such local matters as "codes, licensing and apprenticeship laws and other legislation; political appointments to inspectors' jobs and other jobs less directly connected with union welfare . . . contracts, help in strikes . . . and often their share of political graft. The common theme was jobs for members."[21] William McFetridge, former president of the Building Service Employees International Union and the most powerful leader in the CFL for many years, abandoned his life-long Republicanism during the regime of the exceptionally skillful and powerful Democratic leader and mayor, Richard J. Daley. But personal friendship with Daley and respect for the Democrats' increasing dominance of Chicago politics motivated McFetridge's change more than any commitment to the welfare-state issues of the national AFL-CIO and the Democratic party. His practicality typified the CFL's general approach to politics. In 1954, the CFL's paper, *The Federation News,* supported a compromise reapportionment that gave the Democrats a chance to control the Illinois house but left Chicago underrepresented (by population) in a firmly Republican and conservative senate:

> Those who adhere to an all or nothing policy in any form of political action [the *News* argued] usually wind up with nothing.
> Trade unionists are practical people. They know that the adamant "whole hog" attitude in collective bargaining doesn't always bring home the bacon.
> This is even more true in the complex field of politics. . . . The easy way out of a fight is to take an extreme position and retire from the arena because you don't like the rules.[22]

The similarity of political styles and specific material goals helped produce close personal ties—even friendships—between the CFL and Democratic organization leaders. Meyerson and Banfield ascribe many of the difficulties of the Chicago Housing Authority in the late 1940s to the middle-class background of the authority's staff, which differed dramatically from that of the party leadership. By contrast, the CFL leadership shared with most party leaders a lower-class, usually Irish Catholic background, and the native ability and toughness that helped both groups achieve organizational and economic success.[23]

This web of relationships is well illustrated by the career of CFL President William Lee, an anti-Hoffa leader of the Teamsters and former president of the Chicago Bakery Drivers Local. By 1962, Lee had replaced his supporter, ally, and patron McFetridge as the strongest figure in the CFL-CCIUC, and he was far stronger than the presidents of the Detroit and Los Angeles union executive organizations. After the Teamsters were expelled from the AFL-CIO, Lee joined the Building Service Union in order to remain eligible for CFL office. He played an increasingly independent role partly because McFetridge lost the presidency of his international union and partly because Lee had control over WCFL patronage and finances. But the most important reason for Lee's influence may have been his close relationship with the mayor. As one of Daley's most trusted allies in civic affairs, Lee served as a loyal administration spokesman on the Mayor's Citizens' Committee, which nominated Chicago school board members, and on numerous other civic committees. In 1965, he personally negotiated an agreement that avoided a politically damaging school strike. For some years he was a Chicago civil service commissioner, an important post for a representative of organized labor. Within the CFL he firmly opposed any proposal that might offend the party leadership.*

The CFL-party alliance also depended, of course, upon a complex exchange of specific favors and benefits and only some of which were even indirectly related to the maintenance of the national union-party alliance that had taken shape during the New Deal. For the party organization, CFL endorsements helped maintain the Democrats' popular image as the representative of lower-income groups. CFL unions also contributed financially, both by supporting individual party candidates and by backing other fund-raising events. The unions, for example, bought tickets for fund-raising functions held in off-years, when normal campaign contributors were less in evidence. Lee and others also dependably represented the mayor's interests when they served as union representatives on committees that purported to represent the entire community, like the governing board for the Chicago War on Poverty programs and citizens' committees for various bond issues.

In return, the party provided CFL leaders with a wide range of benefits. Union leaders believed the attitudes of the city's police department and judges toward strikes to be quite satisfactory.[24] Apart from appointing union leaders to prestigious or well-paying public positions, party leaders also enacted favorable ordinances governing the construction industry, maintained high wages for union members employed by the city, and had its legislators take prolabor positions in Congress and in the Illinois legislature.† This list of benefits demonstrates the party's dominant position in the alliance.

---

* Lee, of course, was not the only Chicago labor leader who has had a government appointment from the party. McFetridge has had one of the few paid appointments on the Chicago Park District Commission, an important dispenser of party perquisites. Labor has two positions on the school board, and one on the Chicago Housing Authority. Labor representatives have held lesser positions, on the Library Board and on the Tuberculosis Sanitarium Board.

† Symbolic gestures can also be important. Many labor leaders were flattered to be guests of the mayor at a luncheon in honor of the visiting Queen of England.

The party could find money and dependable allies in other groups, and partly derived its reputation as the representative of the less well-to-do citizens from the national party's reputation. But the CFL unions, especially given their concern about local ordinances in the construction industry, had no fully satisfactory alternative to alliance with the party.

Nor, indeed, was there an alternative for individual labor leaders. Richard Rovere observed that Sidney Hillman's eminence in labor politics reflected his skill in building upon his position in both the labor movement and the Roosevelt administration by continuously drawing strength from one position to bolster his position on the other. He became the political leader of the CIO, in other words, because of his entrée to the New Deal, but this entrée also reflected his position within the CIO.[25] Although Hillman also benefited from his leadership of a fairly sizable union, this observation does suggest the important way in which an informal elite network, by cutting across formal party and union structures, permits individual leaders to pyramid or multiply their power. Several CFL leaders, including McFetridge and Lee, thus significantly reinforced their power within the labor movement by acting as the channel for the mayor in his dealings with other union leaders. The mayor's position in the party was marginally improved in turn, of course, because he enjoyed close personal relations with important labor leaders. As a result, the alliance between the party and the CFL rested on a pyramid of mutually reinforcing, if unequal, relations among their top leaders. The importance of these relations meant that this mutual interpenetration enabled each partner to influence the other organization's internal decision-making processes on political questions.

Significantly, this interpenetration also occurred, as we shall see in Chapters VIII and IX, where the Democratic party and the local unions were committed to social reform. But in the case of the CFL and the regular Chicago party, the exchange of favors, the similarity of styles and the personal friendships permitted an intervention in each other's decisions that actually impeded efforts to elect issue-oriented liberal congressmen. In fact, the CFL and the Chicago Democratic party organization typified very well the potentially conservative tendencies of such working-class organizations and are thus consistent with Michels' analysis. Each flourished during the generation after the New Deal because their shared emphasis on narrow goals rather than broad changes in governmental welfare policies contributed to a mutually profitable modus vivendi with each other and with the Chicago business community as well.

This pluralist alliance with the party was the CFL leadership's most obvious motive for limiting the development of a strong COPE organization. At any time COPE unions might upset the partnership by opposing regular party nominees as insufficiently liberal or issue oriented. Consistent with the voluntarist perspective on maintaining their organizational position, however, the CFL leaders had several additional reasons for fearing COPE operations as a threat. For one thing, these officials, who were at least middle-aged in the late 1950s and early 1960s, distrusted issue-oriented campaigns for the national Democratic party, partly because such precinct work was unfamiliar. More specifically, a union political organization concerned with electing Democrats who favored welfare-state policies appeared to be a possible competitor for their members' loyalty. Members who actually participated in COPE might develop organizational skills that would help them challenge existing union leaders. In at least a few cases, such political activists were put on the union payroll as employees of their union officers, reducing the possibility that they would become insurgents. Most dangerous of all, perhaps, COPE's campaign activities—provided they did not challenge party activity—might prove more valuable to the party than the CFL's traditional personal relationships and financial support. Rather than antagonize the party, COPE leaders might begin to rival the CFL leadership as the party's most important allies in the labor movement.

Before merger with the CIO's Cook County Industrial Union Council (CCIUC), these considerations led the CFL leadership to curb the activities of Labor's League for Political Education (LLPE), COPE's AFL predecessor in Chicago. In order to maintain the appearance of compliance with AFL national policy, the CFL followed a common practice of Mayor Daley's city administration. It established a bureaucratic structure whose formal table of organization and operations faithfully conformed with national policy, but was also one that had only severely limited impact on actual campaign work. In particular, the LLPE maintained an extensive file system of union members by place of residence. In theory this system singled out un-registered union members so that LLPE workers could urge them to register and then vote for labor-endorsed candidates. National polit-ical action leaders considered this structure the best in the country. The inevitable problem of constant changes in address aside, how-ever, many unions flatly refused to submit their membership lists. Some feared that the lists might be obtained and exploited for their own purposes by employers, rival unions, or clothing and tool sup-pliers. Other unions simply disliked LLPE's entire enterprise. One of the most powerful CFL leaders ordered a local under his control to withdraw its membership list immediately when he heard that it had sent it in to LLPE. Some locals supported LLPE secretly, and only contributed money for district headquarters. Few actually supplied significant numbers of precinct workers who might have used the registration lists as a meaningful campaign device. In 1958, James McDevitt, then director of national COPE, complained publicly that:

> Here in Chicago you have one of the finest political education facilities anywhere in the country . . . a registration program second to none . . . [but] I am gravely disturbed at the lack of interest shown by the unions and their leaders. . . . [Among our] serious problems . . . is our inability to get to the membership . . . and one [local] leader can keep us from reaching many members.[26]

Even apart from precinct work, Chicago LLPE faced greater re-strictions than in any comparable city. The Illinois Federation of Labor (IFL) controlled endorsements for state candidates, and the CFL insisted on making all endorsements in local elections. "We felt we had to go outside the federal field," one LLPE leader recalled, "but every time, we felt the CFL or the IFL pushing against us. After all, they could threaten any time to take over LLPE and kill it."

Rather than destroy LLPE, however, the CFL let it struggle for support and money without benefit of per capita contributions by the affiliated local unions. Finances had to come from a variety of fund-raising affairs and whatever local unions happened to contribute. Even after merger, the CFL maintained its casual attitude toward political action by adjourning for the summer in 1962. Its first meeting, in October, was thus held well into the campaign and after registration closed. An even more serious obstacle was the lack of strong leadership. LLPE lost its most powerful chairman when Joseph Keenan of the International Brotherhood of Electrical Workers (IBEW) became secretary-treasurer of his international union in Washington. His IBEW Chicago successor later demanded that one of the local's business agents resign as LLPE chairman on account of the organization's liberal policies. Indeed, several LLPE chairmen, often because of pressure from their local unions, entirely abandoned LLPE activities after stepping down from leadership.

These difficulties were not wholly eliminated by the LLPE-PAC merger that formed COPE and made national political campaign activity a direct responsibility of CFL leaders. For one thing, the CIO unions in Cook County that favored such political action made up only about one-third of the county's AFL-CIO membership. This disparity and differences over political action contributed to a seven-year delay, one of the longest in the country, from the time of the national AFL-CIO merger in 1955 to the CFL-CCIUC merger in 1962. More fundamentally, as Chapter II showed, COPE and its predecessors indirectly represented the impact of industrialization on the behavior of American unions in national politics. They focused primarily on those policy outputs of the political system designed to satisfy certain demands of the industrial working class and to contain the influence of large industrial corporations. But this concern for policies or ends in principle precluded any emphasis on a political means as a good in itself. COPE could never give first priority to the CFL's organizational and personal benefits produced by an alliance with an issue-indifferent party, precisely because its primary concern was with welfare issues as system outputs. Accordingly, COPE tried to subordinate political means to the official, formally stated ends, by "rationalizing" both the Chicago labor movement's process of endorsing candidates and its entire relationship with the party. It favored *formal* procedures for making endorsements and universalistic criteria for evaluation stands on issues, despite the CFL's primarily *informal* relationships with important politicians and with the party organization as a whole.

We have argued that COPE met with such limited success in this effort because the CFL and the party leaders concentrated so effectively on mastering political techniques and assembling organizational resources, the means to achieve power. For just this reason, as Chapters VI through IX indicate, the CFL and the party were able to control COPE's endorsing procedures and to shape its criteria in order to protect their informal relationships. Insofar as Chicago COPE tried to follow the national pattern as a structural flow channel for welfare demands, it found the party and the CFL strong enough to reduce its channel capacity. COPE did, however, continue to operate; its function as a flow channel was never completely stopped.

COPE's Resources in Chicago

The sheer size, wealth, and organizational resources of Chicago's industrial unions, themselves fairly direct results of industrialization, were indispensable prerequisites for COPE's modest but significant political action program in Chicago. But the political importance of these same unions was substantially, if less directly, strengthened by the impact of industrialization as well as by urbanization, the diffusion of formal education, and the development of welfare-state orientations even in nonfactory unions.

Even though the CFL has been among the most faithful adherents of voluntarist belief and practice among all city central labor unions, it could not ignore the national government's growing regulation of labor-management relations that so visibly affected the AFL and other union federations. As the two parties, nationally and in Chicago, came into conflict over labor and welfare issues, it became difficult for even the most conservative CFL officials to support many Republican candidates. The clearest change involved the CFL's rhetoric—it became far more issue-oriented than the AFL's pronouncements under Gompers. Under its liberal editor, Irving Klass, *The Federation News* took highly issue-oriented and strongly Democratic positions from the early 1950s on without departing from CFL policy.* At the same time, the CFL was pushed steadily closer to endorsing national Democratic party policies by virtue of its alliance with the local Chicago organization, whose legislators and spokesmen regularly supported the national party's welfare-state position.

These trends were furthered by the merger of the CFL and the CCIUC. Of course, the Steelworkers and the Automobile Workers had enough money, members, and skilled leaders to carry on precinct work without the CFL. Open CFL opposition to COPE activities could not have stopped all election work in national campaigns in the industrial areas of Cook County. But COPE supporters also included AFL leaders in the printing trades, and in such unions as the Jewelry Workers, Furniture Workers, and Boilermakers. These leaders happened to be outside the dominant network of personal relations and influence within the CFL. But they were important in working out the unofficial merger of LLPE and the CIO's PAC at the congressional-district level, long before the official CFL-CCIUC merger. Other COPE supporters included service unions in the hotel, restaurant, and retail fields, together with some Building Service locals (once McFetridge was no longer an international union president).

The selection of John Cullerton as the first director of Chicago COPE after the CFL-CCIUC merger indicated that there was substantial support for COPE, provided its activities did not directly threaten the party. Cullerton, who became director of the Illinois Department of Labor in 1963, was admirably fitted for the role of first COPE director. As manager of the joint board of the Hotel and Restaurant Workers, he had an independent position of power in Chicago labor. He was trusted by the CIO and COPE leaders as an articulate liberal who was genuinely committed to political action. Yet as the son of a Democratic alderman and the nephew of the powerful county assessor, Cullerton also had the confidence of the party organization. Partly for this reason, he was acceptable to the CFL as well. Cullerton's position, person, and rhetoric, therefore, functioned to bridge the gap between those who backed COPE and those who distrusted it.

---

* CFL President Lee himself has become committed to national Democratic politics as a result of his alliance with the local party. He has been a delegate to several national conventions. Stephen Bailey, a power in the CFL, was the grand marshal of the party's massive parade for Kennedy just before the 1960 election.

He sought to make COPE effective without upsetting labor's alliance with the party that he thought invaluable to labor. Rather than contest party endorsements, he favored registering prolabor (i.e., Democratic) voters and getting them to vote, activities that would help elect liberal candidates but did not threaten to upset the party's patronage system.

As this formula indicates, Cullerton articulated a policy of stabilizing COPE's position both in the CFL and vis-à-vis the party. Indeed, COPE's precinct work for Democratic candidates may have reinforced its position in the CFL-CCIUC just as some CFL leaders feared. Insofar as COPE simply supplemented party efforts, it was valued as an unorthodox but still cooperative ally, particularly among party leaders outside the inner-city wards. An effort by the CFL to curb these operations entirely might have actually antagonized party leaders. In turn, this modus vivendi with the party was possible because the regular organization was disproportionately strong in Chicago's inner-city wards and relatively weak in the more prosperous residential wards and suburbs where more and more Democrats live.[27] For it is in just these areas that better-educated and better-paid citizens, who are unwilling to exchange their vote for the inducements a precinct captain can offer, are most numerous. For many such voters, good citizenship requires a choice between candidates and parties on the grounds of either personal qualifications for office or issues—that is, the criteria of "good government."

In some suburbs, the Democratic township organizations were so weak that they were sometimes covertly controlled by the local Republican organization, which could offer key leaders local government patronage. In other suburbs, like Evanston and Rich Township, this same lack of material incentives enabled issue-oriented liberals to assume leadership of the party organization. These same factors allowed labor to secure a major voice in party decisions in the Cook County's southeastern suburbs. Even regular-organization precinct captains in the suburbs did not completely resemble their Chicago counterparts. One liberal politician from the southern suburbs observed that:

> They may not be willing to admit it, but almost every captain out here has some concern with issues. There is some patronage from

the county, but not that much. We've had so many defeats, they can't be concerned with just winning. These people know the differences between candidates and they work harder for those they admire.

COPE's Accomodation to Chicago Pluralism

Party weakness was much less pronounced but still important for COPE in some of Chicago's outer residential wards where the voters also responded to "good-government" issue appeals. As elsewhere in the city, the controlling concern was for power and jobs but the basis for an accommodation existed. Where the party already had difficulties in covering the precincts, COPE workers who supported Democratic candidates were sometimes welcomed as an opportunity rather than resented as a threat. But such cooperation at the ward level was not automatic; it depended on the personal feelings of the ward leader. Until he became used to COPE he might be uneasy simply because the issue-oriented style was so unfamiliar. In some areas, however, COPE's general lack of interest in patronage jobs gradually allayed the leader's suspicions so that COPE precinct work was perceived as "free" labor. COPE was particularly welcomed in national campaigns where it could supply campaign literature and workers who are somewhat familiar with the issues, as many party captains were not.

Similar accommodations also took place between the individual precinct captain and the COPE worker. The Steelworkers in particular instructed their men to explain their activities to the precinct captains and to offer cooperation.* COPE workers in some cases jokingly reassured the captain by claiming, "We have better jobs than you, why should we want your job?" The cooperation of the captain, however, was not cost free, for some of them tried to persuade less sophisticated COPE workers to support local candidates, who control patronage, rather than COPE's national candidates. Indeed, the captain may have cooperated most with personally unaggressive COPE workers who followed the captain's suggestions and were thus less

---

* On occasion, regular channels of communication did develop. One steel worker who was also a party precinct captain reported that his party leader had written a union leader praising his work.

threatening. In these cases, some party workers actively encourage the worker to participate in subsequent elections.

The important point to emphasize is that this accommodation with COPE in "good-government" wards and precincts was part of a much larger process by which the party sought to adapt to local politics after the New Deal. This adaptation involves a wide range of government policies that the party has endorsed in order to appeal to good-government voters. In his study of Chicago politics, Banfield describes good-government as a variable mixture. On one side it includes reform, "the suppression of vice, crime and political corruption," and "efficiency" in the day-to-day administration of the government's business. On the other hand, it involves "progressive," largely New Deal, welfare policies, and "big projects—airports and exhibition halls, for example—to boost the size, business and repute of the city."[28] Significantly, these elements appeal to liberals as well as to conservative businessmen. But such policies also reflect an orientation toward the political system as a source of collective policy outputs for the entire society, in contrast to the machine's view of it as a source of income for its members. "Big projects" and "progressive" policies, of course, are clearly outputs in themselves. Reform and "efficiency" concern the capacity of the city government for the efficient conversion of resource inputs (largely money) into just such policy outputs. In other words, all four elements reflect a post-New Deal view of government as an instrument for social change, an instrument that must be made as administratively effective as possible in order to achieve desirable goals.[29]

Even the good-government forces in Chicago who were less concerned with progressive welfare issues shared with COPE a stress on political policy outputs because both groups saw government as an appropriate agency to regulate the economic and social change sparked by industrialism. In the face of this joint pressure, the Democratic party tried where it could to maintain its appeal in middle-income areas through popular policies that did not threaten its source of material incentives. For example, the Chicago organization used the national party's and COPE's social issues to divert attention from embarrassing local matters. In the spring of 1962, Mayor Daley publicly urged the organization to mobilize behind President Kennedy's national campaign to enact Medicare through Social Security. Party workers dutifully circulated petitions calling for its passage. Significantly, the party enthusiastically embraced this popular issue just at a time when voter unrest over local real-estate taxes and scandals in the Chicago Sanitary District had become most obvious. The party also often chose candidates who appealed to good-government voters to lead its ticket. It recommended such men in statewide and citywide races where these groups are particularly strong. Most of these candidates, including Adlai Stevenson (1948) and Otto Kerner (1960 and 1964) for governor; Paul Douglas (1948, 1954, 1960, and 1966) and Sidney Yates (1962) for United States Senator; and Adlai Stevenson III and Joseph Lohman for state treasurer (1966 and 1958), also appealed to most pro-COPE unions. These steps reveal the effectiveness of an existing pluralist political structure in accommodating to social and economic change without substantially harming its own operations.

Yet, for all this resourcefulness in the face of social and economic change, the good-government predilections of so much of the electorate has detrimentally affected the party's operations in two major ways. First, faced with relatively fewer voters in the entire metropolitan area who responded to material incentives, the party did begin to make its appeals in terms of good-government issues.[30] But these policies were less stable attractions to an at least partially issue-oriented electorate than were favors and perquisites to previous generations of urban immigrants. And on issues like integration there is always the danger that the party can find no generally popular course. The crisis over the integration policies of the Chicago Board of Education may offer an example. The taxpayer's revolt against a series of important bond issues in the 1962 spring elections offer a second instance. At the same time, the party's incentives for its workers became less effective because patronage jobs became increasingly less competitive with private employment opportunities in a prosperous economy. Patronage jobholders have tended to be somewhat less energetic than formerly and are often poorly equipped to appeal to those voters who now desire at least some superficial discussion of the issues. It was this sheer organizational weakness in some areas of the city that made COPE's campaign assistance so desirable.

A second difficulty, as Banfield emphasizes, is that effectively appeasing good-government groups by introducing reforms sometimes mean sacrificing substantive party interests. New administrations in the police department and the sanitary district, for example, reduced the jobs and other material perquisites available to ward committeemen. Indeed, as such good-government issues became important devices for winning elections, even at the cost of patronage, they appeared to have an additional feedback effect on party leaders. To the extent that they wished to defend their activities as desirable rather than merely necessary, they appeared to weaken in their opposition to a policy-oriented form of politics. Certainly such politicians may see real advantages in working with an issue-oriented group like COPE that is not primarily interested in strict reform (as distinct from "progressive") social-welfare issues.

To summarize, a tacit working arrangement between COPE unions and the party emerged, but in a form somewhat unusual in Chicago politics. Ordinarily, the party proved extremely considerate of the specific and often material interests of such groups as businessmen, craft unions, the Catholic Church, and the University of Chicago. But Chicago businessmen were not able to reverse the party's support for social-welfare legislation in Washington. Nor was a Catholic spokesman heeded on urban renewal near the University.[31] By contrast, the party listened to COPE on a wider range of issues, not only on social-welfare policies, but also on the nomination of some—though by no means all—party candidates. Unlike almost all other groups, labor carried on precinct work with tacit party approval in some areas of the city. But COPE exercised decisive influence in few, if any, of these areas. Several other factors, including loyalty to the national party and to its lower-class constituents, constrained the Chicago organization to support social-welfare reforms. Similarly, COPE's precinct workers were the controlling force in only one or two suburbs at most; elsewhere they only supplemented party activities. And COPE had the final influence on nominations only in the same suburbs. All this may have been the best bargain it could hope for. Certainly, it was on these terms that the party incorporated COPE as a usually reliable ally and that the trade unions interested in influencing national politics have found a place for themselves in their local political environs.

Conclusions

Chicago COPE's accommodation with the powerful organizational pluralism of the CFL and the Democratic party was a local variant of the process by which American industrial unions abandoned their quasi-radical goals of the 1930s. Detroit and Los Angeles will provide us with very different examples of this same process, but the Chicago case also emphasizes the important role that the local Democratic party usually has played in producing this political caution and moderation. Yet the capacity of Chicago pro-COPE unions to operate in some national campaigns, given their particularly forbidding local political culture, suggests that industrialization helped push American labor politics very far indeed from Gompers' voluntarism. We thus return to the connection between economic and political change considered in Chapter II. We concluded there that the character and traditions of the American political system do account for American unions' relatively moderate role in national politics, but that the emergence of this partisan role itself must be traced to the impact of economic industrialization. In terms of political systems analysis, these union activities for the party in national electoral politics constituted flow channels for certain nonpluralist welfare demands of wage earners. This pattern of flow channels resembled those provided by social-democratic union-party alliances in Western Europe, but they operated with a clearly more limited capacity to transform these demands into collectivist issues and ideologies.

By creating these channels, even with their limited capacity, industrialization has nevertheless reduced the pluralist character of the American polity. Of course, not all recent economic changes have weakened the labor movement's pluralist political tendencies. In fact, the steady advance in functional specialization and the division of labor has increased the number of distinct economic interests, and automation has reduced the industrial wage earners as a proportion of the work force—creating new sources for pluralist group politics. These trends and labor's potential response in terms of consumer-class politics are considered in the concluding chapter of this study. But as the present discussion indicates, economic development has created particularly severe problems for machine politics as distinct from other forms of political pluralism. The COPE and good-government conception of the state as a major instrument for regulating an industrial economy has weakened Chicago's organized pluralism. By building a political apparatus committed to its own power far more than to any particular public policy goals, urban machines effectively incorporated ethnic groups into American politics. But this same indifference to policy permitted alliances with businessmen engaged in the massive capital accumulation necessary for industrialization.[32] Good-government politics and labor's campaign activities for the national Democratic party seem to reflect very different economic conditions. Whereas the American economy was preoccupied in the late nineteenth century with capital accumulation, it was so developed by the middle of the twentieth century that the process of development became the routinized function of large corporate bureaucracies. As a result, concern for the means of production, which Weber saw as dominant of the early capitalists, came to be supplemented by greater attention to an at least intermediate end with which both good government and the welfare state are concerned—how the society individually and through government programs collectively consumes its economic product.[33] Obviously, these economic changes have generated only a statistical tendency rather than an unavoidable necessity for patronage organizations to decline. As the strongest surviving machine and thus the clearest exception to this trend, the Chicago Democratic party very well illustrated the capacity for political structures to persist after the passing of those economic conditions that originally helped them flourish, by adapting at least partially to a new environment. In systems terms, the party continued throughout the first decade of COPE's life to be the major actor that reduced substantially organized labor's capacity to act as a structural flow channel for working-class demands. Chicago Democrats did so more effectively than the much less organized pluralist groups in other cities. The party organization thus reduced the *rate,* compared with other cities, at which the Chicago labor movement and especially its industrial unions undertook activity oriented toward welfare issues in national politics. Certainly, this movement proceeded far more quickly in Detroit, which in much of the 1960s had one of the least pluralist local political systems of America's great cities.

IV

Detroit:

The Dilemmas of Political Power

Both political and economic factors explain the unsurpassed position of Detroit COPE among labor political action organizations in the twenty years after World War II. The triumph of "good government" far beyond anything Chicago reformers ever approached left Detroit's non–issue-oriented Democrats too feeble to resist the CIO's Political Action Committee (PAC) when it entered the party and won a dominant voice in the late 1940s.[1] This nearly unique partisan role of Detroit unions primarily demonstrates the capacity of a single dominant economic structure, in this case the companies and unions of the automobile industry, to shape the political life of a great city. Given the weakness of regular party organizations, the UAW's size and its tradition of rank and file ideological commitment enabled the Autoworkers to revivify and liberalize Michigan's Democratic party. In fact, the UAW achieved as much by this transformation of the state's party system as any metropolitan labor movement could expect to accomplish.

As the archetype of a powerful partisan campaign organization, Detroit COPE, under UAW leadership, thus illuminates the attributes of labor's campaign organizations throughout the country. Paradoxically, perhaps, Detroit COPE's very success also reveals the limits on the American labor movement's partisan role in systematic campaign work. Because the UAW did so much, it made visible the obstacles to union success that are present elsewhere but are obscured by more obvious difficulties like the power of the Chicago party organization. As in postwar Western Europe, where the militancy of Socialist party and trade union members moderated, even Detroit Autoworkers have only intermittently participated in politics, Even then, they have often ignored the issue-oriented appeals of their own leaders. They have conformed, in short, to Lenin's observation that most workers display only trade-union consciousness rather than a sustained interest in broader political solutions to their social and economic problems.[2]

At the same time, many more consistently issue-oriented UAW officials were inhibited by their caution in the face of political defeats and, equally important, by the capacity of the Detroit political community to co-opt them. In Chicago this capacity of the political system to restrain labor's political activities and to minimize its influence mainly occurred through the Democratic party organization's incorporation of all major social and economic groups as subordinate partners in its coalition. In Detroit, where COPE dominated the formal party organization after 1947, the autonomy of the political system vis-à-vis the labor movement necessarily took a different form. Within the party, the advantages incumbent politicians usually have over challengers in primaries strengthened the Democratic officeholders in resisting labor demands. In addition, the resources necessary for victory in political campaigns, a politician's personal popularity with voters and the capacity to devise effective strategy and tactics, for example, were so widely distributed that labor could not monopolize them. Finally, COPE was restrained by its own role as leader of the Democratic party. With this leadership went the responsibility for party success, that is, to win elections by assembling broadly based electoral coalitions that necessarily include non-UAW members. If Detroit represents the most dramatic impact of industrialization on

American politics, it also indicates the minimum level above which the pluralist character of American politics persisted in the generation following World War II.

However much Detroit and Chicago appear polar opposites, labor political action in both cities involved a process of mutual accommodation with political and economic power structures outside the labor movement. This similarity is not immediately obvious, however. In Chicago, the formidable and widely recognized power of the party organization tended to obscure COPE's contribution to party campaign activities in those marginal areas where the party is weak. In Detroit, the UAW's widely recognized control and strengthening of the Democratic party obscured an appreciable moderation of labor's role in Michigan politics.

The Implementation of Labor's Liberal Ideology

Once it systematically sought to win party offices in 1947, the UAW transformed a weak, lethargic, and relatively conservative structure into one of the most active, militantly liberal, and politically successful state parties in the country. In the process, the union recruited a large number of issue-oriented political activists who maintained vigorous COPE as well as Democratic party organizations in all six of Wayne County's congressional districts. By partially overcoming the apathy of low-income Democratic voters, COPE workers won a remarkable series of electoral victories in previously Republican Michigan. Between 1948 and 1960, Michigan Democrats elected a governor for seven consecutive terms and in 1962 and 1964 continued to sweep all state administrative elections below governor. During the 1950s the party gradually increased its strength in the state legislature and, after reapportionment, won both houses in 1964. In national politics, two liberal Democrats ousted two conservative Republican senators, and under a 1964 redistricting, won a temporary party majority in the congressional delegation.

After reaching a peak in 1956, the Democratic percentage of the two-party gubernatorial vote did fall uninterruptedly through 1966, and the party lost the governorship in 1962. But several special factors partly explain this decline. Governor G. Mennen Williams accumulated numerous opponents in his twelve-year incumbency and in the 1958 election trailed his running-mates. When his Democratic successor, John Swainson was elected in 1960, he found it difficult to establish a public identity of his own. He also alienated suburban voters by supporting a Detroit city income tax and legislation outlawing discrimination against Negroes in housing. These difficulties suggest that, even in Michigan, labor-endorsed candidates faced problems common to many incumbent governors across the country during this period. Still, the seven successive Democratic victories up to 1962 remain an impressive record. Furthermore, until 1966 the party continued to win some lesser state offices in the face of the considerable political talents and popularity of George Romney, the first Republican governor in fourteen years. Only then, nineteen years after the UAW initiated formal partisan campaign activities and in the face of white backlash against civil rights, the Vietnam War, and Romney's great appeal, did the Democrats meet with unequivocal defeat, and the UAW began to lose some of its intraparty influence. Yet even in 1968, the party carried the state for Hubert Humphrey.

The UAW could not possibly have reshaped Michigan politics to this extent had not the automobile industry, and consequently its own membership, been concentrated in the Detroit area. In the course of his careful survey research analysis of party organization activity in the 1956 Presidential election in Wayne County, Eldersveld found that fully 39 percent of all Wayne County Democratic voters were associated with the CIO—and of these an overwhelming proportion were UAW members.[3] These Automobile Workers provided a core of generally responsive voters and a smaller group of activists willing to work in political campaigns. Fully 73 percent of precinct leaders in Eldersveld's sample were union members, as were 70 percent of the top leaders in the congressional-district Democratic parties. Furthermore, about 86 percent of these top leaders (60 percent of all leaders in the sample) were from the CIO. All Democratic precinct workers taken together produced an approximate net increase of about 15 percentage points in Democratic voter turnout.[4] In addition, Detroit COPE profited from the presence of the

UAW's international headquarters. Staff officials there were encouraged to join the COPE organizations in their congressional districts. Seventeen percent of all party precinct leaders in Eldersveld's sample were union officers, that is, either union bureaucrats or local union leaders who formed most of the pool from which such bureaucrats are recruited.[5] The cohesiveness of these UAW leaders and members gave the entire COPE operation a unity that it lacked in the more diverse Chicago and Los Angeles COPE operations. Guided by organizationally skilled union officials, the relatively large group of rank and file UAW activists played an indispensable role for COPE within the local and state Democratic party organizations.

Yet even these activists would have had difficulty in completely wresting control away from a powerful, patronage-based party organization like Chicago's where, among other things, precinct captains owe their position to appointment by the ward leader rather than to election by the voters. Indeed, one of labor's motives for entering the Democratic party in Michigan rather than establishing an independent labor party was the weakness of the regular party organization. This weakness can be traced to the strict merit system in all Michigan government, the state's nonpartisan system in local government, and the formally democratic structure of Michigan parties. All these features, which contrast with the situation in Chicago, were introduced by middle-class Protestant progressives in the heyday of good-government reform between 1912 and 1918. The single most important innovation was the merit system, which eliminated large-scale patronage incentives and thus the most reliable source of party workers.* Any citizen, for example, can volunteer as a poll watcher and appointments are made by career officials in the election commission. These reforms were somewhat less pervasive in county government. A few county officials, usually Democrats, have jobs at their disposal, for example, deputy sheriffs and assistant prosecutors. But the county officials win nominations and elections by their personal popularity. As a result, the party organiza-

---

* Chicago by comparison has had a flourishing, patronage-oriented Democratic party, despite the persistence of technically nonpartisan elections for aldermen. Even the secretaries of the members of the Detroit Common Council are protected by civil service.

tion cannot use these jobs to discipline its members or candidates.*
There are simply too few centrally controlled jobs to allow any
meaningful centralization of party activities.

The mores of nonpartisanship in Michigan local government also
bar the party organization from any formally legitimate role in local
politics. As a result, the Democrats in Detroit could not profit from
the national party's success after 1928, as the party organization in
Chicago did, by establishing firm control over the city's government.
As skillful a Democratic politician as Jerome Cavanaugh, who became mayor in 1962, encountered substantial difficulty in assuming
the role of titular party leader, because he had won election mainly
on his individual campaign and personality. By the same token, the
party organization as such did not even control the temporary jobs
that Cavanaugh and other city officials filled by discretionary appointments. In turn, the lack of party influence in city government
precluded any plausible effort to win support by promising to improve city services in a given neighborhood, a staple technique of
patronage-based organizations.

The third element that made labor's task easier was the legislative regulation of Michigan's political parties. The Wayne County
parties are organized by law on a congressional-district basis. Each
precinct elects a delegate to the district convention that in turn elects
the officers who control the official party organization. This formally
democratic structure, which contrasts with that of Chicago and Cook
County, made penetration by the UAW relatively easy. Because
there are six congressional districts, each with several hundred precincts, control of each convention requires contesting most of the
precinct elections and the cohesiveness to coordinate activities at the
convention itself. With politically active members distributed across
most of the county, the UAW was well equipped for just such an effort.

The dominant Democrat party groups that the CIO ousted in the
late 1940s often did rely on the little county and state patronage

---

* A few jobs are also available at the state level, but they are either memberships on state commissions requiring considerable executive ability or
part-time jobs, like those at the annual state fair, and none of these are
appealing enough to build an organization of job-conscious party workers.

available. But these material incentives were so limited that their organization was inactive and unsuccessful in Michigan politics. Throughout the New Deal period, the party regularly elected governors in presidential years when Franklin Roosevelt ran, but lost the governorship in off years. In this situation, almost any organized group could exercise influence; and AFL unions like the Teamsters played a leading role. But the state party suffered from the gradual erosion of the national party's popularity that began in 1938 and thus prepared the way for the entry of the CIO.

The UAW's sheer size and the weakness of nonlabor Democrats, even taken together, would have meant little without the union's traditions of active rank and file participation on behalf of the class-oriented welfare-state goals first sought in the 1930s. Without this ideological motivation, many fewer UAW members would have worked in the precincts, run for election as precinct delegate, and supported their leaders in ousting less issue-oriented Democrats from power. This orientation itself is directly traceable to the first formative period of UAW history, in the 1930s, which was directly shaped by two major economic factors—the working conditions intrinsic to producing automobiles, and the employee-relations policies of the automobile companies.

From its early development, Detroit was an antiunion, open-shop town. Henry M. Leland, its first great manufacturer,

> . . . picked Detroit rather than Chicago as a location because, having virtually no industry, it was free of labor disputes . . . Leland was determined that Detroit should continue free of labor trouble and to this end he formed the Detroit Employer's Association . . . The association succeeded until the bitter battles of the 1930's that marked the organization of the United Automobile workers.[6]

The bloodshed at the "battle of the overpass" (between UAW members and company agents) and elsewhere, and the semilegal sit-down strikes established the UAW as the leader among the militant industrial unions of the CIO.[7]

In order to overcome this bitter management opposition the union had to quell racial and ethnic hostility within its own ranks, as well as conflicts between skilled and unskilled workers. UAW leaders therefore appealed for solidarity based on their common status as industrial workers.[8] Such appeals led the union to favor improvements for workers generally like an expanded Social Security system that required government action.[9] In general, the struggle for recognition by the auto companies together with the intrinsic tension and frustrations of the assembly line—evidently greater than in any other major American industry—produced the UAW's deep hostility toward management.[10] In turn, this hostility led the UAW to extend into politics its fight against the companies that had begun to enter the Republican party organization as early as 1940.[11] At the same time, the unusual degree to which the union was organized by rank and file workers rather than by professional staff organizers (e.g., this was the case in the steel industry) created a tradition of member participation in union factional conflicts. As a result, many Automobile Workers acquired political experience, skills, and self-confidence far surpassing that of the average factory worker. Even after factional politics declined nationally it continued in many locals. Early management hostility also contributed to the importance of socialists, communists, and other radicals who were committed enough to devote the time and to risk the physical dangers that organizing Michigan's auto plants in the 1930s required. These radicals also fought among themselves. Many, especially in the union's first decade, preferred working for a socialist program and breaking with the established parties, whereas others were attracted to the Democratic party. But almost all agreed that the union should be involved in politics.[12]

For all its success, Detroit COPE did not dominate the Michigan Democratic party to the extent that the regular organization controls the party in Chicago. As we shall see, it has not controlled the selection of all or almost all Democratic officeholders, at least below the level of nomination for statewide office. In fact, COPE's influence in the primaries was uneven and somewhat erratic. But by controlling the district and state Democratic conventions and thus the formal party machinery, the UAW and its allies did become the most important force in setting party policy and in determining the image that the Democrats presented to voters throughout the state.

COPE has consistently used this power to select liberal chairmen of the state and Wayne County Democratic organizations and to nominate men with similar views as Democratic candidates. In 1964, for example, congressional redistricting created two contests between incumbent Democratic congressmen from Wayne County. In one race COPE officially endorsed John Dingell, Jr., against the much more conservative and, COPE felt, much less politically skillful John Lesinski, Jr. According to Dingell's own campaign staff, COPE's support was indispensable in helping him win in a district mostly composed of Lesinski's previous constituents. COPE took no official stand in the second race, where the differences in terms of issue and personal qualifications between the two congressmen were somewhat less pronounced. But most of the UAW's top leaders and local unions supported the more liberal and more articulate Lucien Nedzi against Harold Ryan (see Chapter IX). Key figures in Nedzi's campaign observed that without this labor support he would not have won the primary.

Detroit COPE has often expressed the same liberal ideological commitment in state and local elections, notably in Melvin Ravitz's first election to the Detroit City Council in 1961. As head of the community organizations division of the city planning commission, Ravitz anticipated the War on Poverty's emphasis on the political participation of the poor by organizing neighborhood block clubs. Ravitz not only hoped the clubs would improve the social and physical environment in lower-income neighborhoods, but he also saw them as a source of political support on liberal and civil-rights issues. When the Detroit city administration under Mayor Miriani realized Ravitz's intentions, it reassigned him to the city housing commission, where his program languished. The decision to run for the city council was in part an effort to reverse the city administration's edict at the polls. Ravitz's narrow victory by 2,403 votes meant that every important group of supporters could plausibly claim to have been decisive. Yet labor's support was certainly as important as any other factor. Detroit COPE's formal endorsement identified Ravitz with organized labor for the many Detroit voters who follow COPE recommendations with regard to unfamiliar candidates in nonpartisan elections and bolstered the enthusiasm of his many trade-union campaign workers. It also assured him access to many local union meetings, a major advantage for a little-known candidate in an at-large race. In more tangible terms, COPE contributed three skilled union staff members to help manage Ravitz's campaign, an office secretary, badly needed financial support, and three interviews on a UAW-sponsored television program.

This support was particularly significant because, as an intellectual and professor at Wayne State University, Ravitz appeared almost too liberal to win a council seat in an at-large election in a city that had repeatedly rejected less liberal candidates for mayor. In addition, Ravitz had antagonized some union leaders by withdrawing from a special election to the council in 1960 too late for COPE to find a new candidate. In the face of these difficulties, Ravitz's ideological liberalism was the decisive factor that secured his endorsement again in 1961 in a much harder race against an incumbent councilman—a decision the Chicago Federation of Labor would almost certainly never have made. Ravitz had not only attracted a following through countless speeches to block clubs and civic groups, but he was extremely popular among many of COPE's own campaign workers who participated in political action for ideological reasons. Because these workers were unhappy with COPE's endorsement of Mayor Miriani for reelection, many of them made Ravitz's election their central goal. As one veteran UAW local president observed, "in twenty-five years I don't think I've ever seen the UAW secondary leaders have greater personal enthusiasm for a candidate." COPE workers interviewed in 1962 repeatedly volunteered that "our main problem was electing Mel Ravitz." Why? Because "I heard him speak," "He had a good program." "He's an intelligent person—a professor." Black COPE workers linked Ravitz with the black incumbent councilman William Patrick in their campaign work.

Ravitz generally benefited from the black protest over the police department that helped defeat Mayor Miriani and three incumbent councilmen for reelection. Nevertheless, he would not have won without significant support among white voters, many of whom were evidently contacted by COPE workers. He acknowledged this substantial debt to labor in speeches to local unions and to COPE and Democratic party meetings throughout Detroit. Ravitz's liberalism and personality attracted his campaign workers, but it was the UAW's political commitment that created the pool of activists who responded to his appeals. The election of Ravitz makes clear that *even in local politics* COPE and the UAW often displayed a broad-constituency rather than pluralist orientation. Indeed, the unions' success at the councilmanic level testifies to the substantial liberalization of Detroit local politics accomplished by the Autoworkers and their allies. In the more favorable arena of state politics, COPE achieved an even greater measure of success—at least until 1966—which represented a nearly complete transformation of the pre-World War II party system.

Limitations on COPE's Power

Fay Calkins' *The CIO and the Democratic Party* accurately depicted the UAW's 1948 entry into the Michigan Democratic party as the most ideological, most aggressive, and most ambitious example of labor political action of the time. Although Detroit area COPE certainly retained its preeminence in comparison to Chicago and Los Angeles, the change in its political activities since 1950 was far more subtle but no less important than the cessation of labor's hostility toward the Chicago party. As the special conditions of the 1930s steadily receded with time, the outer limits on labor's political power within the present system became increasingly clear to the Detroit area labor movement itself. The UAW's exceptional resources and the weakness of the Democratic party has enabled Detroit COPE to test these outer limits, as labor in the other large metropolitan centers could not do. In the years since 1948, however, Detroit COPE accepted these restrictions and thus came to terms with the entire political system by moderating its goals and by reducing its capacity to act as a flow channel for lower-class demands.

Significantly, the most impressive illustration of these limits emerged in Detroit's local politics, which, in direct contrast to Chicago, are both formally and informally nonpartisan. Despite the Democrats' overwhelming majorities in state and national partisan contests—often exceeding 70 percent of the two-party vote in the city—the UAW met only repeated frustrations in mayoral contests and only moderate success in at-large council elections. In itself, this contrast demonstrates the causal importance of a political ground rule beyond labor's control, that is, the legal prohibition against designating the candidates' partisan affiliation on the ballot. Specifically, nonpartisan politics in Detroit not only reduced the importance of the Detroit electorate's social and economic cleavages in partisan contests but also limited the effectiveness of so formidable a campaign organization as Detroit COPE.[13]

As a result, from the departure of Mayor Frank Murphy in 1937, through Miriani's defeat in 1961, the UAW never supported a successful mayoral candidate who faced significant opposition in a closely contested election. Nor can these defeats be explained by a failure to raise the social and class issues that became so important in Michigan partisan politics in the late 1940s and the 1950s. During the 1940s, the UAW-dominated PAC of the CIO made at least three major but unsuccessful attempts to elect a mayor, and all three provoked hard-fought ideological confrontations with major conservative groups. The 1943 and 1945 elections were marked by bitter ethnic controversy and by liberal-conservative quarrels over such issues as civil rights, public housing, the right of public employees to strike, and charges of political bossism by labor radicals. The alignment in 1945 is particularly instructive:

For loser	*For winner*
Richard T. Frankensteen	*Edward H. Jeffries*
Wayne Co. Democratic party	Wayne Co. Republican party
The Communist Party	Gerald L. K. Smith
Michigan Citizens Committee	Detroit Citizens League
The Political Action Committee of the CIO (PAC)	The daily press and McGriff community papers[14]

The labor-backed candidate got 45 percent of the vote in 1943 and 44 percent in 1945. In 1949, City Treasurer Albert Cobo defeated a proven vote-getter, former UAW official and then Common Council President George Edwards, with 60 percent of the vote. As mayor, Cobo, an able administrator, alienated most blacks, liberals, and UAW leaders by following conservative policies and rejecting black demands. Nevertheless, the intense ideological conflict of the 1940s did not characterize Cobo's reelection campaigns in the 1950s. In fact, rather than continuing to try to remold Detroit politics, the UAW sought to adjust its own political behavior to the conditions imposed by the formal political system. The union lowered its goals after 1949. It had learned to play by nonpartisan rules and, at least in mayoral races, supported moderate candidates who could appeal to nonliberal voters and groups. In 1951, the CIO-endorsed candidate campaigned against Cobo without appealing to liberal ideology, but Cobo again won with about 60 percent of the vote. Cobo did face a more outspoken, more liberal opponent in 1953, but the CIO did little for the challenger, in part, perhaps, because he was not well known and appeared unlikely to win. In 1957, labor, the business community, and the press supported Miriani, who had become mayor earlier in the year after Cobo died in office. Miriani won in 1957 without significant opposition or any extended discussion of the issues. As we saw in Chapter II, the new mayor's carefully balanced policies kept the friendship of both labor and business leaders. Ironically the UAW made this adjustment to Detroit's nonpartisan politics too well in terms of its own political success. In 1961, Miriani, with the support of the same broad coalition that had helped him in 1957, lost his bid for a second reelection to Jerome Cavanaugh, a political unknown whose campaign appealed to liberals and blacks as well as to many of the UAW's rank and file. Once again the UAW backed a losing candidate.

Although this record dramatically illustrates some of the same advantages unions derive from their Democratic party alliance that Calkins saw in 1952,[15] nonpartisan politics did not in itself completely explain labor's defeats. Rather, it magnified more general obstacles that all AFL-CIO unions encountered in American politics. On one side, these obstacles included the same weakness and absence of class consciousness that had distinguished American workers from their counterparts in Britain and on the European continent. Detroit COPE thus found that the constituency of low-income voters that it sought to mobilize in local elections was much less dependable than the economic constituency of Autoworkers that it represented in collective bargaining. On the other side, these difficulties reflect the fact that the American polity, as a system of behavior substantially independent of social and economic life, operates according to ground rules that tend to limit the total influence unions can achieve.

⌊ The political moderation of American workers was expressed in the 1950s by a lingering feeling, even among UAW members, that labor ought not to be in politics at all.[16] This view did not operate decisively in all cases, even within the Michigan electorate as a whole. In partisan politics, a building-trades-union leader, Patrick McNamara, won two elections to the United States Senate and other union officials have been elected to various state offices. Yet in order to blunt the charge of labor control during his unsuccessful primary campaign for Congress from the sixteenth district in 1960, Carl Stellato, president of local 600, largest in the UAW, publicly asked that the Wayne County COPE not endorse him. Even so, many Democrats in the district attributed Stellato's two primary defeats to his union office.

As a result, COPE leaders recognized the need to maintain the coalition character of the Democratic party lest it alienate nonlabor voters, as Calkins pointed out over fifteen years ago.[17] In 1963, the UAW joined with a relatively small group of nonlabor allies to oust the incumbent state party chairman. They prevailed over the bitter opposition of a former state chairman, Neil Staebler, then congressman-at-large from Michigan, and many other state and federal Democratic officeholders. Yet a year later COPE agreed to nominate Staebler for governor, and in 1965, after his defeat, it acquiesced in his reelection as national committeeman.

This hostility to unions in partisan politics is even stronger in nonpartisan elections, where the prevailing good-government norms emphasize the public interest above that of any particular group. As a result overt labor activity was vulnerable to the charge that it represented the interference of selfish narrow interests. Many observers felt that mayoralty candidates Frankensteen and Edwards were hurt by their careers in the labor movement. Since those campaigns, labor strategists have been reluctant to support a labor official for mayor. In 1961 Councilman Edward Carey, a former UAW official, demonstrated his wide popularity by leading all other council

candidates, as Edwards had done in 1947. Yet the fear of an unfavorable reaction to a former UAW official was one of the reasons
Carey decided not to run against Mayor Miriani in 1961 when, as it
turned out, he might well have won.

Ethnic prejudices and loyalties, which previously reduced class
feeling and hindered unionism among industrial workers, presented
an even more serious obstacle to labor political dominance in Detroit.
Here too the problem was most severe in nonpartisan contests. Anti-
black sentiments were clearly responsible for the substantial majorities that Cobo and other conservative mayoralty candidates amassed
in normally Democratic wards where UAW members were numerous.
These same wards also voted far more heavily for white candidates
for council endorsed by the UAW than for their black running-mates,
and the latter ran far ahead of their ticket in inner-city black wards.[18]
As Wilson shows by comparing these figures with the pattern in
Chicago's partisan elections, this pattern is directly related to the
impact of nonpartisan politics. With the party symbol removed from
the ballot, several Democratic (but anti-black) ethnic groups were
free to vote against candidates who supported civil rights without
breaking with their party. In its own organization, the UAW overcame these divisive sentiments by appealing for solidarity against
management. But even in partisan politics, the labor movement cannot invoke such an immediate and visible symbol of collective self-
interest. For example, anti-Negro feeling may have cost Governor
Swainson reelection in 1962. The official COPE organization in the
old first congressional district could not bring the white, mainly
Polish, majority and the large black minority into a genuinely united
district party organization, despite the presence of many UAW members in both groups. By 1962, COPE leaders in the fifteenth district
expected Congressman John Dingell, Jr., despite his liberal civil-
rights record, to lose the Democratic primary to a black within two
to four years. These problems were only alleviated by the 1964 reapportionment that created a second mainly black district, the fourteenth, and left black voters as only small minorities in the county's
other four districts.

Lower-income voters not only ignore some COPE recommendations, but in other cases fail to vote at all. Even in elections when

lower-income groups do vote, COPE sometimes finds that their limited class feeling and ideological commitment leaves them distressingly partial to popular, well-known moderates and conservatives. Here, too, problems in local politics are paralleled in partisan contests. Apart from Mayor Cobo in Detroit, Republican George Romney not only won the governorship in 1962 and 1964, but carried his entire ticket to victory in 1966. In other words, as an autonomous system of organized conflict, Detroit and Michigan politics rewarded politicians in terms of their personal attributes—and thus clearly limited COPE opportunities for repeated victories. Of course, the UAW has supported many popular liberal candidates like Governor Williams in the 1950s, Senator Philip Hart in the 1960s, and a number of candidates for Congress and city council. But a politician's personal popularity is by no means necessarily related to his political principles or to his party affiliations. Labor could try to recruit personally attractive liberal candidates, but it could hardly keep attractive conservatives off the ballot. This essentially chance distribution of political popularity thus represented a factor that could undo COPE's best campaign efforts.

COPE's problems with popular opposition candidates were exacerbated when the politician was an incumbent. Indeed, incumbency was a second political attribute, in this case a formal institutional status, that offset the UAW's money, numbers, and organizational skills. The incumbent's official acts familiarized the voters with his name. In addition, a public office bestows a certain aura that attracts campaign workers who enjoy associating with the politically important. Like ethnicity, incumbency proved most important in nonpartisan races where the electorate lacked the alternative criteria of party affiliation in evaluating candidates, even though labor sometimes profited from this situation. Mary Beck, one of five labor-endorsed Detroit common council candidates in 1961, had lost much of her former popularity. But her prominence as incumbent council president helped her win reelection although not as its president. Yet Detroit voters not only twice reelected Mayor Cobo but also consistently reelected several conservative city councilmen. In addition, the problem of conservative incumbents also affected COPE in partisan politics. In 1960, COPE opposed for renomination eight Democratic state representatives from Wayne County, most of whom had largely ignored the party organizations in their areas or voted against COPE on such major issues as a graduated income tax and unemployment compensation revisions. Even though labor concentrated its resources in these primary contests, all eight won renomination. COPE had no better success in defeating Representative John Lesinski, Jr. in 1958 and 1960. It ousted him in 1964 only when he ran against another incumbent congressman. In some cases, COPE's opposition may have forced these incumbents to spend more money than usual to win renomination, making them somewhat more responsive to labor's subsequent demands in order to avoid future challenges. But this was not always the case. Lesinski was sufficiently emboldened by his primary victories to defy COPE by joining the few Northern Democrats who voted against the Civil Rights Act of 1964.

Similarly, the moderately liberal independent Congresswoman Martha Griffiths, from Detroit's prosperous seventeenth district, defeated COPE-endorsed candidates in her early primary races and built up a devoted personal following. This organization plus her successful nonpartisan style and independent voting record irritated the Detroit COPE leaders who expected Democratic candidates to display greater party loyalty. In some other cases COPE found itself frustrated not only by the nonpartisan appeals of candidates like Mrs. Griffiths but by the personal popularity and incumbency that an independent candidate could acquire in local nonpartisan politics and then use in the partisan arena.

The career of Tom Anderson, former mayor of suburban Southgate who won election as a Democratic state representative in 1964, provides one illustration. A middle-level management executive at Ford, Anderson was a relatively conservative independent Democrat whose views were clearly to the right of COPE's. After serving as president of a local citizen's association, Anderson won election as town supervisor and then, after incorporation, as Southgate's mayor. As supervisor, he introduced efficient business practices that won him the support of the community press. As a member of the sixteenth-district Democratic party organization, however, he soon had several open disagreements with COPE leaders. On the county board of supervisors, he sometimes voted against the labor position. And in his own political campaigns for mayor, he welcomed Republican support and put some local Republicans on his nonpartisan slate. As a result, COPE tried to defeat Anderson for reelection, and the last time he ran for mayor, COPE brought in precinct workers from other suburban areas. These efforts, however, proved ill-fated. COPE's workers were not familiar with the local situation and could not offset the work of Anderson's own supporters and his general popularity as an incumbent. Indeed, Anderson not only retired as mayor without a political defeat, but after redistricting gave the south suburbs a new state-representative seat, he was strong enough in 1964 to win the Democratic primary and the election. Incumbency, once again, was not a political position that only liberal or prolabor candidates monopolized.

A third political attribute that limited Detroit COPE's success because of a random distribution among politicians was tactical skill. The importance of this attribute was most dramatically illustrated by the Michigan Constitutional Convention (Con-Con) of 1962. Con-Con was proposed and supported primarily by George Romney and other political moderates including PTAS, some building-trades unions, and the League of Women Voters. These groups sought to end a nationally publicized battle over state taxes (see p. 130). Throughout a complicated process in which the voters first established the ground rules for election of convention delegates, then authorized the convention, and then approved the new constitution, Romney's pro–Con-Con forces consistently outmaneuvered the bulk of the Michigan labor movement. For example, COPE objected to the proposed convention because the delegates would be elected from disproportionately (by population) rural state-senate districts, which would probably limit the Democrats to a maximum of 36 out of 102 seats. The Romney forces shrewdly responded with a compromise formula substantially reducing, but by no means eliminating, rural overrepresentation. Not only could the Democrats expect to elect at least 67 of 144 delegates under this plan, but the proposal allowed Romney's forces to appear as honest brokers seeking genuine middle ground. Most labor leaders at first opposed this compromise as well as petitions endorsing it, but the idea proved so popular that, by the time of the referendum in November 1960, union spokesmen were maneuvered into a grudging neutrality and the 144-delegate proposal carried. By the spring of 1961, when a second referendum asked the voters to decide whether or not to call the convention itself, the Democratic candidates running for state office asked COPE to endorse Con-Con in order to improve their chances of winning. Constrained by loyalty to the party it led, labor deferred—without enthusiasm—to its allies.

COPE's subsequent efforts to elect as many favorable delegates to the convention as possible suffered from many of the difficulties it confronted in nonpartisan Detroit elections. In particular, it was unable to stimulate either high turnout among its own supporters or substantial activity among its workers for an election that it never really wanted. Instead of electing sixty-seven delegates, the Democrats elected only forty-five, losing seats in Wayne County and throughout the state that they normally carried. With a large Republican majority, Con-Con produced a rather conservative document that included a ban on a graduated state income tax. Despite COPE's opposition, the voters then narrowly approved the constitution. Subsequently, Con-Con Vice-President Romney won the governorship in 1962 and went on to defeat the Democratic ticket resoundingly in 1966.

COPE and the Detroit Political Community: Moderation and Compromise

The obstacles that limited the UAW's effectiveness also explain COPE's defeats in various political arenas. But these defeats only partially account for the growing moderation of both labor's goals and its relations with the rest of the Detroit civic and political community during the 1950s and 1960s. To explain fully these changes in Detroit COPE we must return to the general question raised in Chapter II that concerned the capacity of American trade unions to act politically as flow channels for lower-class demands. Rather than emphasize bureaucratization as the determining factor, we shall again consider those other conditions that determine political militancy for given levels of bureaucratization.

In Detroit, some of these determining conditions grew out of the internal life of the UAW, whose bureaucracy, it must be emphasized, remained the most politically activist in the American labor movement, continually urging its members to greater political awareness and participation. This posture can be traced in part to the character of the UAW's constituency. On the one hand, the Autoworkers retained their tradition of militancy and member political involvement that set them apart even in the 1930s; on the other, the UAW continued to reflect its members' particularly severe dissatisfactions produced by work on automobile assembly lines. Other constituency characteristics differentiated the political styles of the officials of the Michigan and Wayne County union federations, even though both were dominated by the UAW. Partly because of the craft union's traditional interest in local politics, a much larger group of AFL unions affiliated with the Wayne County AFL-CIO than with the Michigan AFL-CIO. In this situation, President Al Barbour and other UAW leaders of the county federation sought good relations with their more conservative AFL minority to avoid charges of unfairness and to set an example for the overwhelming number of central bodies throughout the country that had an AFL majority. By contrast, few AFL unions, except those liberal groups already sympathetic to the CIO and to political action, affiliated with the state body led by its militant president, August Scholle. This situation may help explain why Scholle could be so much more suspicious of Romney's Citizens for Michigan (CFM) than even the UAW was—a suspicion the UAW later conceded to be justified after the CFM's successful support of Con-Con. At the same time, the county federation's endorsement of Miriani in 1961 not only pleased its AFL minority but indicated a decline of the ideological orientation of the UAW-controlled Wayne County AFL-CIO, in comparison with either the Autoworkers' own behavior in the 1930s or with the activities of the state federation.

By all odds, the best illustration of these developments within the UAW itself concerns the decisive issue of the Michigan state income tax. Because it directly affected income distribution, tax policy was the most ideologically sensitive class-related issue, and one of the most heated sources of controversy, between Michigan's major parties in the late 1950s. The problem became increasingly serious when the popular Democratic governor G. Mennen Williams quarreled with the state senate whose Republican majority was guaranteed by the overrepresentation (by population) of rural areas. The senate blocked any graduated-tax proposals that would have affected higher income groups more heavily than others, whereas Williams and Michigan labor federation president Scholle supported a levy more steeply graduated than the federal income tax.* This deadlock precipitated the state's much-publicized financial crisis, including payless paydays for some public employees in 1959.

As the crisis wore on, however, close and intensive consultation on the tax issue gradually developed between business and labor representatives. Although much of the consultation was informal, organized negotiations took place through the tax committee of the Citizens for Michigan organization, which included Jack Conway, Walter Reuther's chief administrative assistant, and Ford President Robert MacNamara. Remarkably enough, this diverse group unanimously agreed to a corporate income tax, a flat-rate personal income tax that permitted the same exemptions as the federal income tax, and the elimination of the Michigan business activities tax.

The agreement reflected weariness with ideological conflict, a desire to compromise, and a convergence of preferences on certain specific policies. A flat-rate income tax was obviously more regressive and less favorable to low-income groups than a graduated tax. Nevertheless, the UAW found it preferable to further sales-tax increases. Michigan's industrial unions were also naturally sympathetic to reducing high property taxes on machinery that may have indirectly affected their members' employment opportunities. And some businessmen agreed with labor that the Business Activities Tax, which ignored a corporation's profits, discouraged new industries that

---

* The spirit of this position was maintained in the special committee set up by the Detroit common council to study a proposed city income tax. The committee by a seven to five vote favored a tax equal to 6 percent of the federal levy except that each person received a $5 credit and an exemption of $1,000 of income. Again, this proposal was considerably more progressive than the federal tax.

had little immediate prospect of large earnings from locating in Michigan. By early 1962, despite his approaching campaign against Romney, Governor Swainson had united business and labor leaders in a series of conferences across the state designed to secure tax reform. His own 1962 revenue proposals generally followed those of the Citizens for Michigan, although he pleased labor by adding an exemption for food from the present sales tax. UAW Vice-President Woodcock promptly and publicly endorsed Swainson's proposals.

Many UAW activists who had agreed with and defended labor's earlier tax policies were unhappy with this agreement on tax relief for corporations and on a flat-rate income tax. Significantly, however, the UAW representatives who negotiated the Citizens for Michigan compromise eventually gained status in the union organization whereas officials who had been less flexible on the issue did not. By 1963, the union's official position on federal taxes, which emphasized a moderate increase in personal exemptions, had become relatively more acceptable to business spokesmen. One company official felt that this recent moderation resulted from the development within the companies of professional staffs of economists with more academic, technical training—a trend that also appears to have moderated the companies' tax position.*

Most significant of all, perhaps, spokesmen for labor and management, for Democrats and Republicans, continued to adhere to the agreement after 1962 when the boom in auto production ended the immediate crisis and led to a sizable state budget surplus. Rather than an ideological deadlock, a more mundane struggle for tactical advantage between Governor Romney and legislators of both parties delayed enactment of the compromise, with each side reluctant to acquire a "high tax" reputation. As this maneuvering for tactical advantage replaced the previous and atypical (for American politics) ideological confrontation, Michigan's once heated politics increasingly came to resemble the political systems of other American states.

Michigan's fiscal crisis had earned for the state the reputation for having a dysfunctionally divisive conflict between unreasonably

---

* It should be observed, however, that the UAW and its political allies, like Governor Swainson, adopted the essence of the compromise sooner than the companies. The companies themselves were divided.

rigid, inflexible, and doctrinaire parties. "Under these circumstances," Greenstein concluded, "policy oriented parties led to the kind of politics described by the French as *immobilisme,* rather than to popular control, political stability, and effective policy making."[19] The state's reputation for dysfunctional conflict does accord with the social bitterness engendered by the auto industry in the 1930s. Yet, by the mid-1960s, what appeared to be the climactic showdown between belligerent ideological opponents seemed only the final eruption of a fading struggle. In fact, the bitter tax controversy abated dramatically when both labor and business recognized that a permanent basis for cooperation in Michigan politics had almost imperceptibly replaced the earlier bitterness. By 1965, the Democratic legislature and Republican Governor George Romney enacted an almost unprecedented quantity of new welfare legislation.

These developments emphasize the importance of the opportunity for bargaining and compromise with labor's opponents in determining the militancy of Detroit COPE, which equaled in importance internal factors like the composition of its constituency. Furthermore, these political changes in the environment paralleled and in part perhaps reflected economic changes, notably the reduced bitterness of labor relations in the automobile industry. On UAW's side, President Reuther, for example, agreed that all the American Motors automobile plants should be moved to Wisconsin in order to help keep the company viable. The union also assisted the auto companies on tax matters affected by labor contracts and on obtaining government orders for Michigan industries. Such UAW policies implicitly assumed, as UAW leaders sometimes openly acknowledged, that high pay and success in contract negotiations depend on corporate earnings and on the general prosperity of American capitalism. Whether or not such dependence was as important in the 1930s as it was in the 1960s, it was perceived far more readily in the later period. Certainly, these later attitudes are not entirely consistent with the UAW's earlier view of the auto companies' power as an unacceptable threat to American life.

The crucial point is that this moderation partly represented a response to the opportunity for compromise presented by a general change of attitudes among businessmen and other conservative forces in Detroit. During the early 1960s, in the midst of the state's fiscal crisis, the Michigan business community had serious second thoughts about its attacks upon labor, the Democratic party, and Governor Williams. National headlines blaming the UAW hardly improved the competitive position of Michigan's economy in attracting new industry. In early 1962, one leading executive, after surveying the state's needs, pleaded for an end to "the fault finding." "Above all, let's have no more bad publicity." As one high UAW official put it in 1962:

> With the exception of Chrysler, there has been a real change in the industrial relations directors in the auto companies. Lou Seaton at GM is no liberal, but he's much more reasonable than any of his predecessors. And this colors the tone of the city. Seaton doesn't use wildcat strikes as a chance to call unions irresponsible. He puts the community first . . . What is more, the camp followers are no longer encouraged to attack us . . .

Another symbol of the change among businessmen has been the slow but appreciable shift of the Detroit press from the right to the center or even to the left wing of the Republican party. Such shifts have occurred in several other urban papers, but the Detroit change paralleled the larger shift in community sentiment. One union official thought, indeed, that *"The Detroit News* now represents the more civilized wing of the Republican Party. Martin Hayden [the editor] has an institution to protect and he can't relocate in Mississippi." Similar trends affected the Republicans. Even before George Romney—a self-proclaimed moderate—assumed leadership. According to a high official, "In 1958 our [gubernatorial] campaign was based on hanging Walter Reuther, Mazey, and Scholle. In 1960, the issue was dead—it's a good sign."

Of course, the personalities of the key union officials played some role in the labor movement's decision to act on these opportunities for compromise. Michigan labor president Scholle was temperamentally not disposed to seek compromise with conservative groups. And, as we shall see, different officers within both the UAW and the county federation reacted differently to these possibilities. Nevertheless, this reduction in the hostility of its unions' opponents seems particularly important. By 1962, for example, UAW Secretary-

Treasurer Emil Mazey, titular second officer of the union, was widely considered less influential than Vice-President Leonard Woodcock, the director of the union's General Motors department. Two well-informed observers described Mazey in 1950 as "by nature and training a rebel against the social status quo—less the intellectual socialist than the aggressive, 'class-conscious' unionist who has come to a general socialist view through years of labor activity."[20] In the 1960s, Mazey was reported to visit the plants and local union meetings more frequently than other top union leaders, and on some questions, particularly on foreign policy, he stood somewhat to the left of other UAW leaders. Yet he was a relatively isolated figure on the executive board and had little influence over policy.

Woodcock, like Mazey, was an ex-socialist who subscribed to the liberal ideology of the Democratic party's left wing. As a member of the board of governors of Wayne State University, he pressed for higher educational appropriations and he took positions to the left of the Kennedy and Johnson administrations on many domestic issues. Yet Woodcock had a much better reputation than Mazey among some—though far from all—conservative business leaders in Detroit. One Republican leader found him "one of the smartest labor men in the United States—one of the most conservative and far thinking, a moderating force you can trust." Some business leaders admired his ability to seek common ground in private negotiations. And as a major union spokesman on public issues in Michigan, he became the first top UAW official to endorse a compromise flat-rate income tax that precluded proportionately higher tax levels for higher-income groups. In general, then, Woodcock began to assume the role of union representative in civic affairs because his articulateness and his subtle grasp of organizational and bargaining tactics enabled him to convey UAW positions reasonably and persuasively to nonunion audiences. He thus differed from Mazey less on the substance of political issues than in his personal style. The reduced level of conflict in Michigan politics increased the value of such a role for the UAW.

A significantly similar pattern also emerged in the Wayne County AFL-CIO that formally controls Detroit COPE operations. When the Wayne County AFL and CIO central bodies merged, President Mike Novak of the CIO and his vice-president, Al Barbour, exchanged positions, evidently at the prompting of UAW leaders. As president, Barbour maintained a particularly close personal and political relationship with Mayor Miriani and backed him in his losing reelection campaign against the more liberal Jerome Cavanaugh, who received massive Negro support. Again, although Barbour has publicly deplored Dearborn Mayor Orville Hubbard's explicit policy of keeping Negroes out of that city, as a county supervisor Barbour worked with Hubbard on some issues. On practical grounds, Barbour was reluctant to oppose Hubbard's reelection because the mayor controlled four votes on the board of supervisors and, in any case, appeared politically indestructible. Yet, like Woodcock, Novak, and Mazey, Barbour was also a committed liberal. In one notable confrontation within the fourteenth-district Democratic party organization, Barbour denounced more conservative UAW officials and union members for their lack of ideological commitment. Once again, therefore, the major difference between Barbour and Novak appears to have been one of personal style rather than of political orientation. Novak lacked Mazey's general radical perspective, but he shared Mazey's frank, blunt approach. Barbour was apparently chosen to lead the merged federation because of his smooth, articulate manner and his ability to handle parliamentary tangles. These qualities allowed him to work harmoniously not only with more conservative AFL leaders in the merged county federation but also with nonlabor Detroit civic leaders. In sum, Barbour's formal promotion reflected a change in the UAW's definition of its own leadership needs. In turn, this new role put a premium on the ability to recognize both the limits of labor's political power and the opportunities presented by the new moderation of its opponents.

This interpretation is supported by the fact that negotiation was both potentially profitable and possible for President Barbour when he dealt with nonpartisan city governments and with the Democratic government of the county. It also proved rewarding for UAW leaders who dealt with moderate businessmen. Until 1963, however, President Scholle dealt with two very liberal Democratic governors and a legislature in which conservative Republican senators exercised a veto. With the governors, major compromises were usually unnecessary; with the senate, they were usually impossible. The only major social legislation the Republican senate passed, for example, was a state fair employment practices act. Few people pressure for unattainable compromises, but where compromise seems feasible, one's supporters often call for half a loaf. And compromises did occur in state politics after the election of a Democratic legislature and a liberal Republican governor made it possible. Indeed, Scholle himself made commitments that were dictated by his alliances at the state level, which others have criticized on ideological grounds.*

In all these cases, however, the opportunity to reach agreements with opposition leaders depended on the UAW's importance as the dominant force within a revitalized Democratic party. COPE's decision not to oppose the call for a constitutional convention and its later agreement on taxes were both partly designed to alleviate the embarrassment of its own Democratic party candidates. These decisions point to the more general constraints that the UAW encountered because of its dominant party role. According to one local business leader, "We've found it increasingly hard to be anti-UAW and still be a local booster." This observation implicitly conceded that labor through its success in Democratic party campaigns and its influence on party decisions had indeed become an essential part of the structure of political power and influence in both the city and state. But this situation constrained the union as well as the business community. When asked why the UAW agreed to the tax compromise, one union official replied that "We tried to take a responsible position, to work for the benefit of the whole state." Compared with the attitude of other state union leaders this reply seems to reflect more than clever rhetoric; it cannot be fully understood apart from the UAW's position of partisan power.

In most other cities, where the merger of important unions with the Democratic party's electoral organization is less complete, government policies are proposed and executed by elected and appointed government officials after varying degrees of consultation with interested groups, including unions. Because organized labor does not un-

---

* His support of a less programmatically liberal candidate than the candidate supported by the district COPE organization in the first-district special-election primary in 1961 is a case in point.

equivocally lead the party, it does not have to reduce its formal demands, but only accept—unwillingly—a compromise worked out by others. During Michigan's financial crisis, however, it was the UAW itself—largely because of its leadership in the party—that reached the first understanding on taxes with business leaders. As a political negotiator, it therefore encountered the pressures and limitations that elsewhere constrain any party organization to balance against each other not only the demands of its own constituent groups but also the needs of the whole political system. Labor was free to enter the Michigan Democratic party. But once it made this choice it could not merely consider the interests of its own members or even those of all wage earners. This responsibility, the other side of its power, proved a final if unanticipated restraint on labor political action.

Conclusion

Rather than accepting either Michels' or Lenin's analysis of bureaucratization as the decisive variable determining the political behavior of union organizational elites, the historical review in Chapter II provided an alternative set of explanatory categories. This approach explained the political posture of various unions in terms of both their constituency and history and the environment in which they operate. Bureaucratization, it was argued, only amplifies and exaggerates whatever cautious or aggressive trends emerged. The analysis of the UAW and COPE within the Democratic party and in Detroit's nonpartisan campaigns in this chapter has provided more detailed documentation for this argument. The UAW officials' militancy partly reflected the rank and file Autoworkers' extreme alienation from the factory work process, reinforced by a persisting traditional resentment at the antiunion attitudes of the automobile companies.

Economically generated discontent was reinforced, at least for the union leadership, by the imposition in Detroit of a nonpartisan political system with at-large city council elections. This achievement of Detroit's Protestant elite early in the century made it difficult for working-class and racial and ethnic minority groups to attain either symbolic recognition through winning elective office or, later, favorable policies on public housing and the like. More liberal policies were developed only after Cavanaugh was elected in 1961. In these respects Detroit local politics notably diverged from the partisan ethnically oriented systems of all the other very large Eastern and Midwestern cities with large European and black immigrant populations. By comparison with other American cities, Detroit thus presented an extreme case of both the economic grievances that Marx emphasized and the sense of exclusion from the political community that concerned Bendix. Together, these economic and political factors produced the preeminence of Detroit COPE and its predecessors. Accordingly, the pressures that led these militant Detroit labor organizations to a policy of accommodation and compromise may usefully illuminate the larger process that has restricted the capacity of American trade unions to act as structural flow channels for working-class political demands.

Consistent with the argument in Chapter II, these pressures all contributed to the UAW's co-optation and incorporation into Detroit political life. First, in the case of the party system, Democratic leaders invited Michigan labor leaders to involve themselves in the life of the party.[21] But as we have seen, the concern for partisan advantage that accompanied labor's assumption of party leadership restrained the UAW's pursuit of its own policy and issue goals. Second, a variety of political officials, notably Mayor Miriani, successfully wooed individual union leaders, made them advisers and personal confidants, and gave them some of the perquisites of power. Such informal relationships found formal expressions in appointments of union leaders to the Wayne County Board of Supervisors by Detroit city councilmen. In turn, these alliances led to the co-optation of the Wayne County AFL-CIO during Miriani's term as mayor. Finally, business leaders, despite the strong antiunion tradition of Detroit industry, demonstrated considerable willingness to deal with union officials on such issues as taxation.

In all these instances, conservative or at least procapitalist politicians and business officials proved willing to associate and negotiate with union leaders, regardless of social distinctions of status, class, and occupation. The Detroit elite's flexibility may well reflect the lack of feudal tradition in American Society. This same lack of feudal background has persistently undermined proletarian consciousness among American workers, thus encouraging the working-class political apathy and ethnic divisions so starkly revealed in nonpartisan elections. And it was precisely this unreliability of its own political constituency that made entry into the Democratic party so attractive to the UAW. In turn, this entry meant creating structural flow channels within the existing patterns of the political system, limiting the UAW's capacity to convey working-class demands on behalf of welfare issues. Identification with an existing major party operated to reduce the sense of alienation or exclusion from the political community that had distinguished Detroit workers from those of comparable cities. Furthermore, by seeking electoral victories in conventional partisan and nonpartisan politics, the UAW profited from, but was finally limited by, the high electoral payoff for the attributes of political skill, popularity, and incumbency that its candidates could not permanently monopolize. As Chapter VI shows in detail, the process of making economic resources useful politically involved conversion costs that limited the labor movement's political impact.

To summarize, the degree of radicalism, as well as the capacity of American trade unions to act as flow channels for collectivist reform demands, depends in part on the degree of their exclusion or inclusion in the political community. This is true of the American lower classes compared with those of the European nations Bendix studied with respect to suffrage. As this chapter has emphasized, it is also true of Detroit workers compared with those of other American cities. The political moderation of American workers and their union organizations thus corresponds to the American polity's traditional receptivity to lower-class participation. Similarly, the relative militancy of the Detroit UAW corresponds not only to the extreme frustrations of work on the assembly line and to the antiunion policies of the auto companies, but also to exclusion from the city's nonpartisan politics. These considerations in turn explain why the relationship of the UAW to the Democratic party in Detroit, including the year-round congressional-district COPE and party organizations, was closer than its counterparts in other large American cities to the union–Labour party alliances with its branch structure in Britain.

Conversely, the moderation of the Detroit UAW since the 1930s directly reflects its incorporation into the local and state political communities. Even so, however, Detroit COPE remained more militant than Chicago COPE partly because the process of incorporation was carried on so much more effectively by the Chicago party organization. For example, immediately after the Memorial Day massacre of Steelworkers in 1937, the Chicago regular party organization moved to placate the CIO unions. Simultaneously, however, the party's perception of its organizational maintenance needs led it to establish control over the CIO's campaign activities. That it accepted any COPE precinct work at all reflects the political impact of industrialization on even the strongest pluralist organization. Detroit politics reflects this impact far more clearly, partly because it lacked such an effective organizational mechanism for co-optation and incorporation.[22]

This emphasis on a continuum of political inclusion and exclusion, however, assumes a relatively clear line of demarcation between industrial workers and the rest of the political community. But if such a clear distinction depends on cohesive organizational structures, the entire problem may take an entirely different form in areas where a poorly coordinated labor movement must operate in a highly diffused and poorly delineated political community. This situation, which characterizes Los Angeles politics, reflects both the growth of service and technologically skilled sectors of the economy and massive residential mobility. As Chapter V shows, it also posed very different political problems for union campaign organizations.

V

Los Angeles:

The Politics of Disorganization

More than its counterparts in Chicago or Detroit, organized labor in Los Angeles resembled the national AFL-CIO in its political activities. In terms of intraparty influence, if COPE organizations in Detroit and Chicago marked out the range of the labor movement's roles among Northern Democrats (i.e., from dominance to junior partnership), Los Angeles COPE approximated the midpoint between these extremes. This intermediate position primarily reflected the pervasive disorganization of the Los Angeles metropolitan area that limited the political effectiveness of both the labor movement and its potential competitors for influence within the party. Although the unions' own organized political activities were thus harder to sustain, the local alliances that in Chicago limited aggressive campaign work were also much weaker. This situation thus approximated AFL-CIO's position of influence rather than dominance within the national Democratic party.

Similarly, the city's prevailing disorganization made organized

labor's political problems in Los Angeles strikingly similar to those
it faced in a national political system thoroughly fragmented by
federalism. The labor movement responded to this situation by emphasizing the resources of formal trade union organizations as a
partially effective substitute for the much more imposing incentives
commanded by the Detroit UAW or the regular party organization in
Chicago. Yet, just as pro-COPE unions in Chicago had to come to
terms with CFL leaders and the party organization, while the Detroit-
area UAW achieved tacit compromises with more conservative elements within its community, the unions in Los Angeles COPE were
themselves noticeably affected by the very social and political disorganization whose impact they sought to minimize.

Los Angeles typified far better than either Detroit or Chicago
the contrasting styles that most American unions adopt in national,
as opposed to local, elections. In Detroit, the UAW followed its welfare-state orientation at all levels of government. In Chicago's highly
pluralist system, no union could ever entirely avoid the voluntarist
pattern of Samuel Gompers. Primarily because of the city's political
disorganization, Los Angeles unions, on the other hand, conformed
to the more general pattern in the nation as a whole by combining
pluralist activity in local politics with a more issue-oriented posture
when campaigning for state and especially for national office.

Conservative Consequences of Disorganization

The most obvious fact about political life in Los Angeles is not
the power of a political party organization, as in Chicago, or an
economic industry, as in Detroit, but the fluidity of southern California's social institutions. This social fragmentation is in turn a direct result of the area's unrelenting population explosion. Except for
the economically depressed 1930s, California as a whole grew by at
least 44 percent in every decade of the century—a tenfold total increase from just under 1.5 million in 1900 to about 15.7 million in
1960.* In the same period, Los Angeles proper grew almost twenty-

---

* Even in the 1930s the state grew 21.7 percent, which was just under
three times the national increase.

five times, from just over 100,000 in 1900 to just under 2.5 million in 1960. Yet, in recent years, the city's extraordinary increase could not match the expansion of the area's suburbs, most of which lie in Los Angeles County. Whereas the city grew about 70 percent between 1940 and 1960, the population of the outlying areas, excluding the city of Long Beach, more than tripled.[1] The effect of this immigration has been reinforced by the massive migration within the area. More than one-fourth of the people in the Los Angeles urbanized area did not live at their 1949 address in 1950. The comparable figure in 1960 for the entire metropolitan area was 32.5 percent.[2]

Social Fluidity

These social conditions contributed directly to political fragmentation by severely weakening party organizations. The vast immigration into the state produced significant changes in the electorate between successive gubernatorial campaigns. Even with the most favorable legal arrangements, such conditions would have made it difficult to sustain a traditional patronage-based precinct organization. For one thing, many voters had arrived too recently to identify with the politics of their new state or neighborhood or to form the stable core of supporters that the Chicago precinct captains acquired. Indeed, party patronage organizations depend upon the precinct workers' personal influence and contacts with their constituents, which are usually cultivated over many months or even years. In Los Angeles, where at least half the voters in an average precinct and many precinct workers themselves move away between elections, such relationships could have a very limited importance.

Political Disorganization

Such massive social dislocations, even combined with middle-class resistance to machine politics, would not by themselves have ruled out a strong formal party organization if patronage were available. Party workers might cultivate the more stable residents in poorer areas and help some of the isolated newcomers adjust to the neighborhood. Because turnout is usually low, even a small group of loyal supporters in a few areas might ensure control of at least some important primaries. Party workers might also effectively register poorly motivated party supporters and get them to the polls in general elections. Before 1909, state law provided for a series of interlocking party conventions that chose candidates and helped establish a relatively clear party hierarchy.[3] But this relatively organized structure was wholly destroyed by the legal and institutional reforms initiated during the progressive period.

> Between 1911 and 1913, a presidential primary election and the direct election of United States senators were authorized, straight-ticket party voting was made laborious by eliminating the party circle from the ballot, the legal party organization was fragmented and reduced to impotence, all city and county elective posts were made non-partisan, and cross-filing was introduced. The result was the creation of a political vacuum which has never been filled.[4]

As in Detroit, the good-government forces struck an even more important blow by introducing a merit system that effectively eliminated all but a few hundred appointive jobs at the state and local level. After this attack, party leaders emerged with few if any organizational resources that could be used to stimulate voter turnout.[5] In the 1960s, the formal organizations of the two major parties remained among the weakest and most open of any in a competitive two-party state in the country. Political novices or recent migrants to California regularly achieved major leadership positions in both parties after a few years of activity within the party.[6]

This deliberate destruction of party organization in California reinforced the impact of massive intrastate mobility and influx of immigrants. In the end, almost all the stable institutions with which lower-class citizens could meaningfully identify had been eliminated. The region's unfailing climate, natural beauty, and social and economic growth may have made California, as McWilliams describes it, a land of exceptional opportunity characterized, according to Wilson, by "the pervasive optimism with which the future is viewed."[7] Yet the weakness of institutional life meant that southern California was also marked by a widespread sense of social rootlessness, or in McWilliams' words, "a vast drama of maladjustment, social, familial, civic and personal." Instead of well-established ethnic institutions available to many in the East, California immigrants had to rely on state-of-origin societies to renew ties with the past and, as best they could, to assist "the newcomer in making an adjustment by placing him in touch with others of his kind." McWilliams adds that "the popularity of the cafeteria in Los Angeles is primarily due to the loneliness of the people. A cafeteria is a friendlier type of eating place than a restaurant. A possibility of meeting someone—just *someone*—is much greater . . ."[8]

Despite the area's pervasively suburban character, local residential communities often proved equally ineffective as a source of stability. New residential communities tended to develop so rapidly that the population outstripped all existing public facilities. Still more important, because so many residents were relatively recent arrivals, the entire community often lacked a stable status and class structure, strong civic organizations, and widely respected or even recognized elites. As a result, there were few institutions that might guide public opinion and stabilize individual attitudes.*

Because the main political resource of lower-class citizens in a constitutional democracy lies in their numbers, these obstacles to organizing mass political activity through parties and other institutions had a particularly severe impact on Los Angeles workers.[9] Indeed, social life in southern California served to perpetuate well into the twentieth century the disorganization that had characterized the entire American working class throughout the nineteenth century. This situation in turn continually frustrated not only the successful organization of industrial unions but also the emergence of a major political party committed to an extensive welfare state and closely allied with the labor movement. As we have seen, politicians who sought to mobilize such a lower-class constituency in other cities found various solutions to this problem. In Detroit and other manu-

---

* "The first families exist, but they do not perform a vital social function. . . . The average resident has not the most remote idea as to the identity of the first families of Los Angeles, much less to their comparative rating in social distinction. In 1945, Los Angeles gave an enormous civic welcome to General George Patton. In preparing the reception, the city discovered, almost as if by accident, that General Patton is not only a Native Son, but that he belongs to one of the early first families." McWilliams, *op. cit.*, p. 240.

facturing centers, large concentrations of industrial workers who could be organized for political as well as economic action made the industrial unions the most important backers of COPE in the 1960s. CIO unions in Los Angeles, however, were substantially less important than in Detroit or even in Chicago, where the leaders of the Chicago Federation of Labor have opposed an active political action program. Whereas former CIO unions made up 33 percent of the CFL-CCIUC at the time of merger, the comparable proportion in Los Angeles was only 16 percent.[10] Bernstein adds:

> These figures may overestimate the importance of the former CIO unions . . . because much of their membership was concentrated in branch plants of nationwide companies. The unions that represent their employees locally, however, have looked for leadership to the centers of power in Pittsburgh, Detroit, Akron, Washington and Chicago.[11]

CIO unions took only ten of the thirty-two executive board positions in the merged Los Angeles Central Labor Council. In 1962 no CIO official held a full-time policy-making position in either the state or city central bodies. As it was, the Los Angeles CIO did succeed in having representation on the board by union rather than by geographical area within the county. The latter form would have meant almost no CIO representation.

In Chicago, the principal method by which the lower classes overcame the obstacles to their political organization was to build a patronage-oriented local party. In addition to the merit system that made strong party organizations so difficult, the political isolation of Los Angeles' individual lower-income citizens was intensified by local elections that eliminated even the party label as an orienting symbol. In fact, this system presented, in a more extreme form, the same obstacles to labor's electoral success that the UAW encountered in Detroit although there the UAW could at least elect a significant block of liberal councilmen. Los Angeles thus represented a highly pluralist system based on narrow group self-interest, but one that was much less organized than its counterpart in Chicago. Indeed, freed from the restraints of certain group affiliations, Los Angeles citizens supported many more emotional ideological clashes than did the participants in Chicago's organized pluralist system. And Los Angeles unions did become involved in several of these controversies that appeared to involve broad constituency coalitions. Usually, however, the unions participated at least in part because of their own more immediate self-interest. For example, a broad coalition of labor and middle-class reformers worked from the progressive period until the mid-1930s to establish city ownership of electric power facilities. Most of labor's contribution, however, could be traced to the Electrical Workers (IBEW) Local 18, which represented the employees of the city department of water and power. Public ownership would clearly increase the local's size and protect its members' jobs.[12] Once the battle was won, the local did not undertake any significant political-action program. A similar mixture of organizational self-interest and ideology characterized the labor movement's role in the conflicts over public housing and rent control in the late 1940s and early 1950s.[13]

More recently labor participated vigorously in a liberal coalition against ideological conservatives in school-board politics. Los Angeles trade unions contributed money, campaign workers, a speakers' bureau, and extensive mailings to the liberal victories of 1955 and 1957. When liberal control was threatened in 1965, labor again participated quite actively in a successful campaign to elect the first black to citywide office. As in the housing controversy, some unions, particularly those from the CIO, shared the general liberal position, which, in this case, opposed the elimination of materials about UNESCO from the curriculum and the censorship of purportedly unfit books. But many union leaders were also concerned with the impact of the conservatives' antiunion position on the school system's personnel policies.

Such limited-goal pluralism also characterized labor's activities in local politics in the 1960s. In 1961, COPE's efforts to build an active campaign organization through its participation in the mayoral campaign were undermined by its endorsement of Mayor Norris Poulson. A conservative former congressman, Poulson encountered labor's opposition in his successful 1953 race for mayor because he had opposed public housing and supported overriding Truman's veto of the Taft-Hartley Act. During his two terms, Mayor Poulson had terminated the city's public housing program, vetoed several pay raises, and defended Police Chief William Parker against Mexican and Negro charges of police brutality. He had also taken some more liberal positions, for example, in support of public garbage removal, and he had made several appointments that labor found satisfactory. But COPE endorsed Poulson in 1961 primarily because the support of the press, most leaders of both parties, and most business interests made him appear a certain winner. In any case, his opponent, Sam Yorty, a former Democratic congressman, antagonized most labor leaders and other Democrats by supporting Richard Nixon in 1960. As a result, Los Angeles unions saw no real alternative.

Poulson's overall record, however, made it difficult to stimulate activity among those trade unionists sufficiently issue-oriented to be interested in campaign work in the first place. COPE did open a few headquarters in the city, but as one leader described it, "Nothing happened; we had the wrong horse and couldn't sell him to our members." Poulson, who suffered from a controversy over the Dodgers' baseball park and from his poor television performance, lost to Yorty by a sizable margin.

When Yorty ran for reelection in 1965, labor was still not enthusiastic. And with little effort on its own part, COPE found that it had a highly acceptable candidate in Congressman James Roosevelt, who had compiled a strongly prolabor record on the House Labor and Education Committee. Yet labor's support for Roosevelt only demonstrated once again its limited commitment to political action in local elections. Roosevelt's campaign staff estimates that less than 500 COPE workers volunteered for the campaign and that more than half of that number worked only on election day. One of the biggest unions affiliated with Los Angeles COPE, the UAW North American Aviation Local, responded to an appeal by President Reuther by making a financial contribution, but, at most, 200 of its members worked in the campaign, far less than in 1964. Another major COPE union, the Lockheed International Association of Machinists (IAM) local, could supply only fifteen or twenty men each night during the height of the campaign. Labor's lukewarm support contributed to Roosevelt's generally poor campaign performance.* Despite expenditures of over $250,000, Roosevelt received only 247,000 votes (36.5 percent) to Yorty's 392,000 votes (58 percent). The issue-oriented COPE workers who did participate in the elections concentrated on the school-board campaign, which resulted in the election of a black to citywide office for the first time.

Interest Group Pluralism

In fact, nonpartisan local politics in Los Angeles conformed to the larger pattern of California's political pluralism. With its deliberately enfeebled parties, the state's politics was characterized by a politics of competing individual candidates stressing personal rather than organization or partisan appeals.[14] As elsewhere, organizations were also important, but they produced a deeply entrenched and at times notorious system of strong functional economic interest groups rather than parties with a broader class orientation. According to Wilson, "Unions, businesses, and individuals with interests they are anxious to advance are . . . likely to give money directly to candidates, particularly incumbent candidates."[15] As Cresap observed in 1954, no one runs the state, it is "almost entirely devoid of any well-defined, responsible leadership. Rather, public policy is determined by the many influential individuals who gravitate from one amorphous alliance of interests to another."[16] Indeed, individual politicians and groups dealt directly with each other without worrying about larger interests. As a result, some legislators simply worked for particular constituencies, often without apology or embarrassment. Politicians felt little need to worry about the party's overall record,

---

* Reflecting on the campaign, pro-Roosevelt local union leaders reported that many of their members were attracted to Yorty by his skillful TV performances and shrewd four-year battle as the self-proclaimed underdog against the city council. By contrast, Roosevelt's campaign organization was weak, and he was evidently little known outside his own district. Moreover, he did not maintain the clear stand on civil rights that might have attracted liberal and minority voters.

and the interest groups had the resources to finance the campaigns of individual candidates.* According to Cresap:

> The fact that brewers in California pay an excise tax of only 62 cents a barrel as compared with an average of $2.03 in other states, that medical care in California is the most expensive in the nation, and that the ashes of cremated persons in California are required to be deposited in a cemetery or mausoleums, attests to the influence of the brewers, the doctors, and the cemetery and mausoleum associations respectively.[17]

The formal partisanship of California politics, did not, therefore, distinguish pluralist state politics from the equally pluralist nonpartisan politics of Los Angeles. Rather, California unions themselves participated in this dominant interest group politics. As established organizations with ample financial resources, they often found that their easiest course was to press for immediate organizational interests in the legislature rather than for the class or income-group interests of the entire labor movement. They achieved considerable success along these lines. The California legislature passed laws regulating licensing provisions, prevailing wages for craft unions, and factory inspection and safety regulations for industrial unions. In addition, unions and employers in a particular industry often cooperated effectively for common goals—attracting defense contracts, for example.

This moderate and cautious pattern even in the legislative politics of the 1960s is illustrated by an article in the *Los Angeles Citizen,* the weekly paper of the Los Angeles Central Labor Council. Union lobbies in the legislature are accepted by politicians because union members own property and pay taxes "except for those who have had tough luck or are relatively new to the labor movement." In fact,

---

* The system of powerful interest groups dominating California politics reached its climax in the career of Arthur Samish, self-proclaimed governor of the California legislature. As lobbyist for scores of separate interests, Samish controlled enormous sums of campaign finances throughout the state, and was acknowledged by observers familiar with the legislature as the most powerful political figure in California politics for much of the period between 1932 and 1950. On Samish, see *ibid.,* pp. 80–81; McWilliams, *California: The Great Exception, op. cit.,* pp. 198–209; and Lester Velie, "The Secret Boss of California," *Collier's,* 124 (August 13, 1949), 11ff. and (August 20, 1949), 12ff.

union members seemed middle-class citizens "prominent in the American Legion, the VFW . . . in civic activities and . . . public office." Today, the article continues, labor's representatives "are hollered at down the corridors and engage in back slapping with the best of them."[18] Even during the Republican period of control before 1959, Executive Secretary Cornelias J. Haggerty of the state labor federation enjoyed close relations with Governors Earl Warren and Goodwin J. Knight and with many Republican legislators. Haggerty succeeded in blocking many antilabor bills and in passing some prolabor legislation.[19]

J. W. Buzzell, who led the Los Angeles Central Labor Council through the 1930s and early 1940s, not only preferred narrow group politics but militantly opposed on principle any ideologically oriented political activity.[20] Even under his liberal successor, William Bassett, much of the council's energies continued to be devoted to improving the wages of city employees in local unions, securing friendly police attitudes toward strikes, and preventing the use of city employees who were not craft-union members on city projects. Political action in elections remained secondary.

Even considering this union activity, then, the net effect of government by interest groups appears to have primarily benefited upper-income and upper-middle-income groups, which possessed most of the available money and organizational resources.[21] Although the Great Depression made politics unusually salient, the voters of that time were not cohesive enough to form permanent political organizations. In general, lower-income groups tended to leave partisan politics in California to those who had the requisite motivation, skills, and financial resources to participate in the costly interest-group process. As in the nonpartisan politics of Detroit, in which conservatives did far better than they did in partisan elections, California's partisan but highly personalized statewide campaigns generally helped those interests that enjoyed incumbency, press support, and organizational skills. All of these factors—including incumbency until 1960—favored the Republicans, although some of the most successful, like Earl Warren, Hiram Johnson, and Goodwin Knight blurred party differences by enunciating liberal prolabor positions, including opposition to right-to-work legislation.

Unstable Mass Protests

Nevertheless, California politics until the 1950s mixed together the organized pluralism typical of twentieth-century American politics and a series of emotional but disorganized lower-class protests typical of American workers after the Civil War. In other words, this pluralist politics of weak parties and strong interest groups, together with social rootlessness, produced the most immediately striking feature of southern California politics, the wide variety of poorly organized lower-class mass-protest movements that somewhat resembled the area's frequent religious revivals. These working-class movements included Kearnyism in the nineteenth century and the Union Labor party after the turn of the century. The depression of the 1930s produced still others, most notably Upton Sinclair's End Poverty in California (EPIC). The middle-class progressives, whose most successful politician was Hiram Johnson, flourished from 1910 to 1916. All these protests reflected the isolation of individual Californians, which, McWilliams argued, led to a common pattern, that is, "[A] mass revolt, in an amazingly brief period, [which grasps for] power with little preparation or formal organization."[22] In other words, the prevailing disorganization meant there were few groups or elites with broad constituencies that could restrain and channel discontent before it burst out—or sustain protest groups once they were formed. As McWilliams points out, these movements quickly disappeared without having any lasting effect on organized political life. In most cases, the lower-income voters were thus capable only of intense outbursts. They could not support sustained efforts at reform.

In seeking to make the Democratic party a stable and permanent vehicle for advancing their social-welfare goals, Los Angeles' unions thus encountered the same social and political fragmentation that has hitherto made lower-class politics so unpredictably sporadic. The California electorate consistently supported liberal Democrats only in highly publicized Presidential elections that presented a relatively clear choice between a liberal and a conservative. California voted for liberal Democratic candidates Wilson, Roosevelt, Truman, and

Johnson, in all their successful Presidential campaigns, and almost voted for Kennedy. But until 1958, Republicans dominated both legislative and gubernatorial elections. To help reverse this picture, organized labor had to mobilize its members to undertake campaign work for the party. But the ever-present political disorganization and social fluidity made it difficult to arouse even union activists. In fact, we shall see that Los Angeles unions found themselves immobilized by social and political fragmentation in the same way, although not to the same degree, as the individual lower-class voters.

Tradition and Disorganization—Sources of Labor Political Action

Although Los Angeles' pervasive disorganization creates particularly severe difficulties for labor unions trying to build a stable coalition on behalf of the Democratic party, this fragmentation actually affected union behavior very differently at different points in the political process. However pluralist labor's participation in local politics and (to a somewhat lesser extent) in lobbying the state legislature with regard to partisan election campaigns, Los Angeles was dramatically distinguished from both Detroit and Chicago by the enthusiasm of many nonfactory unions formerly in the AFL. Indeed, many of these Los Angeles unions regularly outstripped the contribution to political action made by the Detroit and Chicago affiliates in their international unions.

This enthusiasm for partisan campaign work was symbolized by William Bassett, secretary-treasurer of the AFL Central Labor Council, who later held that post in the merged county federation. Bassett demonstrated a strong commitment to political action projects over a decade before the AFL-CIO merger. He launched the United AFL Voters' League four years before the national AFL initiated Labor's League for Political Education. This group proposed that all local unions "precinct" their members and appoint committees to work with the league in each congressional district.[23] At that time the league could not overcome the opposition of some conservative union leaders. But once the merger established COPE as a committee of the county council, Los Angeles unions undertook a sizable political-action program.

Although the largest CIO unions, the Steelworkers and the Autoworkers, were very active during the 1960's, they were by no means large enough to assume the dominant role common elsewhere. For example, the IAM (which was never in the CIO, although it has many industrial locals) played a much more active role than in Detroit or Chicago. Furthermore, the general obstacles to effective precinct work in Los Angeles meant that most political campaigns relied at least as much on direct mailings to reach the voters as on the door-to-door campaigns that the large industrial unions were equipped to undertake. As a result, two relatively small unions, the Ladies Garment Workers, (ILGWU), formerly AFL, and particularly the Amalgamated Clothing Workers, (ACWA), formerly CIO, proved far more important in Los Angeles than in either Detroit or Chicago. Both unions used retired and temporarily unemployed garment workers who accepted their unions' commitment to political action and had the leisure time and dexterity to handle mailings efficiently.

The contrast between union campaign activity in Los Angeles and Eastern cities was still more dramatic with respect to many of the city's nonfactory unions. The most active service union that cooperated with COPE's activities on behalf of the Democrats was the Building Service Union, despite its extremely conservative role in Chicago. This activist stance reflected the influence of International Vice-President George Hardy, who led the union in California from his San Francisco headquarters. Hardy's staff representatives in San Francisco employed a liberal rhetoric very much like that of CIO officials in Detroit and Chicago. In Los Angeles, Hardy evidently tried to move his staff in a similar direction by hiring as business agents college graduates who were much more inclined than older agents to include political campaign work among their duties.

Still more surprising perhaps was the activity of many building-trades locals, the traditional centers of voluntarist opposition to political action in both Detroit and Chicago. In 1960 and 1962, for example, many building-trades locals sought to stimulate membership registration by identifying unregistered members through a central file system. This enterprise, Voters Registration Service, was not affiliated with COPE, and some COPE leaders criticized it as ineffective and divisive. But the service itself was designed to foster political action, and most unions participating in the service followed COPE's endorsements of candidates (see Chapter VI).

On the other hand, the activities of the service did not even begin to match those of Local 11 of the IBEW. This local was not only more active than the Building Service locals and easily the most active building-trades local in COPE, but also, according to Democratic party leaders, was the most effective COPE union in the area except perhaps for the UAW. The local's leaders were much less ideological than some of George Hardy's own staff in Building Service, reflecting in part perhaps the much more prosperous economic position of the union's members. They more often justified political action to their membership in terms of the work rules in the construction industry, and they emphasized welfare issues of particular interest to their members like health insurance for retired workers. Nevertheless, these leaders were highly partisan Democrats; the local's former manager, George O'Brien, was rewarded for outstanding service to the party by appointment as Los Angeles United States Marshal. Local 11 was only the most outstanding example of the nonfactory craft unions that played an appreciable role in political action, including Carpenters', Painters', and, at times, Sheet Metal Workers' locals. Indeed, these groups displayed a commitment to partisan campaign work dating back two decades to Bassett's Voters' League.

At least three peculiar features of California life explain this unusual taste for political action in national partisan politics among Los Angeles' nonfactory unions. One factor, the traditional militancy of the entire California labor movement* originated in San Francisco, the state's first major economic center. The city's early isolation from the Eastern United States not only meant a chronic labor shortage, but also gave its fledgling unions great bargaining power. Aided by a general fear of Oriental workers competing for jobs, labor organizers built powerful unions that secured passage of a series of

---

* This militant tendency was encouraged by the traditional autonomy of west coast unions, so that even unions with very conservative national heads, like the Carpenters, have had militant leaders in California.

advanced labor laws during the nineteenth century and supported several successful though transient labor parties. By 1900, "San Francisco was recognized as not only the most tightly organized city in America but as the stronghold of trade unionism in the United States."[24] As Los Angeles began to grow, the northern California labor movement sent in its organizers to protect itself against low-wage competition. In the process they communicated the militancy of the San Francisco unions to their Los Angeles affiliates, some of whom remain under northern California influence in the 1960s. The impact of these attitudes in the 1960s could be detected in some important Los Angeles unions, including Building Service and, less directly, the Carpenters.

Another factor encouraging militancy was Los Angeles' own open-shop tradition, strongly fostered by the city's determinedly antiunion business community led by Harrison Gray Otis of the *Los Angeles Times*. In addition, socialist-oriented unions appeared likely to elect a mayor in 1911 until two labor leaders confessed to bombing the *Times* just before the election. Together with unfavorable laws and strenuous employer resistance, this disaster kept Los Angeles an open-shop city until the New Deal.[25] This forbidding local environment meant that, like the Autoworkers in Detroit, nonfactory unions in Los Angeles faced both repression by employers and substantial exclusion from their city's nonpartisan electoral system. As a result, these unions only achieved a reliably secure position as a result of the Wagner Act and the creation of the NLRB. AFL unions in Los Angeles, therefore, resembled CIO unions elsewhere in the sense that they flourished only under the New Deal. By contrast, the views of many nonfactory union leaders in the East were molded by Gompers' voluntarist interest-group perspective. The younger leaders who gradually replaced Gompers' contemporaries rose in organizations where internalizing these views favored their advancement. But in Los Angeles, the rapid expansion of the labor movement after the Wagner Act was passed has created a new generation of nonfactory union leaders whose political views were formed under Franklin Roosevelt. Consequently, these leaders take for granted welfare-state politics, federal protection for unions, and the importance of supporting Democrats in national politics.

A history of antiunion repression and consequent political militancy cannot, however, entirely explain the commitment of Los Angeles unions to campaign work for the Democratic party. The Chicago Federation of Labor supported a left-wing labor party in the 1920s, and some of Chicago's CIO unions fought bloody struggles for recognition in the 1930s. Yet as part of their understanding with the Democratic party, both groups agreed to limit COPE activities. Much of the difference between Chicago and Los Angeles nonfactory unions must therefore be attributed to southern California's social and political disorganization. For one thing, Los Angeles' rapid population growth and mobility during this period directly affected the internal structure of many of its unions. Labor leadership expanded so markedly that business agents who were college educated, and often as a result COPE oriented, found easy access to leadership positions in such nonfactory unions as Building Service, Painters, and Carpenters. Of course, Los Angeles nonfactory union leaders, like their Eastern counterparts, were also concerned about building codes, licenses, inspection, and police practices that affected their members' job interests. In Eastern states, these interests have led nonfactory unions to build particularistic alliances with often conservative or at least non-issue-oriented local party politicians, a maneuver that often reduced their commitment to COPE's campaign activities in national politics. In California, however, many license and code matters were regularly handled by state contract and licensing boards, and partisan patronage was so limited that, even immediately before elections, personnel for vital jobs had to be actively recruited by state officials. As a result, union officials accumulated few political debts to local politicians by requesting that union men be appointed inspectors. They had difficulty persuading even their older members to take this less strenuous but also less well-paying job. In any case, the unions dealt with nonpartisan councilmen and the mayor, who usually were not concerned with the union's role in partisan state or national politics.

The important point is the extent to which these conditions weakened the constraints under which such unions usually operate in politics. Nonfactory unions were able to join with more ideological allies, including industrial unions and middle-class issue-oriented

Democrats that were to their left both in local controversies and in partisan politics, because they had few alliances with more conservative politicians who might oppose such activities. The impulse to join in political action, in other words, did not encounter countervailing commitments like those that have hindered Chicago COPE.

Labor and Increasing Party Organization

Beginning in the mid-1950s, the California party system increasingly reflected the New Deal realignment in national politics as each major party began to appeal to a more economically distinct body of supporters. The clarity of the partisan choice presented to the electorate was considerably increased by eliminating from the law a cross-filing provision that in practice had substantially weakened the formally partisan character of state and federal elections. By allowing candidates to run in both Democratic and Republican primaries simultaneously, cross filing had helped incumbents, most often Republicans until 1960, win both primaries and thus retain office without a clear-cut party confrontation. Once each candidate's party allegiance was listed on the primary ballots in 1954, these double victories sharply declined, increasing the number of partisan contests in the general election. After they came to power in 1959, the Democrats ended the system entirely.

Changes in the structure of party campaign organizations have reinforced this change in the electoral law. Some Republican candidates attracted support from a variety of right-wing, issue-oriented groups. The Democrats, on the other hand, have acquired the very liberal Democratic club movement. These groups in the two parties represented elements of both innovation and continuity. Like some of the state's earlier mass political movements, they displayed an emotional commitment to ideological positions on issues less common in much of the East, where patronage politics was well entrenched. But their stress on organizational maintenance and systematic campaign work differs sharply from the earlier, poorly organized mass movements that often appealed to otherwise isolated individuals. In fact, both left- and right-wing groups were relatively cohesive middle-class organizations strong enough not only to undertake extensive precinct work but also to persist in the face of much public criticism. On the Democratic side, the clubs organized themselves on a statewide basis into the California Democratic Council (CDC). Modeling itself after the older California Republican Assembly, the CDC sought to bring peace and order to the confused Democratic primaries by making endorsements before the primaries were held, thus designating a semiofficial organization candidate. In addition, the CDC claimed a major role in helping liberal Democrats win the party's primaries and capture the statehouse, the legislature, and the congressional delegation in 1958.

Although the CDC's actual effectiveness in campaigns may be questioned,[26] the club movement did seem important enough to be imitated by a group within the party who objected to its militantly liberal stand on issues as doctrinaire and counterproductive. Particularly since the 1958 victory, this group, including many of the party's incumbent officeholders and their associates and supporters, have been united by Jesse Unruh, the state assembly speaker and dominant Democratic party figure in southern California. In the spring of 1964, the Unruh forces withdrew from the CDC board with considerable publicity, and formed the Democratic Volunteers Committee of California (DVC). According to one of its own pamphlets, the DVC "believes that the leadership of the Democratic Party is vested, and properly so, in its elected office-holders." The Unruh forces appeared particularly upset by the CDC's criticism of the Johnson administration's Asian policies, its sniping at party incumbents generally, and its resolutions that expressed views that were, it seemed, far to the left of most voters. The DVC appeared to draw its members from a group of somewhat lower status than the original club movement, finding support in some parts of the San Fernando Valley and Los Angeles' less prosperous Negro and southeastern sections where the club movement was weak.

Like the party organization in Chicago, the DVC looked at issues as means to win votes for party candidates. It relied on the gratifications of political involvement, association with political figures, and general socializing, as incentives to political activity, whereas the Chicago party organization depended on material incentives. But this meant that the DVC tended to be controlled by officeholders, unlike the Chicago party, which usually controlled the candidates it elected. The DVC could not even hope to imitate the Chicago party by excluding or fully controlling COPE or other party groups. On the contrary, the southern California labor movement paralleled the national role of organized labor in strengthening the Democratic party in campaigns and pressuring for a welfare-state orientation.

To carry the similarity with national politics a step further, just as the heightening of party differences in the New Deal contributed to union involvement nationally in Democratic campaign work, union efforts in California were stimulated by the unusually ideological state election of 1958. This campaign brought the Democratic party to power and enabled it to end cross filing entirely. The interest of both unions and low-income voters in this election was particularly spurred by the controversy over a right-to-work referendum, endorsed by the Republican candidate for governor but opposed by every major Democrat. As one knowledgeable observer concluded, "it is generally agreed by business, labor and party leaders that organized labor in California made the greatest political effort in its history in this campaign."[27] In the face of such a direct organizational threat, labor launched a massive public relations campaign against the referendum, stressing the proposition's big-business support, coining such slogans as "right-to-work for less and less," and inducing many religious leaders to speak out against the proposition.[28] These steps, as well as a coalition with Catholic leaders against both the right-to-work proposal and an attempt to end tax exemptions for private elementary and secondary schools helped change a 51 percent to 44 percent majority for the right-to-work referendum in an April 1958 poll to almost 60 percent opposition in the November referenda.[29]

The campaign was also significant for the unprecedented enthusiasm generated within labor's own ranks.* Union members and leaders throughout the state contributed $2.5 million of which almost

---

* "Four groups with an overwhelmingly Democratic registration [voted against right-to-work] . . . labor unionists, Jews, Negroes, and Mexican-Americans. Union members voted 85 per cent in the negative while voters without union family connections voted 49.6 per cent in opposition." Anderson, *op. cit.*, p. 291.

$600,000 came from Los Angeles labor's Save Our State Committee. Several Los Angeles building-trades locals received contributions averaging $4 or $5 per member, with many business agents contributing much more.

These financial contributions were matched by the unprecedented campaign activities of individual union members, ranging from speakers' bureaus to extensive mailings, including over 1 million pieces by the Amalgamated Clothing Workers alone. Almost every paid union official in the county participated in the campaign as part of his union duties; in addition, most large unions put some rank and file workers on their payrolls for the duration. According to Anderson, "one hundred or more union-paid precinct workers were supplied to each assembly district office on election day."[30] Interviews four years after the campaign confirmed this general picture but suggested that the number of workers varied considerably— larger groups were assigned to the lower-income and minority-group districts. The quality of the union members' political campaign work was as unprecedented as their numbers. Campaign workers canvassed lower-income neighborhoods before the election to register people, distribute literature, and explain the right-to-work issue. In some areas, where few houses had ever been covered before, most houses were covered more than once. One rank and file member recalled that "I detest precinct work, but I walked several precincts with my wife to beat right-to-work." As a nonunion club leader said, "I guess they were really scared."

The election saw a rare confrontation in which different classes employed their most basic political resources; labor's organized manpower against the mass-media influence of the business community. Although subsequent elections by no means duplicated these conditions, the 1958 election cemented the labor-Democratic alliance in the state. For one thing, simply registering the groups that could be expected to oppose a right-to-work referendum amounted to registering primarily Democratic voters. Beyond that, COPE workers opposing right-to-work not only put in a word for the entire Democratic slate but often integrated labor's campaign organization into the overall party effort. Indeed, the unions maintained and staffed the headquarters for Democratic candidates in twenty-nine of the thirty-one assembly districts in Los Angeles County, hiring nonlabor Democrats to run them if necessary.[31] Often, labor put up a sign advertising the headquarters that had the Democratic candidate's name in the largest letters and a smaller, though readable, legend urging a vote against right to work.

Labor's political participation fell off sharply in the years following 1958, even in Presidential elections, but its subsequent organizational relationship with the Democrats was permanently affected. The 1958 campaign brought into politics on the side of the Democrats many local unions that had previously avoided any partisan commitment. As the leader of a building-trades local reported, "it really woke them [the rank and file] up. Once we started making endorsements in 1958 they started asking each year, where's our slate this year?" A club leader reported that in his district, "some of them [the labor workers], less than half, came back to work in 1960. But those that did really had learned something; they had a sense of accomplishment, and they really wanted to work."

The outcome of the 1958 election reinforced these trends by emphasizing partisan differences so that most unions perceived no alternative to supporting Democratic candidates. The victory of so many liberal Democrats enabled the party to cater to the interests of individual union members, union organizations, and labor's broader social-welfare demands under Democratic Governor Edmund G. Brown. At the same time, with Republican moderates no longer in control of the governorship, the ideological right wing of the party has assumed greater prominence, and this shift culminated in the election of Governor Ronald Reagan in 1966. Taken together, these developments made labor an integral part of Democratic campaign operations. Typically, the widely distributed Democratic state party calendar for 1962, which indicated important dates in the months preceding the election, routinely included, along with the deadlines for voter registration and the dates of official party meetings, the dates for the annual state labor convention. The state party leadership thus recognized in a semiofficial way the California labor movement's contribution not only to Democratic campaigns but also to the organization and coherence of all party activities.

The Persistence of Political Disorganization

The participation of Los Angeles unions in California's party realignment should not disguise the effect that the general disorganization of southern California life had on organized labor's campaign organization. In fact, COPE shared the predicament of the individual voters confronted with the same political fragmentation. We have seen that the UAW's power within the Democratic party and the Detroit labor movement paralleled the dominant position of the automobile corporations in Detroit business and civic life. Again, the internally monolithic, but pluralistically oriented, Chicago Federation of Labor resembles the dominant party in ethos and structure. Similarly, the Los Angeles Labor Council typified diffusion of power in Los Angeles by its own factions, conflicts, secessions, and the autonomous joint boards that united locals of various international unions long before political action became a major issue.[32]

This fragmentation also directly affected union political activities. Although a wide variety of unions favored political action, many demonstrated a greater tendency to undertake independent projects outside COPE than they did in either Detroit or Chicago. This pattern was followed by unions with traditions of independent political operation (e.g., the IAM and to a lesser extent the Steelworkers). The case of the craft unions, which supported the Voter Registration Service that operated in 1960 and 1962, provides an even clearer example. Many of the locals that helped organize the service, including the Engineers, the Carpenters, the Painters, and the Sheet Metal Workers, together with a few locals of Rubber Workers and Communications Workers, did not play an important part in COPE itself. As a result, COPE leadership feared the service as a potential competitor and refused to cooperate with it. As one well-informed observer put it, "The Building Trades people then got angry, everyone got their backs up, and they decided to carry on the work themselves."

Los Angeles union leaders apparently felt more keenly than most that operations explicitly conducted by COPE would benefit the central organization much more than the individual unions. Consequently,

Los Angeles COPE functioned much more as a roof organization, which affected the political preferences of its constituent unions by endorsements, than as an organization that coordinates and supervises precinct work.

Los Angeles COPE did perform an important function because its endorsements provided a link to the Democratic party in general elections. But an examination of labor's alliances with party groups reveals the effects of this same political disorganization. In the 1962 state legislative and congressional primaries, for example, labor generally sided with Unruh's group of incumbent party officeholders in their successful campaign to oust the officers of the Los Angeles County Committee who favored the club movement. Most labor leaders had described these men as impractical ideologists. As Chapter IX shows, COPE also endorsed some of the state legislative and congressional candidates Unruh favored. In one congressional primary, however, the COPE leadership endorsed a congressional candidate who had fought Unruh in the state legislature and was closely associated with the club movement. In other races COPE was too divided to take any position at all, and in one case the COPE delegate body demonstrated the basic diffusion of power within Los Angeles labor by rejecting its executive board's endorsement recommendation for one of Unruh's candidates. Despite Unruh's tactical brilliance and unequalled influence in the California legislature, he could neither impose unity on a divided labor movement nor offset its gratitude to his political opponents who operated as independent political entrepreneurs.

Two years later even this partial alliance with Unruh was in disarray. According to the compilation made by the state labor federation, whose secretary-treasurer was on very bad terms with the state speaker, Unruh ranked in the lower half of the Democratic assemblymen in the 1963–1964 legislature. Led by the UAW, anti-Unruh forces in the Los Angeles COPE delegate body passed a resolution explicitly refusing to endorse him in the 1964 primary although the executive board had previously agreed to take no action. Los Angeles unions also endorsed Comptroller Alan Cranston's bid for the senatorial nomination against Unruh's candidate, former Presidential Press Secretary Pierre Salinger. In defying Unruh, organized labor followed its accustomed practice of rewarding friendly incumbents. On other occasions this criterion had led it to support the speaker and his allies. Indeed, these same considerations led COPE and some of Unruh's closest allies among individual unions, including IBEW Local 11 and the UAW's sometimes dissident North American Aviation local, to support Congressman James Roosevelt against Mayor Yorty in 1965, even though Unruh opposed him as a potential rival.* In fact, labor's differences with Unruh emphasized the capacity of almost all partners in Los Angeles political alliances to act independently of each other when they see fit. For example, Unruh's own senatorial candidate against Cranston, Pierre Salinger, broke with Unruh after winning the primary.

This same fluidity of alignments meant, however, that even labor's break with Unruh was not decisive. The speaker's relations with many Los Angeles unions, apart from the top UAW leadership, was not wholly ruptured. Such groups as the Teachers, Building Service, and the Building Trades sided with the Unruh-backed DVC organization because it shared labor's tendency to support rather than to criticize most of the party's officeholders. COPE also endorsed Unruh in the 1964 general election and the COPE director, Thelma Thomas, and her superior, Secretary Bassett, joined Unruh's successful campaign in the 1964 primary to keep control of the Los Angeles County Democratic Committee.

Significantly, however, labor found this problem less serious in general elections for state and federal office, where formal, legally sanctioned party competition simplified labor's choices and consequently made it easier to recruit COPE campaign workers. In November 1964, COPE maintained a headquarters in every congressional district that was not strongly Republican and carried on extensive campaign activities in several important areas. In central Los Angeles, the UAW's North American Aviation local, one of the most active in the city, spent $35,000, hired five full-time staff men and

---

* Labor also generally supported the CDC-oriented liberal in the 1964 primary in the twenty-third congressional district, where the Democrats incorrectly expected to pick up an additional seat.

supplied 150 deputy registrars and other volunteers. In the highly Democratic thirty-first and twenty-first congressional districts, these workers helped register 35,000 new and overwhelmingly Democratic voters. Approximately 500 of the local's members worked on election day. In east central Los Angeles, the Meatcutters supplied 150 volunteers to work on election day, half of whom were Mexican-Americans. But this activity contrasts dramatically with other campaigns. Neither local was particularly active in the 1965 mayoral campaign or in the important 1964 senatorial primary in which intraparty bitterness apparently contributed to the Democrats losing a senate seat.

This mixed pattern of participation helps us specify more precisely the changes that labor helped bring about in the California party system. We have seen that up to the middle of the 1950s individual Democratic politicians and rank and file voters had to fend for themselves in partisan elections as well as in primaries and local nonpartisan contests. Decisions had to be made about particular contests (whether to run or not, whom to support, whom to vote for) in isolation, that is, without the benefit of a framework of organizational commitments and with little regard to other campaigns either past or future. As this chapter indicates, such individualism with regard to partisan contests was reduced by the increased strength of the party campaign organization as well as by the end of cross filing. Nevertheless, factions within the party not only combined differently in different congressional districts in a single year, but also different factional patterns emerged in successive campaigns. Organized labor's position in Los Angeles politics, in other words, came to parallel but not duplicate this long-time predicament of California's individual lower-income voters. Like these voters, the labor movement was most active in Presidential elections and the crucial ideological confrontation over right to work in 1958. Similarly, labor political activity resembled the relatively low interest of the electorate in primaries and in nonpartisan local politics, where COPE usually does little. COPE's position diverged most from individual behavior in the intermediate case of partisan state and congressional general elections. It is primarily in this area that labor's organizational skills, manpower, and money appear to have helped reduce substantially the disorganization of its political environment.*

Conclusion: Los Angeles as a Microcosm of Organized Labor in National Politics

The position of organized labor in Los Angeles politics suggests at least three respects in which partisan labor politics in Los Angeles, far more than in Detroit or Chicago, resembled the AFL-CIO's position in the larger American political system during the Kennedy and Johnson administrations. First, with regard to the labor movement's power and influence, it is clear that, by comparison with the situation in Chicago, Los Angeles COPE played a much more important role in the Democratic party coalition, even though it had fewer precinct workers and poor internal cohesion. The influence of Los Angeles unions within the Democratic party, however, did not compare with that of the Detroit-area COPE and UAW. To be sure, Los Angeles COPE was not constrained by the power of a regular party organization (as in Chicago) or by its relations with business leaders and its own position as party leader (as in Detroit). Such restraints were ruled out by the persisting, if recently modified, political disorganization. Rather, this disorganization was itself the constraint that denied labor reliable allies or enemies. The labor movement excercised influence, but found it difficult to play any consistent political role, to find the fulcrums to control Los Angeles' political world.

The second point of resemblance between labor politics in the nation as a whole and in Los Angeles directly concerns their common disorganization, which contrasts with Detroit's and Chicago's more orderly systems. Socially, Los Angeles is so diffuse that some observers half seriously refuse to call it a city at all. Yet, American society also tends to be composed of congeries of geographic, economic, and

---

* COPE's position in Los Angeles resembles Detroit COPE's ineffectiveness in Detroit mayoral campaigns and its rebuffs in Democratic primaries. On the other hand, Detroit COPE is able to mobilize its resources in primaries and local elections far more effectively than Los Angeles COPE—and has somewhat more success in both arenas.

ethnic interests. By comparison, European societies are generally made up of a set of large class groups. Politically, by comparison with most European parties, America's national party organizations have been heterogeneous coalitions,[33] just as Los Angeles parties are riven by autonomous factions. In Durkheim's terms, because American society lacks a feudal past, it never even approximated the level of mechanical solidarity within social classes—a cohesiveness fostered by a shared sense of similarity—that characterized medieval Europe and formed the basis for proletarian class consciousness. In turn, the lack of such solidarity doomed socialism in America and delayed and inhibited the growth of industrial unions. Precisely similar factors have weakened, without suppressing, Los Angeles unions in their political activities.

To be sure, these instances of disorganization have rather different causes. In southern California the principal agent producing social dislocation is massive population growth and movement. By contrast, for the nation as a whole, massive foreign immigration to Eastern and Midwestern cities ceased over forty years ago, and social fragmentation nationally results from the physical extent of the country and its economic and cultural diversity. Politically, the weakness of Los Angeles parties is specifically traceable to the reforms of the progressive era that made them the prime example of ineffectual party organizations in a competitive two-party state.[34] By contrast, the weakness of national party organizations derives primarily from the nature of the American federal system, which still disperses party hegemony among state leaders, and even more often, among leaders of county, city, and ward organizations. Despite these different causes, both this chapter and Chapter I have shown that disorganization in Los Angeles and in the nation as a whole had similar consequences. Both adversely affected the political position of the lower classes.

It is true that over the past century industrialization and urbanization have functioned through the agency of lower-class political organizations to offset somewhat the fragmentation of American society and to increase working-class political unity by reducing ethnic and regional differences.[35] But these tendencies have been most important with respect to workers in individual cities like

Chicago and particular industries like the automobile industry. Traditional urban patronage organizations (in Chicago, for example) have effectively increased and coordinated lower-class political activity. But these machines have depended on the largely mechanical solidarity of relatively stable local communities often united by a common ethnicity that enabled precinct workers who typify these ethnic traits to win the confidence of constituents. The case of Detroit indicates that, as this ethnic consciousness among European immigrant stock declined, the relatively stable shop societies in industrial plants sometimes provided a partial substitute in terms of a commonly perceived status as workers in a particular industry.[36] But like the ethnic neighborhood that (with the primary exception of Negro ghettoes) faces erosion as city dwellers move to the more prosperous suburbs, the importance of the shop society could decline as technological change eliminates face-to-face work groups in manufacturing. To that extent the problem of concerting the political activities of the lower classes in such cities may come to resemble the problem in Los Angeles and in national politics.

From this point of view, the AFL-CIO's COPE proved especially significant as a national organization that was more than merely a collection of local industrial-union-based political-action groups. In other words, it did not rely for its cohesion entirely on the partially mechanical solidarity of the shared status of industrial wage earners or on other similarities. Rather, because its main inducement was less a social friendship network than shared political values and attitudes, COPE could be relatively independent of face-to-face groups. It thus represented organized labor's answer not only to the general fragmentation of American politics that affected the Democratic party, but the more specific decline of the machine and the erosion of face-to-face industrial shop societies. In particular, national COPE drew upon varied skills and resources of campaign workers and voters and thus relied on a still more organic solidarity than the shop societies. This partial shift from mechanical to organic solidarity as the basis of the labor movement's political activities and the possible accompanying shift to consumer-class politics will be examined in a more extended way in Chapter XI. It is clear at this point, however, that Los Angeles COPE represented a significant innovation in labor politics precisely because it too tried to offset social and political disorganization without recourse to Chicago or Detroit COPE's primary dependence on industrial unions. And as Chapters X and XI suggest, this reliance on such a formal political organization, rather than on the mechanical solidarity of factory unions, paralleled much of organized labor's partisan political activities nationally.

Trade-union political activities in Los Angeles in the 1950s and 1960s resembled union politics nationally in a third respect—a sharp contrast between a welfare-state orientation in national election campaigns and pluralist attitudes in other spheres of political activity. This contrast involved two dimensions, one of which is characterized by the *homogeneity* (as opposed to diversity) of the interests present in the constituency of a union organization. As the size-of-political-unit analysis indicates, such homogeneity is ordinarily greater in small constituencies, while larger constituencies tend to be more diverse. The second dimension deals with the *cohesion* or unity—with respect to government policy outputs—of the interests in any given constituency. We have already seen that *interest homogeneity* is greater in craft unions as opposed to the more economically and ethnically diverse industrial unions. At least as important, homogeneous constituencies are much more common in local as opposed to national politics. The federal government is far more diverse in terms of the number of citizens and variety of interests it comprises than the states or localities. Even apart from economic and social composition, the national system must deal with the competing claims of different localities and states which are not present in local politics itself. In local politics, with fewer interests to be satisfied than in national politics, the possibilities of making particular arrangements with individual interests—in the style of the Chicago party—is increased.

Los Angeles unions, for example, conformed more closely to Gompers' pluralist prescriptions in nonpartisan local elections than in national elections where constituencies tend to be larger. Indeed, organized labor's electoral participation locally, even on strongly ideological issues, also reflected a pluralist concern for the organizational interests of particular unions. Unions supported a conservative incumbent mayor in 1961 and displayed little enthusiasm for a liberal candidate in 1965. Yet, the same unions pursued welfare-state goals in partisan election campaigns for state and especially national office on behalf of relatively liberal Democratic party candidates. Similar but smaller differences between union behavior in national and local elections were apparent in Detroit and Chicago. Detroit COPE was relatively less programmatically oriented in local elections than in national ones, and in Chicago the predominantly pluralist Chicago Federation of Labor did conform somewhat to national COPE's welfare-state posture in at least some congressional district contests. More generally, most labor efforts in local politics have remained the preserve of those relatively pluralist nonfactory unions least interested in COPE. But as we have seen, a greater number of ideological industrial unions have devoted most of their resources to national politics. In part because of their greater diversity, these industrial unions and the state and national union federations have often found it more advantageous to unite their members through broad welfare-state programs than to rely too heavily on congeries of perhaps divisive particular interests.

The second *interest cohesion* dimension explains differences in trade union behavior in terms of different types of political issues and different types of electoral party systems. In the case of different types of issues, many union organizations, including the AFL-CIO, have frequently lobbied effectively for their own narrow organizational and economic interests in spite of the labor movement's extensive work for welfare-state measures in Congress. On these pluralistic issues with highly divisible outputs, which Lowi calls regulatory or distributive, a large number of small particular interests may be satisfied without having to unite through a common ideology or program.[37] If such interests, including particular unions, can obtain small outputs without disturbing other interests, there is little advantage in building large, issue-oriented coalitions, including those within a political party. Cohesion among interests is therefore low. This case may be typical of legislation affecting the working conditions or contracts of particular industries, or the economic health of particular regions.

On those broad welfare-state issues (which Lowi calls redistributive) where the policy outputs are large and indivisible, the various political interests have a powerful incentive to unite in a programmatically cohesive coalition. The more indivisible the output, and thus the larger the number of interests affected by any given set of outputs, the greater is organized labor's incentive to assemble a diverse, rather than homogeneous, aggregation of interests. Only a large coalition is likely to be strong enough to control the decision-making process. Under such conditions, a major, issue-oriented political party becomes an increasingly convenient organizational instrument for producing unity. As a result, welfare-state oriented unions that support COPE have tended to sway the individual voters' and even campaign workers' loyalty away from particular unions or other subgroups and toward the Democratic party, as a larger, more inclusive entity. In other words, such union members and leaders, both as individuals and as organization officials, promote interest cohesion by taking the role and perspective of a larger group, that is, the party.

Contests under the electoral system promote interest cohesion through a two-party system of competition in which partisan labels effectively guide, organize, and restrict the voters'—and the organized interests'—choice between candidates, in contrast to the less organized primaries and nonpartisan or multiparty elections. The extreme, and most important case, presents the voters with a forced choice between only two significant Presidential candidates, a factor that limited the final popular vote total of George Wallace in 1968.

To summarize, the unions' pluralist, as opposed to welfare-state, orientation, is a function of the *interest-cohesion homogeneity ratio*. The smaller the magnitude of the ratio (i.e., the smaller the cohesion between interests and the greater their homogeneity), the more likely it is that the union will adopt a pluralist position. As we have noted, this is more likely to occur in local, small constituency politics and on issues that involve divisible outputs, and in less organized primaries and nonpartisan elections. The greater the magnitude of the ratio (i.e., the greater the cohesion between interests and the less their homogeneity), the more likely it is that labor will adopt a welfare-state position. As we have indicated, this is most common among industrial unions, national and state federations, on redistributive issues, and in general elections in a two-party system. In

Table 1 this ratio is greatest in the lower right-hand corner and smallest in the upper left-hand corner.

TABLE **1**   **Interest-Cohesion Homogeneity Ratio**

	Low Interest Cohesion	High Interest Cohesion
High Interest Homogeneity	Ratio small (voluntarist orientation)	Mixed cases
Low Interest Homogeneity	Mixed cases	Ratio large (welfare-state orientation)

As suggested earlier, this ratio explains the differences between voluntarist and welfare-state oriented behavior within the Los Angeles labor movement and the national AFL-CIO more accurately than it does the cases of the Chicago and Detroit unions. However, a limited contrast consistent with the ratio could be observed between the activities of Detroit unions in local and national politics. The Detroit UAW did concentrate primarily on partisan state and national elections (where the ratio was large). Nevertheless, it was strong enough to stage large-scale campaigns on behalf of liberal mayoral candidates in nonpartisan contests (where the ratio was small) until the mid-1950s. In addition, throughout the 1950s and 1960s, its campaign workers supported liberal candidates for the Detroit Common Council, thus providing a hitherto unprecedented degree of coherence and organization to the otherwise extremely individualistic, nonpartisan councilmenic elections. In turn, the UAW overshadowed the voluntarist craft unions, which are so important in local politics elsewhere. In Chicago, the industrial unions and their allies did support some liberal congressional candidates in the city's residential areas, but avoided interfering in local politics. Yet the pluralist regular Democratic party organization and the voluntarist Chicago Federation of Labor were strong enough to limit Chicago COPE's issue-oriented activities in national, as well as in local, elections. The city's strongest industrial unions accepted limits on their congressional campaign activities unknown in cities with weaker party organizations.

In these two cities, then, size-of-political-unit analysis, the ratio of decisions to interests, proved less useful in explaining trade-union political behavior than in Los Angeles or in the nation as a whole. An explanation for this deviation may suggest those conditions under which the size-of-political-unit approach rather than other types of analysis is most applicable to the American labor movement. The importance of Detroit COPE in local politics reflects the dominance not of political variables but of socioeconomic factors, specifically the automobile companies and the UAW, in Detroit life. In other words, we can account for the main outline—though not for all the details— of labor's behavior by the social stratification approach within political sociology. By contrast, political system variables were so dominant in Chicago that even powerful industrial unions with ample economic resources could only attain a highly marginal position in the city's politics. To explain the Chicago case, we must turn to the competing explanatory tradition that emphasizes the independent importance of political roles and structures.

It appears, therefore, that differences in the size of such political units as constituency and type of issue-output are most important— at least in explaining the labor movement—primarily when those unions committed to welfare-state politics and those committed to voluntarism command roughly equal organizational resources. Such equality was encouraged by the political and social disorganization of Los Angeles politics and by the equivalent fragmentation imposed by federalism on the already large and diverse American nation. Such disorganization or fragmentation also tended to isolate large-constituency welfare politics from small-constituency pluralist lobbying. In this situation, resources available for national electoral campaign work could not be easily transferred to local politics. Nor, by the 1950s, could unions mainly committed to lobbying prevent welfare-state-oriented unions from undertaking extensive partisan campaign work. Where trade unions had the commitment and strength to function as class organizations, as they did in Detroit, the size of analytic units on the local-national and electoral-legislative dimensions retained only a diminished importance. As in Chicago, where the pluralist norms and institutions of the political system were so thoroughly entrenched that every political actor had to conform to them if he wished to achieve influence, all union political activities reflected a voluntarist orientation regardless of the decisions-interests ratio.

The size-of-political-unit approach is so useful in analyzing organized labor in Los Angeles—as well as in American politics as a whole—precisely because both socioeconomic and political variables operated independently and jointly. As the first chapters argued on the basis of historical data, labor politics in the United States since the 1930s can be understood only as the product of both an institutional and normative political pluralism and the class tensions generated by a heavily industrialized economy. Whereas these political factors have encouraged trade-union voluntarism, the economic ones, through the mechanism of working-class protest, gave shape and direction to the development of the welfare state. In short, the size-of-political-unit approach explains American labor politics to the extent that economic and political variables have equal impact on trade-union behavior. The American labor movement, in other words, functions as a major Democratic party electoral organization within certain limits imposed by its own economic structure and its political environment. The two chapters that follow will examine these internal and external conditions by a comparative analysis of Chicago, Detroit, and Los Angeles.

VI

Labor's Campaign Apparatus:

The Political Incentives of an Economic Organization

In terms of constituency, organizational structure, and campaign activities, the labor-Democratic party alliance through the mid-1960s conformed neither to the branch structure of Western European working-class parties nor to the middle-class cadre structure usually attributed to major American parties. The first two chapters of this study offer a broad historical explanation for the emergence of a union-Democratic party alliance rather than a full-fledged labor party. By examining the particular resources and obstacles of the unions in each city, Chapters III through V explain the considerable intercity variation in the forms of this alliance. It is now desirable to establish an analytic framework that can adequately account for both the variation in the campaign activities of different unions and the constraints common to them all. We shall try to do this by examining the *political incentive systems* of the diverse unions in Chicago, Detroit, and Los Angeles.[1] These systems are comprised of the resources with which trade unions induce individual members to participate in politics, and the environmental variables which make these resources more or less effective. Relevant resources include the size and type (factory or nonfactory) of union and wage and education level of their members. The environmental variables include the inducements available to nonlabor Democrats, and the social—particularly residential mobility—patterns of particular cities. Together these factors account for differential capacities of unions to mobilize their members for extensive campaign work. At the same time, our analysis will indicate some of the major barriers which keep American unions from duplicating the working class-union-party alliances of post-World War II Europe. Chapter VII will extend the discussion by examining the patterns of interaction among union campaign activities in particular cities and congressional districts.

From national COPE's point of view, unions should use their resources to build COPE district organizations that would bring together the rank and file union members in a congressional district to campaign systematically for all Democratic candidates. But apart from patronage machines, such partisan organizations, including those associated with unions, have rarely flourished in working-class areas. Unlike the avowedly socialist-labor parties of Western Europe, the procapitalist Democrats could not arouse workers to do campaign work by appeals to the class conflict between them and their employers. As a result, appeals to class-oriented workers to undertake campaign work had to be provided in large part by the labor movement itself. Yet, even after the founding of the CIO, the labor movement retained its primary status as an economic institution, devoted first of all to its members' immediate economic interests.

As a result, the effective inducements to political activity within the movement were supplied not by local, state, and national federations but by individual international and local unions, which, as their members' bargaining agents, claimed the first allegiance of the rank and file. To be sure, the COPE organizations associated with these federations controlled some campaign funds, coordinated some individual union activities, and made endorsements of candidates. Nevertheless, only the exceptional union member was led into campaign work by COPE directly, and individual unions frequently operated substantially independent programs in order to retain direct supervision over their members' election efforts. As a result, district COPES were most often either the creatures of one union, as in most of Detroit, or a roof organization that combined largely independent union operations, as in much of Los Angeles and Chicago.

The predominant place that these economically oriented unions assumed in providing political incentives for working-class politics indicates in still another way the relatively weak class consciousness of American workers. As this entire study has stressed, a critical factor that distinguishes American labor politics from its European counterpart has been the impact of an open pluralist political system in minimizing rather than reinforcing the grievances of the industrial proletariat. The consequent dominance of these capitalist values meant that private goals and interests played a decisive part in the American polity. Typically, the predominantly economic character of these unions limited their available inducements for involving union members in the public arena of partisan politics. These members, after all, could always ignore COPE campaign activities as irrelevant to the union's admittedly all-important success or failure in collective bargaining. The American labor movement thus confronted the difficult problem of using the chiefly economic resources of trade unions in political life.

This problem proved least serious in the important area of financial contributions to campaigns that involved the union organizations as such, rather than generating incentives for the rank and file. In most state and local elections and in all their nonpartisan registration drives in heavily Democratic areas, unions could spend the dues money their members had already contributed to the treasury without any special need to convince the rank and file of the importance of political participation. Only the funds spent in federal elections required active solicitation by union officials through "dollars for COPE" drives, and most unions found it easier to solicit small sums from individual workers than to persuade them to do precinct work. COPE also apparently learned how to spend its money efficiently in close races and during the important early months of campaigns, thus earning the candidates' appreciation (as indicated in Chapter I).

Nevertheless, liberal candidates have acquired other sources of campaign financing from individuals and groups outside labor, for example, the National Committee for an Effective Congress. But these groups could not provide numerous campaign workers in Democratic working-class strongholds. And it was in this distinctive role as a major Democratic electoral organization that the American trade unions found their primarily economic-based incentive system to be an important barrier.

Limitations as an Economic Organization

The limitations on union political incentives can be illustrated by considering two polar types of inducements that explicitly partisan, and thus primarily political, organizations of the left frequently offer to their campaign workers. At one extreme are the divisible material private-regarding incentives commonly associated with machine politics. At the other end are nonmaterial, public-regarding, disinterested incentives like class loyalty, which are often more ideologically than financially gratifying to the activist. These latter incentives are indivisible in the sense that the rewards generated by the desired political activity (e.g., broad changes in policy) are, as a whole, distributed to large groups rather than parcelled out to particular individuals. After World War II, such collective nonmaterial incentives continued to be found among many of the working-class branch-structure parties of Western Europe, even though these parties were then explicitly reformist, rather than revolutionary. Although COPE's ideology comprised somewhat similar policy goals, working-class European parties had far stronger incentives than any found among American workers because socialist traditions and class consciousness made ideological appeals more effective. Within the American Democratic party, middle-class ideologically motivated liberals, in James Q. Wilson's terms, the "amateur Democrats," could also rely on such ideal benefactions. In Detroit, for example, such workers were more meticulous in their campaign efforts than COPE workers in the early 1960s. But they usually lived in Republican or marginal areas rather than in the less prosperous Democratic strongholds.

The American urban machine had even greater success than these amateurs, particularly in low-income areas. Its highly divisible incentives, including employment for precinct workers and gifts and services to voters, appealed strongly to its lower-middle-class personnel and lower-class clientele. Despite these vital differences, however, European working-class parties, the amateur Democratic clubs in the United States, and the American urban machines were all, unlike COPE, specifically political organizations. They recruited their members on the basis of some *political* commitment, jobs, power, or principle, which the members shared with each other. By contrast, as primarily economic organizations, American unions in the generation after the New Deal had to rely on inducements that fell between these polar types and were less effective than either. Whatever the different political incentives that various unions offered their members, none of them—as applied to the rank and file—matched the effectiveness of the machine's divisible material incentives or of the ideal benefactions that induced political amateurs to campaign.

Typically, the position of the COPE worker with regard to material benefits was anomalous. He did not share the amateur Democrat's unqualified opposition to jobs or to other material considerations as legitimate political goals. But even industrial unions only paid their members a flat fee (about $20 to $25 in 1962) in lieu of lost pay for each day of campaign work. Obviously, such material inducements could not equal those of a party organization whose patronage workers kept their jobs by working in the precincts. Precisely because the unions would protect and improve their members' jobs and income regardless of their political activity, such election-day payments, even though they made possible a paid day's work outside the factory routine, provided at best a moderate inducement.

COPE also relied heavily on appeals to collective material self-interest that emphasized the gains produced by the welfare state. But these arguments were not based on deeply felt class antagonisms. Rather, they depicted union political work as a way of extending and protecting the economic gains secured through collective bargaining. The workers' welfare, it was stressed, depended on favorable government policies, which in turn depended on the election of liberal Democrats, because antilabor legislation could undo the victories won in union contracts. But such election victories depended on political action. Whatever its merits, this argument was accepted without serious challenge by most COPE workers. But it was rather complicated, and collective material "payoff" for the individual worker—better labor and social-insurance laws, for example—were very indirectly related to his actual campaign activities. As a result, he could be motivated neither by the moral and psychological rewards of working disinterestedly for an abstract or deeply felt cause, nor by tangible, personal, and immediate benefits, as in a strike for higher wages.

These deficiences in labor's political incentives were reinforced by the structure of COPE's campaign organization. Both issue-oriented Democratic clubs and patronage machines supplemented their basic incentives with the solidary incentives of fellowship and camaraderie available to members of a year-round organization. Outside of Detroit, such permanent COPE organizations were rare either because labor lacked the resources to maintain them or, as in Chicago, because they offended and threatened the party organization. But even in Detroit where such year-round organizations operated in every congressional district, the impact of these solidary incentives was reduced by the UAW's economic function. Most members of district COPES remain involved in the social life within their local unions which represent them on the job. Indeed, the UAW could not put great stress on social involvement in COPE rather than in the union itself without undermining its primary claim on its own rank and file.

The relatively strong economic inducements to undertake campaign work that unions could offer their own staff employees proved the most substantial exception to the general pattern of limited political incentives. Supplemented during campaigns by temporary union employees recruited from the membership, these officials, as in Detroit, formed the indispensable core of most political-action programs. As individuals they were often more interested in politics, more committed to labor's welfare-state goals, and more sensitive to political regulation of collective bargaining than the rank and file. Their official positions also made many of them particularly aware of the impact of politics on the organizational maintenance needs of trade unions. But these motives were powerfully reinforced by mainly economic incentives in those unions that consider campaign activities a part of their officials' jobs. To be sure, the primacy of the unions' economic function meant that many officials could compensate for a lack of enthusiasm for a political campaign by a good performance in collective bargaining. But because enthusiastic political activity could strengthen their position on the union staff, they were partly motivated by the same divisible material perquisites used by patronage machines.

Interunion Variation

Despite these general restrictions, union incentive systems did vary substantially in motivating rank and file campaign activity. Consistent with the analytic perspective of this chapter, this variation was closely associated with such economic factors as different markets, technologies, and wage levels and with the resulting differences in the unions' economic functions and organizational structures. As a result, the incentive systems of industrial unions committed to political action were more effective than those of service and craft unions, even when the leaders of these latter types were equally interested in providing the party with a campaign organization.

First of all, the nonfactory workers in many low-wage service unions—although this does not apply to those in the building trades —have fewer skills than industrial workers and earn much less money. They often typify the lower-class pattern of little organizational and political experience that makes such citizens particularly reluctant to engage in precinct work among strangers. Perhaps more importantly, nonfactory unionists do not—unlike most industrial-union members—belong to informal shop societies that reinforce their solidarity.[2] By making its members more aware of their common situation and status, the shop societies increase the workers' receptiveness to political action and make the industrial union's political incentives more effective. By contrast, the work units of nonfactory union members are usually too small and often too temporary to provide this stimulus.

The members of industrial unions also tend to work for a smaller number of larger and economically more secure employers than do the members of nonfactory unions. With more traveling and negotiating with separate employers necessary to service the same number of members, the business agents of craft and service unions, therefore, have less time for political agitation than do the industrial-union staff representatives. In addition, the national markets of major industrial unions encourage a more hierarchical structure among industrial-union staffs than among those in nonfactory unions. Most industrial-union officials depend for their jobs on regional or national officers. As a result, those industrial-union officials who are personally indifferent to politics but who are working for leaders committed to political action are much more likely to encourage rank and file campaign work than similarly predisposed nonfactory business agents, who are protected by their more independent positions.

In combination, the shop society and the industrial-union staff organization thus provide an institutionally structured two-step flow of influence by which union officials amplify their political opinions and exhortations.[3] Of course, the messages from official leaders, like other messages, are subject to considerable distortion and can be entirely ignored during this informal two-step process. But the content of a particular message that stresses action for the collective political goals of the working class is reinforced by the explicit character of the shop society as a community of workers.

Differences in the stock of incentives available to different types of unions also obviously depend on two other factors. The number of union members who eventually decide to do precinct work is related to the number exposed to political incentives; that is, to the total membership of the union in a given area. At the same time, the effectiveness of the incentives for a union of any given size is conditioned by the social and economic environment. COPE incentives are less effective if they must compete with those of the Chicago party organization or if all precinct workers are discouraged by the social disorganization found in Los Angeles.

Among those unions desiring to participate in a political action program, this variation in the total stock of political incentives directly affected each union's capacity to operate permanent COPE congressional-district organizations and the form of its participation.

As we shall see, Detroit COPE maintained year-round organizations that at least approximated the European party branches. But smaller industrial unions in less favorable environments and nonfactory unions with less favorable economic and organizational structures had fewer incentives with which to maintain such organizations. A decline in incentives produced less stable congressional-district organizations that did not participate as regularly in Democratic campaigns or did not as thoroughly cover the areas where the party needed assistance. With a still smaller stock of incentives we find the use of the congressional-district COPE as a unit of organization for campaign work often increased when the unions became too weak to maintain their own organizations. On the other hand, these unions relied less on direct incentives to the rank and file in their worker groups and placed more emphasis on providing rewards for the union officialdom and those members involved in the life of the union's formal organization. Such groups also display a marked tendency to mobilize voters on an ad hoc basis for particular candidates in particular campaigns. Finally, in those unions with the weakest incentives, we find no direct attempt whatever to mobilize voters for the party but simply a much more systematic version of Gompers' effort to use the union's organization to make sure its members register and vote.

In general, then, this decline in incentives produced a *variable* tendency to build a COPE district organization structure, but it also produced a *consistently* increased reliance on the formal bureaucracy rather than on informal work groups as the source for recruiting political activists. But even under the most favorable circumstances,

TABLE 2 **Size of Incentive Systems and Union Organization Techniques**

Incentive System	Reliance on Union Staff to Recruit Workers	Reliance on Congressional-District COPE Organizations
Large (Detroit UAW)	Low to Moderate	High
Moderate (Chicago and Los Angeles UAW and USA)	Moderate	Low
Small (Los Angeles non-factory unions)	High	High

as in Detroit, a primary concern with economic functions forced COPE to settle for a basically superficial contact with the lower-class voters it sought to mobilize. In other cities, COPE was even less fortunate. In this sense, an examination of organized labor's political incentives only emphasizes the general limitation that American labor's primarily economic orientation imposed on its political efforts.

Detroit: The Strongest Big-City COPE Organization

Although non-UAW members, most notably the Steelworkers in southwestern Wayne County, participated significantly in Detroit-area COPE and its predecessor, PAC, both organizations were dominated by the UAW throughout the two decades after World War II. Indeed, the Autoworkers had so large a system of incentives that Detroit COPE's unusually systematic and visible operations illustrated the pattern of political activity to which other urban COPES aspire. Of course, unions with less imposing incentives necessarily deviated from this pattern and, as the stock of incentives decreased, the deviations became more important. But equally important, as a primarily economic organization, even the UAW and its union allies in the Detroit area found that their political incentives had only a limited effect. As a result they could not recruit a corps of dedicated precinct workers who approached the thoroughness of the political professionals in the Chicago party or even highly motivated amateurs. During strikes, almost all the UAW's job-conscious members were willing to forego their paycheck for weeks at a time, but this degree of loyalty proved to be specific to the union's economic role. It was not easily transferable to politics.* Few Detroit COPE members displayed enthusiasm for intensive precinct work as an intrinsically pleasant activity. Determining the political affiliations of all voters in a precinct, let alone personally asking them to vote for your candidate in

---

* This specificity, of course, is an American and not necessarily a universal trait. Some radical European unions, whose stated goals are much more explicitly political, may have a much larger number of workers who will readily follow their leaders in a variety of political activities.

a primary, requires considerable time and energy, particularly if there are many new residents. These inquiries may also involve nasty arguments with Republicans and others who resent a stranger's curiosity. Although a small number of its activists did operate at this high level, the UAW simply lacked the economic or ideological inducements that could stimulate most of its COPE workers to play so exacting a role.

Detroit COPE's campaign operations were designed accordingly to use most efficiently the large number of only moderately motivated precinct workers that its incentives provided. Led by UAW members, Wayne County's six congressional-district COPE organizations function as powerful, usually dominant caucuses within the six district party organizations. But even at this level, the limited effectiveness of the UAW's incentives was clear. Taken together, these organizations totaled less than 500 permanent rank and file activists—together with five to ten or more union staff officials in each district, most employed at the international UAW headquarters. Indeed, Eldersveld found that union leaders made up just under two-fifths of the entire top organizational elite at the district level of the Wayne County Democratic party in 1956. Furthermore, these leaders, both union staff officials and local officers who presumably aspired to their positions, numbered one-half of the entire union contingent within the party.[4]

Much of the district COPE's success was also traceable to the coordinator (through the 1950s one was assigned to each district), a UAW staff member who played a crucial role in organizing activities and prodding year-round COPE members to remain active. The coordinators formally operated under the direction of the Wayne County AFL-CIO COPE, but they actually reported to their superiors in the UAW's citizenship department and assumed responsibility for political action within the districts they coordinated. Their responsibilities included smoothing over organizational, personal, and ethnic quarrels, maintaining alliances with nonlabor groups, and helping select COPE and party officers in the district. For more than the first decade of the UAW's participation in the party, the coordinators' control over COPE campaign funds, the time they spent on district matters as part of their jobs, their organizational skills, and their formal status as UAW officials gave them a dominant voice in both COPE and party organizations. They often directed both labor and nonlabor campaign efforts. The importance of the coordinator's position was illustrated by the difficulties in the fourteenth district, where the post was vacant for several years prior to 1964. Although the UAW did have enough political activists and interested staff officials to maintain operations, a series of conflicts broke out between the district COPE leaders and nonlabor Democrats, and then among UAW leaders themselves. As a result COPE's own campaign activities appeared to have suffered (see the discussion of the special 1961 election in Chapter IX).

The coordinators assumed primary responsibilities for the district's precinct-delegate elections, which determined control of the party organization. Persuading enough union members to run for precinct delegate proved relatively easy. "People like to see their names on the printed ballot," as one district party leader observed. As a result, union members—very largely from the UAW—appeared to constitute 78 percent of all Democratic party district leaders in Eldersveld's sample and made up 79 percent of the most upwardly mobile group within the lower ranks of the party.[5] The problem of incentives immediately recurred, however, when the coordinators attempted to convert the delegates into a campaign organization. Popular vote getters did not always prove dependable precinct workers, so that their official position irritated active workers who were not delegates. Because the party organization could replace only those delegates who resigned or moved away, it had to work around and risk alienating those who were not interested in campaigning. COPE had too few incentives, in other words, to maximize both the number of its precinct delegates and the efficiency and morale of its campaign organization.

Even apart from these tensions over precinct-delegate elections, the coordinators faced a formidable problem in maintaining the general level of COPE's incentives for campaign work. The maturing of the union and the general decline in the intensity of its conflict with conservative groups in Michigan appears to have affected the ideological commitment of COPE workers, resulting in a loss of influence within several congressional districts after 1964, a process we have described in Chapter IV. At one COPE rally, a UAW regional director openly urged the active union members to emulate the militancy of the union's retirees. "Here is a group of workers," he said, "who have the same feeling they had in the 1930s, a real unity of feeling that they should work together for liberal programs as they did so many years ago."

Some UAW leaders specifically complained that even though most COPE members were not seeking jobs for themselves, they became involved in the competition among district organizations for the patronage positions available from the state government up to 1963. "The most liberal people in the party," one staff official reflected, "will support a conservative out of loyalty to their congressional district." Another leader added in 1962 that "a lot of people in the Democratic party want political jobs." Some COPE leaders even hoped that the loss of the governorship in 1962 might help redirect the party's and COPE's own political energies to campaign activities rather than patronage infighting. Yet efforts to increase the rank and file's ideological commitment through educational activities in COPE met a lukewarm reception.* And the union's difficulties mounted with the defeat of its Democratic senatorial candidate, former governor G. Mennen Williams in 1966.

Whatever the changes in the UAW's incentive system, by 1963 no district COPE could boast more than a handful of year-round workers who actually covered their precincts well enough to know comprehensively the political affiliations of the residents. A somewhat larger number of workers, usually the regular members of the district COPE organization, canvassed their precincts in the weeks before elections. They distributed literature and talked with some of the voters about the election. Nevertheless, Eldersveld's sample of precinct leaders suggests that 11 percent of the Democratic party's precincts were entirely unmanned on a regular basis in 1956, and, in 45 percent

---

* In 1961, the COPE organization officially joined in the Great Decisions discussion program, which dealt with a number of foreign policy issues. But it caught on only in the fifteenth congressional district, which at the time was already the most ideologically committed. The leaders in the other districts were too busy or otherwise preoccupied. Despite COPE's stress on political education as indicated by its title, political action leaders feel that union members can join the education programs in their own local unions.

of the remainder, the Democrats revealed clearly inadequate direction and coordination. In fact, ". . . half of the [Democratic] precinct leaders were unaware or ignorant of some aspect of the organization critical to their own performance."[6] Significantly, 70 percent of union officers in his study, but only 36 percent of the union rank and file in precinct leadership positions, canvassed their precincts on a house-to-house basis.[7] In order to cover the districts, the coordinators had to recruit large numbers of supplementary workers who left their plants on election day. In effect, therefore, COPE had to rely on even larger numbers of still less motivated workers. In some districts, COPE coordinators even found that the day's pay provided to these workers either by the district organization or by their local union served as an inadequate political inducement. As a result, a number of COPE leaders in some districts spent election day checking on their workers to prevent them from simply relaxing outside the rigors of plant discipline. In his survey, Eldersveld pointed out the limited role perceptions of the union rank and file in the Detroit Democratic party. "This may have been due to ambivalence about party work, or the fact that they had been recruited for party work, or agreed to undertake party work with considerable reluctance or without adequate understanding of party tasks."[8]

In sum, Detroit COPE's election activities provided a widespread and fairly systematic, but essentially superficial, contact with the voters. The contacts were superficial because its workers neither tried to determine the voters' partisan loyalties nor attempted to persuade them to vote Democratic. Instead they simply urged lower-income voters to go to the polls to express their existing Democratic loyalties. COPE's operation was widespread and systematic because its district leaders, particularly the coordinators, methodically concentrated COPE workers in "high-yield" neighborhoods where according to election and registration figures, the Democrats had a majority in excess of 60 percent. COPE concentrated on the same areas in its registration drives. Indeed, 1956 survey results confirmed that Detroit Democrats were much less well organized in the two most marginal congressional districts by comparison with overwhelmingly Democratic ones.[9] Of course, this procedure unavoidably risked turning out some Republicans who would not otherwise have voted, because most COPE workers could not know in advance the party preferences of the people they contacted. But high turnout is associated with higher incomes and Republican partisanship. COPE thus assumed that most nonvoters and the unregistered—particularly in precincts where the majority of voters are already Democrats—would very likely vote according to labor's preferences if they did get to the polls. Supporting this assumption, Eldersveld's stratified sample of Wayne County adults suggests that party campaign activity among those identifying with the Democrats—and this appears to be largely carried on by Democratic workers—did produce a net gain of fifteen percentage points in turnout of Democratic party voters.[10] Because this net gain falls off sharply in Republican and marginal Democratic precincts (those with less than a 60 percent Democratic vote), COPE left them to whatever issue-oriented nonlabor Democrats live in the areas. Such workers, who belonged to explicitly political party groups in some cases, had a strong enough ideological motivation to first learn the party preferences of most precinct residents and to then concentrate on only the laggard Democrats.

This superficial but widespread campaign procedure also strikingly underlined the labor movement's status as a partisan rather than merely a trade-union political organization. Indeed, it explicitly defined the UAW's political constituency in terms of Democratic partisan loyalty rather than in terms of union membership. And by concentrating on the most Democratic and thus the lowest-income areas, COPE often excluded the middle-income areas where many of the UAW's own well-paid members lived.

Even in Democratic primaries and nonpartisan local elections where Detroit COPE could not rely on the party loyalties of these lower-income voters, its contacts remained superficial. COPE workers primarily passed out slates at the voters' homes or at the polls. Their leaders assumed this technique was effective because low-income Democrats, without the party label as a cue, often had no strong opinions in primaries and followed labor's endorsements. In this case, therefore, labor tried to rely on the voters' low interest and poorly defined preferences rather than on their tendency to identify with the Democratic party.

COPE also tried to compensate for its superficial precinct work by systematically concentrating large numbers of workers in the districts with the most important primaries and in the suburbs with the hardest fought nonpartisan elections. Labor used these tactics in the 1964 Dingell-Lesinski primary and in the 1962 special congressional election in the fourteenth district. In such cases, the district coordinator was often released from other union duties and assisted by other union-paid officials and even rank and file workers temporarily taken from the plants.

The operation of Detroit COPE thus consisted of a core of highly motivated UAW officials who tried to offset the weakness of the political incentives they offered by concentrating large numbers of moderately motivated members at the most profitable points in the party system and electoral process. In the Democratic party, large numbers of members were induced to run for precinct delegate in order to maintain labor's influence, even though many did not canvass their precinct regularly. In terms of the campaign calendar, COPE workers were most active at the two time periods most important for increasing Democratic turnout, the last days of registration and election day itself. Geographically, COPE concentrated its workers in the most Democratic, lower-income areas, which tend to have low voter-participation rates.

Reliance on Industrial Union Organizations: Chicago and Los Angeles

The incentive systems and therefore the campaign methods of industrial unions in Chicago and Los Angeles resembled those of the Detroit area UAW insofar as they shared the common features of factory unionism. But, in terms of union resources, the concentration of the automobile industry in southeastern Michigan provided an unusually large number of rank and file members and many staff officials at international headquarters for potential recruitment as COPE members. In terms of major environmental variables, Detroit-area COPE did not have to contend with either a strong patronage party as in Chicago or with the social disorganization of Los Angeles. As one or more of these factors came increasingly into play, the political incentives and thus the activity of Chicago and Los Angeles industrial unions perceptibly diminished. In particular, the unions in these latter two cities could not effectively emulate the Detroit-area UAW, which built upon the solidarity of the industrial shop society by persuading rank and file union members to affiliate directly with a permanent congressional-district COPE organization. Rather, the weaker incentive systems in Chicago and Los Angeles made less feasible the organizational specialization represented by a separate full-time union campaign structure with a rank and file membership. The year-round planning coordination and preparation for campaign work was therefore undertaken primarily by the industrial unions' own regular organizations.

Chicago unions, for example, maintained a number of identifiable congressional-district organizations, but few ever operated on the year-round basis of those in Detroit. In fact, the coordination and direction of most political action by industrial union members was carried out primarily by the regional and subdistrict organizations of the two biggest industrial unions in the area. Estimates by the regional and district staffs of the two unions indicated that in the mid-1960s the Chicago UAW and the United Steel Workers of America (USA) each had in the neighborhood of 65,000 to 70,000 members in Chicago and Cook County, which had twelve congressional districts and a 1960 population of 5,129,725. By contrast, the UAW had an approximate membership of 200,000 in Detroit and Wayne County, which had only six congressional districts and a 1960 population of 2,666,297—barely more than half of Cook County's. In addition, the two major Chicago unions were traditionally too suspicious and competitive to join in a cohesive and comprehensive organization like Detroit COPE.

As Chapter III showed, the Democratic party organization presented an even bigger obstacle to maintaining a permanent congressional-district structure. In terms of incentive systems, the difficulty was less a question of overt hostility to COPE than of the much greater effectiveness of the party's own incentive system, which enabled it to compete with COPE for the allegiance of labor's precinct workers. The party captains, in fact, could often siphon off with material inducements the members of any permanent organizations who were regularly assigned to their precincts. Chicago's political

culture identified the precinct captain as the representative of the
Democratic party, and COPE itself strongly emphasized the labor-
Democratic alliance. Some COPE precinct workers cooperated with
the captains as a matter of course.[11] As one labor precinct worker
explained, "I have no objection to working with the [party] captain;
he pushes his candidates, I push mine."

Detroit COPE leaders positively encouraged cooperation with the
party because they shared similar political goals and similar leaders.
This pattern presented no problem for the Chicago Federation of
Labor unions, which shunned any independent political action and
shared the Chicago party's political outlook. Many building-trades
leaders welcomed their members joining the party because it
strengthened their position as the organization's faithful allies.
Chicago COPE and the party organization, however, had very different political instincts, styles, and interests. Union members who
were affiliated with COPE but who also worked with the party and
then accepted its perquisites were likely to feel a primary political
obligation to the party, even if they reported on their work at COPE
meetings. Certainly they risked losing many valuable perquisites if
they defied their ward committeemen. For example, a party precinct
captain or worker may be given campaign money to spend as he
wishes provided the party does well in his precinct. Another may
want to obtain a summer job for a relative or even a less strenuous
patronage job for himself as he gets older. At the same time, the
union's contract protects the member's job in the factory, no matter
how he ignores the union on political matters. This same consideration limited the party's own discipline over such COPE workers, of
course. Unlike the patronage worker, the job protection that unions
provided their members made it much more feasible for them to
ignore the party on issues they believed important. And in Republican
suburban areas the party also had fewer material incentives to offer.*

Such COPE workers therefore had available a range of intermediate choices that helped them avoid an open break with either organiza-

---

* For some COPE leaders, the problem of workers joining the party
organization is not serious. One felt "people are different anyway." But his
feelings seemed to express his less aggressive personality, which led him to
avoid the issue of party dominance.

tion. Two Steelworkers who were precinct captains for the party in the western suburbs illustrated this middle position. In their own view, they remained neutral when the union and party organizations clashed in the 1960 gubernatorial primary. They passed out the usual party literature, which supported the party's candidate. But in their conversations with the voters they proclaimed their indifference to the outcome. The workers emphasized that the union took no formal position in the race despite the USA's all-out unofficial commitment. Had there been an official position, the captains said, they might have done nothing throughout the entire campaign. They believed that this middle course was not incompatible with their loyalty to the union, and both said they would work for pro-labor candidates in the Republican party primaries (but not in the general election) if the union endorsed them. But adjustments of this kind cannot obscure the process of at least partial absorption into the party organization that these members typify.

Unions could also expect little gain in return for this co-optation of their members, because rank and file party workers could exercise only limited leverage on the ward committeemen. The committeemen, who are elected in the primary, appoint the precinct captains (in Detroit, elected precinct delegates choose the district party officers). Even if union members could elect an insurgent ward committeeman, he could be stripped of patronage and ignored by the county committee.* In any case, those union members who became precinct captains in the party were unlikely to be insurgents both because the organization weeded out potential rebels and because such rebels were not attracted to the party in the first place.

Some leaders of the USA, which openly tolerated and sometimes positively encouraged its members to join the party, felt that this policy helped account for the decline of union activity in the northern part of the south-side second congressional district during the late 1950s and early 1960s. And even though the UAW strongly opposed this absorption, one of its north-side district COPE leaders

---

* Generally the captains in the party have limited influence. At most, they have the ability to veto candidates they find unacceptable, and even here their influence does not extend to blocking blue-ribbon county or state candidates picked to lead the ticket.

estimated that about one-sixth of the UAW workers affiliated with his organization also worked for the party. Others belonged to the regular organization and had no formal COPE affiliation at all. But even when the COPE worker did not formally become a party worker, Detroit COPE's policy of assigning the same precinct workers to a particular precinct year after year would have created problems for the Chicago COPE leaders. Given the material incentives available to many precinct captains, including cash payments, the COPE worker could establish rewarding, even if informal, relationships with the captains that undermined his ability to follow an independent labor line.

All this indicates rather starkly the limitations that Chicago's political environment imposed on the political incentives the city's largest industrial unions are able to provide. If the compensation for lost time at work on election day proved only a mild inducement in Detroit, it seemed very ineffective indeed in comparison with the rewards available to Chicago party workers. In any case, to reduce the likelihood of absorption and to avoid threatening the party by appearing as a serious competitor, Chicago COPE did not follow the Detroit model of year-round district COPE organizations. Instead the UAW and USA built their political activities during the early and mid-1960s around their own organizations. And rank and file workers were oriented to these groups rather than to any labor political organization that operates on a year-round basis in a specific district. Indeed, rather than operate continuously in each district so that the workers could become familiar with particular precincts, these organizations assigned workers afresh in each campaign. This procedure made the character of the COPE workers' contacts with the voters still more superficial than in Detroit, because it reduced the number of precinct workers who operated in the same precinct year after year.

Chicago's industrial unions, it is true, have tried to conform to the Detroit pattern for political action to the extent that, since the early 1950s, they individually assumed responsibility for particular congressional districts. Particularly after the decline in influence of the Chicago Packinghouse Workers, the UAW attempted to cover a relatively large area of the city. It remained continuously active on

Chicago's north side and played an important role in the western suburbs, part of the south suburbs near a Ford Motors plant, and, at times, the south-side black ghetto. Nevertheless, the union did little in many of the city's most heavily Democratic areas. It only apathetically supported one of its own rank and file activists in the inner-city eighth district, and, in response to party pressure, the union for a time abandoned its activities in the black areas (see the discussion of COPE's activity in the inner-city in Chapter VII). Typically, the Chicago UAW concentrated its efforts in the western suburbs (the tenth congressional district) in 1956, when one of its own staff members was the Democratic candidate. Thereafter, its participation in that district continued at a much lower level as the union turned its attention to other areas. By contrast, the Detroit UAW was strong enough to maintain a year-round COPE organization and to control the district Democratic party. As a result, it was about as active against Representative Lesinski in the 1964 primary when he ran against Representative Dingell, as it was in 1960 when his primary opponent was the president of a UAW local.

In some ways, the USA's operations in Chicago depended even more on its formal organization than the activities of the UAW did. During the late 1950s and early 1960s, the Steelworkers not only concentrated their efforts on southern Cook County, where most of their workers and plants were located, but also organized the activities of each of the area's three congressional districts around one of the union's three subdistrict headquarters. Staff officials at these headquarters more or less directly control COPE operations in the area, and by comparison with the Chicago UAW, this arrangement produced a more regular effort at each election. Consistent with this concentration on the areas of its own congressional strength, however, the union was much less concerned about organizing its members elsewhere in the city in order to build a more comprehensive COPE program, and cooperation with other unions was quite limited.

This emphasis on the union rather than the congressional-district organizations also encouraged each union to operate somewhat idiosyncratically, as well as inconsistently, entering some campaigns and districts but not others depending on each union's particular traditions and on the personal feelings of its leaders. Personalities also played a role in Detroit COPE's district organization, of course, as did the Detroit UAW's own ethos. But the presence of a fairly large number of rank and file workers in each formally autonomous district organization encouraged somewhat greater consistency, uniformity, and hence predictability in the Detroit districts' political operations. Indeed, the assignment of each Detroit district COPE organization to a specific political jurisdiction served as a pressure within the UAW to maintain a continuing and stable level of activity from election to election. In Chicago such demands for continuity could not be strongly articulated by district organizations, which only operated vigorously just before general elections. In this situation, the needs of the union staff and the feelings of its top officials operated more freely.

The personal commitment of many UAW leaders in Chicago to the ideological political action characteristic of their Detroit counterparts did help produce some similarities to the Detroit pattern. Political militancy was symbolized in Chicago for many years by the UAW's regional political education director, Willoughby Abner, top black official in the region and an articulate and often brilliant leader.[12] More generally, the Chicago region's campaign organization was also shaped by much the same egalitarian structure and political commitment as in Detroit. The union regularly assigned both staff representatives and on occasion rank and file members to full-time election activities. As a staff representative said, "All of us have worked more or less full time in a particular campaign. That's part of our job." And within its own ranks, the UAW devoted considerable attention to politics. In the absence of year-round congressional-district organizations the regional citizenship council, which is composed of top local union leaders from Cook and suburban DuPage counties formally made the union's major political decisions. The council took positions on issues, endorsed candidates, and raised political funds, principally through COPE dollar drives and per capita contributions for registration activities and local campaigns. In 1962, it levied five cents per member per month on its local union affiliates.

Although partisans of the UAW and the USA both suggested that the other union talked about political action more than they worked at it, some independent observers asserted and interviews with union members supported an impression that the average UAW member is more enthusiastically committed. If so, the causes can be traced to the union's emphasis, traditionally great throughout the country, on political issues and member participation, as well as to its history of radical leaders. The Chicago UAW's attitudes toward black participation support this interpretation. It gave earlier recognition than USA to its black members, particularly in appointments to the international staff. In 1958, it assigned a black member to coordinate UAW members, almost all whites, in the eleventh congressional district. In 1960, only the UAW, out of all the major Chicago unions, conducted its own minorities registration drive. In 1966, it supported liberal insurgent Democrat Abner Mikva against the regular party's candidate in the second congressional district primary. It also supplied workers for Martin Luther King's effort to organize the west-side black ghetto, an attempt that appeared a serious potential threat to the party organization. In both cases the USA refused to oppose the party.

The importance of personalities, however, appears to have produced somewhat greater variation in UAW behavior both from election to election and from local union to local union than is true of Detroit. For example, as the primary organizational mechanism to reach rank and file members, the Chicago UAW established local COPE committees. But the effectiveness of these committees depended on the enthusiasm of the local leadership. In turn, this enthusiasm was influenced by their relations with the local's international representative. "If the men like him," observed one international official, "they'll do a job . . . to help his reputation with the international." Obviously, relations between the local leadership and the staff representative were also important in Detroit. But the fact that the local union leadership also had to deal with the international headquarters and with its district coordinators tended to make the behavior of these local officials more uniform regardless of the international representative. The local union COPE committees in Detroit were somewhat less important because the individual member could work in politics directly through his district COPE organization and its coordinator without having to go through his local.

Personality factors also affected the UAW's overall political role in

Chicago politics. Abner was clearly the most aggressive and articulate if not the most abrasive leader in the Chicago UAW. "The rest are all nice guys and real liberals," a friendly politician observed, "but [personally] they lack the fire the USA has." As an uncompromising spokesman for militant black members and rank and file ideologues, Abner irritated the union's regional leadership. As late as 1960, he opposed the union's efforts to cooperate with the party, for example, by supporting an insurgent candidate for governor. He owed his position mainly to his strong support among black members and to the loyalty of Roy Reuther, director of the UAW citizenship department. Abner's departure to work for Reuther on national political assignments was not visibly regretted by the UAW leadership, and appears to have improved its relations with the party.

The Chicago Steelworkers, the largest CIO union in Chicago, also reflected the prevailing patterns of their international union. As in the UAW, the USA's three subdistrict legislative and educational councils carried out the overall district program, including COPE dollar drives. Typically, however, they supplemented issue appeals with more material inducements—by sponsoring a raffle that offered a car or a similar prize for the winning ticket, for example. Partly because the USA, by comparison with the UAW, stressed leadership more than member participation, the union's political role particularly reflected the dominating, complex, and shrewd personality of its chief officer, District Director Joseph Germano. Consistent with the more pragmatic and power-oriented attitude of the Steelworkers' national leaders, Germano successfully concentrated on maintaining his power within the union and his political influence outside it. For example, he played a significant role in the union at the national level. After helping found the USA by leading the Amalgamated Association of Iron and Steel Workers into the Steelworker's Organizing Committee, Germano emerged as director of district 31, the largest in the union (Germano has publicly pointed out that the district, which embraces many locals, is smaller than only about ten internationals in the AFL-CIO). In the Cook County Industrial Union Council, he was resented by some other leaders for attempting to use his union's money and size to dictate CIO policy. Within his own organization, he suspected those who might not be wholly loyal to him almost as much as he had suspected possible company spies in the 1930s.

By comparison with UAW officials in Chicago, most of Germano's officials did not as easily command a liberal ideological rhetoric, and they appeared less interested in educating their members to think independently in politics. Typically, the union did not object if some of its members joined the party organization, although it recognized that its political influence partly depended on organizing some members into a separate corps of precinct workers. Many union officials also looked askance at lengthy debates over issues that could take up an entire union conference. In their view, it was the leadership's prerogative to set the policy, and there was much less deviation from the district's leadership than in the UAW. "If you know what one steel local is doing in an election," remarked one observer, "you know what they all are doing." In fact, to ensure loyalty to the leadership, the union sometimes supported a rank and filer running for public office, and if he won put him on the union payroll to maintain its influence over him.

But if the locals followed a more uniform course than they did in the UAW, Germano's own complex political attitudes made the union's performance as a whole somewhat more difficult to categorize. Germano chose as his political action director in Illinois his brother-in-law and confidant, John Alesia, a man who strikingly illustrates the complex motives of many American labor leaders. Like Germano, Alesia enjoyed the accumulation and exercise of power and usually employed it for liberal ends. He strove to maintain good working relationships with the most powerful Democratic leaders in the legislature and carefully avoided defying the Chicago party on most issues even when it nominated conservative Democrats. These concerns of both Alesia and Germano led the union to favor as its first choice for the Democratic U.S. senatorial nomination in 1962 Paul Powell, a relatively conservative downstate patronage-oriented politician who was then speaker of the Illinois house. In fact, Powell was far less liberal than the regular Chicago organization's own choice and eventual nominee, Congressman Sidney Yates. The union's liberal allies protested in vain about Powell's voting record and the equity in state-regulated race tracks that he had acquired as a legislator.

Germano nevertheless retained into the 1960s the liberalism that had animated the CIO during the 1930s. He was personally close to one of the most uncompromising liberals on domestic issues in Congress, Illinois Democratic Senator Paul Douglas. In 1962 Germano's letter to President John F. Kennedy prevented the Bureau of the Budget from giving formal clearance to the Burns Ditch Harbor project, which appeared to threaten the Indiana Dunes and was thus a key issue to Douglas and Chicago liberals. Civil-rights leaders reported that Germano quietly assumed the unpaid bills for civil-rights meetings. Germano's support also helped keep his publicity director, Raymond Pasnick, as the CIO's representative on the Chicago Board of Education. Pasnick was the first board member to attack the policies of School Superintendent Benjamin Willis on civil-rights grounds, and the struggle that followed proved politically embarrassing to the local party.

Much more striking than the union's support for civil rights and the Indiana Dunes was the union's unsuccessful opposition to the party's nomination of Judge Otto Kerner for governor in 1960 on behalf of an apparently more liberal candidate. To be sure, defeating Kerner in the primary—an unlikely outcome—could have made the USA the most powerful union in the state. But labor's traditional opposition to the sales tax as a regressive burden on the poor best explains the USA's vehement opposition, after the election, to the new Kerner administration's 1961 sales tax increase—an increase the UAW supported. In fact, on most issues Alesia was widely considered during the early 1960s to be the most effective labor lobbyist for liberal legislation in Springfield. By all odds, for example, he worked harder than any other union lobbyist for the state fair employment practices act that finally passed in 1961.

For all its stress on leadership decisions, the union has also developed issue incentives for political action. In addition to supervising the four-year union education program (which has a strong political emphasis), Alesia personally directed the most imaginative single device for political education in the Illinois labor movement. During the last three months of the biennial legislative session he regularly brought about fourteen local union leaders to Springfield to help him lobby. In addition to contacting key legislators under

Alesia's direction, these members' presence alone suggested the size and resources of the union. During the same period the union supplemented Alesia's efforts with groups of local union officers brought to Springfield for a few days at a time to visit their own legislators, see each house in action, and listen to discussions on issues. Apart from generally reinforcing the union's position in the legislature, the program oriented a relatively large number of union members toward politics. One local union steward reported that after participating in this program he changed his whole approach toward the dollars for COPE appeal. He began to discuss issues with his men in the shop rather than the chance to win a raffle. The whole experience, he added, made him a more conscientious precinct worker.

Reliance on union rather than on congressional-district organizations appears even more obvious among industrial unions in Los Angeles, which had even fewer effective incentives necessary for maintaining congressional-district organizations. For one thing, even the largest Los Angeles CIO industrial union, the UAW, was no larger than the UAW and USA in Chicago. But the limitations imposed on the industrial unions' stock of incentives by the city's general social disorganization were even more important. In particular, Los Angeles' massive residential mobility functioned as an almost insurmountable obstacle to the creation of stable, geographically based campaign organizations. Like the political parties in southern California, unions found that accurate lists of workers willing to canvass in a particular precinct were extremely difficult to maintain at best. The common practice of commuting long distances to work meant that many union members lived in congressional districts miles from their plant and union headquarters. Because most workers wanted to campaign where they lived, the local union proved a relatively inefficient center for political action.

In spite of these limitations on effective incentive systems, the pattern of industrial union political action in Los Angeles did partly resemble the Chicago and Detroit patterns. The rank and file precinct workers of the UAW reflected their union's general ideological commitment, and their union often criticized assembly speaker and Democratic party leader Jesse Unruh as too conservative. As in

Chicago, the union's political decisions were coordinated by a citizenship council. And the UAW's staff representatives as well as rank and file members who were temporarily on the union payroll worked not only in district COPE organizations but also on the campaign staffs of various Democratic candidates. Even by comparison with its performance in Chicago, however, the UAW's role was uneven. Although it had several politically active members in the area, it did relatively little in the east central Los Angeles twenty-ninth and thirtieth congressional districts, which have large Mexican populations. Its efforts in black areas were more extensive, but they were hindered after 1962 by the internal dissension common in Los Angeles unions. The UAW's black citizenship director, Spencer Wiley, was at swords' points with black Mervyn Dymally, an assemblyman who had many friends among UAW members.

In conjunction with COPE's decision in 1960 to establish regular district organizations throughout the area, the UAW ended its more independent operations and took specific responsibility for five COPE assembly-district headquarters. But this activity was concentrated in areas near its very large plants, including the San Fernando Valley (the twenty-second and twenty-seventh congressional districts) and central Los Angeles (the twenty-first and thirty-first). In effect, the union concentrated on areas of union strength rather than areas where the party was weak, thus resembling the pattern of the Steelworkers rather than that of the UAW in Chicago.

The second largest former CIO union in Los Angeles, the Steelworkers, relied on a mixture of material and ideological incentives similar to those employed by Germano's organization in Chicago. For example, the union paralleled Alesia's practice by regularly sending a number of rank and file members to the state capital to instill them with an issue orientation. On the other hand, it took considerable pains to maintain good relations with such powerful moderates as Jesse Unruh, much as the union in Chicago remained close to both the regular party and Speaker Powell. But partly because of its smaller size and partly because of its less aggressive leadership, the Los Angeles Steelworkers did not assume the leadership of a very active COPE program in any group of congressional districts in the early 1960s. In fact, the USA still operated rather independently of the COPE district structures in 1962, concentrating its campaign contributions and canvassing efforts in behalf of carefully chosen candidates. It thus had even less predisposition to build a congressional-district structure than the Los Angeles UAW.

Industrial-union activity appeared to be still more uneven and inconsistent, both from district to district and from election to election, when it was not vigorously supported by a strong leadership from the international union. In particular, the decentralization of the Los Angeles Machinists (IAM) limited the role of its international staff. In any case, the international IAM's large groups of nonfactory local unions—the union was never affiliated with the CIO—weakened its leadership's stress on political action, and the IAM did not work closely with Los Angeles COPE. Given this independence of the IAM's lodges, political incentives were mainly generated by large industrial units, primarily in the 1960s by Lodge 727 in the eastern San Fernando Valley. Yet even in this case the lack of either a full-time COPE district organization or continued urging by the international union as a stimulus to political activity had important consequences. When the Democratic congressional candidate displayed a relaxed attitude toward the campaign, even Lodge 727 did not make its usual contribution to the 1964 political campaign.

Industrial-union campaign activities in Chicago, in sum, occupied a middle position between the activities of the Detroit-area UAW and the Los Angeles industrial unions, thus conforming to the intermediate size of their incentive system. The tendency of the party to absorb COPE workers and the uneven performance of the biggest industrial unions were clear. Nevertheless, the greater numbers, concentration, and residential stability of Chicago factory workers gave their unions a larger stock of effective incentives with which to recruit rank and file workers and thus permitted them to emphasize the congressional district as a basis of operation more systematically than Los Angeles unions could. As Chapter VII will show, the UAW's activity on the north side and the Steelworkers' activity on the south side provided help to the party in areas where the congressional races were closest. In other words, industrial unions in the Chicago area had sufficient incentives to relate more comprehensively to the needs of the party than was true in Los Angeles. It was the far stronger position of the

Chicago party rather than the paucity of the industrial unions' resources that reduced the intraparty influence of these unions below that of their Los Angeles counterparts. On the other hand, the activities of Chicago unions, given their smaller stock of incentives, were more related to the unions' own organizational position and to the personalities of individual union leaders than they were in the case of the Detroit UAW.

Los Angeles: Political Incentives of Nonfactory Unions

Without the stable community provided by the shop societies of industrial unions, nonfactory unions have a significantly smaller stock of political incentives. Indeed, the imposing political organizations of Detroit COPE and the Chicago Democratic party have (except for the north side of Chicago) deterred nonfactory unions from undertaking large-scale political action in both cities. As the previous chapter showed, however, the weakness of other Democratic groups had encouraged some Los Angeles nonfactory unions to play an active role. But the smaller incentive systems of nonfactory unions have led to a greater reliance on formal organizations of union officials. This tendency reflects the greater difficulty in arousing enthusiasm among workers who do not belong to shop societies, which more easily arouse a sense of class loyalties.

Even the leaders of Los Angeles' most politically active craft union, Local 11 of the Electrical Workers (IBEW), carefully took into account the difficulties by paying close attention to the traditional emphasis of the building trades on wages and working conditions of highly individualistic craftsmen. In order to placate considerable rank and file suspicion of political action, these officials took care never to appear unconcerned with economic matters. They not only identified themselves with demands for higher wages (by 1962, the wage exceeded $5 per hour), but, more specifically, also established a constitutional bar against using treasury funds based on members' dues for any political purpose.

Local 11's political activity can partly be explained by its size; in 1962 it had nearly 10,000 highly skilled and well-paid members.

Still, many of these workers became active only because of their contact with the leadership of the local, particularly its manager, George O'Brien, through formal union activities. Indeed, O'Brien made it an explicit policy to recruit campaign workers and consciously used union meetings to preach COPE's message that the electrical workers' economic gains had to be protected through political action. Interviews with several rank and file precinct workers suggested the effectiveness of O'Brien's tactics. One of them recalled how he had only slowly been convinced, at first resisting the officers' efforts to influence him. But he gradually accepted their view. "What they were saying was true; labor has to be in politics, and our best friends are Democrats."

The union's formal organization thus played a central role. Politically active Electrical Workers often participated in the union's regular activities. Indeed, there appears to be a much closer relationship in Local 11 between union activity and political activism than in many industrial unions where the local officers were frequently too busy for much campaign work. Certainly this was O'Brien's goal. He created a political committee to which he appointed about 500 members, hoping to interest them in political issues and then in election activities. At the same time, he divided the union's six units into zones of from three or four to fifteen members each and appointed a captain to head each of them. The captains had responsibility for informing the members of union elections, advising on union benefits, and checking on the use of union labor in construction in their neighborhood, although months sometimes intervened before the same captains contacted their members on these matters. But the system was also intended to perform a political function by enabling the local's leaders to focus their political communications and exhortations to members in particular geographical areas, notably legislative or congressional districts. Participation in the union thus exposed the members to political education and recruited them for precinct work.

We saw in Chapter II that the entire labor movement committed its organizational resources to partisan campaign work in large measure to offset the decline in the intensity of their members' political commitment as the New Deal ended. This chapter has made an analogous point by considering the variation in worker commitment within the labor movement (i.e., variation between unions in one time period) rather than the changes in the entire movement over time. In effect, O'Brien and other craft-union leaders sought to use their formal organizations as functional substitutes for the political awareness generated by the industrial union's shop society.[13] In this way they sought to maximize use of the limited stock of incentives of a nonfactory union.

On the other hand, the diffusion of IBEW members throughout Los Angeles County and the lack of a shop-society structure, encouraged Local 11 to involve its political activists on a geographic basis; that is, in congressional- and assembly-district organizations. Unable to build their own congressional-district organizations, the local's business agents continuously endorsed participation in COPE, a Democratic club, or a candidate's campaign organization. IBEW members joined in such groups throughout Los Angeles County. In some cases, the union's business agents supported particularly enterprising activists with the union's own resources. In an eastern Los Angeles district, Local 11 supplied cars in 1960 for a register-and-vote parade that had been organized by an IBEW rank and file member. It provided funds for an assembly-district Citizens for Kennedy headquarters organized by another member, even though he usually was not a political activist. All of this was not lost on the membership, some of whom contributed as much as $5 per year for political action in 1960 and 1962, far more than the usual COPE target among industrial unions. Political activity, these members apparently felt, was one route to a good reputation with the local's leaders and even to appointment as a business agent.

The Building Service Union, the most active Los Angeles COPE affiliate in the service trades, differed from Local 11 in its members' fewer skills, more limited education, and lower pay. Because these traits affect the self-confidence necessary to campaign among strangers, the union had fewer effective incentives than Local 11 with which to stimulate rank and file activity. It thus placed still more emphasis on its own staff so that fewer of its members even joined or set up district campaign organizations. Typically, the union's main contribution to Democratic party campaign efforts in the early 1960s could be attributed to the activities of its business agents and other paid staff members, most notably John Geagan. A leader in Los Angeles and in the California Young Democrats and a close associate of Speaker Unruh, Geagen served as director of Youth for Kennedy in Los Angeles in 1960—on loan from the union. Other agents played a significant, if smaller, role. One, although much less experienced than Geagen, served in 1962 as chairman of both a local Democratic club and his COPE assembly-district organization. He used his two positions to conduct a joint registration drive in the district's heavily Democratic areas and to recruit the Building Service members in the area to join in COPE activities.

The union was also respected by some Democratic politicians for its timely financial contributions early in the campaign and its elaborate system for mailing its Democratic primary endorsements to its own members. Because the union compiled its membership lists by assembly and congressional district, its staff could send out letters that mentioned only the endorsed candidates in the member's own district. These letters thus did not force the member to determine which, of a long list of endorsed candidates from many districts, were the candidates for his district. When the union's members did become active in campaigns, the business agents were especially important in directing the actual precinct work. In 1960, one white agent drove seven black women members around heavily Democratic Negro neighborhoods where they reminded people to vote. Significantly, the agent took all the initiative, asking his members to work during the specific election and then supervising and encouraging them on the scene.

For all the differences between the Building Service Union and Local 11, each had a staff of agents dependent for their jobs on leaders who were both Democratic partisans and committed to political action. Undoubtedly, their power to hire and fire business agents stimulated enthusiasm for politics among the staff. The lack of just such a hierarchically controlled staff may explain the emergence and operations of the Voters Registration Service, which, as described in Chapter V, was established by several Los Angeles craft unions. In accord with national COPE recommendations, the service identified the unregistered members of affiliated unions through a central file system and then urged them to register and vote. In practice this procedure represented the unions' effort to improve the electoral turnout of their own workers rather than to help the party. Indeed, COPE leaders not only objected to the service as a possible rival, but also persuasively criticized its entire operations as wasteful in Los Angeles' highly mobile and widely dispersed population. In 1960, the service sent registrars from the party and COPE to register union members in key districts. But the members lived so far apart and moved so often that much of the registrars' time was spent traveling. In addition, the members they sought to register had often moved, registered recently, or were simply out when the worker called. One party leader reported that many registrars quit in frustration. Almost every observer agreed it would have been more efficient to work for a Democratic victory more directly by going door to door in party strongholds.

One industrial-union leader suggested that in Los Angeles each local should identify and contact its own unregistered members, thus explicitly distinguishing this enterprise from labor's broader campaign functions for the Democratic party. And in 1962, the service notified some unregistered members by post card, and asked their local unions to provide follow-up contacts. But the fact that the service continued to send out some deputy registrars in 1962 suggests that this procedure filled an at least perceived need of its mainly craft-union affiliates. Once again the critical factors appear to have been the unions' various incentive systems. The leaders of these unions lacked not only the industrial shop society with which to reach their members but also the power over their own business agents that enabled Local 11 and Building Service to mobilize their officials. Significantly, neither of these unions belonged to the service. By contrast, the Painters and the Carpenters, which did affiliate with the service, elected business agents and local union leaders who were rather independent of their top Los Angeles officials. Among the relatively large number of rather small Painter locals, for example, the leaders who were themselves interested in political action, did persuade some of their members to work in campaigns. When the local leaders remained inactive, however, the top county leaders faced major obstacles. A central registration system provided a formal organization with which they could at least urge their own members to register without having to rely on extensive activity by local union officers or business agents. Just as Local 11's activities functioned as a partially effective substitute for the shop-society structure of industrial unions, the Voter Registration Service functioned as a partial and still more limited substitute for the political action apparatus in the IBEW unit. It represented a limiting case in which the very small stock of incentives of some nonfactory unions seriously restrained any attempt to initiate political action.

The case of Los Angeles nonfactory unions in the 1960s demonstrates that increased reliance on staff officials of particular unions increases as incentives decrease. Local 11's leaders relied on formal union activities to promote rank and file precinct work. Its rank and file members joined COPE or party groups where they lived at the urging of their officers. Most rank and file members of Building Service participated only at the immediate prodding of staff officials, usually without any regard to particular congressional districts. For the craft unions in the Voter Registration Service, political activity often meant simply raising the election turnout of their own members with little emphasis, if any, on campaigning. This pattern of relying on union officials was equally true of the powerful Retail Clerks Local 770, which is not considered in this study because it operated politically almost entirely outside the AFL-CIO structure in the early and mid-1960s.

Conclusions

In seeking to function as a major electoral organization of the national Democratic party, organized labor set as its maximum objective fielding a corps of efficient precinct workers large enough to cover all the precincts, at least in every marginal or Democratic congressional district. Theoretically, these workers would then influence all undecided voters to support the Democrats and make sure all Democrats register and vote. Even in Detroit, which has a stable population (by comparison with Los Angeles), very limited patronage, and a powerful industrial union, political action was limited by labor's primary status as an economic rather than a formally partisan organization. The pattern of a branch structure that one finds in some European countries was only approximated in Detroit. COPE did cover every congressional district, but its workers' contacts with voters were extensive and superficial rather than intensive. As the stock of incentives decreased under the less favorable conditions of Chicago and Los Angeles, union coverage became less systematic, and rather than mobilizing large groups of rank and file, the unions increasingly relied on their own officials.

Insofar as its incentive system permitted, this tendency of labor political action to build a quasi-branch structure for a major party functioned in two different ways to depersonalize labor politics. On one side, it submerged in the structure of a formal political organization the feelings and emotions that characterized the politics of radical trade unions. On the other side, by building an alliance with a party, it has worked against the personal relationships with individual politicans that characterized the politics of conservative voluntarist unions. These personal considerations and feelings of both voluntarist and radical types found little place within a formal union political organization that ordinarily assumed responsibility for campaigning on behalf of much of the Democratic party ticket. Political action through the congressional-district structure thus led to predictable, "responsible" behavior on which labor's party ally could depend, both in framing its campaign tactics and in making long-range strategic plans. As an organizational form, it represented very well the historical impact of the labor–Democratic party alliance in restraining the radical impulses of the early CIO and in liberalizing the AFL.

At the same time, unions that had either a very large or a very small stock of incentives were inclined to rely on relatively distinct district COPE operations, whereas the organizations with intermediate incentive systems placed greater stress on their own political action organizations. At one extreme, the Detroit-area UAW operated within congressional-district COPE organizations that preserved some measure of independence. Indeed, their formal status as units of the AFL-CIO enabled them to attract at least a few non-UAW members in every district COPE; still other trade unionists operated as UAW allies within the Democratic party itself. The UAW was strong enough not only to establish and to direct these COPE operations but also in some cases to tolerate and even to welcome members of other unions.

Near the other end of this incentive continuum, many of the craft locals in Los Angeles, like Local 11, IBEW, and the Painters units, as well as some officers of Building Service, encouraged their members to join or even to lead (as we shall see in Chapter VII) local COPE or Democratic party organizations in the districts where they lived. By comparison with the Chicago UAW and USA, these unions were too small and their membership was too widely scattered to operate congressional-district organizations of their own. For them, as for the active craft unions and the UAW itself on the north side of Chicago, relatively stable geographically based interunion organizations offered obvious advantages. On the other hand, the largest industrial unions in Chicago and Los Angeles had sufficiently strong incentive systems to operate their own political action programs, but could not establish and control district organizations that were freely open to others throughout the city. Given the limitations on labor's political incentive system, labor political action derived much of its importance from the lack of substantial alternatives to COPE activity within the Democratic party. But these weak formal party organizations—outside of machine cities like Chicago—persisted largely because many Americans have been hostile to the overt accumulation of political power. Organized labor has conformed to this norm by remaining primarily an economic organization that is mainly concerned with the members' private interests, rather than concentrating on the acquisition of political power. It did not form an avowedly labor or working-class party on the European model that might well have antagonized moderate Democratic party supporters with a spectre of class conflict or merely with the suggestion of a lust for power. It was the same political culture which restricted labor's political incentives by encouraging a primarily economic orientation, which also created its political opportunity. As this consideration indicates, organized labor's response to such opportunities through its campaign organizations and activity can be fully explained only by examining the political, social, and economic context in each congressional district.

VII

Political Action in the Congressional Districts

The AFL-CIO's primary orientation toward Congress and national political campaigns determined COPE's choice of the congressional district as the common unit for its activities.* Of course, the district COPES within a particular area tended to resemble each other and differ from those elsewhere. But, in the 1960s there were significant differences among the district COPE organizations in Los Angeles, Chicago, and even Detroit, where a single union, the UAW, dominated. This variation reflected social, political, and economic differences within and between metropolitan areas as well as the different incentive systems of the major unions.

---

* In the early 1960s Los Angeles COPE subdivided its congressional-district organizations on an assembly-district basis.

A Typology of Congressional-District
COPE Organizations

The variation among COPE organizations can be categorized by typology of organizational structures:

I. COPE district organizations dominated by (usually one or two) industrial unions

II. COPE district organizations mainly composed of leaders from many different unions who happened to live in the district

III. Districts where many COPE workers joined the campaign organizations of individual candidates (usually candidates for Congress)

IV. Districts where COPE workers were absorbed by powerful organizations of the regular Democratic party

Each of these analytic types was approximated, although not fully realized by one of the four most common forms of district COPE organizations empirically observed in this study. The four types, however, are also systematically interrelated because they represent polar cases on two important organizational dimensions. In that sense the typology is logically exhaustive. One dimension measures the relative size of the resources available to labor and to the party for building an electoral organization. It thus indicates the relative importance and independence of labor as opposed to nonlabor Democrats in the district. The second dimension concerns the relative importance of individual politicians and labor leaders, operating on their own, as opposed to either labor or nonlabor Democratic party organizations whose members are more cohesively tied together and directed by acknowledged organizational leaders. These relationships are indicated in Table 3.

As the analysis in this chapter will show, whether labor or some nonlabor group is dominant, the degree of dominance depends on the degree of organization. In other words, COPE organizations based on industrial unions, as in Detroit, undertook more consistent political action, and played a more active role in party affairs than did organizations of individual union officials. Similarly, the strong organi-

TABLE 3   A Typology of Congressional-District Organizations

	Organizations Predominate	Individuals Predominate
Autonomous Labor Activity	Type I. Industrial unions dominant: All of Detroit; 22nd District, Los Angeles; and 4th District, Chicago*	Type II. Union officials dominant: 11th District, Chicago (14th and 17th districts in Detroit show some traits of this type)
Labor Activity Within or Absorbed by Party	Type IV. Strong party organizations dominant: Most Chicago inner-city districts	Type III. Candidates dominant: Los Angeles, e.g., 25th, 29th and 30th districts

* The districts discussed in this chapter were in effect in 1962. Over the next four years, reapportionment changed them substantially in Detroit.

zations of nonlabor Democrats, as in Chicago, are more effective in absorbing union campaign workers than are the personal organizations centered around individual candidates that one finds so frequently in Los Angeles. In effect, therefore, the gross density of resources available for campaign work within the Democratic coalition increases as one moves left in Table 3 from districts in which individuals predominate to districts in which cohesive organizations predominate. Similarly, the allocation of resources available for organized labor, as distinct from other Democratic party groups and candidates, increases as one moves up the table.

Many of the district COPE organizations in Detroit, Chicago, and Los Angeles take intermediate forms. Nevertheless, by systematically stating the differences among them, the typology helps us identify the social, economic, and political factors that produce the different patterns of resources and COPE structures. Following the discussion of these factors, a series of tables will summarize the relationship between resources and type of COPE structure as well as their joint relationship to the political orientations and goals of union campaign workers. These factors, however, do not explain all the observed difference between various congressional districts. The chapter will therefore conclude by considering the independent impact of two other factors, the difference in priorities of top union leaders and in the ideological commitments among rank-and-file union members in particular districts.

Type I: Industrial Unions Dominant

As Chapter VI indicated, the most visible and active congressional-district organizations were usually dominated by large industrial unions whose members were organized into local union political action groups. These district organizations occurred most frequently in the Detroit area where, before the 1964 reapportionment, sizable UAW local unions were located in all but the residential seventeenth district. Even in this exceptional district, the COPE organization depended on the large number of UAW members, officers, and international officials who were district residents. Not only were all these Detroit-area COPE organizations active, well-financed, and professionally led, but each also played a dominant role in the Democratic party in its district.

This pattern was only approximated in Chicago and Los Angeles, and then only in districts with unusual concentrations of industrial-union members. For example, an active COPE organization developed in the twenty-seventh district in the eastern part of Los Angeles' San Fernando Valley. The two most prominent groups in the district COPE organization were large industrial unions, a UAW Chevrolet local and the somewhat larger IAM Lodge 727. In order to reach those members who were not registered and to contact possible campaign workers in particular areas, the IAM unit listed its membership by precinct and put this information on an addressograph machine. In a number of respects, however, the district did not conform to the pre-1964 Detroit model. The COPE organization was far more dependent than Detroit district COPES on the relationship of its constituent unions with particular Democratic candidates, a situation common in Los Angeles. As indicated above, the IAM lodge had a close relationship with former Democratic Assemblyman Tom Bane, the ill-fated 1964 congressional candidate. The lodge originally encouraged Bane to run for the state assembly, but its efforts fell noticeably in the 1964 campaign when Bane underestimated the seriousness of the Republican challenge.

Another difference was the significant number of nonfactory-union members prominent in the district COPE. A Carpenters local, two Painters locals, and a few activists from IBEW Local 11 made the building trades the third active group in the district. All union groups together accounted for perhaps a third of the precincts covered by various organizations working for Bane's election in 1960 in the old assembly district (which covered much of the twenty-seventh congressional district created in the 1962 reapportionment). According to Bane's campaign staff, labor covered about 150 precincts on behalf of Democratic Councilman Everett Burkhalter throughout the newly drawn congressional district in the 1962 campaign.

The party organization is so important within the city of Chicago, that during the early 1960s the fourth-district COPE organization in Chicago's Republican south suburbs probably approximated the Detroit-area industrial type more closely than any of the COPE organizations in Democratic congressional districts within the city itself. This approximation was particularly close in terms of COPE-party relations. Even though the fourth district was primarily residential and heavily Republican, the concentration of large industrial plants in the eastern part of the district gave former CIO unions, particularly the Steelworkers (USA), unusual influence in party affairs. COPE itself was largely directed by its CIO co-chairman, Sam Perish, who was the USA subdistrict director. Although some AFL local unions also had headquarters in the district, they were relatively inactive. In 1962, the AFL COPE co-chairman, an IBEW business agent, was largely preoccupied with servicing the many small shops in his area and had little time for COPE activities.

Republican control of most suburban towns in the district was a critical factor that enabled unions to play a major role in the party because it deprived the Democratic town organizations of the inducements necessary to recruit nonpatronage-oriented workers. As in Chicago, many Steelworkers joined the party organization as precinct captains and assistant captains. But the suburban township organizations lacked the ample material incentives with which the city ward organizations could persuade union members to follow the party rather than the union in politics. For example, many, though not all, of these captains supported USA's candidate Joseph Lohman rather than the party candidate Otto Kerner in the 1960 gubernatorial primary. In two townships Lohman ran ahead of Kerner.

The USA exercised its influence on the party's own decisions most dramatically in the nomination and election of Anthony Scariano to the seat usually won by the Democrats in one of the three-member state-representative districts in the southern suburbs. Scariano, one of the few issue-oriented, good-government Democrats in the legislature, won considerable publicity and liberal praise for his opposition to the Democratic Kerner administration's 1961 sales-tax increase as a regressive tax on the poor. He also publicly protested corruption in the Illinois legislature and advocated a generous policy on welfare payments, although his maverick liberalism did not make Scariano a hero to the party regulars in the Illinois house, and eventually led to his climactic break with the USA itself. Scariano sought election to the legislature after the 1956 reapportionment created a new Democratic seat in the south suburbs. His first backer was Frank Lynch, a liberal Rich Township committeeman, who lacked the influence to have Scariano slated by the party committee. Director Perish, however, was able to influence the party organization in the other somewhat less prosperous townships in the district where the steel union's plants were concentrated, and he had Scariano slated as one of the two regular Democratic candidates in the primary. Perish subsequently led Scariano's successful primary campaign, which won his candidate the crucial first position on the general election ballot.

In a few townships the USA also exercised great influence on internal party matters, partly because of its close relationship with Scariano, who had established a devoted following among the district's Italian Democrats. In Bloom Township, the union helped oust the Democratic committeeman who had alienated Scariano and who had aroused the union's suspicions that he was working with the Republicans. The union also persuaded the entire Thornton Township organization to break with the county party leadership in 1960 and publicly support Lohman for governor. Significantly, however, after Lohman's defeat the union could not save the township chairman's position when the county leadership cut off all patronage. More typically, even after Lohman's defeat the regular party leaders conceded the union a veto on nominations for offices in the district rather than direct control. "Where labor is about equally favorable to two candidates," one leader observed, "we can act freely even if labor actually prefers one of them. But where labor insists on a candidate, then we have to have their backing . . . " For example, in 1962, the union was consulted on the party's congressional candidates. Quite apart from campaign workers, the union's financial support was vital in so Republican a district even in undertaking a serious, let alone victorious, campaign.

The important point here is that the Steelworkers provided such a large, active, and independent campaign organization, as well as an important source of funds that Democratic leaders were reluctant to antagonize them. Most committeemen in the district resented the USA's influence, particularly because the able and aggressive leadership of Director Perish made this influence so effective. As one Democrat from an adjoining city ward said, "Perish and the committeemen watch each other like male dogs. They have to cooperate, but they don't trust each other." The union was too big, too rich, and too well led to be ignored by party organizations that had so little patronage for their own workers. But it was not strong enough to take over the Democratic party organization outright in most of the south suburban towns. In any case, such an open bid for power in the party might have provoked hostile and costly opposition of the Democratic leadership at the county level.

Type II: Union Officials Dominant

COPE district organizations of type II depend upon union leaders from many local unions operating mostly as individuals rather than upon more sizable groups of rank and file members from a few large, cohesive, and strongly motivated unions. These officials are themselves white-collar rather than blue-collar workers, who earn somewhat more than the average service- or industrial-union member and are normally motivated to participate in a district COPE by their ideology and organizational position rather than by membership in a solidary shop society. As a result, type II COPE organizations usually developed in middle-income white-collar residential districts, for example, the highly residential middle-income eleventh district in northwest Chicago. Because few industrial plants were located in the northern portions of Cook County, rank and file industrial-union members also played a more limited role in the ninth and thirteenth congressional districts as well as in the eleventh. In the 1960 census, these three districts ranked first, third, and fourth in the percentage of resident white-collar employees among all districts in the city, which indicates their middle-class character. The eleventh ranked highest of all nine city districts.

The degree of political orientation and interest was so high among the union officials who lived in the eleventh district that an active political action organization emerged several years before the AFL-CIO merger produced district COPE organizations in the city. Interested officials from AFL and CIO unions began to meet in the early 1950s. With the help of the central LLPE and PAC offices, they identified important locals in the area and collected the names of other officers. Gradually the committee expanded to include part-time officers and rank and file members, and, according to one district leader, reached "unions which haven't worked before at all."

The eleventh-district committee developed an impressive letterhead that listed the wide variety of participating unions. It requested each of its members to send a letter under his signature to his membership urging participation in COPE.* The single largest group of COPE workers came from the UAW, which in several elections also supplied a full-time staff official to help direct its members' efforts. According to UAW leaders, their members accounted for perhaps a third of the COPE workers who actually covered precincts and for a smaller proportion of the entire group that participated in the campaign in some fashion. But the majority of active workers did not belong to industrial unions. And the variety of unions represented on the letterhead allayed the fear of some AFL officers that CIO unions would dominate the organization.

In the early 1960s, the COPE co-chairmen were officers of two small unions, the Retail and Wholesale Workers (CIO) and the

---

* Not every leader on the letterhead actively participated. In fact some, for example those in the building trades, only lent their names in order to increase the range of unions involved. Yet their willingness even to lend their names suggests the extent to which COPE and Democratic Congressman Pucinski inspired union leaders in the district.

Jewelry Workers (AFL). In 1958, the chief full-time coordinator for the campaign was a Furniture Workers official. Other prominent unions included locals from the printing trades, especially from the Mailers, the Milk Wagon Drivers (a Teamsters local long under liberal leadership), the Steelworkers, the Boilermakers, locals from the garment trades, Carpenters, and at one point a Building Service local. Such smaller unions as the Inside Dairy Workers provided only one or two door-to-door campaigners, but they were often highly motivated and were considered among the most effective in the district. By 1956, six years before the Chicago merger, a working relationship had been established. In 1958, the group's early support helped persuade the party organization in the district to reslate Democrat Roman Pucinski as their congressional candidate, even though he had lost in 1956.

With the passage of time, the district COPE organization successfully involved some of the previously inactive AFL leaders. From his first race in 1956, Pucinski proved a vigorous campaigner for whom labor leaders felt they could work enthusiastically. As chairman of a subcommittee of the Education and Labor Committee in the Eighty-Sixth Congress, he filed a report denouncing the National Labor Relations Board under the Eisenhower administration for overturning prolabor precedents. His active support for labor, his Polish background, and his criticism of civil-rights groups appealed to many of his constituents, although not to many COPE activists. Although party leaders did not select Pucinski as leader of the Chicago Democrats in the House after the death of Representative Thomas O'Brien, many union leaders viewed him as an articulate spokesman for their interests.

The COPE organization had an important role primarily because the Democratic party organizations in the middle-income wards were weaker than in the central city. For example, Illinois elections have been marked by charges of vote stealing made by both parties. Whatever the validity of these charges, COPE leaders feel that Pucinski would have been elected in 1956 had every precinct been covered by a Pucinski supporter throughout election day and then during the count. After 1956, COPE tried to supply these workers in precincts where they appeared to be necessary.

COPE also tried to use its own work for Pucinski to offset the greater enthusiasm of some Democratic captains for local candidates who dispense patronage. When an area appeared to be short of Pucinski posters, COPE sometimes sent in its own workers. As a result, COPE's relations with the party were rather delicate. On the whole, however, the district COPE exemplified labor-party cooperation in those wards where patronage workers were not completely effective, so that COPE, the party, and Pucinski's own volunteers attempted to have all precincts covered at least on election day. Accordingly, COPE did very little in the thirty-fifth ward, a party stronghold. Its greatest effort often occurred in the forty-first ward, the most Republican in the district, where Democratic captains were less numerous and less effective. COPE leaders reported that the ward committeeman at first resented COPE workers but eventually realized that they posed no threat. He even told COPE where his own precinct organization was weakest and where his workers needed help. Chicago COPE leaders often cited the eleventh first district COPE as their first or second most effective. Although survey research documenting this claim is not available, it was strikingly and publicly supported by Pucinski himself after his narrow victory (by less than 5,000 votes) in 1966 in the face of a powerful white backlash against civil-rights demonstrations (despite Pucinski's own verbal attacks on the demonstrators). "We've been in a fight and we know it," he said after the vote. "This has been a team effort. But I must say that organized labor really came through for me today."[1]

Despite the strength of the UAW organization, a similar tendency to rely more on union officials can also be detected in white-collar middle-income sections of the Detroit area. UAW officials were most prominent as regular COPE members in the two least Democratic districts, the seventeenth and fourteenth, which (before the 1964 reapportionment) had the highest proportion of white-collar workers in the city and ranked first and third highest in median incomes.

Type III: Individual Candidates Dominant

The third type of district, in which the most active union members attached themselves to the campaign organization of a specific candidate, appeared most clearly in Los Angeles where the lack of patronage weakened party organizations and encouraged candidate-centered politics. Of course, this pattern emerged primarily where the Democrats also nominated candidates who were personally attractive to union members and leaders. Congressman Pucinski's appeal to union leaders meant that even the eleventh district COPE in Chicago displayed some type III attributes. It remained primarily a type II district, however, because the union officers in such upper-middle-income areas had the organizational ability to establish their own autonomous COPE organization and never found it necessary to simply merge into the congressman's personal operation. Similarly, in those areas where a strong industrial union was present, type I districts predominated no matter how attractive the candidate. By a process of elimination, then, candidate-centered districts proved most common in those lower-income and lower–middle-income parts of Los Angeles where both party organizations and industrial-union campaign groups were weak or nonexistent. Many union activists in these areas of Los Angeles were encouraged by their leaders to join the party's, or more often the candidate's, organization. For example, candidate-centered COPE activities were apparent in the twenty-ninth and thirtieth districts, which ranked thirteenth and fourteenth in median income of Los Angeles County's fifteen districts. A majority of the trade unionists who did campaign work in these two east-side districts operated as much or more in the personal organizations of Congressmen George Brown and Edward Roybal as in the district COPE organizations themselves.

Apart from their unions' urging, such campaign workers were attracted by a variety of inducements. A small number owed the candidate a favor or were looking for one. A few were simply attracted by the candidate as the official party representative. Others were his personal friends or associates in local civic affairs. Many enjoyed the aura of working with an incumbent, particularly if he was well known. By comparison with more ideological middle-class, issue-oriented Democrats, union members were often less offended by the compromises on issues that many incumbents felt they had to make.

Is there any meaningful sense in which these union members

were part of labor's political effort, and thus distinct from other Democrats in the candidate's organization? The answer to this question is necessarily complex. Many union members in type III districts had no organizational link with COPE, yet they were loyal to the labor movement and worked for Democratic candidates as the most practical way to realize labor's political goals. Some participated in party activities simply because their union indoctrinated them in the importance of political action—most preferably as a Democrat. Some unions told their members to report for campaign assignments to a particular candidate's headquarters. The garment workers and other industrial unions with large groups of members in minority areas frequently followed this strategy. As one candidate said, however, there were others who "think labor on labor issues but are basically loyal Democrats." Often their unions were not even aware that these members were active in the party. Finally, there was an intermediate group that saw no sharp distinction between labor and the party, particularly when labor and party activities were led by the same man.

The complexity of such workers' motivation in type III COPE organizations can be usefully illustrated by examining the activity of union members in the 1962 campaign in Los Angeles' twenty-fifth congressional district. This rapidly growing east-side district contained both manufacturing areas and large lower–middle-class rather than lower-class residential areas. In 1960, it ranked ninth out of the county's fifteen districts in median income, tenth in education, and twelfth in the percentage of white-collar workers. Although the Democrats claimed over 60 percent of the partisan registration, party voters in the district tended to be conservative, often fundamentalist, Protestants. The district's clubs were generally more conservative than the California Democratic Council.

In 1962, Assemblyman Ronald Cameron, who had the COPE endorsement, won the Democratic primary and went on to win the November general election (see the discussion of this endorsement in Chapter IX). With no strong industrial unions and few CIO members in the area, COPE as a separate organization did little in the primary. Nevertheless, organized labor played a major role through the union members who worked in Cameron's campaign. As elsewhere, these workers' motives, attitudes, and activities varied. One Democratic club president who supported Cameron considered himself a loyal union member, particularly because of his bitter experiences during the Depression. Yet he deliberately disassociated himself from the central labor council's factional role inside the Los Angeles County Democratic committee in order not to split his own club. Another club, made up mostly of union members and their wives, actually fought labor on every intraparty issue in the primary.

Cameron's COPE endorsement, however, appears to have helped him acquire the support of most union members who worked in the primary. But by far the most important single labor contribution during the 1962 campaign was made by one member of Local 11, Howard Jones. Jones, who had been an officer of his unit in the local, served in 1962 as an officer of both party and COPE organizations in the district, encouraged his wife to serve as chairman of a suburban Democratic club, and effectively directed COPE activities in the two assembly districts that made up the twenty-fifth.

Jones' many positions enabled him to organize and coordinate much of Cameron's entire campaign effort. As COPE chairman he collected the names of trade unionists in the district and persuaded many of them to work in Cameron's own organization. Jones also called on other members of Local 11, some of whom he met at union functions, to join their local Democratic clubs. He personally pointed out to Cameron several IBEW members who looked like good prospective campaign workers. According to Cameron's congressional office, Jones' most impressive activity probably was his staging of a series of coffee parties throughout the district at which Cameron's campaign organization chairman asked each guest to visit fifteen other Democrats on behalf of Cameron. Cameron's assistants felt that this personal persuasion was important in a primary, because the voters could not rely on party loyalty in making their decision. Under Jones' direction a coffee party was held for every three precincts, which enabled Cameron to cover the entire district before the primary.

At that time Jones was personally close to Cameron and concentrated all his energies on electing him. Yet much of Jones' unusual motivation for political action, and that of the IBEW members he recruited, could be traced to their membership in Local 11. According to one of Cameron's staff, Jones himself put loyalty to the labor movement ahead of partisanship. "Howard would support Nixon if the labor movement was for him," one remarked. Of course, Jones was only a single union member, even though he recruited others and himself directed much of the campaign. Nevertheless, as his work illustrated, under certain circumstances the labor movement served as a channel that directed its members to campaign organizations of the Democrats it endorsed. More generally, it motivated these members to engage in politics in the first place. In this sense, Jones' efforts must be counted among labor's contributions to the Los Angeles Democratic party's campaign activities.

Type IV: Party Organization Dominant

In some ways, type IV districts, in which COPE activity has been effectively absorbed by strong regular party organizations, were a polar opposite of those dominated by industrial unions. In 1962, for example, no meaningful COPE organization really functioned in Chicago's first, fifth, sixth, and seventh congressional districts, where the party usually amassed its largest majorities. Almost all the union members who worked in campaigns in such districts operated within the regular party under party rather than labor leadership. As noted earlier, this pattern was most common among unions in the building trades whose locals are often more concerned with the friendship of professional politicians than with national policy issues. Even in Detroit, some building-trades members supported a caucus of largely nonideological Democratic politicians opposed to the COPE organization in the east-side fourteenth congressional district. Although this dissident group lacked the patronage in the 1950s and early 1960s to challenge COPE successfully, it subsequently gained considerable strength in the aftermath of the party's loss of a United States Senate seat. Nevertheless, nonlabor party organizations completely absorbed the union workers only in Chicago, particularly in the inner-city wards. Even the most formidable nonlabor Democrats were not nearly strong enough to do so in Los Angeles and Detroit.

Sources of Variation Among COPE
District Organizations

The discussion of each of the types individually has already suggested that those districts that approximated one or another of the four types were far from randomly distributed. Every COPE organization that approximated a pure type was primarily a function of one particular social, economic, or political factor which operated with unusual importance in its district. Type I, the industrial-union–dominated COPE organization, was clearly the product of the district's economic structure, that is, an unusual concentration of large manufacturing plants organized by industrial unions. Type II districts basically reflected the particular social class of their residents. The union officials who, acting as individuals, comprised these COPE organizations differed from their members less in their higher income than in their middle-class style, ambitions, and verbal and intellectual skills. Type III districts, in which COPE activities were centered around a particular candidate, depended first on the general importance of candidates as opposed to party organizations in the local system, and, then, on the candidate's personal attractiveness to union leaders. Conversely, the absorption of COPE activities by a powerful party organization, which occurred in type IV districts, reflected the access of these organizations to political patronage.

Of course, no actual district perfectly conformed to one analytic type, partly because no one factor entirely determined the form the COPE organization took in any one district. Rather, all four factors affect COPE—either positively or negatively—in every district. Each COPE organization, in other words, was affected by the presence or absence of industrial unions, middle-class residential areas, patronage-oriented parties, and appealing candidates. On the other hand, these four factors were not equally important. Given the importance of organization, the predominant role of individuals (types II and III) were likely to become important only in areas where union and party organizations were not strong, as in much of Los Angeles. Even in the most prosperous districts of Wayne County, the power of the UAW created COPE organizations that most closely resembled the industrial-union type. Meanwhile, the eleventh congressional district COPE organization operated in the shadow of the Chicago party organization. Finally, in districts with neither a strong party nor industrial-union organization, the controlling factor was more likely to be the social and occupational character of the district rather than the candidate's personality. In prosperous areas where union officials were more numerous, they often maintained their own organization even when they worked for a candidate, like Pucinski, whom they found appealing. Only in lower-class and lower–middle-class areas with fewer union officials, did the rank and file members of nonfactory unions tend to join the candidate's own organization.

These observations enable us to establish the relationship between the four types of districts and these four basic factors, first for each type individually and then for all four types simultaneously. The industrial-union–dominant type I district organizations were likely to emerge wherever there were large numbers of industrial unions, except in lower-income neighborhoods with strong patronage-supported party organizations. They were unlikely to appear where industrial unions were rare. Type II district organizations, which are dominated by union officials, tended to appear in residential middle-income and upper-income districts. They were unlikely to emerge in lower-income districts and in districts with many industrial unions.

Type III candidate-dominant district organizations were likely to be found only in lower–middle-income areas. Even in such areas, however, these districts were uncommon if there were many industrial unions, patronage was available, or the candidate was not personally appealing. Obviously, type IV party-organization–dominant districts depended on the availability of patronage. But this form did not emerge in the upper-income districts and in those middle-income districts where industrial unions were numerous, even when patronage was available. As this discussion implies, the frequency of these four types can be depicted simultaneously in tabular form, indicating the importance of each factor in the context of the other three, as shown in Table 4.

The analysis up to this point has essentially considered the effect

TABLE 4 Likelihood of a Particular Type of COPE District Organization to Appear in Certain Districts

	Many Industrial Unions		Few Industrial Unions	
	PATRONAGE AVAILABLE	PATRONAGE UNAVAILABLE	PATRONAGE AVAILABLE	PATRONAGE UNAVAILABLE
Upper- and Middle-Income Districts	Industrial union type, some union officials type features	Industrial union type, some union official type features	Union officials type, some candidate-centered features	Union officials type, some candidate-centered features { Union officials type
Lower-Middle-Income Districts	Party organization type, some industrial union type features	Industrial union type	Party organization type, some candidate centered features	Party organization type, some union officials features { Candidate centered type.
Lower-Income Districts	Party organization type	Industrial union type	Party organization type	Union officials type
	CANDIDATE APPEALING OR UNAPPEALING	CANDIDATE UNAPPEALING	CANDIDATE APPEALING	CANDIDATE UNAPPEALING CANDIDATE APPEALING UNAPPEALING

of social, economic, and political variables on the distribution of the resources available for campaign activities. In turn, this distribution affects the structure of the district COPE organizations. This causal relationship is indicated in Table 5, which restates Table 3. But

TABLE 5 **The Structure of COPE Organizations**

	Many Organizational Resources	Few Organizational Resources
Control of Sizable Resources by Labor Groups	Type I: Industrial union dominant	Type II: Union officials dominant
Control of Bulk of Resources by Nonlabor Democrats	Type IV: Party organization absorbs COPE	Type III: Candidate's organization absorbs union campaign workers

the various types of congressional districts also differed in the orientation, tone, style, and goals of their members. The differences in organizational resources and structures brought about these behavioral differences because they produced intervening attitudinal variables, that is, different normative or value orientations toward politics. Different types of organizational resources, in other words, evoked and fostered political activity among union members with differing political motivations.

We can indicate the source of this relationship between resources, structures, and attitudes by considering the resource dimensions in Table 5 in terms of incentives. It then appears that the availability of resources (the horizontal dimension) corresponds to the *material or nonmaterial* character of the incentives to political activity offered most union members in the district. Material incentives are most important in types I and IV, and nonmaterial incentives appear to predominate in types II and III. With respect to the vertical dimension, when union members and officials participated in union-dominated district COPEs (types I and II) they responded to *indivisible incentives* that appealed to all union members. When they participated in party-dominated districts they responded to *divisible incentives* offered by party organizations (type IV) or particular candidates (type III). We can conclude, therefore, that industrial-union–dominant districts (type I) exemplify a pattern of material but divisible incentives, particularly the CIO's ideological welfare-state commitment. The union officials pattern (type II) represents the sophisticated political commitment of labor leaders from both factory and nonfactory unions who accepted the AFL-CIO's welfare-state ideology and perceived the impact of the larger party cleavage on their unions. Thus, their incentives were in large part indivisible and nonmaterial. Type III, candidate-centered districts, represent the response of union members to the personal gratifications of association with individual candidates, that is, divisible but nonmaterial incentives. Party organization dominant districts (type IV) represent the familiar accommodation of often voluntarist unions to the pluralist patronage party in terms of divisible material incentives. Table 6 restates Table 5 in incentive terms.

TABLE **6** **Dominant Incentives of Different Types of District COPEs**

	Material Incentives	**Nonmaterial Incentives**
Indivisible Incentives	Type I: Industrial unions dominant	Type II: Union officials dominant
Divisible Incentives	Type IV: Party organization dominant	Type III: Candidate dominant

It is now possible to consider these four types of districts as the poles of two attitudinal dimensions, while preserving the *relative* position of each type to the other three indicated in Table 6, by rotating the axes, or dimensions. These relative positions can be preserved because, as we have just seen, the attitudes of union members who became active in each particular type of COPE organization were systematically related to that organization's resources and, therefore, types of incentives. The first of these new dimensions, which runs from lower left to upper right in Table 6, can be categorized as *personal economic gain versus disinterested economic welfarism.* Specifically, this dimension indicates the union member's concern for his own personal material improvement against a somewhat more disinterested concern for the interests of workers generally.

Type II districts, which were composed of middle-class union officials, represent the polar form of such disinterestedness. Apart from concern about political threats to labor's organizational security —which usually leads to lobbying—these officials participated in COPE to expand the welfare state. But such programs at least purport to benefit the less well-paid rank and file union members and the still poorer unorganized workers more than better-paid union leaders. Type IV districts represent the polar opposite. The union members incorporated into a patronage-based party organization were in most cases primarily concerned with the divisible material incentives that the party supplied to them as individuals. On this dimension, the other two types of organizations represent intermediate cases. The rank and file members who made up the bulk of the industrial-union–dominated organization (type I) stood to benefit more directly than better-paid middle-class union officials from the welfare-state policies that COPE advocates. However consistent with their orientation toward material but indivisible incentives, they would benefit in this way collectively as a class rather than individually. They were thus less self-interested than members of a patronage-oriented organization. By comparison with the rank and file members of these COPE organizations, the members of a candidate-oriented political organization (type III) were interested in more direct individual gain, but the gain was more psychic than economic, that is, in nonmaterial but divisible incentives. The typical Los Angeles candidate, for example, rewarded his campaign workers by associating with them on a personally friendly basis because he had few material rewards to distribute. In terms of public policy, these workers tended to be more issue-oriented than union members in a patronage party organization, but less so than union officials in a middle-class district.

The second and cross-cutting dimension, *orientation to formal governmental office,* indicates the degree to which the individual COPE member's participation was motivated by concern with politics on its own terms—exemplified by the desire to elect a specific individual to a particular public office—quite apart from underlying social cleavages. This dimension runs from the upper left to lower right corners of Table 6. Obviously, this motivation is dominant in the candidate-centered organization (type IV). By contrast, the industrial-union–dominated COPE district organization (type I) recruited its members with very little regard to the particular office or candidates. Moreover, membership in the union, which is itself a private economic organization, was the primary basis for recruitment, and the organization was directed and sustained by leaders of the union who self-consciously maintained their union role. On this dimension, types II and IV (dominated by union officials and party organizations, respectively) districts are the intermediate cases. The union members absorbed into the party organization were certainly concerned with electing its candidates to office. But they were not basically oriented to any specific offices or candidates. Moreover, the basis of recruitment was ultimately the individual member's own private gain, not the gratification of seeing one's favorite politician elected. By comparison, the members of type III (union-officials–dominant) COPE organizations were usually more focused on the particular office of congressman from their district. They were recruited on the basis of their residence in the congressional district rather than their membership in a particular union. But they retained a primary identification as union officers and members of the labor movement, and they maintained a formally independent COPE organization.

TABLE **6A**   **Incentives and Political Orientations in District COPEs**

	Material Incentives	**Nonmaterial Incentives**
Indivisible Incentives	Low orientation to particular political offices	"Disinterested" economic welfarism
Divisible Incentives	Personal economic gain	High orientation to particular political offices

Deviations from the Typology: The Role of Individual Motivation and Political Strategies

We have related economic, political, and social characteristics of particular congressional districts to the distribution of resources, and the primary political orientation of the district COPE. Nevertheless, all these relationships between resources and the types and levels of activity are only statistical tendencies. The entire variation of union member motivation and behavior between congressional districts cannot be entirely explained by variations in these economic, political, and social resources. Admittedly, the resources approach accounts for much of our data. For example, in the case of Chicago districts, the COPE leadership's perception of an unfavorable distribution of resources reduced their enthusiasm for campaign activity. Conversely, such enthusiasm was encouraged in Chicago's eleventh district by a congressional candidate with a strong personal appeal to labor leaders. The motivation and thus activity of a particular COPE organization also reflects, however, the independent political attitudes of two key leadership groups within the labor movement.

One such set of attitudes, at least in Chicago and Los Angeles, involved the intensity of ideologically based political commitment to campaign activity among the political activists in the district itself. The larger the commitment, the more active the COPE district organization. Because the distribution of such committed union political activists was not specifically correlated with the social, economic, or political character of the district, it appears to have operated independently of other causal variables. A second such independent factor was the choice of campaign strategies made by county and state COPES and affiliated union leaders. On one side, Chicago COPE decided to concentrate on electing the maximum number of liberal congressmen, and this strategy meant emphasizing activity in the politically marginal districts where either party might win, rather than in districts that were safely Democratic. With some exceptions, Los Angeles unions adopted Chicago COPE's approach. By contrast, Detroit COPE set as its main goal the election of candidates running in statewide elections, which meant concentrating on safely Democratic districts in order to build up large Democratic majorities. Both strategies meant deemphasizing suburban, well-to-do Republican districts where COPE efforts would produce little return. As a result, there was significant COPE activity in Republican areas only when such areas had sizable groups of industrial unions, vigorous leaders, and the opportunity to elect Democratic state representatives through a modified proportional representation system. For example, such conditions accounted for labor activity in Chicago's suburban fourth and tenth districts.

But when we turn to areas without a solid Republican majority, the choice of different strategies in the early 1960s led to very different consequences in districts with otherwise similar socioeconomic and party voting attributes. In Chicago COPE largely ignored those inner-city districts where a strong Democratic organization was certain of victory. In addition, the low levels of income, education, and white-collar employment in these heavily Democratic districts meant that, as in Republican strongholds, labor had a relatively limited pool of motivated and skilled leaders and activists. By contrast, Chicago's middle-income politically marginal districts provided better-paid, more potentially effective recruits for campaign work. Nevertheless, Detroit COPE systematically placed greater emphasis on heavily Democratic rather than on marginal areas in order to offset heavy Republican majorities outstate. The Detroit UAW systematically overcame the limited number of potential precinct workers by committing its own staff officials and organizational resources.

The operation of Chicago's eighth district in the early 1960s simultaneously illustrated the importance of both ideological commitment among activists at the district levels and the strategic political decisions of top leaders. Since 1959, the district had been represented in Congress by Daniel Rostenkowski, the son of a powerful ward leader. Rostenkowski became the informal leader of the Chicago Democratic delegation in the House in 1964, and by COPE standards compiled an excellent voting record. In other respects the district generally typified those in which COPE hesitated to operate extensive campaigns. In 1962, it was the fourth most Democratic in the city and thus extremely unlikely to go Republican. It also ranked eighth among the twelve Cook County districts in median income and percentage of white-collar employees, reducing the group of well-paid unionists available for precinct work.

In most other inner-city districts, the COPE organization involved little more than two or three meetings every two years among a handful of leaders. Nevertheless, a group of political activists emerged in the eighth district in the 1960s and managed to operate a relatively continuous COPE organization, assigned precincts to be covered, held monthly meetings and tried to educate the members on the issues. This group reflected on the whole the commitment of the most politically dedicated industrial unionists. Nevertheless, only twenty union members in 1962—perhaps twice that number in 1966—could really be said to be active. A handful of this core group belonged to AFL unions. Because most Steelworkers who attended were not encouraged by their union to continue, Autoworkers made up the majority of active COPE members. Recruiters encountered such obstacles, however, that even the politically oriented UAW staff officials who lived in the district were inactive. This inability to recruit more than a few of the thousands of union members in the district left the leadership thoroughly frustrated. "We discuss recruiting at every meeting," one said in 1962. "You know I'm so damn disappointed, even the local officers of the UAW don't come and we depend on them." "Even [door] prizes don't work," he continued. "Some guys win the prizes and never come back."

Given the core of activists, these recruitment problems might have been overcome with vigorous backing, but the district COPE received little support or encouragement from union leaders. The big industrial unions were mainly helpful through their standard procedure of compensating members who work on election day for lost pay without regard to particular districts. By 1966 this group numbered as many as 100, but many of them showed limited enthusiasm for serious precinct work and participated only on election day itself. Equally disturbing, the district COPE's efforts, at least in the early 1960s, were partially offset by the strategic decision of higher COPE leaders to concentrate on elections where the outcome was more clearly in doubt. Indeed, some active COPE workers who lived in the district were regularly sent into neighboring districts where the congressional race was closer. This set of priorities could be partially rationalized by citing the relative weakness of the liberal Northern Democrats in the House of Representatives compared with the comparable group in the Senate from 1959, or even earlier, to at least 1964. Concentration on liberalizing the more conservative House thus seemed to be the most effective way for COPE to maximize labor's policy goals.

Of course, Chicago union leaders were also reluctant to disturb the party in one of its strongholds, and this tactic meant that labor's efforts were concentrated in those geographical areas where the party needed, and was most likely to welcome, outside assistance. Chicago COPE's stress on marginal districts therefore could be entirely explained as an accommodation to a more powerful party organization that resented labor activities in the most safely Democratic wards. The two districts where labor was most active, the marginal eleventh and third, included some of the weakest ward Democratic organizations in the city party. Moreover, labor's concentration on congressional elections also complemented the party's determination to control by itself the campaigns for the local offices that dispense patronage.*

Indeed, the importance of the party's wishes might indicate that COPE's concentration on marginal districts was nothing more than a rationalization for its accommodation to the demands of the Chicago organization. This contention is refuted, however, by comparative analysis. Los Angeles labor leaders who never needed to concern themselves with the type of party pressure likely in Chicago, also stressed marginal districts in their campaign operation. The disorganized situation was obviously more complicated than in Detroit or in Chicago. Los Angeles unions did make some effort to build up statewide Democratic party margins, particularly in the city's black areas. And the Los Angeles party welcomed these efforts (similar incursions into the black first district in Chicago had aroused party suspicion and hostility). Moreover, union campaign work also occurred in several other relatively poor Los Angeles districts, specifically the harbor areas and east central Los Angeles (the twenty-ninth and thirtieth districts). However, when we examine these districts closely they begin to resemble the situation in Chicago's eighth district where campaign work was undertaken by a core of activists living in the area and did not depend upon a massive commitment of resources by top union leaders. Together with the eighth district, these areas illustrate the wide diffusion of political activism among

---

* Of course, the party has some interest in congressmen, witness the Fields-Finnegan affair, but, particularly for the precinct worker, Congress is of considerably less interest than many local positions. See Chap. IX.

certain local union leaders and members of the American labor movement.

The Los Angeles harbor-area COPE, for example, primarily operated in the seventeenth and thirty-second congressional districts, which ranked tenth and eleventh out of fifteen in median income. In percentage of white-collar employment, the securely Republican thirty-second district ranked sixth out of fifteen whereas the securely Democratic seventeenth ranked fourteenth. In these districts the active COPE leadership in the area appears to have reflected a militant and somewhat separatist tradition that has been characteristic of west coast harbor areas since the early years of the century.[2] On the one hand, the local unions in the AFL had a separate harbor-area central body that only merged with the Los Angeles County central body at the time of its merger with the CIO. By 1962, on the other hand, the COPE leaders had established a perhaps unusually good working relationship with harbor-area leaders, including the secretary of the Long Beach Building Trades Council and leaders from the Retail Clerks, Operating Engineers, Steelworkers, Autoworkers, and Carpenters. Somewhat earlier this harbor group had been impatient with the Los Angeles Central Council for its delay in setting up area COPE organizations. In 1958, building upon the strong union feeling against the state right-to-work referendum, the group formed a COPE organization for the general election.

The commitment of these individual leaders could not entirely overcome the lack of either large unions committed to political action or a large group of motivated union officials. The leadership remained informal and decentralized and decisions were often made at the assembly-district level. The organization met only once or twice during off years to endorse local candidates and to fill leadership vacancies. It even hesitated to endorse any Democrat against the thirty-second district's well-entrenched Republican Congressman Craig Hosmer. Although it concentrated its registration activities in poor Democratic areas, its coverage of these precincts in the 1960s was neither thorough nor systematic.

The COPE organization in east central Los Angeles in the twenty-ninth and thirtieth congressional districts developed around nuclei of local union officers and leaders who were united—and animated

—by minority group leftism. The twenty-ninth district included such older immigrant groups as Mexicans and Italians in the west and better-educated younger Catholics in the east. In 1960 it ranked first out of fifteen in the county in percentage of Spanish surnames. The thirtieth district ranked second in percentage of Spanish surnames in the county and third in percentage of Negro population. In addition to having large ethnic minorities, the two districts were less prosperous than the harbor area, ranking thirteenth and fourteenth among the county's fifteen districts in median income and ninth and tenth in percentage white-collar employees among their residents. The leadership cadre had worked closely together during the 1958 campaign, when most of the area was in the nineteenth congressional district, and decided to continue operating in future elections. Perhaps the central figure in 1962 was COPE District Chairman Harold Dunne, a Jewish Autoworker who had a Mexican wife. In 1962 he was recording secretary and political action chairman of UAW Local 216, and recording secretary of the UAW's Area Citizenship Council. A second important leader was David Fishman, president of a Painter's local with mostly Jewish members that had been the first of his union's Los Angeles units to admit many Negroes. By the early 1960s, the local was about half Jewish with large Mexican and Negro groups. In 1960 as many as twelve Painters came out on some weekends to work for Kennedy in the Presidential election. Another leader, J. J. "Rod" Rodriguez of the Butcher's Union, was the leading Mexican trade unionist in Los Angeles and a Central Labor Council vice-president. His union had perhaps half a dozen members out on weekends during 1960 and nearly 100 workers on election day who worked precincts and took voters to the polls. The union's turnout for Johnson in 1964 was still larger. The leadership group also included Steve Blancarte of Local 11 of the IBEW, Del Coffey, a Negro Steelworker, and Art Takai, a Japanese-American board member of Clerks Local 777.

In 1960, this COPE group concentrated on shopping centers, sending out perhaps six to eighteen workers on a weekend and also sending some members door to door for registration work and election day get-out-the-vote efforts. Like the harbor-area COPE, however, the leadership lacked the manpower in its low-income area to sustain a year-round program, and meetings often included only a few active leaders.* In the 1962 primary, the group strongly supported George Brown in the twenty-ninth, but its efforts disappointed both Brown's own campaign staff and the COPE leaders themselves. In the thirtieth district these leaders supplied a somewhat larger group for Edward Roybal, but he faced less formidable opposition. As one COPE leader commented, this group and the harbor-area COPE were important mainly because the size of the average campaign organization in any one assembly district (usually one-half a congressional district) rarely exceeded fifty to seventy workers. In his view, "weak as we are we are stronger than almost anyone else."

In fact, however, organized labor seemed to be less active in these four districts where one party or the other seemed well-entrenched than in the thirty-first, the twenty-fifth, and the twenty-seventh, which were the second, third, and fourth most closely contested in 1962. All three sent newly elected Democrats to Congress in January 1963, suggesting the high priority top union leaders gave to marginal districts. In the thirty-first and twenty-seventh both industrial- and craft-union members were prominent; the twenty-seventh district was notable for the already-mentioned activities of Howard Jones of the IBEW. Most striking of all, COPE made its biggest single effort through the combined efforts of the UAW and the building trades in 1962 and 1964 in the closest district in the entire county, the twenty-second in the western San Fernando Valley. This district in particular, given the feeble character of the party organization, confirms the assertion that the concern for marginal districts in Chicago was more than a simple concession to party pressure. In economic terms, the twenty-second actually should have voted Republican because it ranked second in median income and fifth in percentage of white-collar employees of all Los Angeles County districts. Only the personal popularity of the Democratic candidates and former City Councilman James Corman; a sizable number of upper- and middle-income Jewish Democrats; and the major effort of COPE, the Democratic clubs, and Corman's own sup-

* One rank and file unionist interested in political action but hostile to the district COPE leadership found it difficult to find out about COPE meetings.

porters account for his victories from 1960 to 1966. COPE's workers came primarily from the UAW and a number of important craft unions including the Operating Engineers, Sheet Metal Workers and particularly Local 11 and Carpenters Local 844—all of whom were close to Corman when he was a councilman. Together these groups accounted for about one-third of Corman's workers in 1960 and 1962. In any case, Los Angeles Democrats rated the overall effort on behalf of Corman as perhaps the most effective union campaign work in the entire county.

The stress on marginal districts in Chicago and, less exclusively, on districts like Corman's in Los Angeles, clearly reflects a particular definition by the labor movement of its role within the Democrats' overall electoral activities, that is, helping secure liberal Democratic party control of the U.S. House of Representatives. Specifically, COPE defined its functional responsibility in the party in somewhat narrow institutional and geographic terms. In Chicago this arrangement meant a division of labor in which COPE concentrated its issue-oriented workers in areas with better-educated middle-income voters, and the party used material incentives in less well-to-do areas. Over time, however, the unions' narrower functional definition of their role came to be valued for its own sake. To be sure, some COPE workers in Chicago's eleventh district tried to reassure party precinct captains that "We're just here to help you." Nevertheless, when COPE workers in the district encountered Republican voters in their canvassing, they often concentrated on persuading them to vote for Congressman Pucinski. To avoid losing the vote for Congress by getting into a partisan argument, the COPE workers ignored even Presidential and senatorial races. Whatever the effect of this tactic, which some of Pucinski's own volunteers adopted, the congressman usually ran ahead of the ticket in the early and mid-1960s. In a still more striking case, described in detail in Chapter IX, the previously active twelfth district COPE organization practically stopped functioning in 1960 after a quarrel over the party's choice of congressional candidate. As a result, organized labor did relatively little in that Presidential election in the northeast corner of the city even though Illinois was a pivotal state in an extraordinarily close election (the city lost the twelfth district in the 1961 reapportionment).

Chicago COPE's emphasis on close congressional races and Detroit COPE's concern with statewide races produced a dramatic contrast in which the party candidates and organized labor reversed their functional roles, primarily with respect to mobilizing party support. Congressman Pucinski, although he needed Republican votes, had to proclaim his party loyalty because he depended on the party for renomination. It was labor that searched out Republican voters, for instance, among the district's numerous Scandanavians, and asked them to vote for Pucinski even if they otherwise voted a straight Republican ticket. Yet, in Detroit's rather comparable seventeenth district, Congresswoman Martha Griffiths used a consistently nonpartisan appeal that evidently attracted enough middle-income and even upper-income Republican voters to carry the least Democratic district in Wayne County. Indeed, Mrs. Griffiths enraged UAW leaders when, consistent with this appeal, she demonstrated how to vote both for Eisenhower and Griffiths on a labor-sponsored television program. She had no right, one UAW official complained to "spend our money to tell people how to vote for Ike." In any case, because Detroit COPE tended to concentrate on the most Democratic areas in the city in order to produce Democratic majorities in the state, it could give only second priority to winning congressional seats in the marginal areas that Chicago COPE emphasizes. By thus assuming leadership for a wide range of party activities, Detroit COPE appeared to have sacrificed some of its freedom to emphasize districts that determined control of the House of Representatives.

Of course, given the opportunity, even Detroit COPE committed unusual numbers of workers and large financial resources to some particularly important and doubtful congressional contests. One notable example occurred in the special congressional election in early 1962 in the fourteenth district, which is described in Chapter IX. Yet, the UAW was able to concentrate its resources in a relatively marginal district at that time only because it was a special election in which there were no statewide races to consider.

It is clear that this difference in function is related to a difference in the voter constituency that each COPE chooses to seek to mobilize. Chicago COPE tried to bring to the polls politically marginal, middle-income, and middle-status groups, who might be persuaded to vote

for Democratic congressmen. By contrast, the Chicago party organization relied most heavily on poorer voters. This difference in support was graphically suggested by a party leader's retort when a
COPE leader, who admired the district congressman, accused him of
nominating candidates for other offices who were not committed to
liberal policies. "You know it's rough dealing with you guys—it's
okay to be a knight in shining armor—but you dislike me because I'm
in the party. How the hell do you think we elected the Congressman?
I went to the whore houses, the gamblers, and the taverns and said,
'Unload the dough.' " The COPE leader admitted that this answer
"was a shock to me. Where do you draw the line? We [sometimes]
get liberal candidates [from the party], but dirty guys elect them. I
don't know. . . . Or what happens when the west side block [which
has alleged syndicate ties] votes perfectly on social legislation? They
were poor, and they want to take care of poor people."

Although the issue-oriented UAW did not make the same appeal
to these interests in Detroit, it did concentrate resources on bringing
to the polls voters from those areas of the city that correspond to the
strongholds of the Chicago party organization. In fact, by spurring
lower-class electoral turnout, the party in Chicago, the UAW in Detroit, and to a lesser extent both COPE and party groups in Los
Angeles all functioned to offset the greater political participation of
wealthier, better-educated Republican voting groups. In other words,
COPE's supplementary role in middle-income congressional districts
in Chicago is likely to continue as long as the Democratic party
maintains its strength. Should the party suffer enough defeats to lose
its patronage base and thus its effectiveness in low income areas, the
motivation for Chicago COPE to organize this lower income constituency would substantially increase.

Conclusions

This chapter first categorized and explained organized labor's
campaign activities in different districts by a two-dimensional typology; that is, by the density and allocation of resources available to
unions and to nonlabor Democrats. Deviations from this typology

were then accounted for by political attitudes independent of each district's configuration of resources; that is, the ideological commitments of individual activists and the strategic choice of priorities between marginal congressional contests and statewide races. Taken together, these differences in resources, attitudes, and priorities account for the bulk of the variation between the three cities that we considered in different terms in Chapters III, IV, and V. It should be emphasized, however, that these two attitudinal variables only accounted for *deviations;* the *central tendencies* were expressed by the typology based on resources. For example, in most lower-income districts with powerful patronage organizations, such as four of Chicago's five inner city districts, the party organization in 1962 had largely absorbed COPE operations. In maintaining a life of its own, the eighth district COPE was the exception rather than the rule. Moreover, the difficulties of this group, and the evolution of the COPE organization in Chicago's black first district (discussed in Chapter VIII) suggests that very large deviations from type IV (party organization dominant) districts under these conditions would be very unlikely.

Similarly, the unusual commitment of individual local union activists in Los Angeles' twenty-ninth and thirtieth districts enabled them to maintain an independent COPE organization even though we would expect them to be absorbed by Democratic congressional candidates (type III). As pointed out earlier in the chapter, however, much of their activity actually involved supplying workers to the organizations of Congressmen Brown and Roybal rather than to sustaining their own independent campaign operation, confirming the analysis in the typology. In a case where the ideological commitment of the local leaders was unusually weak, for example, in the fourteenth congressional district on Detroit's east side, the COPE organization encountered both difficulty in maintaining a coordinator and open quarrels among top COPE leaders. This case also deviated from the typology. Nevertheless, the UAW was able to sustain a COPE organization that generally resembled those in other Detroit districts, and thus approximated type I (industrial union dominant).

The second attitudinal variable, the strategic choice between marginal congressional districts and statewide races, affected the level of COPE operations more than the type of organization. For example, it helped explain the somewhat greater strength of the Detroit COPE organization in inner city rather than in the marginal and more closely contested middle-income districts. Similarly, the presence of a large UAW contingent that supplemented the union officials in Chicago's eleventh district reflected in part the emphasis of COPE leaders in that city on marginal congressional contests. In both cases, however, the specific COPE organizations generally conformed to the typology.

These references to labor's choice of political strategy, which actually means its choice of role within the party, emphasize the importance of the party system as a context within which COPE operates. Union campaign activities cannot be understood entirely in terms of the internally generated incentive systems discussed in Chapter VI, and the environmental factors in particular districts that we have just examined. If we are to fully understand organized labor's impact on the American party system since World War II we must now explicitly consider organized labor's place as an operating partner in the Democratic party coalition of the early and mid-1960s.

VIII

🐝🐝🐝🐝🐝🐝🐝🐝🐝🐝🐝🐝🐝🐝🐝🐝🐝🐝🐝🐝🐝🐝🐝🐝🐝

The Labor-Party Alliance

The American labor movement's activities during much of the 1950s and 1960s as a faction within the Democratic party pose substantial difficulties if we are to apply the widely acccepted distinction between American parties and pressure groups. In this influential view, a distinguishing objective of the two major parties is to win elections for public office. E. E. Schattschneider, a leading American theorist of party government, has defined a political party as "an organization formed for the purpose of winning elections in order to get control of the directing personnel of government. Having taken possession of the principal offices, the party obtains general control of the government." It follows, according to Schattschneider, that "The ultimate [aim] of the party is . . . conquest of the power to govern. The point of attack, or the method, is to nominate candidates and to support them in an election campaign. The methods and the objectives of the parties are inseparable." By contrast, Schattschneider sees the pressure group as "an association that tries to bring about the adoption and execution of certain public policies without nominating candidates for the great offices, without fighting election campaigns, and without attempting to get complete control of government."[1] To further its policies, the interest group applies pressure and uses other inducements on politicians and parties. David Truman, perhaps the most influential theorist of group politics in the United States, has formulated this process in terms of access:

> The political party has come to be thought of as the instrumentality through which choices are made among aspirants for office. Access to this instrumentality, therefore, may be important to a political interest group, although . . . it cannot be the only, and may not be the most important, point of access to government.[2]

It is generally recognized, of course, that this distinction can be easily overstated. Clinton Rossiter points out that some groups, including labor, not only work with a single party but actually take a major role in the party's election campaigns.[3] Moreover, winning public office is not the only activity of the major parties. As a leading American government text observes:

> In general, the party is primarily interested in winning control of and operating the government; the pressure group is primarily interested in shaping public policy. On the other hand, having won control of the government, a party can hardly avoid the responsibility of shaping public policy; whereas to influence public policy, the pressure group may find it necessary to try to elect its supporters to public office.[4]

Even if this qualification is accepted, the party's typical role in shaping policy has been frequently seen to be somewhat different from that of the pressure group. Whereas pressure groups ordinarily originate demands for particular policies and programs, parties are thought to combine and reconcile the diverse and conflicting demands of a plurality of separate and particular interests. Gabriel Almond labels these combining functions—for our purposes we shall term them activities—interest *"aggregation,"* which he distinguishes from interest *"articulation,"* an activity that is most prominently performed by pressure groups. Almond carefully specifies that party systems are not the only political actors or structures that aggregate interests and he points out that they perform other functions as well. But adhering to the basic distinction of Schattschneider, Truman, and others, Almond asserts that, on the whole, parties aggregate the interests articulated by pressure groups.[5] It may not be accidental that the analysis of aggregating and articulating activities has been stressed by scholars concerned with comparative politics, for such analytic concepts seem particularly appropriate for the comparison of similar behavior by apparently dissimilar political actors. These concepts are useful here in analyzing systematically the overlapping activities of such organizations as the Democratic party and the labor movement, which appear to have very different structures and goals. Nevertheless, organized labor and the Democratic party do not conform to the usual party-pressure group distinction that we have just discussed.

Direct Political Aggregation:
Labor and Minority Groups

The Democratic party's efforts to incorporate the industrial working class into American political life during the New Deal meant aggregating labor's interests with other elements of the party's constituency. As Chapter II emphasized, this aggregation did not fully take place until the workers were able to articulate their interests for themselves. But this capacity depended first, upon the emergence of organized groups, specifically the CIO unions, and second, upon the workers' voting in larger numbers and with greater partisan unity. These developments, which Roosevelt and his party often deliberately fostered, made the workers' interests sufficiently important for the party to aggregate them through its nominations, rhetoric, and programs, all of which helped build political coalitions. From the workers' perspective, the party under Roosevelt had helped them articulate their interests more satisfactorily by providing new access to the political authorities. From the party's perspective, the workers' better organization and higher voting rates were the first step in aggregating, that is, in combining, altering, and even resisting some demands, in order to unite the workers with other party groups.

We call these activities aggregation because the interests the party first evoked and then "combined" and "reduced"[6] were not its own but those of the unions and workers generally. In the three cities studied in this book, organized labor in varying degrees assumed just such an aggregating posture toward relatively new groups of urban immigrants who felt excluded from American political life in the generation after the New Deal, notably blacks and Spanish-speaking Puerto Ricans and Mexicans. At a minimum the labor movement helped these groups to organize and vote so that they could begin to articulate their own demands, which labor as a party faction then helped aggregate into programs and slates of candidates.

This direct aggregation was least important in Chicago where the regular party's strong ward organizations resisted any intervention by outside precinct organizations. In the early 1950s, militant blacks in the CIO did attack the south-side organization of Congressman William Dawson for its reliance on patronage politics, moderate rhetoric, and limited demands for civil-rights legislation. In 1950, the first district Political Action Committee (the CIO predecessor of COPE) unsuccessfully ran Willoughby Abner, citizenship director of the regional UAW, in a state senate primary.[7] Through most of that decade, the PAC organization remained among the most vigorous in Cook County. Imitating the Detroit COPE organizations, it continued to operate between elections with support from a largely UAW membership and to pressure the Democratic party to heed a greater range of black demands. In effect, CIO unions tried to help Chicago blacks articulate civil-rights demands that the national party had already begun to aggregate into its program, but which the pluralist, local party organization preferred to minimize.

After 1958, however, Abner's organization disintegrated. Repeated defeats in primary elections had gradually eroded its members' morale; more importantly, the Chicago party leadership made clear its opposition to such open insurgency. The UAW reduced its material and verbal support, and the leadership urged the district organization to stop opposing the party in primaries and to concentrate on helping in general elections. Because members and leaders felt this left them with no significant function, Abner and other black UAW members turned to the Negro-American Labor Council, but this group never became a major campaign organization. In the 1960 and 1962 elections Abner received national assignments that took him out of Chicago, and in 1963 he was transferred from the Chicago region of the UAW.

Chicago unions met less determined party opposition when COPE's efforts at aggregation were limited to increasing the black vote rather than affecting party policies and personnel. For example, a new first district COPE began to operate on a year-round basis in the mid-1960s with as many as 200 members. But it supported rather than opposed the party and backed Congressman Dawson in his hard-fought 1966 primary contest against a much more ideological civil-rights militant. The party organization also raised no general objection to the 1960 national COPE drive to register voters among Democratic Spanish-speaking and black groups. Registering new and perhaps undependable voters from these groups may have unsettled some Chicago party precinct captains, but it was much less threatening than the open primary contests staged by Abner's organization. Even so, Phil Weightman, an assistant national director of COPE, carefully went outside the party's allies in the Chicago Federation of Labor when he selected John Yancey, a close personal friend, to lead the registration drive in Chicago. Yancey's bargaining and organizing activities for the regional AFL-CIO had kept him out of Chicago politics. Although he consulted COPE's central card file and a committee of union staff personnel, Yancey in turn relied primarily on his own union contacts to recruit the thirty-five workers whom COPE hired for the drive. These workers, who canvassed door to door for about four hours a day in such apparently promising areas as public housing projects, contacted the residents regardless of union membership. Yancey's workers belonged to unions not usually interested in political action. One south-side black waiters' union had a business agent and six waitresses distribute a leaflet that publicized registration procedures. The agent and the waitresses personally knew most of the precinct captains in the area, and they emphasized to the party that they were not troublemakers but only wanted to register more Democrats. In the sixth ward, the agent spoke directly to the alderman, who had been supported by his local in previous elections.

Reflecting a similar prudence, Yancey did not try to multiply his limited staff by recruiting unpaid volunteers. Even so, the entire operation hardly aroused the party's enthusiasm, and the south-side party ward organizations generally left the COPE workers to fend for themselves. This was not the case, however, in the far more politically sensitive west-side twenty-fourth ward. Although the incumbent Jewish precinct captains who lived outside the ward wanted to control the organization to protect their jobs, the black assistant captains were already beginning to struggle among themselves for future control. Both groups feared that the COPE workers would register voters who could not be counted on. As a result, both groups tried to turn their friends against the COPE canvassers as "intruders." In the end, national COPE was extremely dissatisfied with the registration drive in Chicago's black areas, blaming the general political situation in the city, rather than Yancey or his workers. Chicago did not participate in national COPE's 1964 drive.

Yancey's registration activities among Spanish-speaking Mexicans and Puerto Ricans encountered much less party opposition. This minority was much less numerous and it was so spread out geographically that it could not hope to control any single ward organization. The fact that there were only a few Spanish-speaking party captains throughout the city and that the party was generally reluctant to register these minorities made Mexican and Puerto Rican organizations eager to cooperate with COPE. Yancey did not speak Spanish, and he assigned direction of the COPE program to Rachel Guajardo, a Packing House Workers staff member. Because there were few Spanish-speaking leaders in Chicago unions, Miss Guajardo turned to Mexican and Puerto Rican civic organizations affiliated with the Cardinal's Committee for the Spanish Speaking to provide most of the workers. As an outside figure, she helped the two communities coordinate their efforts. With COPE funds she hired six field leaders to instruct the workers in registration techniques, to schedule assignments, and to supervise door-to-door activities in areas where Spanish-speaking residents were numerous.

The organizations associated with the cardinal's committee thought the registration drive so successful that they decided to "finish the job" with a get-out-the-vote drive. For a week, members of the two communities contacted by mail or in person newly registered voters with Spanish surnames. COPE played no official role; Miss Guajardo returned to her union duties and only participated during her spare time. Yet the original stimulus of COPE's initiative and money increased the capacity of a small but heavily Democratic ethnic group to articulate interests that the party might consider and aggregate.

In Los Angeles, party opposition could not have blocked labor's aggregating activities among minority groups. On the contrary, party and COPE organizations were both so diffuse that they jointly, if not always harmoniously or successfully, tried to bring Mexicans and black voters into the party coalition as active partners. Indeed, their aggregating efforts extended beyond voter registration to the election of blacks and Mexicans to public office. This symbolic and psychological reward also increased the likelihood that the interests of these groups on public policy matters would be considered by the party. The political emergence of both minority groups was hindered not only by their lack of money, weak political consciousness, and disorganization but also by the general fragmentation of Los Angeles politics. Until 1963, only one Los Angeles black assemblyman, Augustus Hawkins, held any major elective office. Meanwhile, a series of short-lived black political organizations followed one another in bewildering succession without establishing a channel for political influence.[8] The Los Angeles labor movement itself had fewer important black leaders than Detroit or even Chicago unions, and the local Negro-American Labor Council exercised almost no influence.

The growth of the black population, as well as redistricting, did enable the black voters to elect several important officials in the 1960s. In 1962, they elected two assemblymen and sent Hawkins to Congress; three blacks gained seats on the city council in 1963, and in 1965 another won a seat on the city board of education in an at-large election. In these contests, labor and party leaders both played a significant but characteristically uneven role. Whereas Hawkins easily won election to Congress in 1962 on his own (labor and the party did endorse him), both groups worked enthusiastically for Douglas Jones' 1965 election to the school board. The victories of the two black assemblymen presented a similarly mixed picture. Because blacks made up a clear majority of the Democratic primary vote in the redrawn fifty-fifth district, both labor and party leaders had urged veteran white Assemblyman Vernon Kilpatrick to retire. When he refused, they finally agreed to support him in one last campaign. Kilpatrick then lost the primary to a politically unknown black minister, F. Douglas Ferrell, who relied mainly on his church associations and the straightforward assertion that a black man ought to represent a black district. No organized party faction, including labor, played any role other than to resist the change. None even considered Ferrell as a possible winner.

Although the outcome in the other overwhelmingly black assembly district also surprised many leaders, the two major primary candidates were better known, and some unions figured in the outcome. The victor, Mervyn Dymally, an ally of Assembly Speaker Jesse Unruh, had belonged to the UAW for ten years and to the American Federation of Teachers for five. Dymally had also served as treasurer of the California Young Democrats and as minorities coordinator for the 1960 Kennedy campaign in southern California. He had successfully agitated to keep open a popular state-subsidized child care center for working mothers and organized a group of black Democratic clubs that helped him win the primary endorsement of the Democratic club movement.

Dymally ran against Congressman Hawkins' brother Edward, a former city commissioner who evidently lacked Dymally's personal dynamism. Hawkins had the support of the top Democratic club leaders with whom he had previously worked as treasurer of the county committee, Central Labor Council Secretary Bassett, and the labor council's two Negro vice-presidents, Willard Pollard and Spencer Wiley. Dymally's supporters charged that Pollard and Wiley feared a young, ambitious leader who might challenge their position in the black community. But opposition of these three men meant the COPE board was likely to endorse Hawkins, providing him with a presumably valuable asset in the lower-class black area. To block this development, Dymally could count on his own teachers' union; the laborers' union, whose black leader disliked Pollard and Wiley; and the Amalgamated Clothing Workers, because the son of its manager had worked with Dymally in the Young Democrats. Most important, another Unruh supporter, John Geagen, of Building Service

Employees International Union (BSEIU) arranged for Dymally to join the BSEIU's state employee local and to become a delegate to the Los Angeles Labor Council where he met other labor leaders. Geagen helped win over the influential IBEW Local 11 and the Steelworkers. Finally, BSEIU's black representative at the crucial COPE board meeting loudly protested that Edward Hawkins did not live in the district, that he was not a union member, and that Pollard and Wiley were not the only black labor leaders in Los Angeles. Together, these efforts kept COPE from making any endorsement.

During the campaign, the Building Service Union sent two enthusiastic mailings on Dymally to its many members in the assembly district, gave him considerable publicity in its paper, and provided the largest of his union financial contributions. Union members also accounted for many of the precinct workers who worked in the Dymally campaign.

Labor has also played an uneven role in dealing with the Los Angeles Mexican community. Like black voters, the Mexicans made an increasing number of political demands during the late 1950s and early 1960s, ranging from charges of police brutality and job discrimination to claims of exclusion from public, union, and Democratic party office. A Mexican candidate's ethnic appeal almost defeated an incumbent liberal assemblyman, Edward Elliot, in the 1962 primary, and Mexicans did win four Democratic primary contests for the state assembly and one for Congress. All but one of the assembly candidates won in the November general election. In some ways, however, the Mexicans were even less well organized than the Negroes. For its part, organized labor tried to encourage this largely Democratic group to increase its political activity. But the unions found themselves confronting a problem typical of those faced by any political leaders who attempt to aggregate a group into a partisan coalition. Like party leaders, the union officials could accede to some demands but had to resist others. Typically, the only Mexican officeholder in Los Angeles up to 1963, City Councilman and later Congressman Edward Roybal, established a durable reputation by articulating the feelings of both Mexicans and Negroes against discrimination and alleged police brutality. But he did not receive labor support when he first won election to the city council by defeating an aging prolabor incumbent, and his unsuccessful race against another councilman for county supervisor attracted major union support only from the industrial unions. The building-trades unions and the large AFL Central Labor Council honored their commitments to Roybal's veteran opponent. Some Mexicans in Los Angeles concluded that labor generally passed over Mexican candidates as unelectable. They pointed out that Henry Lopez was the only Democratic statewide candidate in 1958 who was not endorsed by labor.

Most union leaders also opposed the incorporation of the predominantly Mexican East Los Angeles area as a separate city, although they did little except putting out a few mailings and encouraging a speech against incorporation by Mexican labor leaders. One union official who opposed incorporation conceded that this opposition partly reflected the reluctance of some union leaders to deal with a suburban government controlled by Mexicans. But he also asserted that the opposition was consistent with similar stands against the incorporation of small cities throughout the county. Labor spokesmen consistently argued that by comparison with the county government that controlled such unincorporated areas, these new cities were often more easily influenced by business interests, paid poorer wages, and were harder to organize. Some liberal labor leaders also felt that once incorporated, East Los Angeles would be a lower-class Mexican ghetto with a permanently inadequate tax base. In this case, aggregation of many interests into a single political program meant resisting and antagonizing some Mexicans.

On the other hand, Los Angeles unions did try to incorporate Mexicans into political life as Democratic party supporters. The Central Labor Council opposed Roybal very reluctantly when he ran for supervisor and supported him for lieutenant governor in 1954. It also endorsed Roybal's reelection campaigns to the council and broke with Speaker Unruh by supporting Roybal in the 1962 Democratic congressional primary. Although J. J. Rodriguez was the only Mexican officer of the Central Labor Council in the early 1960s, COPE helped elect James Cruz of the Brick and Clay Workers as third vice-president of the Democratic county committee in 1963. Finally, labor increasingly concentrated its registration activities on Mexican as well as on black areas that had many Democrats. It directly subsidized the registration activities of the Mexican Community Service Organization (cso), which at the same time strengthened cso itself. Organized labor's relations with Mexicans thus followed the same somewhat sporadic pattern of aggregating activities that characterized its relations with Los Angeles blacks.

In Detroit, the liberal UAW extended its efforts to aggregate the demands of blacks (the city had relatively few Spanish-speaking residents) in an attempt to alter the basic policies and power relationships within the Democratic party and the city's entire political system. Indeed, the UAW helped build and lead a powerful labor-liberal-black coalition that deliberately and systematically sought to include black organizations in civic affairs and in partisan and nonpartisan politics. This coalition successfully sponsored a series of highly qualified black candidates who won election to positions on the city board of education, the Wayne State University Board of Governors, the Detroit city council, and state judicial and executive bodies. Detroit COPE also pursued its aggregating role with respect to policy. It insisted that Democrats in Michigan politics and labor's nonpartisan local candidates take strong positions in support of civil rights.

The 1957 nonpartisan city council elections in Detroit may have marked the high point of this close cooperation. The UAW enthusiastically supported William Patrick, Jr., who became the council's first black member. In turn, black leaders backed state representative Ed Carey, a former UAW international representative who formed a joint campaign team with Patrick. In 1960, despite Senator Kennedy's rather moderate record on civil rights and some other domestic issues, which had antagonized some black militants, the state party leaders decided to support him as the most likely liberal to win the nomination. At this point the leading blacks in COPE cooperated with UAW leaders and Governor Williams in swinging the Michigan delegate caucus to Kennedy at the national convention. By 1961, however, strains were clearly evident. Black leaders went into open revolt in the Miriani-Cavanaugh mayoral election.

Despite the rift, the UAW-led liberal coalition, by bringing together a wide range of black groups, helped organize the black community to play an independent political role in articulating civil-rights demands unusual in Northern cities before 1963. Although black professional and business groups were often rather quiescent politically in Northern cities, Detroit's Cotillion Club took the initiative in suing the city's white realtors for conspiring to segregate the real estate market. In both 1957 and 1961, the club worked closely with labor for liberal civil-rights candidates in local election campaigns for councilman. But in 1961 it joined black union groups in backing Cavanaugh against COPE's candidate Miriani, illustrating the limits of COPE's power.

Within the UAW, many black shop stewards, committeemen, and rank and file members also acquired unusual political experience and sophistication by participating not only in campaign work for the Democrats but in the union's usually intense factional life. Many of these members, for example, organized block clubs, which in 1962 were much more common in Detroit than in either Chicago or Los Angeles. Like the precinct captain in the patronage-oriented party organization, the clubs concerned themselves with improvement of such city services as garbage collections, street lighting, and street paving.[9] Unlike the captains, however, clubs also encouraged their members to become politically active and demanded a moratorium on mortgage foreclosures during Detroit's high unemployment in the years before 1963. The clubs' political program also included support for ordinances curbing flophouses and pawn shops and opposition to permits for commercial or industrial zoning variances in black residential areas.

From one point of view, then, the Detroit-area UAW's success at aggregating blacks into the Democratic party coalition in effect simply encouraged the city's blacks to articulate their own demands independently. But as blacks approached a third of the city's total population (the nonwhite, mostly Negro, population in Detroit itself rose from 16.4 percent in 1950 to 29.2 percent ten years later), the party and COPE itself became increasingly dependent on black support. During the early 1960s the Trade Union Leadership Council (TULC), the most active and effective local affiliate of the Negro-American Labor Council, became the major instrument for this pressure.*

---

* Significantly, although TULC had members from other unions, including the laborers, Hotel and Restaurant Workers, Steelworkers, bus drivers, and

TULC made discrimination against blacks within the trade unions themselves an important target. Despite the UAW's outstanding record on race relations as compared with other American unions, TULC attracted many black local officials in the UAW who felt that racial discrimination retarded their advancement to higher union positions. During World War II, the union's communist fraction had proposed a constitutional provision reserving a black seat on the UAW board. The Reuther caucus, supported by several TULC leaders who were present, rejected the proposal as inverted racism.[10] But by 1962, there was still no black representation on the board, and TULC accused the Reuther caucus of bad faith. Its leaders started to make public protests, published magazine articles on the issue, and threatened an embarrassing floor fight at the 1962 convention. All this threatened to hurt the UAW's position as a leading liberal force within the Democratic coalition. When the Reuther caucus agreed that a black should be elected, TULC leaders joined with black militants in Chicago and insisted on either their own most influential member, Horace Sheffield, or Willoughby Abner from Chicago. But the Reuther caucus considered these two leaders unacceptable and angered TULC and its allies by choosing Jack Edwards, a black staff member who had worked on negotiations more than on civil rights or political activities.

In 1961 TULC carried its fight for more black officers to a number of UAW local unions, including the largest, Ford Local 600. The council complained that this local, by its sheer size a force in Dearborn politics, had not really fought Mayor Hubbard's public policy of excluding blacks from the city. After failing to enlist the international union as an ally, TULC turned to an extreme left group. Carl Stellatto, incumbent president of Local 600, responded by running an unprecedented all-white slate and won narrowly.

TULC's critics in the 1962 struggle over the executive board positions accused it of racism, citing the Local 600 election for con-

---

dairy employees, most of its members were Autoworkers. TULC reinforced its ideological and political appeals to this diverse group with the solidary incentives of a private club. Its members were encouraged to spend their leisure time at its headquarters, which functioned as a clubhouse with a liquor license. The council also maintained an active program of social, educational, and social action activities.

firmation. They saw in it an unpleasant resemblance to the special caucuses, communist, socialist, Catholic, and others, that had divided the UAW in its early years. They pointed out that TULC attacked racism, but did not support Lucien Nedzi, a white who was the one major candidate in the 1961 primary election in the first congressional district who openly opposed the rampant racial appeals in the campaign. TULC leaders felt such criticism was motivated by self-interest. "We have to deal with a lot of insecure people," said one, "and TULC is a challenge to their interests; the most important thing to them is their jobs." They conceded that in the 1930s the CIO brought the black worker a new protection for his job through seniority and equal treatment in the plant. But, in their view, blacks were now demanding an equal voice in policy and leadership positions, and would not tolerate subordination to white leaders.

At the same time, however, TULC and other Negro groups applied pressure in partisan politics. Before the 1964 reapportionment, black Democrats regularly attacked Polish domination of party and COPE organizations in the first congressional district. In the fifteenth district, blacks also attacked both the white congressman and the party chairman although both men had liberal civil-rights records and had even earned the support of some TULC leaders. These problems were eliminated in 1964 only because black Democrats in the legislature, acting independently, supported a Republican redistricting plan that created a second black-dominated congressional district.

Conflict between unions and black groups in Detroit is somewhat restrained by the considerable overlap of their constituencies. Most of Detroit's blacks are workers, and many of them are members of the UAW. In addition, unions and the blacks have been among the biggest and the most faithful supporters of the liberal-Democratic party coalition. Conflict was further contained at times by divisions within the Detroit black community itself as black militance increased. In 1964, TULC lost much of its power when its candidate for the newly created black congressional district narrowly lost the Democratic primary to John Conyers. The winning candidate belonged to another, equally radical, faction that had split off from TULC and created a rival organization. Significantly, Conyers enjoyed the support of Jack Edwards, the UAW staff official who had been elected to the UAW Executive Board over TULC opposition. Similar splits also appeared in Los Angeles, although typically they have taken a much less organized form. Spencer Wiley of the UAW sought to recoup some of the prestige he lost in futilely opposing Mervyn Dymally by siding with Congressman Augustus Hawkins and anti-Unruh civil-rights militants against the administration of the War on Poverty programs in Los Angeles. Nevertheless, as black demands mounted, the capacity of the UAW in Detroit to control them declined. Even the regular party organization in Chicago lost influence. By the mid-1960s, black militancy not only produced the election of several insurgent black aldermen and state senators in south-side Chicago wards, but a reduction of UAW influence within the Democratic party organization in Detroit's black congressional districts.

Organized labor's efforts to aggregate minority groups into the party show the intimate relation between interest aggregation and articulation. By aggregating, that is, incorporating the party's constituent groups directly, the unions encouraged them to articulate their own interests through political activity. As a result *the labor movement subjected itself to the pressures that articulating interest groups usually bring to bear on parties*. The Detroit UAW in particular invited this pressure by helping channel black grievances and frustrations into the party system, which then became pressure on COPE as a party leader. For very different reasons—the blacks' own disorganization in Los Angeles and the resistance of the party organization in Chicago—these grievances were not as extensively articulated in the early 1960s in the politics of Los Angeles or Chicago. But the political militancy of Detroit's unions enabled them to open up their city's political system to their black allies so that by 1961 black voters could play a decisive role—in the face of COPE's own disapproval—in ousting an incumbent mayor. In this sense, by providing an opportunity for relatively moderate political protest, organized labor, as its left-wing critics claim, did function as part of the "establishment." Of course, neither the labor movement nor its leaders belong to a social establishment in terms of status, nor to an economic establishment in terms of wealth. But, in addition to the moderation of union militancy described in Chapter II and its relatively conservative position on many foreign policy questions, the labor movement's efforts to aggregate the interests of minority groups in response to charges of conservatism by Negroes and Spanish-speaking voters indicate how completely it became a part of the established American political order as represented by the two-party system.

As Almond and others have observed, peak associations of interest groups like the AFL-CIO frequently carry on aggregating activities outside the party system.[11] In the cases described here, however, labor has helped aggregate groups that are much more completely in the *party*'s political constituency rather than in the ranks of union members themselves. Labor was acting more as the party's electoral arm than as a separate pressure group. Miss Guajardo, for example, helped register Spanish-speaking citizens in Chicago even though so few of them were members of trade unions that she had to rely on Catholic civic groups to undertake the operation. In Detroit, many of COPE's black allies, including some UAW members, believed that they owed more loyalty to the Michigan Democratic party, or to some racial or civil-rights group, than to their union. Yet these same facts also demonstrate that the interests and membership of the labor movement were sufficiently diverse to overlap with the interests and membership of those ethnic groups it sought to activate politically. Labor's large membership, by far the biggest of any organized Democratic party group, obviously facilitated its efforts to aggregate non-labor groups. The breadth of labor's economic constituency, in other words, enabled it to act on behalf of the still larger political constituency of the party.

Aggregation and Intraparty Factionalism

The preceding chapters have made clear that organized labor's political energies were by no means entirely absorbed by the direct aggregation of particular ethnic groups into the party's constituency. In addition to its campaign activities, the labor movement had a strong incentive to influence the party's selection of policies, tactics, and candidates who might appeal to all party groups and thus serve to aggregate diverse interests. These concerns, of course, meant involvement in factional partisan conflict with both professional, patronage-oriented politicians and ideological amateurs. The battles with professional politicians, as described in earlier chapters can be attributed to three factors: first, an overt conflict of organizational interests; second, disagreement over questions of government policies; and third, differences in political style. In the latter case, COPE emphasized the collective benefits of welfare-state politics whereas the professional politician stressed individual patronage and advancement. COPE mainly recruited its workers by appeals to welfare-state issues rather than offering them specific material inducements, and in turn these workers used an issue-oriented approach when they talked with voters. Pro-COPE unions in Detroit and Chicago, therefore, favored much more attention to explicit issues criteria and formal endorsing procedures in selecting candidates than did the professionals.[12] As a result, party regulars had an obvious organizational interest in resisting the influence of independent COPE organizations that not only had candidates of their own, but also threatened the professionals' entire mode of operating, which depended on personal understandings and informal alliances.

James Q. Wilson, several years before the present study was written, used these same three areas of conflict—organizational interest, policy preferences and political style—to explain organized labor's disputes with the issue-oriented amateur Democrats. He pointed out, for example, that in Los Angeles the political style of the lower-class Harry S Truman Democratic Club differed decidedly from that of middle-class clubs. Its working-class members primarily wanted "to defeat the incumbent Republican assemblyman and elect a Democratic President who would deal with bread-and-butter issues." With the help of a UAW local, the club was active in the 1960 campaign, but it

> was quite unlike a middle-class CDC unit. It never had more than thirty members, only fifteen of whom were active and most of whom quit as soon as the election was over. The club never had regular meetings [and] never drew up a constitution . . .[13]

In 1962, after Wilson completed his research, there were a considerable number of working-class clubs throughout Los Angeles County, for example, in the twenty-fifth congressional district, that persisted longer, held more regular meetings, and discussed more issues than the Harry S Truman Club. These issues, however, were usually those immediately relevant to the membership. For example, a Negro group discussed the new state fair employment practices act, and the Jimmy Roosevelt Club considered local zoning problems. Many lower-class and lower–middle-class suburban clubs were more interested in those same local issues (e.g., schools and streets) that concerned the precinct captains in Chicago than in more remote state and national issues. In the 1962 county committee fight, some of the labor members who voted for the Unruh-labor slate reported that they were put off by the middle-class style—the rhetoric and mannerisms—of the club candidate for county chairman.

These differences were paralleled by conflicts over government policy outputs. Labor felt that these policies reflected the very different constituencies of the clubs and trade unions. Some labor leaders, for example, wanted a less conciliatory foreign policy toward Communist China than did the clubs; others agreed with the clubs; and still others were indifferent. Almost all, however, were more concerned with domestic issues and feared that militant left-wing positions on foreign policy and civil liberties would hurt the party and reduce the possibility of passing liberal welfare legislation. Of course, the middle-class club members publicly and emphatically favored these same programs. But the programs claimed to provide relatively more economic benefit to most union members and to other wage earners than to middle-income liberals. For example, middle income club members might be hurt economically by the redistributive tax policies they favor. In addition, unions also had a more direct organizational interest in the outcome of partisan conflict over domestic issues than the clubs, because union activities were directly regulated by the federal government. As Wilson suggested, the club members' commitment to their vision of a good political order may have been more important to them than electing moderate Democrats who simply favored further extensions of the welfare state. At any rate, many labor leaders concluded that as representatives of the workers they had a greater immediate stake in the party's victory than did the issue-oriented amateurs.*

These differences were intensified by a clear conflict of organizational interests. Apart from the clubs, whose conventions regularly endorsed candidates in Democratic primaries, and the Citizen's Committee for Old Age Pensions, unions were the mass-membership organizations most closely associated with the party, and their pre-primary endorsements were highly valued. As the party's chief endorsing organization, the club movement, which also had a "grass roots" membership, challenged labor's position. As one labor leader put it, "We'd just like to have more influence; perhaps we haven't gone into the clubs enough." Indeed, labor leaders and others charged that in 1962 the clubs were no longer, if they ever had been, grass roots organizations, but that they were run by power-hungry leaders for their own ends. In effect, this meant a recognition that the power of labor was threatened by the clubs, at least under their leaders in 1962. In 1962, union leaders also felt that the county committee leadership favored the clubs and ignored labor whereas the anticlub state committee leaders had inaugurated bimonthly meetings with top union officials. One Los Angeles labor leader actually made the same complaint about the clubs that some Chicago COPE leaders made concerning the Democratic organization in Chicago, "they were treating us as if we had no place else to go."†

In terms of organizational interest, then, both the clubs in Los

---

* Of course, civil liberties and foreign policy issues have important consequences—and often for more people—than do domestic issues. However, none of these issues, with the exception of the peace issue, affected the club members personally because they were usually from higher-income groups and had less to gain from welfare-state measures. On the other hand, it is also true that labor did not find its relations with Speaker Unruh, the club's arch enemy, wholly satisfactory. Unruh backed some Democratic candidates who were conservative on welfare issues, and labor was sometimes unhappy with Unruh's own record in the legislature. Meanwhile, however, labor's opposition to the clubs also increased in the middle 1960s. The California Democratic Council's president openly attacked the Johnson administration's Vietnam policy, much to the distress of many California union leaders.

† Consistent with Los Angeles' factional fluidity, these leaders were much less hostile to some of the clubs' favorite officeholders, like Lieutenant Governor Anderson and State Senator Richards, who did work with labor.

Angeles and the regulars in Chicago saw labor as a competing faction within the party. On questions of issue and style the professional politicians resented labor's tendency to emphasize public issues as criteria for policy making and formal organizational procedures. Yet the amateurs made the opposite complaint. They charged that in order to win elections the labor movement too willingly compromised even its own limited goals. But questions of style and issues, that is, decisions on personnel and policies, involve the main techniques by which a party aggregates interests within its electoral coalition. The contradictory complaints of its fellow Democratic partisans thus illuminate organized labor's intermediate position—between purely ideological and purely pluralist orientations—in the party's factional competition over the proper method of aggregation. Indeed, although he points out that they are analytic definitions of pure types rather than descriptions of reality,[14] Wilson's picture of the typical amateur and professional politician makes clear that questions of aggregation are a major source of intraparty conflict.

In the professional's view, as Wilson puts it, politics "consists of concrete questions and specific persons who must be dealt with in a manner that will 'keep everybody happy' and thus minimize the possibility of defeat at the next election." He aims "not at producing the good society, but at gaining power and place for one's self and one's party." By contrast, politics for the amateur "is the determination of public policy . . . [which] ought to be set deliberately rather than as the accidental by-product of a struggle for personal and party advantage. Issues ought to be settled on their merits."[15] Although these differences conform in part to the size-of-unit approach frequently referred to in this study, both groups try to win electoral majorities, that is, to assemble large partisan constituencies. The basic issue, therefore, is less the scope or size of the constituency than how to aggregate it. The professional politicians, who dominated the Chicago party, *aggregated pluralistically* by dispensing many discrete benefits to a constituency that they saw as a collection of relatively small and distinct groups, each with its own interests. Classic examples of such aggregation include congressional logrolling on rivers and harbors or tariff legislation in which each area or industry backs other groups' projects in return for support on its own projects.[16] The legislation that results, represents an aggregation of various group interests and demands, but not a common program that appeals—as a whole—to its supporters. By contrast, programmatic issue-oriented politicians, such as the amateurs, saw their constituency as a group united by a set of common or at least generally compatible political interests. They tried to *aggregate by principle,* for example, by uniformly distributing the collective benefits of welfare-state programs to the entire constituency of lower-class voters. These programmatic politicians were less likely to cater individually to numerous particular ethnic, regional, or narrower economic interests.[17]

Organized labor quarreled with both the programmatic amateurs and the more pragmatic professionals, because most unionists did not fully agree with either's method of aggregating. On the one hand, the AFL-CIO unmistakably favored the expansion of the welfare state, a policy that served to unite union members politically, and it adopted an ideology appropriate to this viewpoint. Competition for narrower benefits distributed more pluralistically by region or by industry might have divided the AFL-CIO's own membership and thus weakened the entire movement.[18] In addition, labor favored programs designed to benefit wage earners as a whole. Yet, unlike the amateur Democrats' ideological concern, the labor movement's goals specifically included the organizational interests of particular unions, the regulation of picketing, for example, as well as the economic interests of workers already organized in unions. Moreover, the unions were less outraged than the amateurs with a view of politics that emphasized material benefits as a primary reward for the political activists. As Chapter X shows, the interests of unorganized workers like migrant laborers were sometimes given a lower priority. In sum, organized labor favored aggregating the party constituency by principle provided that one left room for the pluralistic aggregation of some of its narrower interests. It is within this context that many of the basic cleavages between labor and other factions within the Democratic party can be best understood.

Aggregation Within the Party:
Organized Labor as a Democratic Faction

As in the case of organizer labor's direct aggregation of Democratically inclined minority groups, union influence as an intraparty faction varied with the distribution of organizational resources in different cities. In every case, however, labor could not entirely avoid conflict or at least tension with other major party groups.

Given their exclusion from most party decisions, some pro-COPE unions in Chicago occasionally combined with issue-oriented liberals to back insurgent candidates, especially in the fifth ward area around the University of Chicago.[19] The most direct clash occurred in 1950 when labor supported UAW Citizenship Director Willoughby Abner for state senator. In most cases, however, these conflicts with the party reflected unusual circumstances. Insurgent Leon Despres had liberal and labor support in his successful campaigns for alderman in 1955, 1959, and 1963, although his 1955 support for Robert Merriam, a Republican mayoral candidate, deprived him of many formal union endorsements in his first race. As a labor lawyer, Despres had acquired a large number of union acquaintances who personally served on his campaign committee and secured financial contributions. Moreover, two middle-level CIO leaders, Willoughby Abner and Walter Schaible of the Steelworkers, on their own initiative sent black campaign workers into the black areas of the ward where Despres' white middle-class supporters were not particularly effective. By 1959, Despres' public support of most Democratic candidates in the 1956 election and his prolabor record on open occupancy, public housing, and grievance procedures for city workers led to wider union support.* In 1956, most unions also strongly supported Democratic insurgent Abner Mikva for state representative for the same south-side area. As a labor lawyer himself and a law partner of Arthur Goldberg, who was then USA general counsel and special counsel for the CIO, Mikva appealed to a variety of unions.

---

* The most important exception in 1959 was provided by the Steelworkers, who were then trying to build a close relationship with the party.

These special circumstances reduced the significance of labor's break with the party. State representatives and aldermen did not directly affect the party's supply of patronage. Moreover, Despres succeeded a series of independent aldermen from his ward, and in 1963 and 1967, he was even supported by the party's own ward organization. In Mikva's case the district had been newly created by reapportionment, so that he did not oust an incumbent Democrat. In addition, the party ward organizations had been themselves divided, and the party finally nominated a little-known candidate. When Mikva proved a popular legislator, the party followed a common pattern and endorsed him for reelection.

Those factors continued to affect the possibility of labor challenging the party. In 1962, John Carney, a liberal Catholic with an impressive record as a lobbyist and citizen in the field of race relations, the adjustment of Puerto Rican migrants to Chicago life, and liberal legislation in Illinois, ran for state representative against Harry Bauler. Labor gave him little support, although liberal union leaders made a few financial contributions. In his quest for labor support, Carney was handicapped by labor's perception of his poor chance for success, his failure to contact labor leaders early enough in the campaign, and the commitment of the party to electing Bauler, the son of a well-known ward committeeman. Moreover, Carney, unlike Mikva or Despres, was not a labor lawyer. Indeed, in the Mikva and Despres campaigns, the party recognized the unions' special obligation to each man just as it recognized that Democratic ethnic groups sometimes voted for Republicans out of ethnic loyalty. Both men, and later Robert Mann, a liberal state representative from Mikva's district, were seen as spokesmen of their labor-liberal supporters in the area, much as Polish Democrats, for example, represent Polish voters elsewhere.

Even these mitigated conflicts, however, became relatively less and less common. When Mikva tried to oust an incumbent congressman in 1966 the party bitterly opposed him as did the Steelworkers and the second district COPE the union controlled. Although the UAW and some smaller unions supported Mikva, the first congressional district COPE, in which the Autoworkers were an important force, opposed a black insurgent who ran in the same primary against Willoughby Abner's old antagonist William Dawson.

In the 1960s, the rest of the Chicago labor movement increasingly contented itself with trying to influence the party organization's decision before the primary. In this case too, union influence varied considerably, as illustrated by labor's role when the party nominated nonincumbent candidates for governor in 1960 and senator in 1962. In 1960, the organization chose Cook County Judge Otto Kerner.[20] A Protestant who would help balance the Kennedy ticket, Kerner presented a good-government image that party leaders hoped would attract independent voters to the ticket and thus defeat Cook County State's Attorney Benjamin Adamowski, a Republican. For a number of reasons the party leadership did not seriously consult union officials in choosing Kerner. COPE was already totally committed to work for the ticket because it strongly supported both Kennedy and Senator Paul Douglas. In any case, the unpopularity of the Republican incumbent, William Stratton, made Kerner a likely winner. And the party particularly wanted to make the decision itself because the governor controls a sizable block of patronage in Illinois.

The reaction of the two strongest COPE unions to this *fait accompli* illustrated their limited but not entirely powerless position within the party. Kerner faced two major opponents in the Democratic primary. Former Democratic National Chairman Stephen Mitchell, a downstate candidate who lacked experience as a public official, was not seriously considered by most Chicago labor leaders. But the liberal stands of the other candidate, State Treasurer Joseph Lohman, impressed many labor people, particularly the Steelworkers. Lohman's many speeches at the union's meetings had earned him wide popularity among local union officers and members, as well as the gratitude of the USA's top leaders. And if Lohman had then won the election, which was a possibility if Mitchell had withdrawn, the Steelworkers would have dominated labor politics in the state for many years. In any case, the union could hope that an independent stand would elicit more respectful treatment from the party.

A minority of UAW activists led by Willoughby Abner also supported Lohman as the more liberal and promising candidate, because Kerner was not on public record on many liberal issues and had little administrative experience. They also felt that this race allowed the union to protest the tendency of the party to ignore it. But the UAW leadership, bent on improving its relations with the party, found Kerner quite promising and Lohman too ambitious and unreliable. The UAW officially voted to support Kerner. After Kerner easily won the primary and the general election, he handsomely rewarded the UAW for its support and pointedly ignored the USA. When two Chicago Federation of Labor leaders, Steven Bailey and William McFetridge, both insisted on naming the new state director of labor, Kerner appointed UAW Director Robert Johnston as an interim compromise. As director, Johnston rejuvenated factory inspection programs, hired qualified inspectors, and initiated stringent regulations of migrant labor. He also helped pilot through the legislature large increases in workmen's and unemployment compensation as well as a Fair Employment Practices Commission (FEPC) bill. But, as indicated above, UAW officials were made particularly uncomfortable when, as members of the administration, they had to support Kerner's sales-tax increase, which the USA felt free to oppose.

This episode did not indicate that pro-COPE unions were totally impotent politically. The Steelworkers' support for Lohman was much more a calculated demonstration of independence than a complete rupture of relations. The union gained little influence at the state level, but this defeat did not visibly reduce the Steelworkers' influence on the policies and appointments of the Chicago party organization. It may even have increased the party's estimate of the union's importance. For its part, the UAW leadership traded acquiescence on Kerner's nomination for considerable subsequent influence on policies and, thus, on the party's overall appeal to its varied constituency. Even when they were not consulted in advance, the big industrial unions exercised some indirect impact on policy decisions.

There were also some circumstances where labor more directly influenced the party's behavior, although it almost never controlled it. Democratic party chieftains apparently still remember that in 1950 labor's apathy hurt the entire ticket when labor refused to work for Senator Scott Lucas because he had supported the Taft-Hartley Act. In 1956, labor was also unenthusiastic about the party's unsuccessful gubernatorial candidate. Under certain conditions, then, the party actively tried to anticipate labor's reaction.[21] It asked not whom labor wanted but whether or not the choice of a specific candidate would prompt labor to lose interest in the campaign.

The 1962 senatorial campaign offers a case in point. Mayor Daley asked UAW Director Johnston to speak before the party slating committee on behalf of liberal Congressman Sidney Yates. Despite the mayor's influence in the party, he still had to persuade the committee to slate his candidate, and he knew Yates' record and political style attracted the industrial unions. If Johnston expressed his support before the committee, he would indicate the congressman's wide appeal and hence suggest that independent sources of campaign funds would be available. For his part Johnston was willing to support the nomination of a candidate popular with COPE-oriented unions.

The party's greater solicitude for labor's opinions about Yates than about Kerner directly reflected the very different situation in 1962. By comparison with the governor, a U. S. Senator controls relatively little patronage, and the party had less to fear from outside influence. Moreover, running against the formidable incumbent Republican Everett Dirksen meant that Yates needed labor support far more than Kerner did. There were also no other top statewide candidates, like Kennedy and Douglas in 1960, who would have assured labor's enthusiastic participation.

As noted in earlier chapters, this generally marginal but somewhat varying role also characterized the union's participation in party decisions at the congressional-district level. Theoretically, COPE district organizations interviewed candidates and made recommendations to the state executive board. But as one leader euphemistically observed, "We don't try to dictate to the party. They have their own choice and we shouldn't interfere." In fact, the frequency and meaningfulness of these interviews were dubious at best. In the south suburban fourth congressional district, the Steelworkers acquired real influence, and in the tenth district in the western suburbs, where unions provided much of the congressional candidate's support, the interview at least enabled the COPE leaders and the candidate to become acquainted. In both areas, of course, the regular party organization had much less patronage than in the city. In the north-side eleventh district, COPE leaders may have helped sway the party slating committee to renominate Roman Pucinski in 1958, but the party ordinarily gave losing congressional candidates like Pucinski a second opportunity in any case. Because patronage was plentiful in the city, COPE had little more influence on party decisions in such middle-class areas as the eleventh district than in the poorer inner-city core, where the district COPEs often did very little. In most such cases, therefore, formal interviews would have had no meaning and COPE did not even attempt to conduct them.

The analysis of union influence on the Los Angeles Democratic party is complicated by the absence of meaningful party structures in the atomized politics of southern California. Nevertheless, labor achieved a significant although not decisive voice in the diffuse decision-making process that had emerged by the early 1960s. This role can hardly be compared to the UAW's position in Detroit, but it was certainly more important than that of Chicago COPE. Indeed, Los Angeles' professional Democratic politicians (i.e., the incumbent officeholders and their close associates), usually welcomed labor support in the 1960s. Most of these professionals were much closer to COPE's liberal position on domestic issues than members of the Chicago party were. Yet they also shared with most union leaders (outside the UAW) an enmity for the ideological Democratic club movement. Indeed, in the 1962 primaries, labor joined a coalition of party candidates headed by Speaker Jesse Unruh that ousted the leaders of the Los Angeles County Committee who favored the clubs, increasing at least its formal influence in party circles.

The Unruh forces triumphed by electing a majority of the members of the county committee, which included the party's legislative nominees and seven delegates from each assembly district. Because many unknowns ran in each district, winning usually depended on the candidate's place on the ballot (chosen by lot) and his occupation, which was listed on the ballot.[22] To secure firm control in this situation, the Unruh forces had to mount an unusually well planned and coordinated campaign to assemble a reliable majority. The coalition mailed a yellow card, or in some cases a sample ballot, to the registered Democrats in twenty-five of the county's thirty-one assembly districts. The card endorsed pro-Unruh candidates on behalf of several organizations, including the AFL-CIO. To increase its authentic appearance, the sample ballot, a photostatic copy of the official ballot, included the assembly, congressional, and state candidates who were endorsed by all party factions.

Organized labor participated prominently in the county committee election contests because COPE Director Thelma Thomas, who recognized an opportunity to increase labor's formal party influence, committed COPE immediately and later secured her board's approval. Labor's participation was not absolutely vital. It paid $1,500 for printing the yellow cards and helped distribute them in some districts. But the Unruh group had money of its own and could have used professional delivery firms throughout the county as it did in some districts. Similarly, almost all of the twenty or so county committee members who belonged to unions would probably have voted for the Unruh slate simply because they were already close associates of particular pro-Unruh assemblymen, or were themselves personally hostile to the clubs. In any case, the Unruh forces estimated that among the county committee members they had perhaps twenty votes in reserve that they could have produced by insisting on an open ballot—their successful technique in the previous state committee election. The AFL-CIO's most important contribution, therefore, was its simple presence in the coalition. Unruh and his associates sought this participation to acquire, as one said, "a cloak of respectability" for the operation. They felt that the AFL-CIO name on the yellow cards was somewhat more effective than the endorsement of individual unions, which could have easily been obtained from Unruh's labor allies. Certainly labor's open opposition would have been so damaging, one Unruh aide reflected, that "we never would have gotten into the fight in the first place." Labor's support thus lent legitimacy to one of the contestants in a critical intraparty contest.

Labor was rewarded for its efforts. Paul Posner, a labor attorney and son of the Amalgamated Clothing Workers' manager, was elected first vice-president of the county committee, and two years later became county chairman after the Unruh-labor coalition won a second victory. In addition, three union officials, including a Negro woman and a Mexican, were chosen second vice-president, third vice-president, and assistant treasurer of the committee in 1962. By themselves, these officers could do no more than provide labor points of access to a county committee that had extremely limited influence and resources. By fostering a more moderate party image through control of one of its formal bodies, however, COPE did further its view on the best way to aggregate the party's constituency. Certainly in the eyes of most labor leaders, this image would best aggregate the diverse congeries of Democratic groups, not all of whom responded to strongly ideological appeals.

COPE's influence in Detroit, of course, was still more obvious than in Los Angeles. Although the UAW lacked the votes itself to control the Detroit-area and Michigan Democratic party organizations, the union joined liberal and ethnic groups to secure a majority at the district, county, and state levels. For example, the UAW, with a small number of nonlabor Democrats, used this power to elect Zolton Ferency chairman of the state Democratic party in 1963. In ousting incumbent Joe Collins, they defeated most Democratic state and congressional officeholders, including Neil Staebler, national committeeman, congressman-at-large, and former state chairman. The UAW felt that Collins had irritated several key Democrats during his two-year tenure to the extent that he had divided rather than united the party. But Ferency could not have won without the votes of the Detroit area Autoworkers who went to the convention at their leaders' urging and won over five of the six Wayne County district delegations. This case demonstrated the Detroit UAW's ability to affect substantially the choice of policies and personnel by which the party aggregated the interests in its coalition.

A survey of the Wayne County congressional districts in the early 1960s (before they were substantially redrawn by the 1964 reapportionment) reveals a similar pattern. Despite this overall labor dominance, union influence among Detroit district party organizations was affected by two variables, the social class of district residents and availability of public office to political activists.[23] Specifically, COPE control was limited in some cases by the presence of middle-class Democrats in certain districts, as well as by the existence of strong patronage-oriented groups in the suburban sixteenth district. Overall, however, labor stood out as the strongest party faction in each district.

In the first district, which in 1960 had the lowest median education level and the second lowest median income in Wayne County, the UAW was so strong that COPE's only organized opposition came from Negroes, including some UAW members, who resented the Polish domination of the district party. The middle-class party chairmen in the district were selected by the COPE coordinator and depended on him for support. In fact, the coordinator unobtrusively controlled both the party and COPE organizations partly by the force of his personality and partly by dispensing payment for work on election day—a popular inducement in poor neighborhoods.

COPE was equally and more obviously dominant in the other inner-city district, the thirteenth, which, until 1964, ranked sixth in income and fifth in education of the six districts and was the only one in Michigan represented by a Negro in the U.S. House of Representatives. In 1960, when the UAW decided that the district's chairman, an official of the Garment Workers, had opposed COPE's influence, COPE easily ousted him and his supporters from office. As a result, all but one or two of the district party officers in 1962 belonged to COPE and it had the only district party chairman in Wayne County openly identified with the Autoworkers.

Within Detroit itself the west-side fifteenth district organization had the most active group life. The district included both lower- and upper-income areas, and ranked fourth in both education and income. A largely middle-class Jewish organization of amateur Democrats, who had first formed to work for Adlai Stevenson, covered the most northern section of the district. By 1962, over half the district's Democrats were black (as were over 46 percent of the district's entire population), and several black groups actively competed for patronage and party positions. Blacks were relatively well organized in the district—the home of TULC—because Detroit's west-side UAW locals traditionally elected more black officers than east-side locals.[24] Even so, the UAW remained the strongest force in the district. As a result, cooperation among these various groups directly reflected the preferences of a succession of able COPE co-ordinators who could have followed a very different policy had they wished to do so. In all three districts, the first, thirteenth, and fifteenth, COPE remained on relatively good terms with the incumbent congressmen.

Middle-class Democrats were more numerous and influential in the more prosperous and less overwhelmingly Democratic fourteenth and seventeenth Districts, although labor exercised firm control in both party organizations. In the seventeenth district, which ranked first in both income and education, a middle-class Democrat served as district party chairman for a decade until 1961. But as many of the most influential nonlabor liberals became absorbed in state party affairs under Governor Williams, their relations with labor began to deteriorate. In contrast to their position in the fifteenth district, members of Volunteers for Stevenson were ignored after the 1956 campaign in favor of the district's less independent Young Democrats. A group of nonlabor Democrats sporadically opposed COPE within the district party organization but had little success up to 1964. The middle-class character of the district was expressed, however, in the success of Congresswoman Martha Griffiths, who with the help of these insurgent Democrats won the 1954 Democratic primary over COPE opposition and then won the general election. From the first she pursued a highly independent course, refusing to consult labor as frequently as did most other Detroit Democrats in Congress.

In the early 1960s, COPE did not have a regularly assigned co-ordinator in the fourteenth district, which ranked third in both median income and education. As a result, the district party organization was controlled by a group of UAW local union leaders who dominated its executive board, effectively controlled the nonlabor chairman, and maintained close ties to Congressman Harold Ryan after he was elected early in 1962. The alignment in the district was somewhat complicated, though, by divisions both within the UAW and the nonlabor Democrats. Opposition to labor control had always been particularly strong in the district, usually led by a group of less programmatically oriented, predominately Irish Democrats. This group was usually opposed not only by the UAW but also by upper-income issue-oriented Democrats who lived in the residential eastern portions of the district, which included the well-to-do Grosse Pointes. But by 1962, these liberals, as well as top UAW leaders, had been alienated by the district party executive board's concern with appointments to party and public office. With the 1964 reapportionment, the UAW citizenship department assigned one of its ablest coordinators to the district, and for a time he succeeded in reasserting control at the expense of the local union leaders. Under his leadership a more independently minded and programmatic nonlabor Democrat became district party chairman.

In these five districts the solidity of COPE's dominant position before the 1964 reapportionment was inversely related to the educational and income levels in the districts. COPE was strongest in the first, thirteenth, and fifteenth districts where these levels were lowest; it faced the most persistent opposition in the fourteenth and seventeenth districts where these levels were relatively high. COPE also had to share power in the suburban sixteenth district, but the district's high income and educational levels were not the only, and probably not the most important, reason. Labor's position was also directly affected by the district's forty independent suburban governments, which provided a relatively large number of officially nonpartisan elective offices for district residents to fill. Since the sixteenth district was predominantly Democratic, most of the offices were likely to be filled by Democrats and the endorsement of the local Democratic club was a valuable asset. Accordingly, many aspiring politicians joined and worked for their local clubs in order to merit future support.[25]

The sixteenth district COPE, therefore, confronted a multitude of fairly active and independent party organizations whose patronage goals differed from labor's policy concerns. COPE's strategy was to work out an accommodation with these groups rather than try to drive them out of the party organization. In striking these bargains it could always rely on a large group of politically active UAW members whom it could send from nearby areas into towns where labor faced a particularly difficult challenge. But as a district-wide organization mainly interested in legislative candidates and in district and state party officers, COPE was able to trade concessions to the clubs on endorsements for local nonpartisan offices in exchange for support at the higher levels. Most of the district party, for example, joined the UAW in opposing the conservative Democratic incumbent in the 1960 primary. As one leader summed up COPE policy, "We never object if one of our boys wants to run for office—a guy deserves the extra money. . . . But we never push our guys . . . unless labor issues are involved. And that way we can insist on their listening to us on party questions."

This pattern of union influence within the party reveals both similarities with and contrasts to union efforts to mobilize Democratic voters through district COPE organizations described in Chapter VII. In some respects, voter mobilization appears closely related to the faction-aggregating activities discussed here. Indeed, organized labor's effectiveness in mobilizing voters sometimes increased its influence within the party, for example, in the nomination of Chicago Congressman Yates for United States Senator. Conversely, the influence of Detroit COPE encouraged an identification with the party which, in turn, increased labor's own efforts to mobilize Democratic voters. It could even be argued that interest aggregation and voter mobilization were two highly correlated components of a single, larger process.

Some support for this argument emerges when we consider the labor movement's voter mobilization and aggregation activities in the three cities. First, let us consider two behavioral indicators of voter mobilization. In terms of *campaign strategy,* Detroit COPE concentrated on lower-class areas; Los Angeles unions concentrated primarily but not exclusively on mobilizing voters in politically marginal, more prosperous areas; and Chicago unions emphasized such marginal areas almost exclusively. Because the Democratic party in all three cities relied more on a lower-class than a middle-class constituency, these findings suggest the following ranking of labor's importance to the party in voter mobilization: 1.) Detroit, 2.) Los Angeles, and 3.) Chicago.

A similar ranking emerged with respect to a second indicator of voter mobilization, the *structure of* COPE *district organizations.* As Chapter VII showed, Detroit district COPEs conformed entirely to the industrial-union type; Los Angeles districts had primarily industrial-union and candidate-centered types; and Chicago combined the industrial union, absorbed by the party organization and union official types. Ranking these types from the most favorable to the least favorable for union as opposed to nonlabor Democrats in terms of the relative distribution of resources, we find parties organized as follows: 1.) industrial-union dominant 2.) union officials dominant 3.) candidate-centered, and 4.) absorbed by the party organization. It follows that by comparison with the resources of nonlabor Democrats, union resources were most important for voter mobilization in Detroit, less important in Los Angeles, and least important in Chicago.

Crucially, the same rank order emerges on two indicators of labor's aggregating activities as a party faction. First, COPE had appreciably more *influence* within the Democratic party in Los Angeles than in the Chicago party, but it had still more influence in Detroit. Second, the range of *direct aggregation of minority groups* that labor undertook in Detroit in the early 1960's went far beyond its efforts in Los Angeles, and COPE's activities in Chicago were largely limited to registration drives.

This identical rank order *by city* on all four indicators, that is, Detroit first, Los Angeles in the middle, and Chicago last, suggests that both voter mobilization and interest aggregation reflect some underlying variable such as labor's relative organizational strength. But this conclusion is not wholly confirmed when we consider the variation *between congressional districts* in the same city. On two of the four indicators, to be sure, such within-city comparisons are not possible. The decision as to which congressional districts the unions emphasized, the safely Democratic lower-income or politically marginal middle-class areas, must be compared between cities rather than between districts in the same city. Similarly, the extent to which labor aggregated black interests is better compared on an inter-city basis. (Indeed, these two indicators may be closely related. For example, Detroit COPE's emphasis on mobilizing voters in inner-city districts was very nearly equivalent to the first step in the process of aggregating the interests of the largely black population in these same districts.)

But the other two indicators, the structure of the COPE district organizations that sought to mobilize voters and the influence that union groups exercised on party policies which affect aggregation, did not vary together (change in the same way) from district to district in either Chicago or Detroit. As indicated in Table 7 this pattern becomes clear when the districts in Detroit and Chicago are considered in terms of their socioeconomic composition. Los Angeles congressional districts were characterized by the location of many industrial-union locals and attractive Democratic candidates across a variety of socioeconomic areas. Combined with the absence of patronage, this pattern created extremely complex interaction between socioeconomic factors and the balance of organizational resources, which together influenced the structure of the district COPE organization.

In Detroit and Wayne County the organizational balance of resources so consistently favored the unions that a single COPE *structure,* the industrial-union type, predominated in every district—even the suburban sixteenth—regardless of socioeconomic composition. Yet, we have seen that these same socioeconomic differences apparently did affect union *influence* which ranged from full control in lower income areas to sharing and bargaining for control elsewhere. In some districts this influence declined still further in the mid-1960s.

The highly unfavorable balance of resources in the city of Chicago meant that the district COPEs had consistently little *influence.* But to complete the contrast with Detroit, we must note that their *structures* varied from the party organization dominant type, in most poorer areas, to union-official and industrial-union types in better off outlying districts. To summarize, in Detroit, where the balance of organizational resources consistently favored unions, the socioeconomic variation between districts affected intra-party influence rather than structure. In Chicago, where the balance favored nonlabor Democrats, socioeconomic variation affected structure but not influence. Thus, a favorable balance of resources made almost complete union dominance possible in some districts, but not all, whereas an unfavorable balance excluded union influence in every case.

This finding reinforces the view that mobilizing voters and aggregating interests are at least partially independent activities. We can

TABLE 7 Influence and Structure of COPE District Organizations as Functions of Socioeconomic Composition and Organizational Factors

	Socioeconomic Composition	
	LOW	HIGH
Balance of Organizational Resources (early 1960s)		
NONLABOR (CHICAGO)	COPE INFLUENCE LOW* and party-organization type dominant	COPE INFLUENCE LOW and union-official or industrial-union type dominant
LABOR (DETROIT)	COPE influence dominant and INDUSTRIAL-UNION TYPE DOMINANT	COPE bargains in order to control and INDUSTRIAL-UNION TYPE DOMINANT

* Similarities in structure or influence, despite differences in socioeconomic composition, are indicated by capital letters.

now add that they differ in part because seizing power to shape the party's aggregating activities with respect to candidates and policies is more difficult than sharing in the often noncompetitive tasks of arousing the voters. This observation parallels and supports a major argument in Chapter VI: As economic organizations, American trade unions have much more difficulty in generating incentives for rank and file political activity than do avowedly political organizations attached to political parties. The next section of this chapter makes explicit a related difficulty implicit in the present analysis: Even in Detroit the union's status as an economic organization directly interfered with labor's efforts to aggregate the constituent interests of a political party.

Limits on Aggregation

The conflict between organized labor's dual goals of articulating its own economic interests and aggregating the political constituency of the party should have been least important in Detroit. Indeed, the UAW's control was so great through the early 1960s that in some cases it all but eliminated an independent party organization. Yet a close examination indicates that, to facilitate aggregation, even Detroit COPE found it necessary to tolerate and even to encourage party leaders whose partially independent position vis-à-vis the labor movement became an asset for COPE and for themselves inside the party. At any rate, the influence of nonlabor leaders within the party was greater not only in higher-income as compared to lower-income Detroit neighborhoods but also in the higher as compared to lower levels of government and party office where aggregation of diverse interests was particularly important. In part, the independence of nonlabor Democrats simply reflected the power and prerogatives of office, which conservative politicians also successfully used in defying COPE. For example, on the death of Arthur Vandenberg, Governor Williams appointed as United States Senator a candidate labor had never even considered, newspaperman Blair Moody. Williams had less influence within the party itself. At the 1956 national convention, he failed to keep Michigan uncommitted after UAW

President Walter Reuther announced for Adlai Stevenson. But he could safely ignore labor in appointing a senator partly because of his formal powers as governor but also because during the 1950s he appealed so successfully to the party's larger constituency of liberals, ethnic groups, and outstate voters.[26] Even within the party, Neil Staebler, the state chairman during most of Williams' administration, achieved influence because of his deft handling of patronage, his success at reconciling party conflicts, and his ability to stimulate support for the party in outstate areas where unions were weak if not suspect. Both men achieved independent influence through their ability to attract and thus aggregate nonlabor interests in a union-dominated party.

Equally striking, a similar pattern emerged even in the Wayne County congressional districts where UAW members were particularly numerous and where the party constituency was more homogeneous. Indeed, this tendency appeared no matter how much influence COPE exercised in the district. For example, the fifteenth district party received considerable cooperation from its very active and competitive constituent groups partly because the veteran chairman who held office for a decade until 1962 was so successful a mediator. A devoted Democrat who was known to advance his own money for district expenses, he was respected by all groups and often attended their meetings without identifying himself with any one. After each primary he played a particularly important role in apportioning seats on the executive board proportional to each group's precinct delegate strength. Despite COPE's overall dominance, he exercised considerable independent influence on endorsements in primaries as well as on allocation of intraparty offices. The professional politician who served as chairman of the sixteenth district in 1962 played a somewhat different mediating role between labor and the district's patronage-oriented suburban clubs. According to one observer he ran "the district the only way you can, high-handed but eminently fair." In the process he built alliances with local club leaders that on occasion enabled him to defy COPE or even to insist that it change its position on policy questions.

Unlike the chairmen of the more heterogeneous fifteenth and sixteenth districts, the middle-class nonlabor chairmen in the overwhelmingly working-class first district could not possibly have based their independent influence on the power distribution between labor and nonlabor Democrats. Indeed, they required direct and continuous support of the COPE coordinator. Yet these chairmen consistently played an independent mediating role, for example, among the first district's various ethnic groups. In the face of mounting Polish-black conflict the coordinator selected an Irish lawyer, who was a figure acceptable to both groups, as party chairman in 1961. Indeed, precisely because they were directly associated with the dominant Polish UAW groups, this chairman, and even his Polish predecessor, Lucien Nedzi, who was later a congressman, continuously sought to minimize Negro-Polish conflict, an activity that the UAW's Polish coordinator could not carry on alone. For example, in order to placate black Democrats, the district party decided to remain neutral rather than to endorse the incumbent congressman, Thaddeus Michael Macrowicz, for renomination in 1960. Although the coordinator provided indispensable support, Nedzi took the initiative in making this decision.

Given the fact that throughout the early 1960s labor commanded the bulk of those party organizational resources that were available to party factions, some of the districts did have chairmen closely associated with or controlled by COPE. Significantly, COPE leaders often sought to replace leaders who were so closely identified with COPE by successors who could undertake a more neutral mediating role. In 1962, the chairman of the thirteenth district was a UAW member openly identified with the district COPE organization. He had been recently elected because COPE felt that the previous chairman, rather than mediating between rival factions, actually favored the non-COPE elements in the district. But the resulting hostility and charges of "labor dictatorship" led COPE leaders to elect a non-COPE chairman as a replacement in 1965. Equally important, during the tenure of the UAW member as chairman, the COPE leaders also encouraged a lawyer, a friend of COPE but not directly connected with it, to undertake some of the mediating activities performed in other districts by the party chairman.

In the fourteenth district the non-COPE chairman elected in 1960 was effectively controlled by UAW local union leaders on the party executive board, to the dismay of other Democrats and even of top UAW leaders. But when the district was realigned by the 1964 reapportionment, the UAW assigned it to one of the ablest coordinators in the union, who limited the influence of the local union leaders and helped elect as party chairman an issue-oriented liberal with ties to the more ideological group of disaffected non-COPE Democrats. The top COPE leadership was also unhappy with the situation in the seventeenth district, where, until he resigned in 1961, the veteran party chairman had joined some UAW leaders in excluding nonlabor liberals from the party leadership positions. His successor, although personally popular, lacked both the articulateness on issues and the personal forcefulness that could attract many of these programmatic Democrats. Party leadership, including mediation between various suburban factions, increasingly devolved on the coordinator. But the UAW's obvious economic and organizational interests made it difficult for any UAW official to mediate among party factions. In 1963, union members elected a much more forceful nonlabor chairman, and by 1965 the UAW replaced the coordinator himself. Indeed, the UAW citizenship department entirely revised its policy and assigned each coordinator at least two congressional districts, reducing the possibility that any of them would exercise too dominant a voice.

Detroit COPE's search for nonlabor mediating figures reflected a pessimistic judgment about its own capacity to aggregate, by itself, the interests in the Democratic party's constituency. If the structure or organization that aggregated the diverse interests included within the party became clearly identified with any single constituent interest, the possibility of alienating the others increased, as Calkins observed in her study of the Michigan UAW in the early 1950s.[27] Large and diverse as its own constituency may have been, organized labor was not large enough to play a neutral aggregating role in every situation. Just as labor's primarily economic status limited its recruitment of precinct workers, as we saw in Chapter VI, its character as an economic pressure group thus limited its role as a party faction. COPE, therefore, recruited as party leaders politicians who were sympathetic to unions but independent enough to aggregate labor's interests with those of other Democrats.[28] Such politicians were disinterested with regard to their individual constituents, however much partisanship they showed when they represented the interests of their constituency as a whole vis-à-vis other groups outside the party.

COPE's reliance in Detroit on both ideologically oriented liberals in the fifteenth and first districts and more pragmatic professionals in the sixteenth and (in 1962) seventeenth districts suggest that both polar types of Democratic politicians could achieve this neutrality. Whereas the professional politician approached the aggregating function by disinterestedly distributing particular benefits to his constituent groups, the programmatic politician constructed an intellectual vision so general that it could claim to comprehend a variety of interests within one overall program.

Conclusion

This chapter has indicated that in some cases organized labor rather than the formal party organization directly aggregated such Democratically disposed groups as ethnic minorities into the party constituency by bringing them into politics. In addition, as a party faction, labor sought to control or at least to influence the party's efforts at aggregating various voter interests by influencing the selection of party officials, candidates, and policies. Apart from conflicts of sheer organizational interest, the labor movement's conflicts with other party factions turned on the proper methods of aggregating the party's constituent interests. On the other hand, the labor movement's handicaps as an economic organization encouraged it to call upon other more disinterested Democrats to take formal positions of party leadership. This latter point, however, by no means simply confirms a pluralist view of organized labor's role in national party politics. It underlines the potential importance of the union-party alliance for the consumer-class politics of the 1970s described in Chapter XI. Moreover, as the next chapter shows, party leaders themselves have narrow interests that under certain conditions prevent them too from aggregating the diverse interests of the party's potential supporters. Combined with organized labor's capacity to speak for most of the party constituency, these narrow interests of the formal party leaders have led to a pattern of conflict and tension between union and party officials wholly contrary to our usual distinction between parties and pressure groups.

IX

꧁꧁꧁꧁꧁꧁꧁꧁꧁꧁꧁꧁꧁꧁꧁꧁꧁꧁꧁꧁꧁꧁꧁꧁

Party Pressure on Labor

Pressure groups are commonly associated with the articulation of interests in American politics because pressure is a demand to have one's interests considered in the formation of public policy and in the selection of public officials. As a result, party leaders on whom such pressure is applied are ordinarily thought to aggregate such interests in order to hold together their partisan constituencies. Chapter VIII depicted organized labor's contribution to the overall aggregating activities of the Democratic party. This contribution included the direct incorporation of certain Democratically inclined, but often inactive, ethnic groups into the party coalition, as well as the effort to influence the selection of candidates and policies that would help unite the party's entire constituency. In all these cases, however, union activities complemented or supplemented the official party leadership as the major aggregating force among the Democrats. Even the exceptionally strong Detroit COPE organization did not fully replace nonlabor Democrats as party officials, because it recognized that labor's particular economic interests limited its aggregating role. As a result, Chapter VIII depicted the party and individual nonlabor party leaders in relatively passive roles. They allowed organized labor to aggregate for them; they responded by accepting or rejecting labor influence; or they were called on by labor to play an aggregating role.

The analysis in Chapter VIII, then, only served to qualify rather than to actually contradict the usual distinction between large-constituency parties that aggregate interests and narrow-constituency pressure groups that articulate them. This chapter carries the analysis a step further by suggesting that, even suitably qualified, this distinction is not valid at all points in the political process. In fact, there is no obviously compelling reason to assume that this relationship is so invariate that, under all conditions, the major American party organization represents and tries to aggregate larger constituencies than interest groups. Similarly, there is no reason to assume that, in all circumstances, party leaders are relatively more passive than their labor counterparts. Admittedly, the most active and effective interest groups in American politics are usually well organized, while in most places American parties are poorly organized indeed. Nevertheless, election campaigns, as distinct from the legislative and administrative arenas, are one point in the political process at which the narrow, specific, organizational interests of American parties are particularly salient. Indeed, parties as organizations are uniquely fitted to fight these elections.[1] If party organizations, including nonlabor party leaders, are to survive politically, they must above all control the access of specific individuals to particular political offices. To secure this long-term goal, controlling party nominations is often thought even more important than winning general elections. But as the adjectives "specific" and "particular" imply, this concern must be relatively narrow. The aggregation of social interests by taking stands on policy issues that are popular with large numbers of voters loses its paramount importance.

Organized labor in the congressional politics of the early and mid-1960s differed from many other party factions because it was relatively more concerned with defeating the Republicans than with deciding among competing Democratic factions, all of which, outside the South, were likely to be prolabor. A number of possible Democratic candidates would be equally attractive to COPE on the basis of its issue criteria. In close districts, labor tended to seek the strongest vote getter, that is, one with a broad enough appeal to all party segments to win the election. In more safely Democratic districts, labor sought to elect strongly liberal candidates to strengthen the appeal of the party as a whole in Congress. In both cases the labor movement tried through the selection of Democratic party candidates to maximize its capacity to aggregate the party's constituent interests. And it is in this aggregating role that labor was subjected to the pressure of nonlabor party leaders who wished to articulate their own individual or organizational interests. This proposition will be supported by considering the most revealing conflicts over the Democratic congressional nominations in the early 1960s that took place in Detroit, Chicago, and Los Angeles. In each case, the boundaries of the distinction between party and pressure group were not simply blurred but actually reversed. The party, to further its particular interests, attempted to change labor's position on a number of candidates for United States congressman. In David Truman's terms, the party sought access necessary to influence labor's decisions, that is, to exert pressure on the pressure group. Significantly, these instances of party pressure took place in all three cities despite the dramatic differences in their overall political systems and the specific alliances between labor and the Democrats.

Detroit: The Party Vetoes One of Labor's Alternatives

The death of Representative Louis Rabaut, Sr., in late 1961 created a vacancy in Detroit's fourteenth congressional district that was to be filled by special primary and general elections in early 1962. Detroit-area COPE and UAW leaders immediately started looking for the party's best possible candidate, because the fourteenth district could well have gone Republican in a special election. But COPE soon found itself involved in a protracted search that produced repeated frustrations and disappointments. Significantly, an important cause of its difficulties was Governor John Swainson, leader of the Michigan Democratic party.

Three potential candidates appeared to be unsuitable to labor at the outset. The fourteenth district Democratic party chairman, according to all groups in COPE, lacked the articulateness, experience, and forcefulness necessary either to campaign successfully or to operate effectively in Congress. A second candidate, a liberal lawyer from the wealthy suburb of Grosse Pointe, impressed some county COPE leaders and several top UAW officials. But his intellectual, middle-class approach to politics antagonized the less issue-oriented leaders of the UAW local unions—especially Local 7—that controlled the executive boards of both the district COPE and the party. In the face of labor opposition, both the lawyer and the party chairman withdrew from consideration.

By contrast, Louis Rabaut, Jr., the late congressman's son and the third candidate unacceptable to labor, felt he was strong enough to run without any COPE support. Indeed, Rabaut announced his candidacy for his father's office without consulting the COPE leadership. As the son of the former incumbent, Rabaut inherited both his father's electorally valuable name and the loyalty of the district's politically active Belgian community. With these advantages he was clearly a major contender in the primary. Nevertheless, COPE leaders felt that, except for a period during which he served as an assistant to his father, Rabaut had no significant political experience and that he had shown himself both less astute and more conservative than his father. Rabaut's defeat in a special election for delegate to the Michigan constitutional convention also suggested that if he won the primary, he might still lose the general election. Equally disturbing to COPE, Rabaut had the support of the more conservative elements in the district Democratic party, which had fought COPE for control of the fourteenth district party organization.

COPE was also worried about the dynasty problem. In two other Detroit districts, former Democratic congressmen had been succeeded by their sons who relied on the voter's familiarity with their fathers' names. In the fifteenth district, John Dingell, Jr., proved quite acceptable to COPE. But labor considered Representative John

Lesinski, Jr., in the sixteenth district too unskilled and conservative. A third Detroit representative, Charles Diggs, Jr., from the thirteenth district, had relied on his father's reputation as a state senator from a district similar to the thirteenth to become the city's first black congressman. Although Diggs had a liberal record, many COPE leaders felt he lacked energy and initiative. For many reasons, then, COPE was determined to find a candidate who would not only win the election and serve effectively, but who would also defeat Louis Rabaut, Jr., in the primary.

Union leaders in the district believed they had a number of attractive candidates who were both personally popular with the leaders of UAW Local 7 and ideological enough to appeal to higher union officials and other liberals in the party. For many years UAW officials had expected Detroit's able and popular city councilman Ed Carey, a former party leader in the state legislature and a former UAW official, to replace Louis Rabaut, Sr. But Carey had had the good (or bad) fortune to win the presidency of the Detroit common council, by running ahead of all other council candidates in the 1961 city election. Carey risked an unfavorable voter reaction if he resigned the city's second highest office just after winning it.

It seemed certain that former Governor Williams, who lived in the district, would easily win the election if he agreed to make the race. Williams, however, held too important a position as an assistant secretary of state in the Kennedy administration to agree to campaign for Congress, although he did run unsuccessfully for the United States Senate in 1966. Bernard J. Youngblood, Wayne County registrar of deeds, a proven vote getter and a convinced liberal, also appealed to many trade unionists. But at age sixty-five he was unwilling to begin a new career in a strange city. Finally, Al Barbour, Wayne County AFL-CIO president and another resident of the district, was briefly considered. However, his obvious union affiliation appeared to be a handicap because the fourteenth district Democrats relied on many nonlabor voters.

Among the other Democratic officeholders who lived in the district, only the party's minority leader in the state senate, Harold Ryan, seemed strong enough to defeat Louis Rabaut, Jr., in the primary. Ryan, whose senatorial district covered more than half of the fourteenth congressional district, had planned an attempt to replace Rabaut for some time. Fearing Louis Rabaut, Jr., would also try to succeed his father, Ryan had even secured passage of a state law that provided that if an incumbent's son ran for his father's seat, the ballot would specifically state that the son was not the incumbent officeholder. This provision evidently hurt Rabaut in the primary. From COPE's standpoint, Ryan offered a number of advantages. In the UAW's view, Ryan seemed likely to make a more effective liberal congressman than Louis Rabaut, Jr. As a state senator Ryan had loyally supported most of the liberal program of the Williams administration and had introduced some prolabor legislation. His record appealed to many rank and file COPE workers, and, most important of all, he enjoyed strong support in the powerful leadership of Local 7.

Even some of Ryan's supporters, however, conceded that he was unusually inarticulate and that he made embarrassing slips in his public speeches. Equally disturbing to many COPE leaders, Ryan's instinctive liberalism was nonideological. Like many traditional urban Democrats, he had a general desire to side with the "little man" but possessed little of the UAW's more systematic liberalism, which envisioned a comprehensive program of social reform. Out of deference to the homeowners in the district, for example, he had not taken a clear stand on Rule 9 of the Michigan corporation and securities commission. An administrative ruling against racial discrimination by real estate brokers, Rule 9 was of great symbolic importance to the UAW. In general, Republicans thought of Ryan as a moderate, and many of his Democratic backers were well to the right of Detroit COPE.

The preference of many top COPE leaders, therefore, settled on Zolton Ferency, a very able labor lawyer and at that time administrative assistant to Governor Swainson; he was later elected state party chairman, and became an unsuccessful candidate for governor. Ferency's articulate, intellectual liberalism appealed to the top UAW leaders; his career as a labor lawyer and his long association with local leaders made it likely he would prove acceptable to the officers of Local 7. The enthusiasm of COPE members for Ferency and his ability as a speaker made him a strong candidate in the primary.

In fact, Ferency had once won the COPE endorsement for county attorney against the wishes of the county COPE leaders by dramatically rallying many local union officers to his side. COPE concluded that Ferency would make not only a strong candidate but also the able, militantly liberal congressman they had sought. Nevertheless, like Carey, Williams, and Youngblood, Ferency proved unavailable. Swainson's first few months as governor had been troubled by quarrels over his appointments and general dissatisfaction in the party. As the governor's administrative assistant, Ferency had quickly improved the situation. If Ferency won the election, he would be lost to Swainson. If Ferency should happen to lose either the primary or the general election, the damage to his political prestige would seriously impair his effectiveness as Swainson's assistant. Furthermore, Swainson could justify his retaining Ferency with the argument that the Democratic party's control of the Michigan government rested on the success of Swainson's administration. Along with Ryan's popularity with Local 7, these considerations led COPE to yield, reluctantly, to the governor's wishes. Labor's very power in the party had accustomed it to assume an aggregating role by successfully uniting a coalition of diverse interests around a liberal program that had broad appeal. This effort might well have been jeopardized if the party under Swainson fell into confusion and bickering and as a result did poorly in the coming elections. (As it was, Swainson did lose to George Romney who elected with him a majority in the legislature.) It was now clear that the responsibilities brought by power sometimes involved heavy burdens.

Feeling it had no choice, COPE formally endorsed Harold Ryan. The endorsement, however, was a bitter blow to many liberals in the district party organization as well as in the labor movement. One party member complained that "we've never had a really inspiring liberal congressman, but COPE always promised that once Louis Rabaut stepped aside, we'd get someone first rate. Then they ended up with Ryan." Some liberals turned to one of the minor candidates in the Democratic primary, Roland O'Hare, a labor lawyer active in the American Civil Liberties Union but not in the party. O'Hare announced his candidacy too late to build up much labor support, but COPE now felt only Ryan could defeat Louis

Rabaut, Jr. Few of O'Hare's own supporters felt he could have won the labor endorsement even if he had declared earlier.

To make sure Ryan did win, organized labor committed more money and manpower to the special primary and general elections than in any comparable campaign in memory, according to the president of the Wayne County AFL-CIO at a delegate meeting of his organization. In all, COPE contributed several full-time union officials, a full-time secretary for the Ryan headquarters, and hundreds of campaign workers. Labor also gave Ryan the opportunity to speak at union meetings, undertook extensive mailings on his behalf to union members, and published a Ryan campaign newspaper. With this considerable union help, Ryan ran ahead of Rabaut in the primary by a comfortable but not an over-whelming margin. COPE felt its rejection of O'Hare was confirmed because he finished a very poor third. But in the final election in February 1962, the Republicans almost ended the Democrats' fifteen-year supremacy in the district—Ryan received only 50.7 percent of the two-party vote.*

To be sure, Ryan did carry the district in the November 1962 regular election by a 3 to 2 margin, and the district appeared to be safe for the party. To many COPE leaders, however, it was a dis-turbing partial victory. It seemed at the time that Detroit COPE had lost the chance—perhaps for another generation—to add to the strength of the ideologically liberal wing of the Democratic party in the House of Representatives. Only an unexpected Republican redistricting subsequently led to Ryan's departure from Congress. Insofar as COPE had tried to increase the party's capacity to aggre-gate its constituent interests more effectively by nominating articulate liberal candidates, the entire episode was a failure. In describing the search for a candidate, one UAW leader observed, "We just had a string of bad breaks. The fourteenth district was a case of tough luck." One of the worst breaks was the failure to obtain Ferency as

---

* COPE leaders believed a treacherous ice storm that developed just at quitting time kept even the most loyal union members away from the polls. Some COPE workers, however, were not so sure. They felt the Democratic voters were simply less excited about Ryan than Republican voters were about their more articulate candidate.

the candidate. In part, this last misfortune reflected Ryan's popularity with Local 7. But it was also partly inflicted by Governor Swainson, a liberal ally of COPE and a leader of the Democratic party that COPE itself controlled, who acted mainly out of concern for his own survival as a politician. The pressure he exerted on labor in articulating his own interest was certainly a curious consequence of labor's remarkable political success in Michigan.

Los Angeles: The Party Influences
Some Labor Endorsements

The 1960 United States Census awarded Los Angeles County three new congressional seats. After redistricting by the Democratic legislature, the Democrats in the county expected and, in fact, did gain a total of six new seats in the 1962 election. Because no Democratic incumbents were involved, six candidates who would very likely go to Congress would be selected in the primary. But COPE's endorsements in these contests were conditioned by its alliance in the same primary with the group of Democratic politicians associated with Assembly Speaker Jesse Unruh. With the labor movement's help, Unruh and his associates were successfully attacking the leaders of the Los Angeles County Democratic Committee who favored the Democratic club movement. While COPE and Unruh warmly supported the primary winners in two of the six districts,* they were in less perfect accord in the other four contests, where the candidates favored by the speaker faced more formidable opposition. Significantly, the speaker's ability to influence labor's endorsements and campaign activities in these four races varied considerably depending on the situation in each district.

In a bitter contest in the twenty-fifth district primary, Assemblyman Ronald Cameron defeated former Congressman George Kassem. During his one term in Congress, Kassem had acquired a

---

* COPE and Unruh agreed on the twenty-first district, which went almost by default to popular Negro Assemblyman Augustus Hawkins, and on the twenty-seventh district, which was overwhelmingly won by Los Angeles City Councilman Everett Burkhalter.

number of devoted admirers in the labor movement by compiling an
excellent labor record and by taking a militantly liberal position
on other issues. In fact, the national leaders of several unions were
determined to return him to Congress in 1962. This enthusiasm for
Kassem led union members from the Machinists, the Operating
Engineers, the Postal Employees, some Teamsters locals and some
Railroad brotherhoods, to do about a third of all Kassem's campaign work in the primary. Nevertheless, Cameron won the COPE
endorsement, and most unions active in the district worked for his
election. Cameron appealed to labor because he had sponsored a
number of bills on regulating medical practice for the Brown administration. These bills provided, among other things, safeguards
against expensive but allegedly unnecessary surgery, and they had
aroused the opposition of the California Medical Association, an
AMA affiliate. Both the bills and the association's enmity recommended Cameron to many labor leaders. Others supported him as
a stronger campaigner than Kassem. In 1960 Kassem had agreed to
a series of debates with his Republican opponent and leader of the
John Birch Society, John Rousselot. According to several labor
leaders, after Kassem was out-debated in the first meeting, he cancelled the others, turning a defeat into a disaster. Many union leaders
concluded that in 1962 the shrewd and popular Cameron would
do much better than Kassem against Congressman Rousselot.

Yet labor's support for Cameron did not rest only on its evaluation of his record and abilities as a campaigner. Much of his union
backing was accumulated by the shrewd strategy of Cameron's
mentor, Unruh. The speaker secured a letter from White House
assistant Lawrence O'Brien that expressed President Kennedy's
admiration for Cameron's work on medical legislation. Unruh also
bluntly reminded several key labor leaders that he had a major voice
on all labor legislation in the state. The state labor leadership passed
the warning on to the locals and the Machinists, for instance, felt
considerable pressure not to work for Kassem. This pressure helped
produce Cameron's comfortable majority among COPE delegates.
And with labor's help and COPE's endorsement, Cameron won both
the primary and the general election.

If Unruh helped secure the COPE endorsement for Cameron in

the twenty-fifth district, he was almost solely responsible for obtaining labor support for the winner in the thirty-first district, Assemblyman Charles Wilson. Wilson's record as an assemblyman was described by a supporter as "closer to the center politically than most other Democrats [such as Cameron or Unruh] but to the left of the Republicans." For example, Wilson supported most civil-rights legislation, but he opposed an open-occupancy proposal as punitive. As another Wilson supporter put it, "He wasn't liberal enough" for labor; a third added that "He just isn't a sure labor vote."

Wilson did maintain a close working relationship with the liberal Building Service Union for a time. He successfully sponsored precedent-setting legislation authorizing a medical plan for non-professional school employees in Los Angeles, who were represented by the union. Later, he sponsored another Building Service bill to help organize hospital workers. After it became evident that Unruh and Wilson lacked the votes to report the bill out of committee in the assembly, the union picketed the homes of the recalcitrant Democratic committee members. Wilson denounced the pickets, pleasing many of his colleagues but infuriating the union, which had contributed heavily to his campaign funds. During the transit strike in Fresno, Wilson alienated other labor leaders by attacking it as illegal under the Fresno transit act. Union leaders bitterly claimed that the act, which Wilson himself had sponsored, allowed such strikes. One of Wilson's colleagues added that "it had to or it wouldn't have passed."

Wilson's major opponent was attorney Jerry Pacht, son of a leading liberal Democrat and himself active in civil-rights organizations. Pacht had unsuccessfully run for Congress from a more Republican district in 1960, and had recently moved into the thirty-first. In the campaign, he attacked Wilson from the left by stressing civil rights and the danger of the nuclear arms race. But Pacht was at a great disadvantage as a relative unknown in politics. Moreover, the congressional district, at Unruh's insistence, included substantially all of Wilson's old assembly district. At the same time, Pacht could not match the tactical brilliance of the Unruh associates who worked in Wilson's campaign. As his most important campaign mailing, Pacht reproduced and distributed a letter from John Kennedy (who was then a Senator) endorsing Pacht against a Republican Congressman in the 1960 general election. Although the 1960 date appeared on the letter, the clear implication was that the 1960 endorsement in the general election applied to the 1962 primary.

Unfortunately for Pacht, however, the letter appeared just early enough to give the Unruh forces time to respond. With the help of Unruh's considerable influence with the Kennedy administration, Wilson's supporters procured a telegram from White House Assistant O'Brien stating that the President did not endorse "Mr. Pacht or any other candidate." A Wilson campaign piece reprinted the telegram with the bold headline "KENNEDY REPUDIATES PACHT." For purposes of emphasis, heavy black lines were drawn around "does not endorse Mr. Pacht," which also carefully obliterated the words "or any other candidate." The effect was devastating.

Wilson's campaign also profited from the authentic looking sample ballot that was mailed throughout much of Los Angeles County in the 1962 primary by Unruh and his associates. The ballot suggested that Wilson, and others supported by Unruh, were the candidates officially endorsed by some unspecified party agency.* Plainly, Wilson depended heavily on Unruh's efforts in his behalf, which constituted repayment for Wilson's accommodating the Speaker in the 1962 reapportionment. Because of population changes the three assembly districts of Wilson, Unruh, and Don Allen, a veteran assemblyman, had to be combined into two districts. Neither Allen nor Unruh, whose power rested on his position in the assembly, wished to give up his seat. Wilson agreed to do so if Unruh would help him win a seat in Congress.

In helping Wilson win the primary, Unruh placed considerable importance on the COPE endorsement. He first persuaded the leaders of the county COPE organization to promise that they would secure the necessary two-thirds majority for a COPE endorsement. But at

---

* The ballot looked so official to many voters of the thirty-first district that thirteen of the fourteen candidates for county committee marked on the ballot were elected. Yet these candidates were not more advantageously situated on the ballot than the slate favored by Pacht.

the executive board meeting Wilson and Pacht each failed to obtain
even a simple majority. Unruh then decided he would have to use
his own influence to secure the COPE endorsement for Wilson. As one
union leader ruefully observed, "Jesse put the screws on, real hard."
He and Wilson's campaign manager, a business agent of the Boilermakers, personally contacted important union leaders, and where he
could, Unruh demanded repayment of several political obligations.
As a result, Wilson's supporters assembled a diverse coalition of
unions that achieved the necessary two-thirds majority at a second
board meeting.

Wilson's backers included conservative unions from the building
trades as well as the Bartenders and such liberal unions as the UAW
and the Steelworkers, the two most important industrial unions
formerly affiliated with the CIO. The Steelworkers voted for Wilson
primarily because they usually cooperated with Unruh. The more
ideologically liberal UAW, however, was at first attracted to Pacht. It
reversed itself, in the words of one UAW leader, only after "Jesse
had to remind [us] . . . that we owed him a few things." In particular,
the UAW owed Unruh, among others, its gratitude for the state
assembly's passage of a bill permitting women to work overtime in
California defense factories. This bill was designed to help California
companies organized by the UAW to compete for defense contracts.
The state labor federation opposed the bill in order to increase employment by limiting overtime. With labor divided, Unruh's support
became instrumental in passing the bill through the assembly. In
return, the UAW eventually supplied most of the campaign workers
Wilson received from labor in the primary. The members of one
UAW local union provided about thirty to fifty man-hours per week
to help put out the mailings that made up the bulk of Wilson's
campaign effort.

Wilson's position as an incumbent officeholder, together with
Unruh's powerful support, made him the strong favorite over Pacht
in the primary. Consequently, the help he did enjoy from labor was
probably less significant than the substantial number of union
leaders who defied Unruh by opposing Wilson. The Building
Service Union and the Garment Workers, for example, helped provide Pacht with twice as many precinct workers in the primary as

Wilson had. In fact, Pacht's supporters easily reversed the executive board's endorsement of Wilson when it came up for ratification at the COPE delegate meeting. Wilson failed to get the necessary two-thirds majority vote, and could not even obtain a simple majority of the delegates, although Pacht was also not endorsed. The anti-Wilson coalition included strong Pacht supporters and also many of Kassem's supporters, who were still angry with Unruh because of the pressure tactics he had used on behalf of Cameron. Finally, Wilson suffered because of his own labor record. One Hotel Workers leader spoke for his own union and others like the railroad brotherhoods when he asserted that "Gompers told us to reward our friends and punish our enemies, but here we are asked to vote for an anti-labor assemblyman." Unruh's political power swayed the county COPE leaders and the UAW. But it could not overcome the accumulated grievances that many COPE delegates had against both Wilson and Unruh himself.

The limits on Unruh's ability to pressure COPE were even more clearly demonstrated in the other two contested Democratic congressional primaries in Los Angeles County. In the twenty-ninth district, Edward Roybal, Los Angeles' Mexican-American city councilman, decisively won the Democratic nomination despite Unruh's well-known enmity. Although Unruh had long fought Roybal within the Democratic party, he realized that Roybal would almost certainly win in a district that included many Mexican and black voters. He quietly supported Roybal's opponent but took no overt part in the campaign. Unruh also made no attempt to block Roybal's endorsement by COPE, an effort that would have been futile in any case. The same county COPE leaders who were so responsive to Unruh in the Wilson-Pacht race arranged for Roybal's endorsement by COPE early in 1962, before the speaker or anyone else could organize effective opposition. This early endorsement, moreover, was highly popular with almost all Los Angeles unions. Roybal's issue orientation and reputation as defender of the city's black and Mexican minorities attracted those unions that had liberal political leanings and many minority-group members. Roybal attracted the more conservative unions (those in the building trades, for example) that had fewer black and Mexican members, because of his consistently prolabor record on the council. Even if Roybal lost the primary he would have remained on the council and on its personnel committee, where he directly influenced the position of the building trades members working on city projects. The immediate job interests of the construction trades greatly strengthened their loyalty to Roybal, despite Unruh's feelings.

A somewhat similar situation developed in the thirtieth district, where Assemblyman George Brown won the nomination on a liberal programmatic platform similar to those of Pacht and Roybal. Although Brown had compiled an excellent labor record, COPE itself was divided between him and a prolabor city councilman close to the building trades unions and to some other nonfactory unions. Brown's union supporters included the Machinists, some railway unions, the Butchers, the Steelworkers, the UAW, and some smaller CIO unions. Only twenty or so of their members worked for Brown directly through COPE, but they did a sizable proportion of the limited precinct work in his primary campaign. Their efforts were supplemented by those of other union members working in Brown's own campaign organization. Brown received this support, even though his opponent, like Roybal, would remain on the council if he lost, while Brown himself had given up his assembly seat to run for Congress. Of course, these unions were less affected by city council decisions than those in the building trades, and they rightly suspected Brown would win the primary. Nevertheless, Brown had a long history of conflict with Unruh in the assembly, and his union supporters would still have had to deal with the speaker in the legislature whatever the outcome in the thirtieth district.

Brown's retirement from public life as a consequence of defeat in the primary would undoubtedly have gratified Unruh, who quietly supported Brown's opponent. But the speaker also doubted that Brown could be defeated, and, as in Roybal's case, he made no serious effort to change COPE from a neutral to an anti-Brown position. Here too, he simply lacked the power. One illustration of Unruh's difficulties was the UAW's enthusiastic support for Brown, even though the union had reluctantly supported Wilson at Unruh's insistence. In demanding support for Wilson, Unruh had reminded the UAW that he had pushed through the women's overtime bill. But the speaker could not use this argument as effectively to turn the union against Brown. In the first place, Brown himself had supported the bill, thereby putting the UAW in debt to him. In the second place, by supporting Wilson, the UAW had already repaid its debt to Unruh in a race that indirectly involved the speaker's own seat in the assembly. Unruh knew this, and as one UAW leader summed it up, "Jesse can't push everything. If he tried to, we'd be likely to go all out against him. He knows his limitations and he didn't make the Roybal and George Brown fights his main objectives."

As Speaker Unruh's efforts to influence labor in the Wilson-Pacht and the Cameron-Kassem primaries indicate, Unruh sought labor support to supplement his own impressive political power. The Los Angeles Democratic party had so few effective precinct workers in working-class areas that the COPE endorsement carried far more weight in the Democratic primary than a similar endorsement did in Chicago. It implied not only money and some campaign workers, but also the votes of loyal union members. Unlike the general election in which the party label guides the voters, these members could not rely on their partisan loyalties to tell them whom to support in the primaries. Nor could they consult the regular organization precinct captains so important in Chicago. Had Assemblyman Wilson won the COPE endorsement from the delegate body, his campaign would have been more enthusiastically supported by more unions, and less labor support would have gone to Pacht. Unruh would have had to commit fewer of his own resources, and some of his associates felt that if COPE had backed Wilson at the outset, Pacht might not have entered the primary at all.

The same limitations on Unruh's power that made labor support so helpful to him also enabled some unions to resist his pressures on behalf of Cameron and Wilson and to ignore altogether his opposition to Roybal and Brown. The decisive factor in Roybal's case was the councilman's almost complete independence from any party faction or leader. Unruh lacked patronage to use against Roybal or his supporters. Perhaps more importantly, Roybal's position as a nonpartisan city councilman, his seat on the council's personnel committee, and his personal popularity with minority groups gave him an impregnable defense against any possible attack Unruh could make. The UAW's support for George Brown demonstrated further that even the basis of Unruh's power—his enormous influence on legislation in California—had its limitations as an instrument for pressuring labor. Despite Unruh's enmity, Brown built his own personal record in the assembly and put the UAW in his debt. If the UAW were to maintain its reputation of supporting proven friends, it had to oppose the speaker by supporting Brown for Congress.

Unruh's problems must be traced to the fundamental disorganization of California politics. Because California parties are so diffuse, Unruh assembled his power through the strength of his personality and his agility in political manipulation, as well as through his formal position as speaker. However, he lacked in 1962 the party machinery with which he could have stabilized and institutionalized his position. Because his power was so personal it could be defied when other personal factors intervened; factors like Wilson's unpopularity and the popularity that Roybal and Brown enjoyed among the leaders of Los Angeles unions. Curiously, perhaps, the very confusion and weaknesses of political structures and alliances allowed labor in several cases to support candidates who appealed to a wide variety of Democratically inclined groups. In particular, labor was able to support Brown and Roybal, both of whom were popular among Mexican and black groups. Far more than in Chicago, COPE found itself able to resist the pressures of the party leadership.

Chicago: The Party Dictates a Labor Decision

The Chicago party organization's ambivalence toward COPE and dominant position in their partnership emerged dramatically in a struggle over the 1960 congressional nomination in the old twelfth congressional district. Before it was eliminated by the 1961 reapportionment, the twelfth district covered the middle-income residential areas in the northeast corner of the city along Lake Michigan. The district included traditionally Republican middle-class Protestants, many liberal Jews who were political independents, as well as some more conservatively inclined, but still Democratic, Catholics who were often Irish. The predecessors of COPE had helped Democratic Charles Boyle take the district from the Republicans in 1954 and hold it in 1956 and 1958. In 1956, for example, COPE campaigned for Boyle among the many Catholic Democrats in the district who favored Eisenhower, while it ignored most other Democratic candidates on the ticket.

When Congressman Boyle died in an automobile accident, several Democrats hoped to replace him as the party's 1960 candidate. One leading candidate, Frank McCallister, the labor education director at Roosevelt University, had a wide range of labor contacts, including influential allies within the Democratic party leadership. Many labor leaders also admired state representative Esther Saperstein, an issue-oriented liberal who had recently accepted a city job from the party. The final choice, however, inevitably belonged to the Democratic organization, which rejected both Saperstein and McCallister in favor of a personable forty-ninth ward precinct captain, Edward Finnegan. Finnegan appealed to party leaders on several grounds. The party disliked spending its own resources on congressional races, which involve little if any patronage, and Finnegan could provide his own campaign funds. This reason by itself was not decisive, since McCallister and Saperstein also had financial support for the campaign. A more important consideration for the party, however, was that, unlike the other two, Finnegan was popular with the party rank and file because he had worked his way up through the regular party organization. Finally, Finnegan's selection maintained the delicate ethnic and political balance within the party organization on Chicago's north side. Like Boyle, Finnegan was an Irish Catholic member of the forty-ninth ward organization. McCallister, by contrast, was a Unitarian, and thus a member of a religious group that had no political importance in the area. Saperstein, of course, would have appealed to her many Jewish coreligionists in the district, but two aldermen, a state senator, and Congressman Sidney Yates from the adjacent ninth district already represented the party's north-side Jewish supporters. Another Jewish congressman would have seriously disturbed the ethnic distribution among the party's candidates.

The district COPE leadership, however, was furious at the party's selection of Finnegan. The party had held informal "hearings" at which COPE argued for a friendly liberal like McCallister or Saperstein, but COPE now felt that the hearings had not affected the decision at all. In particular, they called the selection of Finnegan a "joke," "an insult to our intelligence." In their eyes he was undistinguished by personal liberalism or any marked intellectual abilities. Worst of all, when the COPE leaders had asserted at the informal hearings that they would not stand for an "incompetent party hack" as a candidate, the party leaders bluntly replied that labor had no alternative to the Democratic candidate. The COPE leaders, who almost always did endorse Democrats for Congress, were stung by this taunt, and a quarrel ensued.

Somewhat unexpectedly, however, the COPE leaders discovered that they did have an alternative. The twelfth district Republicans, instead of choosing an impeccable conservative like the other Illinois Republicans already in Congress, nominated a liberal Jewish civic leader, Theodore Fields. In his campaign, Fields supported admission of Communist China to the United Nations and actively sought labor backing. In addition, as a former football star with a good singing voice and an attractive personal appearance, Fields appeared to be a popular vote-getter. COPE in Chicago was too weak to contest directly the party's choice in the primary. But a Fields victory helped by COPE support would demonstrate labor's power to the party without depriving labor of a liberal congressman. Presumably it would force the organization to listen more closely to labor's wishes on congressional candidates. The election of Fields would also encourage the Republicans to nominate other liberals, creating still more opportunities to pressure the Democrats. The district COPE organization, therefore, endorsed Fields, subject to ratification by the Illinois COPE organization.

Before the state COPE could act, however, the Democratic organization subjected the entire COPE structure to intense pressure on behalf of Finnegan. The party appealed to national Democratic leaders, as well as to the national COPE director, to secure Finnegan's endorsement. Representative Thomas O'Brien, the powerful leader of the tightly disciplined Chicago Democratic delegation in the House, made it clear he wanted another wholly reliable Democrat from Chicago, rather than a maverick Republican, to bolster his negotiating position in Congress. And O'Brien had proved one of labor's closest and most powerful friends in Congress. Leaders from other COPE districts also appealed to the twelfth district COPE not to imperil their relationships with the party or with top labor leaders. They feared that, rather than contribute to COPE organizations that had antagonized the party, several important unions might directly support individual congressional candidates. In the end, the COPE organizations might well be left without funds. Finally, the leaders of the Steelworkers and the UAW, the strongest unions in COPE, openly spoke out against Fields. Pressure from so many sources had its effect. "We felt like the roof caved in all around us," one twelfth district COPE leader recalled. "Everyone kept saying to us, 'you're right—but so what? We could lose the whole COPE structure.'"

Conveniently enough, Finnegan, unlike Fields, was both a trade-union lawyer and a union member, and his backers could therefore argue that he was entitled to labor support. Amid much embarrassment ("but we already endorsed Fields," one COPE leader pleaded), the state COPE set aside the Fields endorsement. A twelfth district COPE meeting then reversed the earlier district endorsement, declaring both candidates acceptable. Significantly, the district COPE called the meeting during normal working hours, when only paid union staff officials could attend. The rank and file COPE members in the district, who worked in campaigns mainly out of ideological commitment, were attracted to Fields as the more articulate liberal and were less amenable to their leaders' pressures. Because the meeting was held during working hours, few could attend.

The result was disastrous for COPE's 1960 campaign activities in the twelfth district. The COPE leaders met occasionally, "just to give the impression we were actually working," but little was done. One district leader reported that a major union offered several thousand dollars, without conditions, to use in the campaign. But the leaders refused the money, blandly asserting that everything was going well. Another union asked one of its staff representatives to step in and organize a labor campaign for Finnegan. But this union's rank and file COPE workers in the district were incensed at the rejection of Fields, and the staff representative refused to involve himself. During the course of the campaign it became clear that the 1960 Presidential race in Illinois not only was extremely close, but might also be decisive in the national election for President. Along with countless other factors, labor's support for Senator Kennedy, in so close an election, was indispensable for the Democrats' victory. In this situation, the apathy in the twelfth district dramatically indicated the extent of disaffection within COPE. The party could reverse labor's decision, but it could not, after all, force the COPE workers in the district to campaign enthusiastically.

In the election, Finnegan barely carried the district against Fields, partly as a result of COPE inactivity. Yet as a congressman, he compiled a good labor record and proved adept, in the style of a traditional precinct captain, at running constituent errands. As one labor leader put it toward the end of Finnegan's first term, "It's quite true Ed's inarticulate, but there are only two or three articulate Democratic Congressmen from Chicago." Because COPE regularly supported cooperative incumbent Democrats, it endorsed Finnegan in 1962 against a conservative Republican. Finnegan won easily in a district that had been given more Democratic voters by the 1961 reapportionment. Only when Yates wanted to return to Congress from a new district that combined the old ninth and twelfth districts did Finnegan step aside to become a judge. The district COPE, however, felt it gained little from its rebellion, because the party remained essentially free to choose congressional candidates as it wished.

The reversal by the state COPE of the twelfth district endorsement in a congressional race was unprecedented, but it did not surprise many labor leaders. In the first place, Fields had no established record as a friend of labor. Beyond this, in terms of COPE's own criteria he simply came from the wrong party. Chicago unions instinctively favored Democratic candidates for national office against the strongly conservative candidates nominated by Illinois Republicans. Many labor leaders, for example, feared that once Fields was in Congress he would be an isolated liberal in the Illinois Republican delegation and thus vulnerable to party pressures. These very fears were an implicit concession that COPE in Chicago had no alternative to accepting the regular Democratic nominee. Indeed, it was hard to specify exactly what organized labor would lose by helping to elect Finnegan. One COPE leader concluded toward the end of Finnegan's first term that he "is a guaranteed vote for progressive legislation. You can't criticize his voting record." Nevertheless, the decisive reason for Finnegan's endorsement was the direct political pressure of the party organization. All the perquisites of labor's alliance with the party, which included public appointments, friendly police treatment, and favorable votes by state and national Democratic legislators from Chicago, were, to a degree, endangered. Of course, a quarrel over one congressional district, however serious, could not wholly split the alliance. But there are degrees of cooperation, and if labor's opposition to Finnegan had continued, the party might well have been perceptibly less cooperative.

Chicago COPE leaders who asserted their loyalty to labor's traditional nonpartisanship usually explained that COPE endorsed only Democrats for federal office because it could find no acceptable Republicans. But the attempt to endorse Fields in the twelfth district suggests that the alliance with the Chicago Democratic party rested on considerations far more pervasive than a case-by-case evaluation of individual races. The alliance proved so beneficial to both sides that it became a comprehensive agreement between entire organizations, between labor and the party as whole entities. Labor, therefore, was no more free to support an appealing Republican like Fields for Congress in 1960 than the Democratic organization was free in 1958 to permit one of its congressmen to vote for clearly anti-labor legislation. If either the congressmen or the twelfth district COPE demonstrated such independence, the entire alliance would have faltered. In fact, no congressman from Chicago, and no COPE district organization, was independent enough to break the terms of the alliance in such a serious way.[2] In labor's case, moreover, the alliance had gone beyond beneficial exchange of support to become a matter of political loyalty that conflicted with and partially supplanted the nonpartisan tradition. COPE was ideologically committed to the national Democratic party as the political friend of unions and workers generally. In turn, this ideology reinforced the alliance by making support for Republicans appear illegitimate. Once such an ideology was accepted, exceptions based on the peculiarities of one district in one election were not readily countenanced. In part, then, labor's decision not to endorse Fields was a necessary concomitant of its broader political commitments. Of course, COPE's liberal ideology was itself the source of its discontent over the nomination of Finnegan, who could be expected to vote favorably but not to work enthusiastically and effectively for broadly liberal measures. Paradoxically, labor's attempt to aggregate the diverse interests in the party's constituency with a broad, liberal program drove it to support a Republican. By doing so, it sought to force the powerful party organization to nominate more issue-oriented candidates. But the Fields-Finnegan episode suggested the difficulty labor has in playing this aggregating role outside the Democratic party, at least in Chicago.

Aggregation, Articulation, and Pressure in the Labor-Party Alliance

Although party pressure on labor occurred in all three urban areas, its specific form reflected the very different local political cultures of the three cities. The selection of Finnegan in Chicago, like all other major decisions, was made by the party organization. When challenged, it invoked its overwhelming political power. By contrast, the primary victories of Cameron, Wilson, Roybal, and Brown in Los Angeles reflected that metropolitan area's almost chaotic politics, in which factional alliances shifted from district to district and no group maintained complete control over the whole county. Each winning congressional candidate in Los Angeles was a well-known officeholder in his district and, except perhaps for Wilson, his personal following clearly played a major part in his victory. Such personal factors as the candidates' popularity or Unruh's tactical brilliance would not have been so crucial if there had been one large influential organization like the Chicago party or Detroit COPE. In Detroit, to be sure, the absence of a partisan patronage organization also increased the importance of such personal followings as Harold Ryan's, which extended to some members of Local 7. Indeed, labor's frustrating search for a candidate indicated limits on Detroit COPE that, in the early 1960s, did not seriously handicap the still more powerful Chicago party organization. Even so, the organizational strength of the UAW enabled it to influence, if not to dictate, major party decisions.

In sum, the party did pressure labor in all three cities, but the degree of pressure varied directly with the general distribution of power between the two groups. Whereas the Chicago party organization invoked its uniquely formidable network of influence and sanctions to reverse the Field endorsement, Unruh's somewhat similar pressures in Los Angeles had only mixed success. In Detroit, COPE was so strong that direct party pressure was out of the question, and a division in the UAW's own ranks proved to be a more important factor. But in relinquishing the otherwise available congressional candidate who most nearly met labor's criteria for an active liberal congressman, COPE also deferred to the party's leader and to his perception of the party's overall welfare. Given Swainson's position, he could argue plausibly enough that his success as governor would be more important to the party at the next election than finding the best congressman in one district. The pressures thus varied in directness as well as degree. In Detroit a major party leader merely helped to block one possible choice rather than dictating labor's actions as the party organization did in Chicago. In Los Angeles, party leaders could effectively intervene in some labor decisions but not in others.

Obviously these cases selected from one limited time period, the early 1960s, are not representative enough to specify the frequency with which party pressure of this sort occurs. But the available evidence does allow us to hypothesize the most important conditions favoring the recurrence of such pressure. Significantly, each case examined here involved, first, a race for Congress, which, second, the Democrats had a good chance to win, and in which, third, there was no Democrat incumbent. Each of these three conditions deserves attention. Organized labor is most likely to clash with party leaders in national races, including congressional contests, because they most obviously involve aggregation "by principle"; that is, they relate to the social and ideological issues that motivated most COPE members. Moreover, the ideologically oriented COPE organizations are most likely in such instances to make issue-based judgments of candidates. They are less likely to pay heed to matters of personal and factional ambition that affect many nonlabor Democratic leaders. On the other hand, party leaders are most likely to take a major interest in contests in which the Democrat is likely to win, and they are thus inclined to pressure an independent-minded labor movement in such elections. Independent Democrats are tolerated far more readily, even by the Chicago party organization, in suburban areas where they are unlikely to be elected. Finally, the presence of an incumbent is likely to reduce labor-party conflict because neither group is likely to oppose a sitting congressman unless severely provoked. Party pressure on the labor movement should appear most frequently when all three of these conditions are present.

By themselves, however, such hypotheses about frequency (i.e., statistical association) even if supported by the analysis of many more cases than those considered here, do not fully explain the phenomena. We want to know *why,* even under favorable conditions, the usual pattern of groups pressuring parties should be so decisively reversed—and in three such different cities. As the conflict in Chicago's twelfth district illustrates, a fully satisfactory explanation will force us to reformulate systematically our notions about interest, aggregation, and constituency as they apply to American parties and interest groups.

Finnegan's selection was partly the result of a party effort to satisfy its Irish Catholic supporters. Taken together with the recognition of other ethnic groups in other nominations, this tactic conforms to the process described in Chapter VIII as aggregating pluralistically. One aim, in other words, was to help unite the party coalition by giving a specific though symbolic benefit to a particular Democratic group. Nevertheless, the party's first concern was clearly its own organizational interest. Finnegan's ethnicity was almost certainly less important in his selection than his membership in the forty-ninth ward organization, which as a political faction felt it deserved a congressional seat. More important still, the Chicago party organization's vigorous reaction reflected its perception of a threat to its dominant position in the selection of all Democratic candidates. In acting from these motives the party was not aggregating at all, but protecting its very different role (or "function") as the agent for selecting public officials against interference. By contrast, Chicago COPE was not primarily articulating either its own organizational interests or the immediate economic interests of its members. Labor knew it could count on Finnegan—and all the other likely Democratic candidates from Chicago—to vote for specifically prolabor legislation. Instead the district COPE organization was primarily trying to aggregate by principle or ideology, that is, to strengthen the liberal block in the House of Representatives that in turn would attract a wide variety of potential Democratic voters who favor a broad range of welfare-state programs. In short, labor found itself under pressure insofar as this effort to aggregate by principle interfered with the party's role of controlling the selection of public officials.

This situation was also true in the other two cases. Patronage appointments were less important in Michigan, but the same basic concern for his position as an officeholder motivated Governor Swainson, a programmatic liberal whose political style was much closer to that of the Detroit-area UAW than to the style of the Chicago organization. The same consideration also moved Speaker Unruh, whose political style represented an intermediate case. It is very unlikely that these various party leaders pressured labor out of concern for their own efforts to aggregate the party's interests. As Chapter VIII showed, Unruh, Swainson, and the Chicago leaders disagreed with each other on precisely this question of the proper method Democratic leaders should follow in aggregating the party constituency. They pressured labor because COPE's concentration on the candidates' articulateness and general issue attitudes excluded a primary concern for the interests of particular party factions or leaders. Whereas Los Angeles COPE tended to evaluate congressional candidates in policy and ideological terms, Unruh supported both Cameron, a liberal Democrat, and the appreciably more conservative Wilson, because each was a political ally. Of course, labor preferred some candidates over others. The important point is that COPE's criteria did not specifically single out particular individual candidates or officeholders. In the twelfth district, Chicago COPE would have enthusiastically supported Saperstein or McCallister, or any other liberal, just as Detroit COPE considered a whole range of liberals to succeed Rabaut. But just this choice among specific candidates affects the party leaders' entire network of obligations and understandings by which they ordinarily seek office.

As a result, both the party and labor—but at different times—deemphasized the aggregating role. In such instances, each applied pressure on the partner who continued to attempt to aggregate. The interests labor articulated when it exerted such pressure were the familiar organizational maintenance needs of the unions themselves and the somewhat more general demands of organized workers, as distinct from those of such unorganized groups as migrant farm laborers. By contrast, party leaders and candidates applied pressure to protect their general control over nominations or, more narrowly, to secure the particular interests of individual officeholders. In both cases, the aggregating partner was associated with an orientation toward a broader partisan constituency than the partner who applied political pressure. This basic difference appears to explain those conflicts just described in which labor found itself pressured by party leaders.

All of this has relevance to the general treatment of parties and pressure groups in the literature of political science. As Chapter VIII indicated, the activity of interest articulation is often depicted as a function performed by interest groups, whereas interest aggregation and the selection of government officials are thought to be functions performed by parties. The cases described here, however, not only depict an economic interest group alternating its relative emphasis between interest articulation and aggregation, but also suggest that party leaders also alternate between aggregation of broad constituency interests and the narrower concern with selecting government officials. To illustrate, Chapter VIII showed that organized labor's need to articulate its own interests interfered in some cases with its aggregating role in the Democratic party organization in the Detroit area. Detroit COPE had to turn to nonlabor district party chairmen whose neutrality among party factions better enabled them to unite the Democratic groups. In other circumstances, labor's aggregating role, which forced it to balance a number of competing interests within the party constituency, sometimes limited its ability to pay heed to the specific demands of deprived groups in the society. For example, labor resisted some claims of blacks in Detroit and of

Mexicans in Los Angeles. In turn, both these groups have pressured COPE on occasion, as they would a party. Similarly, the entire point of this chapter has been to show that nonlabor factions ordinarily thought to aggregate the Democratic party's constituent interests actually sacrificed their aggregating role by choosing candidates in terms of their immediate factional interests.

These considerations suggest that the traditional view of narrowly based groups articulating particular interests and pressuring more broadly based aggregating parties is incomplete. The present analysis suggests that the labor movement's immediate trade-union interests are more relevant in the legislative and administrative processes than in the electoral process. Of course, this contrast is only one of degree. As the conclusion of Chapter V indicated, administrative and particularly legislative actions at the national level also affected the general interests of wage earners and low-income citizens. Indeed, Chapter X documents in detail organized labor's concern with these broader ideological issues, and the labor movement in the 1960s constituted the core of the entire liberal lobby on these issues. Chapter XI explains that both the unions and the party may well have begun to reorient themselves during this decade to a set of class-related issues that divide consumers from producers. Nevertheless, the large number of individual issues to be decided in the legislative and administrative arenas permitted labor lobbyists to pay particular attention to the interests of their organizations and immediate union membership. By contrast, the limited number of possible outcomes in a basically bipartisan electoral system made it difficult for COPE to avoid supporting the entire partisan coalition that endorsed the expansion of the welfare state. Because welfare-state issues tend to divide the two parties (in most districts outside the South), COPE furthered the interests of lower-income citizens, as it defined those interests, by supporting liberal Democrats. In turn, the lower-income voters, to which the Democrats appealed since the New Deal, have become a potential electoral constituency of the labor movement. Insofar as labor sought to build a precinct organization that could mobilize this entire partisan constituency, it tended to rely on aggregation by principle or ideology. Indeed, it may be significant in this connection that the AFL-CIO since its founding in

1955 has maintained separate political-action and lobbying organizations nationally and these two have somewhat different ideological perspectives.

The party's situation presented a curious mirror image. Insofar as it appeals to lower-income groups, the party represents a large constituency very similar to labor's in that the party has tried to aggregate by framing and enacting legislative and administrative programs attractive to a majority of the electorate. (Narrower regional or economic issues are less often partisan issues in Congress.) In this situation the party has frequently been pressured by unions who are articulating their narrower organizational interests. This is the typical party–pressure group relationship. But, as we have seen, the choice of party candidates—particularly in primaries where the party makes its own decision—directly affects the party's most narrow constituency, those politicians vitally interested in the Democrats' successful attempts to gain and hold office.[3] With personal and factional survival at stake, such politicians articulate their narrower interests; that is, they try to influence—as best they can—labor's role in the selection of party candidates.

Individually, many of these observations are already familiar. The literature on American parties and pressure groups emphasizes that parties can be "responsible" to the interest of some broader constituency, or to the entire public, for the framing and execution of public policy. Yet the same literature also recognizes that parties often act on the basis of self-interested concern for staying in office. Similarly, the very notion of a pressure group implies some self-interested concern, but it is widely recognized that some pressure groups initiate and favor public policies oriented toward a larger group than their own members. Certainly the evidence presented here powerfully reinforces these conventional qualifications to the accepted distinction between parties and pressure groups. Nevertheless, even with these qualifications it is apparently assumed that the behavior of any particular party or group will be stable; that is, consistently oriented toward either a broad or a narrow constituency. It is recognized that a particular interest group may emphasize aggregation and that a particular party faction may emphasize aggregation as opposed to seeking office. Any change on the part of such a party faction or group is likely to be a gradual long-term evolution rather than a systematic and recurrent alternation. As Chapter I indicated, the literature also assumes that parties and interest groups are essentially atomistic entities that remain fundamentally independent, each performing a separate set of activities. Parties and groups may cooperate with each other on occasion, or even for an extended period. Ultimately, many writers have assumed an implicit bargaining model with each individual group or party operating independently.

The last two chapters have presented data that, it appears, cannot be conveniently fitted into this model save as awkward exceptions that require a series of special ad hoc explanations. However well the present model works for much of our political behavior, we clearly need an alternative model to account for the range of party–pressure group behavior described here that may well become increasingly important in a more and more complex society. This alternative model must take into account at least four aspects of the labor-party relationship depicted in these pages. First, the party and trade unions have actually *interpenetrated* each others' decision-making councils in a systematic way.* Second, the existing view is correct in asserting that the groups and parties continue to be distinguished by the different activities they undertake. But the activities that are genuinely distinctive do not include interest aggregation, at least if it means building partisan coalitions. Rather, the labor movement distinctively articulates particular economic interests of their workers and their union organizations, whereas party leaders are distinctively concerned with access to political office by specific politicians. Third, we find in some cases that labor and the party *systematically alternated* the relative emphasis that they placed on aggregation. First one and then the other played the more prominent aggregating role—depending on whether the context in the particular

---

* Recent government intervention by the Democratic Johnson and Kennedy administrations in collective bargaining suggests that labor and the party also jointly participate in what was once thought to be the independent economic activity of setting wages. Thus the joint performance of certain activities remains symmetrical.

case was the legislative or the electoral process. Taken together, these considerations suggest a fourth element rightly emphasized by Leo Snowiss.[4] For practical purposes, labor and the party operated within a political coalition *as partners* who found that mutual consultation and planning were often more advantageous than pressure or access. This last development was clearest perhaps in congressional politics in Washington.

X

Labor and Congress:

Unions as a Constituent Party Interest

Marxist and pluralist interpretations of organized labor in national politics share, at many points, the reductionist assumption that trade-union political behavior can be adequately explained in terms of functional economic interests or of broad economic classes. Although this study provides considerable evidence for both of these approaches, Chapters VIII and IX emphasize a very different *political* factor, the American labor movement's position within the Democratic party. By analyzing the unions' place in congressional elections and in the legislative process from a national perspective, this chapter will expand this partisan interpretation by distinguishing between the nominal and formal Democratic party leadership and its constituency of organized socioeconomic interests.

We noted in our earlier analysis of labor politics in the Chicago, Detroit, and Los Angeles metropolitan areas that Mayor Daley, Speaker Unruh, and Governor Swainson differed politically not only in ideology and in style but also in the quantity and quality of the resources they commanded. Nevertheless Swainson, Daley, and Unruh were the most important nonlabor leaders in parties that shared the same Democratic label and that acknowledged formal allegiance to the same national organization. Equally important, these local parties were based on coalitions that favored the same welfare-state policies and appealed to the same socioeconomic groups, including organized labor.

Each of these attributes generated its own type of partisan loyalty. On one side, the party continued to attract the pro–welfare-state coalition that took form in the New Deal, and could thus be considered the Democrats' socioeconomic constituency. Given our focus on organizational elites we can define the party's organized constituency as the leaders and active members of those organized interests which have not only supported Democrats in national politics but influenced the party's decisions on both candidates and policy in national conventions and elsewhere.

Of course, not all politicians and ordinary voters respond to such policy considerations. Some traditionalist partisans, for example, respond to the favorable connotations and associations of the *name* "Democrat" or "Republican" as a symbol.[1] More generally, such nominal supporters include those voters or political factions for whom party success is a good in itself regardless of its consequence for government policy. Such feelings characterize not only voters but many of the party's elected officeholders, its nominees for public office, and its leaders and workers. These groups, in Weber's phrase, live "off" politics as a source of income, or they become swept up in the competitive "game" or contest between the parties. Consistent with our organizational concern, this chapter will consider the symbolic or nominal sector of the party to be the Democrats' formal leadership, insofar as they set party victory above policy outcomes as their primary goal.

Empirically, relatively few political leaders or voters embody such analytically pure sources of party support or of political motivation. For example, the traditionalist voters who exclusively support the major American parties out of loyalty to the party symbol constituted no more than 4 percent of the 1956 random sample of the electorate analyzed in *The American Voter*.[2] And many politicians display a lively concern with particular issues, even though they may adjust their issue orientation to help win reelection. On the other side, as Fay Calkins noted in the early 1950s, and as American unions have found since then, union members and even leaders transfer much of their loyalty to the Democratic party as a political symbol once they become active in campaigns. They consider themselves loyal Democrats, without having to make an issue-by-issue assessment of their party's current performance on policies affecting union organizations and working-class people generally.[3]

The distinction, therefore, may be most relevant in analyzing those individuals who become incumbents of leadership roles in either the organized constituency or the formal party. Union members tend to support the union's policy positions and campaign activity more strongly after they become union officials.[4] Conversely, issue-oriented individuals may concentrate more on winning office after they become candidates and formal party leaders.

Of course, even holding positions in the party's formal leadership or in the organized socioeconomic constituency need not mean an exclusive concern with either government policies or personal political success. Nevertheless, the distinction does enable us to expand our propositions about the American labor movement's attitudes and behavior. Earlier chapters primarily compared the unions under various social, economic, and political conditions in three cities. We can now explicitly compare these union attitudes and activities with those of its allies in the national party leadership. Such comparisons are especially important because, unlike the party organizations in Chicago, Detroit, and Los Angeles, the Democratic party in Congress numbered among its nominal adherents many conservative antiunion Southerners. Moreover, since the formal party leadership lacked the resources to coordinate the fragmented national party, but, as officeholders, had to enact a general legislative program, they were forced to bargain with these conservatives.

Consequently, as a constituent socioeconomic interest group, organized labor had both more resources and greater freedom of action than the formal party leadership. The unions not only took over coordination of the Democrat's election efforts in 1966, but throughout the 1960s attempted to reshape the formal party along more liberal lines by extending the New Deal partisan realignment to the South. Even on certain welfare issues in Congress, labor lobbyists rather than the formal party leaders coordinated the Democrats' efforts. To be sure, on other welfare issues the formal party leaders played an equal or greater role, and as a constituent interest group organized labor remained free to pursue the pluralist organizational interests typical of many pressure groups. But the distinction between the formal party leadership and its organized constituency identifies the dimension along which the relative positions of the unions and the party as allies varied in the electoral and legislative processes at least in connection with domestic issues.

Congressional Elections: Organizing the Party's Constituency

Because almost all Democratic candidates outside the seventeen Southern and Border states supported welfare-state programs, labor's goal throughout the North and West coincided with the formal party leadership's desire to elect the maximum number of Democratic candidates. National COPE thus confronted only the instrumental problem of providing the most efficient support for the party's nominees in congressional elections. By the 1950s, as Scoble pointed out, the pattern of almost exclusive support for Democrats had been well established.[5] As in Chicago, and to some extent in Los Angeles, national COPE concentrated its resources on those districts and states that seemed most likely to affect the balance between congressional liberals and conservatives. In theory, COPE committed about $2,000 in 1964 to each liberal Democratic congressional candidate and up to $10,000 in Senate races. However, liberals from safely Democratic districts and overwhelming favorites for the Senate, like Edward Kennedy of Massachusetts, actually received much less, whereas liberal Democrats in closely fought contests received much more.

This liberalism did not, of course, extend to all issues of foreign policy, in particular, the Vietnam War. Indeed, labor's support for the Johnson administration's policies helped account for its powerful influence on behalf of Hubert Humphrey at the 1968 national

Democratic convention. Interestingly enough, this close alliance with formal party leaders—which led to the nomination of a weak Presidential candidate—not only conformed to the partisan interpretation of the national political role offered here, but by contributing to the victory of Richard Nixon actually hurt the unions' working-class and pluralist goals. This judgment is confirmed by the lack of union enthusiasm, at least in the critical early weeks of the campaign, for two important antiwar liberals running for the Senate, Clark of Illinois and Gilligan of Ohio. Each man subsequently lost in close contests to Republicans who were clearly less sympathetic to union objectives concerning labor-management legislation and broader welfare-state issues. Nevertheless, the union leaders' powerful counterattack among their own members against the anti–civil-rights Wallace candidacy indicates their continuing commitment to the party's pro–welfare-state coalition—which the formal party leadership, including both Johnson and Humphrey—still aspired to lead.

The formal party leadership and the labor movement, however, commanded very different resources with which to implement their shared objectives. As a result, much of national COPE's activity by the mid-1960s was actually an effort by the strongest element of the Democrats' organized constituency to offset the formal leadership's normal organizational weakness at the national level.[6] Concerned about the difficulty of holding the forty-one seats that the Democrats had taken from the Republicans in the 1964 landslide, COPE sought to coordinate and organize the election campaign activities of much of the party's socioeconomic constituency. Collaborating with such groups as civil-rights organizations, senior citizens' associations, rural electrification organizations, and the Farmers Union, COPE systematically set out to increase the new Democratic congressmen's visibility among their constituents by financing radio and television programs and by organizing trips back to the districts to meet the voters in person. In fact the Democrats suffered a very substantial net loss of forty-eight seats in the 1966 off-year election. Nevertheless, the party retained twenty of the forty-one newly Democratic seats that COPE had sought to save. Fully thirty-one of the fifty-two seats that the party lost had first been won in 1962 or earlier and, accordingly, should have been less vulnerable. This consideration tentatively suggests that COPE efforts may have had some limited impact in retaining the newer seats for the Democrats. But for the present analysis of union-party relations, the most important point is the preeminent role that COPE assumed in this overall party effort.

Since the Democrats' official House and Senate campaign committees primarily made financial contributions to nominal Democrats of substantially varying ideologies and President Johnson sharply limited all campaign activities of the Democratic National Committee, the unions sought to fill the vacuum. As columnists Rowland Evans and Robert Novak reported after the election, "President Johnson's dismantling of the National Committee's campaign staff" meant that "the AFL-CIO's Committee on Political Education took over party functions to try to save pro-labor Democratic candidates." Many in the AFL-CIO were dismayed, Evans and Novak reported, at so explicit an involvement in the party machinery, but labor partisanship was so widespread that "over the past generation, union leaders in state after state have dropped any pretense at non-partisanship."[7]

This situation reflected certain general recurring constraints as well as the particular circumstances of the 1966 campaign. President Johnson apparently resented for many years the National Committee's role in attacks from within the party on his moderate rather than liberal record as Senate Democratic Leader. Beyond this, the administration evidently desired to concentrate power in the White House rather than in a potentially independent, and thus troublesome, party headquarters. As these two considerations illustrate, many formal party leaders are constrained by their alliances with the party's conservative, mostly Southern, minority, including many key congressional committee chairmen. In the 1950s the National Committee had divided rather than united the formal party by complaining about these ties. At the same time, most elected politicians gave their highest priority to protecting their own political positions vis-à-vis other political actors—in essence, maintaining sufficient power to fulfill their governmental responsibilities and maximize their chance for reelection. In the case of the President, this meant securing control over his own administration and the national party apparatus. COPE leaders, in contrast, operated much more freely as leaders of the party's organized socioeconomic constituency, because they had no personal ambition for public office. In addition, the unions' political leaders could call upon a stable bureaucratic organization, well endowed with both money and politically experienced officials. The National Committee, with its uncertain constituency and changing leadership, simply lacked equivalent resources.[8]

These differences partially conform to Schattschneider's distinction between parties, whose "ultimate objective" is "conquest of the power to govern," and pressure groups, which seek "the adoption of certain public policies."[9] In this case, however, the distinction refers to activities which took place within a single party coalition. As a result, the formal party leaders concentrated on running the government, and the Democrats' largest organized constituent interest assumed much of the responsibility for electing party candidates who conformed to their pro–welfare-state policy preferences.

Labor and Party Realignment: The Urban South

In congressional elections in the eleven states of the old Confederacy, organized labor went beyond the instrumental problem of most efficiently organizing available resources on behalf of all Democratic candidates. Faced with the conservative antiunion attitudes of so many Southern Democratic congressional candidates, the labor movement tried to develop a more liberal, formal Democratic party leadership and thus helped drive the conservatives into the Republican fold. By 1965, a sizable cohort of conservative Republicans and liberal Democrats had substantially reduced the number of conservative Democrats in the House of Representatives.

That year Republicans numbered seventeen of the 106 Southern Representatives. As a group they were clearly to the right of their Southern Democratic colleagues. Not one of the seventeen voted even once in accordance with COPE's position on the 13 issues by which COPE evaluated United States Representatives in the Eighty-Ninth Congress. By contrast, forty-one, or almost half, of the eighty-nine Democrats voted correctly according to COPE's criteria at least three times, and only twenty-three or just over a fourth matched the Republicans' conservatism.[10] Moreover, twenty-four of the Southern Democrats in the Eighty-Ninth Congress voted with COPE on more than half of these thirteen issues, and fourteen voted "right" nine or more times.

The electoral success of these conservative Republicans and liberal Democrats during the 1950s and 1960s partly reflected demographic and legal changes. The growing urban and suburban areas increasingly responded to the two parties like metropolitan voters elsewhere. The importance of the areas increased with the effective enfranchisement of Southern urban Negroes and congressional redistricting. At the same time, both the Republicans and the liberal Democrats acquired increasingly important campaign organizations, based on the political activism of middle-class urban Republicans and, very often, the resources of organized labor among the Democrats. In each of these ways, the partial transformation of Southern congressional delegations represented a belated extension of the 1928–1936 party realignment into the South.

In order to estimate organized labor's contribution to this overall trend, all the liberal Southern Democrats first elected to Congress between 1961 and 1964 were selected for interviews in May 1965. Since the Eighty-Ninth Congress had only recently begun, liberalism was defined as a vote—later included by COPE in its 13—to weaken the power of the House Rules Committee, long a formidable obstacle to welfare-state legislation. The selection of relatively junior members concentrated the interviews on the unions' more recent activities. In all, eight congressmen met these criteria, three from Tennessee, two each from Florida and Georgia, and one from Texas. They constituted almost half of the eighteen Southern liberals who voted for the Rules Committee change and one-third of all twenty-four Southern Democrats elected in 1961 or after. As expected, the rules vote proved an excellent predictor of the Southern Democrats' general domestic liberalism as measured by COPE. Those Southern Democrats who voted against COPE on the rules issue had a mean score of only 2.2 "right" votes on COPE's other 12 key issues, compared to 9.9 out of 12 for the eighteen southerners who agreed with COPE. The eight junior members selected for special study (who all had 9 or more right votes out of the total of 13) ranked in the most liberal 20 percent by COPE standards of the eighty-nine Southern Democrats.

The constituencies as well as the votes of these liberals reflected a trend to party realignment, because seven of the eight represented urban-metropolitan areas that in the North and West were the heart of the Democrats' strength. Moreover, these seven had all either replaced conservative Democrats or won election from new districts transferred by reapportionment from generally conservative rural areas. Only one congressman of the eight from a rural area had replaced a liberal predecessor.

Seven of the eight congressmen (except Mr. Sam Gibbons of Florida) agreed to be interviewed, as did a number of their assistants. To avoid suggesting the importance of organized labor to the respondents, the subject of the interview was introduced as the "role of the 'liberal coalition.' " In 1965, "liberal coalition" was widely understood in Washington as designating supporters of the Johnson administration's domestic program. Each respondent was asked to rank in order of overall importance the various groups that supported him in a contested primary and in the general election campaigns. The responses of the congressmen are summarized in Table 8. Only after the respondents undertook this ranking did the discussion turn more specifically toward the labor movement.

Of the seven congressmen, one singled out 3 groups and five singled out 2 groups. Only the representative from the rural district

TABLE **8**   **Groups Mentioned as Important in Congressional Campaigns of Liberal Southerners**

Group	MOST IMPORTANT	SECOND MOST IMPORTANT	THIRD MOST IMPORTANT
Trade unions	3	3	0
Negroes and other ethnic minorities	2	3	0
Senior citizens groups	1	0	0
Individual businessmen, Chamber of Commerce members, etc.	0	0	1

did not mention any interest groups.* (Typically the Democratic party in these Southern districts had little importance as a campaign organization.)[11] Three congressmen ranked unions most important, and three ranked them second to either ethnic minorities or senior citizens. These responses are all the more meaningful because many elected officials have an interest in understating their dependence on a single economic group lest they reduce their appeal to other voters.†

On balance, then, the interview data confirm the labor movement's significant contribution to a partial party reorientation in the South. This judgment is reinforced by the unions' frequent refusal to support conservative Democrats, no matter how hard pressed by Republican challengers, lest they encourage the party to nominate more conservatives. In fact, AFL-CIO affiliates tacitly cooperated with some conservative Republicans running against conservative Democrats. When South Carolina Democrats nominated a conservative to run in a 1965 special election against Congressman Albert Watson, a Goldwater Democrat turned Republican, organized labor sat out the campaign. Similarly, the Texas AFL-CIO refused to support conservative Democratic Waggoner Carr in his 1966 race against the conservative incumbent Republican, Senator John Tower. The unions not only sought to drive out conservatives by denying them victory on the party ticket, but also to reduce the number of conservative Democrats eligible for influential committee positions within

---

* Although COPE itself did not endorse this candidate in the Democratic primary, he did receive a sizable number of endorsements and some financial support from individual local unions. He was also enthusiastically supported by COPE in the general election, although his easy victory minimized the significance of labor's efforts.

† Of course, even though the labor movement was not specifically mentioned by the interviewer, the respondents may have exaggerated its influence, or their responses could have been inaccurately recorded. To minimize these possibilities, the responses were reexamined to identify distortions, but this step suggested that the most likely errors probably cancelled each other out. In one case, where organized labor was ranked second, the congressman added that in fact the unions contributed more money even if somewhat fewer campaign workers than the ethnic group that he ranked first. In the other case, the congressman ranked labor second by virtue of enthusiastic support by individual union leaders. But the ethnic-Negro vote was so important that the unions' contribution emerged only on a follow-up probe question.

the Congressional Democratic party as a whole. The election of conservative Republicans rather than Democrats would thus benefit the party's Northern as well as Southern liberals.

These considerations suggest that the failure of three of the eight Southern liberals interviewed in this study to win reelection in 1966 represented only a partial setback for labor's realignment efforts. In each case the liberal incumbent was defeated by a Republican who then could not influence Democratic party decisions on committee assignments and other matters.

It must be emphasized that the labor movement sought these goals in the South very largely as a formal organization rather than as a voting block. Several of the congressmen interviewed for this study reported that they had much stronger support from union officials than from the rank and file.[12] Indeed, these congressmen's support of civil-rights legislation made their appeal to white union members so fluctuating and uncertain that in one case union leaders could not openly endorse the most liberal candidate in the Democratic primary. In the general election, however, the district COPE not only officially endorsed him but also made financial contributions and provided him with publicity and speaking opportunities at union meetings. Relatively unknown candidates, running against better-known conservatives, often valued this exposure to union members. Moreover, union financial contributions also partially compensated for the loss of the party's traditional financial backers on whom more conservative Southern Democrats could rely. Union officials also helped staff campaign headquarters, sometimes on a full-time basis, put out mailings, put up campaign signs, and made telephone calls. Finally, to a more varying degree, unions provided campaign workers who went door to door on registration and voter turnout drives in lower-income and minority areas. Since blacks, who were often not union members, were more reliable supporters of liberal Democrats than white union members, many of these efforts were concentrated on raising the proportion of black turnout. As in Detroit, the labor movement therefore concentrated on the party's political constituency rather than the unions' own membership.

Consistent with the organizational character of their activities, the unions were able to divert their resources to Senate races when they wished to. Two congressmen, from different states, reported that when a hard-pressed liberal was running for United States Senator, union campaign workers concentrated their efforts on the state race rather than on congressional contests. All these union efforts to replace conservative Democrats with liberals were anticipated by the party's formal leadership. After Southern Democrats had begun to vote against his programs, President Roosevelt intervened in the 1938 elections and successfully protected some liberal incumbents, but failed to unseat conservative Democrats. During the years that followed, the growing prominence of Northern blacks in the Democratic party and the emergence of the civil-rights issue strengthened the positions of most Southern conservatives and a desire to cultivate rather than alienate them encouraged subsequent Democratic Presidents—notably Kennedy and Johnson—to avoid intervention in congressional primaries. Once again, the formal party leadership found its freedom of action restricted by its governmental responsibilities, which the labor movement as a constituent socioeconomic interest did not have to consider. These Southerners could at least provide the formal party leaders with the votes to organize Congress, and they might respond to the blandishments of patronage, particularly if the issues involved did not concern social-welfare programs. At any rate, even if they were determined to oppose such conservatives in the primaries, the formal party leaders again lacked many of the organizational resources that the labor movement commanded. The unions could use their resources more freely because they stressed formal party control of congressional committees much less than substantive legislative outcomes, which fluctuated with the number of *liberal* Democrats. Thus, as the strongest organization in the party's socioeconomic constituency, the labor movement was uniquely prepared in the mid-1960s to try to complete the New Deal realignment in congressional electoral politics.

Interest Group Pluralism in Congressional Lobbying

On a number of issues in the arena of congressional lobbying, the formal party leadership rather than the labor movement was the most prominent group of those seeking to unite the Democrats' diverse constituency. One major factor was the intrinsic complexity of contemporary welfare-state legislation. For example, the labor movement strongly supported aid to elementary and secondary school education, in part as an egalitarian measure. Typically suburban upper- and middle-income school districts often spend much more per pupil on their school children than financially hard-pressed central cities that have many lower-class children. Even federal aid strictly apportioned on the basis of population, would have moderately increased school spending per low-income pupil calculated as a fraction of the amount spent on each suburban child. In fact, the eventual formula based federal aid on the number of low-income school children in each district, which dramatically increased the legislation's potential egalitarian impact.

For all its enthusiasm, however, the labor movement, the Kennedy administration, and allied groups could not pass a general education bill in the early 1960s. Indeed, a controversy among school-aid supporters over aid to parochial (mainly Catholic) schools threatened to remain an obstacle even after the 1964 election elected so many liberals it eliminated the obstructive power of the House Rules Committee. At this point the Johnson administration devised an elaborate and successful compromise that provided enough aid to parochial schools to appease—in effect to aggregate—the Catholics, one of the most important groups, which usually supported the Democrats. In other words, the particularly tangled character of the issue made the technical competence of legislative and executive experts especially important so that labor lobbyists played only a limited role in formulating this successful aggregating compromise.

Labor lobbyists encountered a similar situation when they sought to include repeal of the 4 percent stock dividend credit in the 1964 tax reduction bill. As tax issues go, this question was relatively easy

to explain to union members as discrimination in favor of predominantly well-to-do stockholders, and union representatives made
this highly egalitarian step a major goal. Like aid to education it
became one of the key issues that COPE considered when it evaluated
incumbents in the 1964 election. Nevertheless, both congressmen
and staff members who worked for repeal reported that labor's actual
influence was relatively limited. The complexities of federal income
tax legislation, which increased the importance of Treasury Department officials and tax specialists among the Representatives and
Senators, reduced the general access of union lobbyists to the centers
of decision making, especially in the House Ways and Means Committee. Both expertise and incumbency in formal public office proved
valuable resources.

Outright pluralism also inhibited partisan aggregating activities.
Particularly on those issues which specifically affected the immediate
interests of union members and officials, organized labor, as a
typical interest group, pressured the party leaders in their aggregating
role. For example, Section 14(b) of the Taft-Hartley Act authorized
right-to-work state legislation that outlawed union-shop contracts
requiring newly hired employees to join the union. In practice, these
laws inhibited union organization in just those less industrialized
areas where they were already weak. The AFL-CIO made repeal of
14(b) its chief specifically organizational objective in the Eighty-
Ninth Congress and threw its weight behind prompt legislative consideration. Labor strategists hoped that this step would reduce the
risk of alienating potential supporters in the House whom the unions
would later have to pressure on broader welfare legislation. The
unions hoped that early consideration in the Senate would forestall
a possible filibuster as it would delay the favorite legislation of many
other senators.

The formal party leaders in the Johnson administration, however, preferred to pass their broader legislative program which
might help aggregate the interests of the entire party constituency,
before the Congress involved itself in a lengthy and perhaps embit-
tering struggle over 14(b). In order to reconcile their demands for
immediate repeal with these larger party interests, union spokesmen
insisted that success on the issue would have justified welfare state

oriented political action to otherwise doubtful union members. But whatever their objectives, the union leaders failed. As one labor lobbyist put it euphemistically in May 1965, "the President wanted a more opportune time, later in the session, and so do we." But he also agreed that "there is no point in having a needless quarrel over timing," which, in effect, was an admission that labor had yielded to the administration. Clearly, the formal party leadership, at least when it controlled the White House, could resist union pressure more effectively than the leaders in Detroit and probably even Los Angeles. As it happened, labor's worries about the vote in the House proved unfounded. The repeal passed even though it was considered later in the session. In the Senate, however, most other major issues had already been considered and the bills' opponents easily filibustered it to death. Of course, the filibuster might have succeeded earlier in the session, but the delay increased its prospect of success.

Significantly enough, an organizational and therefore narrow interest in the measure evidently weakened the union's position as it did in an earlier fight over the Landrum-Griffin Act.[13] Indeed, the latter issue divided the labor movement into separate and even quarreling factions, notably between former AFL affiliates and the industrial unions from the former CIO. In fact, this tactically disastrous preoccupation with individual union interests contributed to labor's defeat on the issue—its bitterest humiliation since passage of the Taft-Hartley Act. Alan K. McAdams concluded his study of Landrum-Griffin by claiming, "Over the years, the labor movement has shown substantial immunity to that usually great educator, experience."[14] He adds that "there is not, perhaps never has been a labor 'movement' in this country. There is—and has been at least since the days of the Depression—an inharmonious group of autonomous unions capped with a purposely weak and ineffective superstructure, the parent Federation."[15]

This view could not possibly be applied to trade-union lobbying as a whole without very substantial qualification. But, as Theodore Lowi has persuasively observed, organized labor seemed more united and often more effective on broader redistributive issues that affect a very large constituency than on regulative issues that affect narrower ones.[16] The AFL-CIO had apparently greater success when it urged higher levels and more prompt increases in the federal minimum wage than those favored by the Johnson administration. To be sure, a major effect of this legislation would be a reduction in the nonunion lower-wage areas' attractiveness to businessmen considering the location of new factories. The issue was, therefore, very important to several individual unions in the garment trades. The fact that low-income workers outside the labor movement would apparently benefit more than most union members strengthened the AFL-CIO's bargaining position with the White House and with the formal party leadership in the Eighty-Ninth Congress. In the end, the unions secured a compromise on minimum wage that they found acceptable.

Some elements in organized labor took a more pluralist position than others even on broader welfare-state issues. Among the constituent groups of unions organized as departments of the AFL-CIO, the lobbyists from the Industrial Union Department (IUD) were by far the most concerned with welfare-state issues, just as lobbyists in individual industrial unions were usually more active than other AFL-CIO unions on these issues. At the level of rank and file union members, one Southern liberal congressman who supported the 1964 Civil Rights Act reported far more opposition from craft union members in the district than from workers in industrial plants.

To a limited extent, these differences could be detected in the formal organizational structure of the unions' political activities in Washington. The AFL-CIO assigned supervision of its electoral activities to one operating unit, national COPE, but responsibility for lobbying in Congress to another, the legislative department, under Director Andrew Biemiller. Certainly, it was a considerable exaggeration to say, as one congressman did, that "Andy Biemiller is mostly concerned with Davis-Bacon amendments." (These provisions required locally prevailing rates of pay on federally financed projects, which primarily employed construction workers in the craft unions.) Yet the traditional power of the craft unions in the AFL-CIO meant that his lobbyists put less stress on some welfare-state issues than did the industrial-union lobbyists. Even in national COPE—where all the major leaders were primarily concerned with the entire welfare-state program—at least rhetorical differences between former AFL and CIO leaders could be detected.

Apart from differences among former AFL and CIO members, union lobbyists substantially adapted their style and behavior to the peculiar difficulties and problems that the legislative process posed. Indeed, this adaptation produced a final pluralist division among the AFL-CIO's own political specialists in COPE and in Biemiller's office. This division of responsibility could be defended as increasing the functional specialization and therefore the effectiveness of each organization. But it meant that COPE officials sometimes did not speak to congressmen on important pending measures, even if the particular congressmen felt heavily indebted to COPE campaign efforts. "Biemiller is tough about this," one COPE official said, "he would have my head if I were caught lobbying." Another implied that COPE's exclusion from the Landrum-Griffin fight contributed to the unions' defeat. (To minimize this problem, COPE leaders in 1964 tried to obtain commitments from congressional candidates during the campaign that they would vote to repeal state right-to-work laws.)

The important point is that this pluralism, which was generated organizationally rather than economically, reflected the differences between the electoral and the legislative processes. One former CIO official compared it with tension over union organization and collective bargaining that occurs within industrial unions. "There is a natural friction," he said "between organizers in the field and negotiators. The organizers get the rank and file heated up and then feel let down by the 'unprincipled' compromises made in negotiations. The negotiators claim the organizers lie to the men about what the unions can do." A similar disagreement over the merits of compromise is clearly characteristic of the differences between lobbyists and campaign organizers. As this comment suggests, the tension between COPE and the AFL-CIO's lobbyists cuts across the split between industrial and nonfactory unions. One of the lobbyists for the IUD viewed labor's effort to persuade the Senate to include a section that would outlaw the poll tax in state elections as part of the 1965 Civil Rights Act as a futile waste of valuable resources and energy. Yet, from COPE's perspectives the tax was particularly vicious because it discriminated against lower-income groups—and thus liberal Democrats—in election campaigns.

Medicare and Civil Rights: Interest Aggregation in Collaboration with Formal Party Leaders

Clearly, a still vigorous pluralist tradition of union lobbying for more particular goals coexisted with organized labor's contemporary welfare-state orientation and its accompanying emphasis on electoral campaign work. Yet the same ratio of interest homogeneity and cohesion (discussed at the end of Chapter V) that helps explain the difference between the union's legislative and electoral activities also distinguishes between different issues. This ratio suggests that unions would be less pluralistically oriented on welfare-state issues. And in the mid-1960s, the leaders of almost all AFL-CIO departments and factions, emphatically including Biemiller, strongly supported both welfare-state programs and the election of those liberal Democrats who favored them. Equally significant, the same organizational resources and freedom of action that enabled the labor movement to participate so prominently in the Democrats' electoral efforts enabled it to assume a similar aggregating role for the party on a wide range of welfare-state issues.

Many liberal Democratic congressmen from both North and South, as well as their staff assistants, believed that organized labor was by all odds the single most important lobbying group within the party's welfare-oriented constituency. As one strategically situated legislative aide put it, "Both the AFL-CIO and the IUD have skilled lobbyists, they see the connections; they're damn good." In supporting the Johnson and Kennedy administration's medical care plan for senior citizens (Medicare), the union lobbyists had an essentially instrumental relationship with the formal party leadership. Because the unions and the Democratic leadership shared a similar goal, the union's major problem was simply to collaborate as effectively as possible. Much as in the case of congressional elections in the North and West, where the unions and national party leaders also shared a common objective, the labor movement's special contribution primarily reflected its organizational resources.

The Democrats' Medicare proposals appealed to union leaders in at least certain respects as a major egalitarian innovation within the Social Security system. To be sure, the method of financing—a flat-rate payroll tax—had the distinctly regressive effect of heavily taxing the poor. But, the program was profoundly redistributive by sharply reducing the anxiety and sense of financial insecurity of the great majority of old people for whom serious illness had previously meant facing financial ruin or accepting charity. Perhaps for this reason, the first labor officials to urge an active labor campaign on this issue in the early 1950s were political leaders from industrial unions, including Alexander Barkan, who was then assistant director of national COPE, and Roy Reuther of the UAW. But the support they accumulated among nonfactory unions emphasized the extent of the entire labor movement's break with Gompers' voluntarism. Certainly the unions had little immediate organizational interest in the plan. Many of Medicare's beneficiaries were not even retired union members and few could affect union organizational interests by entering the job market, although almost all union members would face financial pressures at retirement.

Apart from their egalitarian ideology, the union's involvement on this issue thus seemed to grow primarily out of their concern with expanding the political constituency of the Democratic party. In the 1950s, when Medicare emerged as a serious issue in Congress, older voters were much less Democratic than other age groups, despite their relatively lower incomes.[17] Support for Medicare, notably in Kennedy's 1960 Presidential campaign, thus represented a major effort by both formal party leaders and by the organized constituency to incorporate, that is, to aggregate, this largely lower-income but relatively Republican group into their partisan coalition. The partisan character of the issue also induced Northern Democrats to make a pro-Medicare commitment a prerequisite for appointment to the crucially important House Ways and Means Committee. Only the Democrats' 1964 landslide, however, enabled the party leadership to overcome the combined opposition of the powerful American Medical Association lobby and of Representative Wilbur Mills, the formidable chairman of the House Ways and Means Committee.[18] Indeed, their success may have been the best illustration during this period of the conservative tendencies of both pressure-group politics and the congressional committee system. But the party landslide might not have overcome such resistance if the senior-citizens organizations had not generated such intense popular pressure on the Democratic party in Congress. The formal leader of this agitation, the National Council of Senior Citizens, not only forged alliances with many friendly organizations but also tried to organize local groups of older citizens who could pressure Congressmen directly. And as many of the Representatives interviewed in this study reported, the council's efforts made a considerable impression. Nevertheless, such groups of retirees often lacked such important resources as energy, money, and organizational skills, which the American labor movement primarily supplied.

To be sure, nonlabor groups like the Farmers' Union helped organize some senior-citizens groups. But even in cities where union officers and members were not particularly prominent, like Kansas City and Los Angeles, unions often provided the local clubs with lists of their retired members and directly encouraged their participation. And in industrial cities like Pittsburgh, Toledo, Bethlehem, and to some extent Chicago, union staff officials played a direct organizing role. According to one liberal Congressman, "There were many letters from older people but a majority were from those who were already labor-oriented." Meanwhile, the AFL-CIO's bureaucracy provided important support in Washington. Indeed the federation's Social Security department under Director Nelson Cruikshank often supplied vital political arguments and technical information to pro-Medicare legislators more quickly and efficiently than the Department of Health, Education, and Welfare did under Presidents Kennedy and Johnson.

Without the labor movement, in other words, both the National Council of Senior Citizens and the entire pro-Medicare campaign might never have attained the formidable level they reached in the mid-1960s. Indeed, the origins and leadership of the council strikingly illustrate the intimate connection between organized labor's political activities and those of the Democrats' national leadership and the broader coalition of constituent socioeconomic interests. The council emerged after the 1960 campaign as the successor organization to the Democrats' Senior Citizens' Committee for Kennedy. Although it officially became nonpartisan in order to attract sympathetic Republicans, James O'Brien, the coordinator for the Kennedy committee in 1960, became the council's assistant to the President and chief operating officer. At the same time, however, O'Brien continued to serve as executive director of the Steelworkers' Committee on Older and Retired Workers, a position he had assumed in 1957, seven years after beginning his career as a union official. These multiple roles of a key official both symbolized and maintained the coalition character of the entire struggle for Medicare.

Both organized labor and the formal Democratic party leadership matched this commitment to Medicare with their determination to pass the Civil Rights Acts of 1964 and 1965, although this effort meant an attempt to retain an already heavily Democratic group. Once again, therefore, the labor movement's goal was primarily instrumental, that is, it consisted of most effectively bringing its organizational resources to bear. But, unlike Medicare, the unions' most important problem was not primarily to arouse popular pressure that would create a congressional majority. To be sure, popular pressure was important in the passing of civil-rights legislation, particularly in 1964, but much of it was generated by important nonlabor groups. Although estimates of their relative influence varied from Congressman to Congressman,* it did seem clear that each major group in the civil-rights coalition made a somewhat different contribution. Black organizations obviously spoke for voters so committed on the issue that they posed a visible, predictable threat to any unfriendly Congressman who had many black constituents. The

---

* In one typical interview, a Southern liberal Congressman who voted for civil-rights legislation ranked labor just behind Negro and religious groups. Another observed that given his constituents' prejudices against Negroes, effective union activity was confined to Washington lobbyists. A liberal from a Northern industrial district—where (until 1966) the opposition of white union members to civil-rights legislation was weaker than in the South—rated labor second to the churches in effectiveness, since Negroes were not numerous in his district. Another veteran liberal Congressman placed labor ahead of even the churches in his district.

predominantly white church organizations had fewer members so single-minded on the issue of civil rights, but they apparently could influence some adherents in almost every congressional district outside the South. Almost alone, therefore, the churches were able to pressure uncommitted Republican Senators from largely rural areas, whose votes were necessary to end a Southern filibuster. Sizable numbers of union members were also scattered across many, though not all, non-Southern states and congressional districts. Yet the unions' contribution could not so clearly depend on any threatened reprisal at the polls. Indeed they could generate much less enthusiasm for civil rights than for Medicare, particularly among white members with only moderate union loyalties. Of course, in heavily working-class areas, union leaders could attempt to minimize the effect of white prejudice. As one liberal representative observed, "It's not just that the top [labor] people are for it, but they protect us against rank and file criticism. All the top leaders in my district do this."

But the unions' contribution primarily depended on the situation in Congress itself. Although the most enthusiastic supporters of civil-rights legislation were mainly—but not exclusively—Northern Democrats, the two-thirds vote necessary to defeat a Southern filibuster in the Senate required the support of many less thoroughly committed members of both parties. This bipartisan block of more than fifty diverse, independent, and often mutually suspicious Senators required effective coordination. In 1964, this group could look to the Democrats' formal party leaders in the Johnson administration and to Assistant Majority Leader Hubert Humphrey. But senatorial resentment of both ambitious colleagues and of the executive branch's too blatant control somewhat circumscribed the effectiveness of this leadership, despite Humphrey's acknowledged skill and personal popularity. The civil-rights forces thus found it useful to rely on an outside group of lobbyists, the Leadership Conference on Civil Rights, to help write speeches, marshall facts, and most of all formulate a generally acceptable strategy. And it was within and through the conference that the labor movement exercised much of its influence.

An IUD lobbyist served as chairman of the Leadership Conference, and labor representatives participated fully in the intricate tactical decisions involving the amendment of the administration's civil-rights proposals. Most important, the unions supplied resources unavailable to church groups, including money, office space, and mimeographing and other clerical services, on which the conference's communication and coordination efforts depended. In addition, union support also meant that vital corps of skilled lobbyists could be depended upon to maintain personal contact with friendly or potentially friendly legislators.

Moreover, as part of the conference the unions went beyond instrumentally implementing a goal that it shared with the formal party leaders. In one case, the conference supported an amendment to the 1965 voting rights act that outlawed poll taxes in state elections, despite the Johnson administration's opposition. Indeed, Director Biemiller himself helped select Senator Edward Kennedy as floor leader. The battle not only succeeded in the House but also exerted such intense pressure in the Senate that the ban was defeated only by the most strenuous efforts of both the administration and the Senate leadership. As one AFL-CIO official put it, "We almost killed ourselves trying to push it through." In the end the administration accepted a compromise provision that resulted in a successful court suit by the Justice Department to invalidate the poll tax as unconstitutional.

The unions' divergence from the position of the formal party leadership in support of civil rights paralleled COPE's greater willingness to oppose conservative Southern Democrats overtly in primaries and at least covertly in general elections. In both cases, the party's formal leaders, but not its organized constituency, placed its interest in the smooth operation of the government ahead of its interest in electing more liberal candidates. Although the ban on poll taxes affected only four states, it seemed likely to help unions and other liberal Democratic campaign groups by increasing the electoral turnout of already Democratic poor whites and even more dependably Democratic poor blacks. The Johnson administration and Senate Majority Leader Mansfield, however, depended on the tacit cooperation of Senate Minority Leader Dirksen to facilitate the passage of much of their legislative program. Because Dirksen opposed the tax ban, they were extremely reluctant to have it included in the bill.

The inclusion of the fair employment section in the 1964 Civil Rights Act provides an even more striking demonstration of the labor movement's concern with the aggregation of the party's constituent interests. The Kennedy and Johnson administrations did not include an employment section in their original drafts, and the Johnson administration favored treating the question in separate legislation. Apparently underestimating the degree of public support for civil-rights legislation in 1963 and 1964, administration leaders evidently feared that too strong a bill might not pass at all. The Leadership Conference, by contrast, was determined to exploit favorable public sentiment to the maximum. In its view, two major civil-rights bills were even less likely to pass in any one Congress than a single inclusive measure. But no restriction on racial discrimination by employers could obtain the necessary Republican support if it did not also ban racial discrimination by unions, which was a common practice of unions in the building trades.

In this situation the AFL-CIO's opposition might well have prevented inclusion of any employment section at all. For one thing, the prolabor members of the House Education and Labor Committee could have claimed jurisdiction and demanded the right to hold hearings, putting great pressure on the House Judiciary Committee to abandon the whole issue. Despite the influential position of the building trades in his own organization, however, President Meany joined members of the Education and Labor Committee in testifying for the ban on discrimination by unions as well as by employers. Indeed, he conceded publicly as AFL-CIO officials had always admitted privately, that he lacked the power to end discrimination by federation affiliates.

However limited this provision's ultimate impact on black employment, Meany's stand represented a watershed in the evolution of organized labor's political attitudes. Samuel Gompers had probably supported laissez-faire pluralism more strictly than the many businessmen who had favored protective tariffs and various government subsidies. Gompers' voluntarism was pluralist largely because he sought to protect union members and organizations rather than all wage earners. His pluralism was laissez faire because he feared government social-welfare programs would undermine the workers' loyalty to their unions and because antiunion government regulation would destroy union power. In the 1930s, the labor movement broke with both Gompers' pluralism and his argument for laissez-faire politics by endorsing welfare programs designed to benefit workers inside and outside unions. American unions supported social-insurance measures as well as the Wagner Act. But President Meany's stand on fair employment and union discrimination went much further by endorsing *coercive* government interference in the internal union matter of admission to membership. Moreover, this provision explicitly sought to protect wage earners outside the union fold.

Because black Americans were generally poor, organized labor's efforts on behalf of civil rights does seem consistent with its egalitarian ideology and with its concern for working-class unity. On the other hand, much of this stand can be reconciled with the unions' own self-interest. Outlawing the poll tax seemed likely to increase the proportion of poor prounion voters in four traditionally antiunion states. Even in the case of fair employment, the memory of black scabs breaking the strikes of lily-white unions undoubtedly persuaded some union officials to accept government pressure for increasing the number of black trade unionists. In fact, however, sufficiently ingenious arguments could reconcile a wide range of divergent political attitudes with union self-interest. At least in the case of fair employment legislation, the fear of black scabs—which existed long before the rise of the civil-rights issue—seems an only partially adequate explanation. The AFL-CIO's position, therefore, can be reconciled with its self-interest only if that "self" is sometimes thought to include the Democratic party's political constituency as well as the economic constituency of the federation's own membership.

Reapportionment: Labor Defends the
Democrats' Electoral Constituency

Organized labor assumed still more direct leadership of the Democrats' electoral constituency in the congressional struggle over the United States Supreme Court's orders requiring reapportionment of state legislatures by population. As when they worked for party realignment in the South and against the poll tax, the unions assumed this leadership role partly because they were more concerned with electing the maximum number of liberals than were the formal party leaders. In order to defend reapportionment, labor representatives had to activate an initially indifferent block of almost exclusively Democratic Senators, rather than arouse the voters as they did for Medicare or coordinate a committed but previously ill-organized majority in Congress as they did for civil rights.

In terms of its long-range political impact on American politics, reapportionment was probably more important than any other issue before the Eighty-Eighth and Eighty-Ninth Congresses. To be sure, the impact of reapportionment on the nominal Democratic party was less clear. The largely Republican suburbs stood to gain as much or more than liberal Democratic inner cities, and Southern Republicans stood to gain even more. Nevertheless, by requiring apportionment according to population in both houses of state legislatures (as well as in the House of Representatives), the Supreme Court severely weakened the influence of the predominantly conservative rural and small town areas of the North and West where the Democrats had been weak since the 1930s. Conversely, it strengthened the urban areas where Northern blacks, union members, and Democratically inclined ethnic minorities were most numerous. Finally, urban and suburban areas increasingly faced common metropolitan problems that left most rural legislators unmoved. Not surprisingly, therefore, the Farm Bureau, some businessmen, rural legislators from both parties, and many conservative Republicans from metropolitan areas joined in a coalition against the Supreme Court's decision. The pro-reapportionment coalition eventually included, in addition to the unions, some civil-rights groups, middle-class liberals in organizations such as the League of Women Voters and the American Civil Liberties Union (ACLU), and city organizations such as the United States Conference of Mayors. Clearly, activists on both sides believed that these changes would encourage the passage of welfare-state legislation.

Because the anti-reapportionment forces commanded a majority in both houses of Congress in 1964, the Senate, where a large, determined minority could hope to filibuster indefinitely, was the decisive arena. The battle eventually focused on an amendment, or rider, offered by Minority Leader Everett Dirksen of Illinois to the foreign aid authorization bill that would initially have delayed judicial consideration of reapportionment cases for two to four years. Dirksen hoped this would give non-reapportionment legislatures time to ratify a constitutional amendment overturning the Court's ruling. The strategy of offering a rider was designed to minimize opposition of many pro-foreign aid liberals.

Dirksen did win the support of Democratic Majority Leader Mansfield of Montana, as well as many other Southern and Western Democrats. Substantial bipartisan support, combined with his close personal relations with the Johnson administration, led the Department of Justice to help Dirksen redraft his amendments. Although the department did seek to moderate the proposal, this step helped prevent any active opposition by the administration later in the session.

Dirksen's strategy might well have succeeded were it not for his senior colleague from Illinois, Democrat Paul Douglas. In a step that no doubt assured him a substantial place in American political history, Douglas declared his intention to speak at length on the Senate floor. Douglas' prospects for maintaining a filibuster, however, suffered from a lack of allies. As a maverick even among liberal Democrats, he could count at the outset on only a handful of other senators, all Democrats, including Mrs. Neuberger of Oregon and Senators Nelson and Proxmire of Wisconsin, Hart and MacNamara of Michigan, Anderson of New Mexico, and Ribicoff of Connecticut. According to one union official, long a close ally and admirer of Douglas, "No one likes a hairshirt, and Douglas has been the liberals' hairshirt in the Senate."

The labor movement, however, was the one large economic interest group with whom Douglas had maintained consistently cordial relations.* Accordingly, he sent copies of his first speech against the rider to President Meany of the AFL-CIO, President Reuther of the UAW and the AFL-CIO's industrial union department, and Director Biemiller of the federation's legislative department. As one union leader admitted later, "we were just asleep at the switch [on reapportionment] until Douglas alerted us." Once aroused, however, the labor movement, in the view of almost every pro-reapportionment informant interviewed in this study, proved not only the first but by far the most important interest group defending the Court's rulings. Middle-class organizations such as the ACLU could provide the substantive data and arguments that gave pro-reapportionment speeches an impressive aura of pertinence and relevance. But only union lobbyists had the necessary contacts with liberal Democrats—in terms of friendships and obligations owed for past support—to insist that they personally join the filibuster. (Nine months later, in May 1965, union officials were much better informed on the details of recruiting speakers to support Douglas than even the most important non-labor lobbyists.)

The effort involved a wide variety of unions. Although representatives of the IUD, whose members mainly lived in underrepresented urban areas, moved quickly to support Douglas, the AFL-CIO legislative department also took a prominent part. Director Biemiller insisted on having one of his staff included in the filibusterers' strategy meetings. In strategy sessions he later joined with a number of key Senators in opposing any compromise that, even by implication, criticized the Supreme Court. With the unions' help, the pro-reapportionment Senators were now sufficiently well coordinated and numerous—they had multiplied roughly three-fold to include about eighteen or twenty—to speak indefinitely. In addition, so many of Dirksen's allies insisted on speaking on other important issues that the rider's opponents usually had to speak for only three

---

* Among other Illinois unions, Douglas enjoyed especially close ties with the Steelworkers. USA District Director Germano, for example, had effectively supported Douglas' campaign to protect the Indiana Dunes lakeshore from industrial development.

or four hours on any single day. Finally, Majority Leader Mansfield, whose refusal to coerce minorities had been the despair of civil-rights groups—and labor itself on repeal of 14(b)—refused in this case to threaten the minority with long hours or late sessions. As had happened in the past, pressures for dropping the whole issue mounted as the Senate remained immobilized. To expedite adjournment, Senator Mansfield successfully moved to emasculate Dirksen's rider. The decisive first battle to protect the Supreme Court's ruling had been won, because time now worked inexorably against Dirksen and his allies. In compliance with lower-court orders, an increasing number of state legislatures adopted apportionments based on population, making ratification of an anti-reapportionment constitutional amendment less and less likely.

In passing the Civil Rights Act of 1964, Senate liberals overcame their frequent lack of coordination and discipline through the combined efforts of the Leadership Conference on Civil Rights on one side and the Johnson administration and Majority Whip (and likely Vice-Presidential candidate) Humphrey on the other. But during the reapportionment debate in August 1961, Humphrey was absorbed in preparing for the campaign, Mansfield was opposed to the cause, and the administration was at best immobilized. No government or party official enjoyed a sufficiently disinterested position as recognized leader to avoid arousing Senatorial suspicions. Because they sought no government or party positions for themselves, labor representatives were able to assume some of these coordinating activities, including the vital matter of marshaling pro-reapportionment forces for key roll calls. As one staff assistant of an important Senator who opposed the rider put it, "On the key amendments we knew how every vote would go—we had them all counted. Labor really helped us here." As they had during the campaign for electoral reorientation in the South and during the debates on the poll tax and job discrimination issues in Congress, the labor movement provided some of the direction that the formal Democratic leadership could not or would not provide.

In 1965 Dirksen offered a constitutional amendment permitting apportionment on the basis of factors other than population in one house of a legislature. This proposal, unlike the rider, would have left untouched the jurisdiction of the federal courts. To coordinate and dramatize the fight against the amendment, Douglas and his union allies established a pro-reapportionment roof organization of lobbyists and staff aides, the National Council for Fair Representation.

Union representatives took care not to appear to dominate the council, a strategy similar to the UAW's tactic of supporting nonlabor Democrats for many top party positions in Michigan. For example, Director Biemiller was instrumental in the selection of Lawrence Speiser of the ACLU as national chairman of the council. Nevertheless, the council depended heavily on the unions' organizational resources. In addition to staff assistants from Senators Douglas, Proxmire, and Hart, the council included representatives from the ACLU, the Americans for Democratic Action, and AFL-CIO's legislative department. But the largest single group came from the IUD and individual industrial unions in the steel, automobile, clothing, and meat-packing industries.* All told, union officials made up half the membership of the council at many of its meetings. Indeed, they provided two of the three members of the fund-raising committee, and two of the four members assigned to taking a preliminary poll of the House of Representatives. In addition, one IUD staff member also worked almost full time on reapportionment during the first part of 1965. Another IUD official maintained liaison with the aide of a pro-reapportionment leader in the House to make preparations in case Dirksen's amendment cleared the Senate. Labor representatives also contacted congressmen and mayors from such cities as New York, Milwaukee, Philadelphia, Cleveland, and Minneapolis, to testify against the amendment in Senate hearings. Finally, only the trade unions had the resources to lobby against the anti-reapportionment resolutions that were proposed in numerous state legislatures, in part by financing a "Vote Shrinkers Pamphlet" and by encouraging articles in the local labor press.†

---

* Material in this section is based on the minutes of the National Council for Fair Representation as well as on interviews.

† During this period national COPE officials participated in the successful and somewhat unexpected defeat of a reapportionment proposition in Ohio that would have seriously injured labor's and the Democratic party's prospects.

Less than a year after the defeat of his rider, the Senate rejected Dirksen's amendment on August 4, 1965, in a roll call that was essentially duplicated in 1966 when he proposed the amendment a second time. Because a constitutional amendment requires a two-thirds majority, the Douglas forces did not resort to a filibuster, but moved directly to a vote. The events leading up to this decision further indicated the labor movement's importance in the struggle. For one thing, union representatives helped influence several pro-reapportionment Senators. According to one key strategist, who was active in the National Council for Fair Representation, unionists had some impact on two of the three Republicans voting against Dirksen, Jacob Javits of New York and Boggs of Deleware, as well as on Democrats Long of Missouri, Pell of Rhode Island, McIntyre of New Hampshire, Muskie of Maine, Hartke and Bayh of Indiana, Bass of Tennessee, and Yarborough of Texas. In addition, at a tactical level, the pro-reapportionment forces were willing to move directly to a roll call only if they were certain that they had enough votes to reject the amendment. Otherwise they planned to launch another filibuster in an attempt to acquire additional votes or to pass crippling amendments. Douglas and his colleagues, however, delayed the vote for several days because they depended for an accurate poll on union lobbyists whose energies were absorbed by the House vote on repeal of 14(b), which took place on July 28th. This situation offers perhaps the best single illustration of labor's central place in the reapportionment struggle. Only after the repeal bill passed the House and thus after union lobbyists could return to the Senate to make their count could the pro-reapportionment bloc be certain that it numbered well more than a third of the Senate.

Trade Unions and Congress: Working-Class, Pluralist, and Partisan Interpretations

Union support for aid to education, repeal of the 4 percent investment credit, and particularly reapportionment, civil rights, and Medicare appears consistent with the working-class politics inter-

pretation so often applied to the CIO in the 1930s. A pluralist interpretation, however, would stress the high priority that American
unions assigned to the repeal of 14(b) during the Eighty-Ninth
Congress as an evidently contrasting concern with immediate organizational goals. Indeed, virtually every congressman interviewed
in this study reported significant and in some cases intense union
pressure on the issue. In this pluralist view, the prominence of the
union's position on welfare-state issues primarily reflected the limited
resources of other liberal groups. The impressive resources of the
National Education Association, for example, helped reduce the
importance of labor lobbyists on education bills. The real test would
be organized labor's priority in allocating resources when forced to
choose between broad social welfare goals and immediate organizational interests. Although this restated pluralist view does not entirely account for the special case of the AFL-CIO's antivoluntarist
stand on fair employment legislation, it might still explain away
much of the AFL-CIO's support for the other welfare measures described here.

It is significant though not decisive, however, that all but one
of the liberal Democratic informants on Capitol Hill interviewed
during this study rejected this neopluralist interpretation. Indeed,
some of the congressmen and their aides found this hypothesis so
foreign to their working assumptions that initially they had difficulty
comprehending it. One knowledgeable congressional liberal dismissed
the notion with a derisive laugh. Even after it was explained, the
hypothesis won partial assent from only one informant, a congressman on the far left wing of the Democratic party in the House who
criticized the AFL-CIO's support of the war in Vietnam. Yet he conceded that labor had not sacrificed such issues as Medicare or civil
rights for repeal of 14(b). On the other hand, a Southern liberal
complained that "just like the Farm Bureau," labor lobbyists were
in fact too broadly involved in general welfare-state issues. "They
send me a letter every week on some issue—they spread themselves
too thin."

As it happened, the agenda of issues before Congress in 1965
when these interviews were conducted permitted a limited test of
these conflicting interpretations, since Dirksen's reapportionment

amendment came to a vote in the Senate before repeal of 14(b). Because Senator Dirksen was also likely to lead the filibuster against repeal, the labor movement thus had the opportunity to try to rescue repeal from a filibuster by altering its adamant position on reapportionment. The leaders of the industrial union department decisively rejected in advance any such bargain. To be sure, organizational self-interest might possibly explain their insistence on reapportionment, because the IUD's membership was more heavily concentrated in underrepresented metropolitan areas than that of other AFL-CIO unions. And, at least with respect to the branch manufacturing plants of many national corporations, the large industrial unions had not encountered insurmountable barriers to organizing in right-to-work states. It was much more significant, therefore, that Senator Douglas also obtained a commitment from AFL-CIO President Meany against trying to bargain over repeal of 14(b)—a commitment that may have contributed to the defeat of the repeal measure.

Although organized labor's refusal to bargain over reapportionment does not support a pluralist interpretation, reflection on the issue's policy implications by no means entirely supports the alternative Marxist emphasis on working-class politics. Of course, the party's New Deal socioeconomic constituency in all regions was likely to benefit substantially from state legislative reapportionment (though not necessarily reapportionment of national House seats). Indeed, from the time of Al Smith's dramatic gains among urban voters in 1928 to Johnson's landslide victory of 1964, the national Democratic party had primarily appealed to an urban or metropolitan rather than to a rural or small-town constituency. But it was obviously fallacious to assume that this urban constituency was also overwhelmingly lower class. New metropolitan-oriented government programs were certain to benefit primarily middle- and upper-class suburbanites as well as less prosperous residents of both suburbs and central cities.

Similarly, the emphasis on equality of opportunity in employment and public accommodations in the 1964 Civil Rights Act benefited middle-class and lower–middle-class blacks at least as much as poor blacks. The latter were less equipped to travel extensively and to compete for jobs made available by fair employment legislation. Indeed, by operating the War on Poverty, the Johnson administration recognized that civil-rights legislation in itself could not provide the much more direct economic assistance that lower-class blacks required. And even within the labor movement itself, collective bargaining and New Deal welfare legislation had pushed many union members from the lower to the lower-middle and middle social strata when measured in terms of income.[19]

Evidently the labor movement vigorously supported Medicare, reapportionment, and civil-rights measures not because they necessarily benefited the lower classes but because their beneficiaries primarily voted Democratic or might be induced to do so. Organized labor operated, in short, neither as a working-class formation nor as a conventional interest group, but as an organized constituent interest of the Democratic party. These observations strongly reinforce our partisan rather than strictly *working*-class interpretation of such nonpluralist union activities as the "self-interested" endorsement of fair employment legislation. The controlling criteria are thus present for potential membership in a group defined in partisan rather than in income or in occupational terms. As American unions attempted to translate their egalitarian values into government policies in the late 1960s, they increasingly focused on assembling victorious political coalitions by adopting the aggregating perspective of the Democratic party. By 1964, COPE's regional conferences had begun to resemble assemblages of the political interests of the Democratic party coalition, including rural electrical cooperatives, civil-rights groups, senior citizens organizations, and the Farmers' Union—none of which had exclusively lower-class memberships. As we shall see, this partisan orientation is consistent with the emergence of class cleavage between producers and consumers. At this point we can note that this partisan perspective, in Easton's terms, "reduced" union demands, that is, prevented the unions from trading repeal of 14(b) for reapportionment and led them to accept the Johnson administration's delay in considering the repeal of 14(b).[20] As Schattschneider would argue, organizational demands were limited by their commitment to a partisan political constituency.[21]

On the other hand, this partisan criteria also excluded some groups that organized labor's egalitarian values might have led it to support—most notably, migrant farm workers, perhaps the most underprivileged group in American society. Admittedly, the AFL-CIO's testimony to congressional committees unequivocally supported legislation to help the migrants, including the exclusion of Mexican *braceros* who competed against the migrants in the labor market. The AFL-CIO also included farm labor issues among the ten votes in the Senate and eleven in the House used to evaluate incumbent senators and congressmen before making endorsements for the 1964 election. Nevertheless, one well-informed labor lobbyist who pointed out that other groups had also been relatively inactive, admitted that none of the larger labor groups except the Meatcutters had assigned specific lobbyists to secure favorable votes on key roll calls for farm labor legislation. And one of the best informed observers on farm labor legislation in Congress explicitly refused to include trade unions as a major element in the coalition that supported the migrants. Even after repeated probes he insisted, "No matter how you ask it, it always comes back to the [Protestant and Catholic] churches." Organized labor's participation, he continued, "was minuscule, all they did was speak for it." Indeed, he attributed some of the coalition's earlier defeats to union inactivity.

Consistent with a pluralist interpretation, this inactivity on farm legislation may reflect in part the organizational and financial security that reduced the empathy of the strongest American trade unions and their members for such a socially and economically depressed group. Neither members nor unions in the early 1960s seemed as moved to attack apparent economic injustice as they had been in the 1930s. Nevertheless the unions did support Medicare as a partial solution to the severe economic deprivation of non-union members. If a pluralist interpretation works well in the case of farm labor legislation and a working class politics interpretation seems more adequate in the case of many other issues, a stress on partisan self-interest seems best suited to account for both. The migrants' social deprivation and especially their geographic mobility made them much less likely than most other groups to register in large enough numbers to help the party's candidates. But the labor movement became increasingly active once the migrants began to acquire powerful—and largely middle-class—support within the party coalition. By 1966 the AFL-CIO unions in California and Texas had joined the economic battle to help organize the farm workers in their states. And the same informant who dismissed earlier legislative labor efforts on behalf of the migrants as minimal reported that in 1966 union representatives had "begun to join the bandwagon" on such matters as a minimum-wage law for migrants.

By itself, of course, this partisan interpretation cannot explain organized labor's highly pluralist effort to place 14(b) ahead of the party's broader welfare-state objectives. But several respondents during the interviews volunteered a second essentially political interpretation of labor's congressional activities that explains this alternation between partisan and pluralist objectives. As one Congressman stated, "They are only working so hard on 14(b) because in this Congress [which had the biggest Democratic majority since the 1930s] they finally have a chance to push it through." Just as Chicago and Los Angeles unions tended to concentrate their workers on those congressional districts where the parties were most evenly divided, the lobbyists in Washington concentrated on those issues, broad or narrow, where they were likely to receive the greatest marginal return per unit of invested resources. As a Democratic party official added, "Labor lobbyists could afford to concentrate on 14(b) [in the Eightly-Ninth Congress] because most of the issues on which they usually worked so hard, such as Medicare and aid to education, would pass easily." Consistent with this view, the labor movement devoted its energies in 1965 to reapportionment and the poll tax as well as to right to work, all issues whose outcome was in doubt.

Such flexibility reemphasizes the American labor movement's position in the Democratic party's organized constituency rather than its formal leadership. This status meant that the unions could remain an interest group on most pluralist issues and thus have sufficient freedom to pressure the party leaders on behalf of their organizational interests. Yet on welfare-state issues labor could adopt an aggregating posture on behalf of the party and in elections it could support the formal party leadership in general even while it was trying to reshape it in the South. The labor movement's status as a constituent socioeconomic interest of the party thus enabled it to avoid most of those situations in which the unions' partisan and organizational goals directly competed. But in cases where a choice between the two seemed necessary, the AFL-CIO's refusal to yield on reapportionment in exchange for concessions on 14(b) indicated, at the least, a considerable reluctance to sacrifice party interests.

Organized Labor and the Formal Party Leadership

Organized labor's partisan orientation was particularly important for liberal politicians in the early and mid-1960s because they believed that the unions possessed substantial organizational resources. Whatever the other effects of bureaucratization on the behavior of trade unions, the labor bureaucracy in Washington provided an organizational infrastructure in the campaigns on behalf of many of the party's most important welfare-state issues in Congress. To this extent the unions' activities paralleled the efforts of such party organs as the office of the Democratic whips in the House of Representatives. But labor lobbyists were far more united on social-welfare issues than the Democratic whips Ripley describes and could concentrate on these issues exclusively, whereas the whips were responsible for all types of issues. Indeed, organized labor was much less constrained by cooperative relationships with conservative Democrats or with Republicans, as well as with other party leadership groups in the Senate, the White House and the national committee, than were the whips.[22] We have seen that organized labor provided technical information for press releases and debates on Medicare, mimeographing services and office assistance to the Leadership Conference on Civil Rights, pamphlets favoring reapportionment, and membership and leadership support for the National Council of Senior Citizens. At least as important, on most liberal issues only the labor movement had the resources to poll and contact 535 Senators and Representatives—resources that, for example, the promigrant churches lacked. As one lobbyist for a liberal middle-class organiza-

tion observed, "Labor has more persuasive power—and more personnel—than any other group. I lobby alone; we have a one-man
office here."

Typically, one labor lobbyist was better informed on how a
doubtful Democratic Representative would vote on reapportionment than the leading pro-reapportionment Representative from his
state. Union staff men thus acted as a vital channel of information
as well as the spokesman for a pressure group, partly because their
bureaucratic structure enabled labor lobbyists to act quickly once
top leaders like AFL-CIO President Meany and IUD President Reuther
gave them clearance.

These trained, experienced, and often very skillful lobbyists were
all the more effective because they so rarely sought political office
or personal power for themselves. It was this trait that enabled them
to expand the number of Senator Douglas' allies on reapportionment so rapidly. Indeed, union lobbyists could also undertake some
coordinating activities that the Democratic Study Group (DSG)
could not, even though this organized caucus of House liberals was
not inhibited by a conservative membership. In 1963, labor and
the DSG resolved to block Representative Landrum's appointment
to the House Ways and Means Committee lest it become more conservative. But it was labor officials rather than the DSG who made the
key appeals to local party leaders in Philadelphia and in Chicago
to have Congress vote against Landrum's appointment. The patronage orientation of these local leaders did not make them particularly
sympathetic to the DSG's issue-oriented style, but they valued the
labor movement's campaign contributions and assistance in campaign work.

Just as the party's formal leaders could act as disinterested
mediators among some of their constituent interest groups, the labor
movement could act as a disinterested broker among some of the
Democrats' competing or suspicious leadership factions. In electoral
politics, the labor movement also performed this function when it
sought to coordinate party and interest group activities on behalf of
freshman Democrats in the Eighty-Ninth Congress. In the urban
South, the unions' efforts extended to unifying the party by supporting the replacement of conservative Democrats with liberals—

a step formal party leaders were also less willing to undertake on their own.

The labor movement thus provided coordination for pro–welfare-state Democrats that the formal party leaders and organizations were too inhibited by geographical, institutional, and factional barriers to provide. This fragmentation of power and authority among the Democrats, which helped prevent concerted activity by formal party leaders, can be compared to the patchwork governmental structure in many American localities. Banfield has observed that the resources of the dominant party organization in Chicago enabled it to "overcome by informal centralization" the area's "formal decentralization."[23] At least with regard to much of the Democrats' welfare-state program, organized labor in congressional politics in the 1960s sought to provide the same centralization, cohesion, and unity for the national Democratic *party* that the Chicago Democratic organization provided for the city's *government*.

We can now refine the concluding proposition in Chapter IX that the American labor movement and the Democratic party alternated in applying pressure on each other—a formulation that itself qualified the usual assumptions about party–pressure group relationships. The unions' predominantly organizational contributions to party activities described in this chapter exemplify the functional specialization and division of labor typical of most contemporary formal organizations. Not only has the labor movement developed a set of political specialists who have very little to do with economic collective bargaining, its political specialists have themselves become functionally differentiated. The IUD and the AFL-CIO legislative departments' lobbyists have overlapping rather than identical legislative concerns, and both differ in outlook and competence from labor campaign specialists. Finally, within each group, particular lobbyists sometimes specialize on particular issues and areas. It was this division of labor within the labor movement that enabled a larger division of the party's aggregating activities between the Democrats' formal leaders and the unions as one of the party's organized constituent interests.

Many observers have noted that legislators allied with powerful organized interests sometimes invite these groups to exert pressure.

In organized labor's case, for example, its allies in Congress invited union pressure in order to make their vote for repeal of 14(b) appear more popular in their district. Again, Senator Douglas' plea for labor's assistance against the Dirksen rider was actually a demand that the unions apply enough pressure to recruit more senatorial allies. These efforts underline the cooperation based on different skills and resources that characterizes the labor movements' overall relationship to the party on welfare issues. We may speak of cooperation because organized labor's pressure was not primarily, and surely not exclusively, based on a belief in the unions' ability to prevent the reelection of any particular congressman. As the preceding chapters make clear, labor's campaign organization was not strong enough to pose that threat.[24] True, in varying degree from district to district or state to state, unions could make a candidate's reelection somewhat more likely and his election campaign considerably less taxing by improving his reputation with certain voters, by contributing to his campaign funds, or by supplying campaign workers. Yet even where labor had provided such help to individual candidates, union representatives exerted influence—particularly on issues like reapportionment—only in part by reminding their allies of assistance in campaigns. Equally important, they appealed to a common ideology, a common concern for the party, and their joint efforts on other welfare-state issues.

In sum, the unions' organizational resources and freedom from the constraints that public and party offices impose on their incumbents enabled the labor movement to undertake a variety of tasks that the formal party leaders could not do as well for themselves. Of course, these public officeholders had resources and opportunities that the labor movement as an economic group did not. But rather than simply create a mutual and alternating pattern of pressure, this division of resources also produced at times a mutual interdependence—in Durkheim's phrase, organic solidarity—that the partnership between the formal and socioeconomic sides of the party operated.

These considerations point out still more general difficulties with the pluralist pressure-group model of the labor movement's behavior in the legislative process. Indeed, any view of the union's political behavior in Washington as primarily the reflex of relatively stable economic and social interests is not only too static but also much too mechanistic. By itself this pluralist approach illuminates the fluid dynamic quality of political life no better than the social determinism in voting research that Key and Munger attacked a decade ago.[25] By contrast, this chapter has emphasized shared values, attitudes, and loyalties. We shall see that these common partisan commitments are consistent with the class politics interpretation of American life offered in Chapter XI, however much this interpretation differs from the Marxist cleavage between capitalists and workers.

XI

Conclusion:
Labor Politics in a Fully Industrialized Society

Any description, let alone explanation, of the American labor movement's complex behavior in national politics encounters formidable problems of conceptualization. This concluding chapter begins, therefore, by setting out in propositional form the basic arguments of the preceding analysis. The reader may proceed directly and without loss of continuity to the second part of the chapter, which considers the connections between unions, parties, and consumer-class politics in a highly industrialized democracy. However, these summary propositions conveniently introduce the major analytic issue on which the concluding section focuses: The causal relationship between the political behavior and the economic basis of trade union organizations.

Summary Propositions

Condensing the argument of the preceding ten chapters into explicit descriptive and explanatory propositions risks both distortion and oversimplification. Yet the specificity of the propositions not only facilitates their modification or refutation, but also suggests a partially statistical formulation of the qualitative data in the present analysis. Specifically, this book's central descriptive thesis can be formulated in terms of a frequency distribution of union behavior in the early and mid-1960s. This study has indicated a range of union political behavior on a continuum from the pluralist laissez-faire voluntarism of the AFL under Gompers to the collectivist politics of the Detroit-area district COPE organizations, whose activities resembled the branch structure of some European socialist parties. Union behavior as a whole, however, was not distributed evenly along this continuum, but clustered in the middle. This central tendency has often been designated in the preceding pages as organized labor's "role" within the Democratic party coalition.

The propositions that follow are accordingly divided into three parts. The first describes the unions' role; that is, it locates the central tendency on the pluralist–welfare-state continuum in terms of activities, influence, goals, and, in consequence, labor's aggregating role. The second set of propositions attempts to explain this tendency by comparing and contrasting relevant political, social, and economic conditions in the United States and in parts of Europe. The third set of propositions attempts to explain the empirically observed variation, once again, in terms of the unions' activities, goals, influence, and aggregating efforts.

Description of Central Tendency

1. In the early and mid-1960s, the American labor movement's role in the national Democratic party represented a *partial* equivalence to the Social Democratic (formerly socialist) party–trade union alliances in much of Western Europe. This equivalence obtained with respect to its activities as a party campaign (and lobbying) organization, its influence as a party faction, and its welfare-state policy objectives. Analytically, the role's most important consequence has been the labor movement's efforts to aggregate, that is, to combine and to reduce many of the demands of social and economic groups, an activity often thought to be a distinguishing attribute of major political parties in two-party systems.

A. Activities. Partial equivalence characterized organized labor's national campaign activities, signifying the spread of formal economic organizations in America from lobbying (which emerged in the nineteenth century) to electoral politics in the generation after World War II.

1. Union members, particularly the most loyal, generally voted Democratic. Union financial contributions accounted for a sizable fraction—about one-fourth—of all Democratic campaign funds in national elections, and union campaign workers ordinarily tried to contact all accessible Democrats rather than simply union members.

2. The Democratic party, however, commanded a less overwhelming working-class vote and relied less on union contributions in this period than did European Social Democratic parties. And, by comparison with European socialist branch organizations, the congressional-district COPE structure had fewer strongly motivated members, was less able to sustain continuous activity, and was less successful in covering all working-class urban districts.

3. In sum, the American unions' political-action enterprise strategy called for offsetting the workers' limited class consciousness with organizational resources and loyalties.

B. Influence. Partial equivalence characterized organized labor's influence within the Democratic party.

1. Labor leaders acquired many influential formal and informal positions among the Democrats, and, as a whole, the national labor movement became one of several important, largely autonomous party factions that influenced party decisions and most party leaders.

2. On the other hand, such influence rarely meant the capacity to determine Democratic party decisions unilaterally. Once compromise seemed possible, American unions typically sought political accommodation with national and local party leaders rather than militantly asserting their own views.

C. Goals. Partial equivalence characterized organized labor's policy goals in national politics.

1. By the late 1930s, both the AFL and CIO supported welfare-state programs that sought to benefit lower-class citizens, many of whom were not affiliated with the labor movement. On occasion organized labor's espousal of welfare-state goals led it into conflict with more conservative patronage-oriented Democrats.

2. Yet even the welfare-state objectives of American unions were less extensive than the welfare program actually enacted in many European countries—and the unions sometimes took positions to the right of the Democrats' middle-class, ideologically motivated amateurs.

D. Aggregation. Consistent with this partial equivalence, the American labor movement aggregated the Democratic party's constituent interests in some but not all circumstances.

1. In addition to mobilizing heavily Democratic nonlabor minority group voters in elections, the unions have sought to help the party satisfy these groups' political demands and include them in the party's councils. One consequence has been the pressure that these interest groups exerted on the labor movement, much as interest groups are thought to pressure the party. Indeed, this broad aggregating orientation evoked analogous pressure on the labor movement by party leaders concerned with their own factional interests.

2. Organized labor did not fully assume the party's aggregating activities. Typically, nonunion party officials often showed greater capacity to mediate among the various Democratic factions, while the unions, by remaining outside the formal party leadership, retained greater freedom to pressure party leaders on behalf of their own pluralist organizational interests.

Explanation of the Central Tendency

II. The central tendency of union behavior in national politics, that is, its partisan role, emerged out of the unique features of the American society and polity and the common impact of industrialization on America and Europe.

A. Social and Political Differences. The weakness of working-class consciousness, together with certain environmental obstacles, limited the American labor movement's partisan activities, influence, and scope of welfare-state goals.

1. Consciousness was limited by the similarity between social classes and, internally, by social heterogeneity within the working class.

a. In terms of interclass relations, the limited consciousness of the workers' common political interests resulted from: first, the lack of feudal distinctions between status groups; second, a belief in the widespread opportunity to rise out of the working class; and, third, the extension of universal male suffrage in America before the onset of heavy industrialization.

b. In terms of the workers' own solidarity, consciousness was limited by differences of race, religion, and national origin, as well as by high levels of immigration and residential mobility.

2. Environmental obstacles—both social and political—hindered the development of both unions and working-class political formations.

a. Unhampered by a paternalistic and prestigious aristocracy, the industrial bourgeoisie attacked trade unions with a ruthlessness rarely seen in Western Europe.

b. As in the case of some but not all European union-party alliances, the Democratic party long predated the emergence of stable unions, and therefore retained a generally predominant voice in the alliance that solidified during the New Deal. Unlike all the major European parties of the left, the Democrats remained procapitalist rather than socialist.

B. Economic Similarities. The cumulative effect of industrialization was the principal factor producing political unity and active partisanship in the American working class.

1. Industrial rather than nonfactory unions were predominant in labor's national partisan role, primarily because of the frustrations of the industrial work process, the particular vulnerability of factory workers to rapid economic change, and the relative ease of recruiting political activists in the stable factory work situation.

2. The support of industrial capitalists for antiunion Republicans heightened worker consciousness by adding political differences to the existing economic differences between workers and middle-income and upper-income groups. The labor movement's shift to Democratic partisanship was in part a reaction to this business-Republican alliance.

3. By fostering assimilation, industrialization reduced the impact of the workers' ethnic and racial heterogeneity.

4. The Depression of 1929 intensified the workers' sense of shared economic grievance at least temporarily minimizing their remaining racial and ethnic antagonisms. This same collapse also stimulated grievances against the American party system, which, up to 1928, had substantially ignored both working-class economic demands and the ethnic aspirations of most urban minority groups.

C. Organized labor's partisan role—as a channel for collectivist working-class demands with a lower capacity to convert such demands into issues than comparable European union-party formations—was thus a function of the superimposition of an industrial economic order on a deeply entrenched democratic, pro-capitalist, and federal political regime. It is this particular interaction of economic and political systems that produced greater variation in the political behavior of American unions as opposed to their European counterparts.

Patterns of Variation

III. The variation in the labor movement's national partisan role was the product of the variation in, first, its party campaign (and lobbying) activities, second, its influence as a party faction, and, third, its national policy objectives. The variation on these three dimensions, in turn, explains the variation in the unions' partisan aggregating activities. All these variations could be observed over a period of time and among different geographical areas and types of unions.

A. Activities. Holding union size constant, the activity of any given union varied with the effectiveness of its incentive system. This effectiveness was a function of a particular union's economic structure, the external barriers to communication among a union's members, the character of political conflict in the union's locality, and the environmental obstacles to precinct work.

1. In terms of economic structures, such incentives were greater among industrial-union members than among nonfactory union members and, accordingly, were greater in those areas and time periods in which such factory union members were most numerous.

a. The repetitive, routinized operations and physical exertion of factory work created grievances that produced more political activists among industrial than among nonfactory unionists.

b. The informal communication within the factory shop society, unlike that in many nonfactory work situations, encouraged a sense of community and thus a feeling of common working-class political interests. However, some nonfactory union officials succeeded in creating a substitute for the shop society through the unions' formal activities, not only in politically oriented local union COPES but also through union meetings and other activities with a manifest economic purpose.

c. The industrial unions' position in a national market, rather than in the local market of most craft and service unions, increased their incentive to become active in national politics.

d. Production for a national market also encouraged union centralization in industrial unions, strengthening the national leaders' ability to stimulate political activism.

e. Incentives to participate in national politics increased with the growth of the national government's regulation of the industrialized American economy.

2. Union political activity decreased as environmental factors such as a rise in residential mobility or the growth of divisive ethnic or racial consciousness reduced communication among workers.

3. Union political activity varied with the extent to which political cleavage coincided with class conflict in the society.

a. Pluralist politics reduced activity by cutting across class cleavages with conflict over divisible material benefits, such as patronage, to individuals or to small groups.

b. Activity of the labor movement as a whole increased over time as the clash over trade-union issues coincided with the division between the parties.

c. Among individual unions, activity was greater if the union had readily available partisan allies in its early, formative years.

d. Given such allies, political activists increased in response to the threat of antiunion governmental activity.

4. Political activity varied with the number of environmental obstacles to union campaign work.

a. High residential mobility and migration into an area inhibited precinct work by disrupting the organization of union precinct workers and hindering cooperation among different unions.

b. The less certain the outcome of the particular election or legislative issue, the greater the union activity.

c. Union activity decreased in response to actual or threatened sanctions by intraparty competitors. The weaker the regular party organization, the greater the likelihood of union activity.

B. Influence. Holding union activity constant, organized labor's intraparty influence varied inversely with an increase in the incentives available to other party groups or in the opportunities of party leaders and Democratic officeholders to exercise the resources that their offices conferred.

1. Union influence decreased as the nonmaterial incentives and the access to public and party office of nonunion Democrats increased.

a. In areas with little patronage, nonunion Democrats were less active in low-income districts than in middle-income districts where residents responded to nonmaterial incentives.

b. In those areas where the unions were outside the dominant local Democratic party coalition, nonunion Democrats had greater access to party offices, such as precinct captain, where such offices were appointive. In areas where the unions were part of dominant coalitions, the access of nonunion Democrats was greater where party offices were primarily elective.

c. The opportunity of nonunion Democrats to win public office varied with the ratio of the number of such offices usually held by Democrats to the total population. This ratio and, hence, the opportunity, was smallest in those suburban areas where Democrats were likely to win many local offices; the ratio was larger in those populous urban centers with few, elected local officials.

2. The opportunity of nonunion party leaders to utilize the resources conferred by their offices varied with the political context.

a. In situations of severe intraparty factional cleavage, nonunion party officers could mediate among the Democrats' diverse social and economic groups more effectively than union officials, a factor that increased the ability of these party officers to make decisions independently.

b. In low-income and lower–middle-income areas with few industrial unions and little patronage, union influence was reduced by the absorption of members into the campaign organizations of appealing party candidates.

c. In primaries, the generally high status of public officials and their familiarity to the electorate reduced union influence by enabling incumbent Democratic officeholders to ignore union pressure with relatively little risk of defeat.

3. Union influence decreased with the availability of patronage to nonlabor party factions.

C. *Goals*. Organized labor's political goals in national politics varied with the scope of the political constituency, ranging from the party's broad welfare-state constituency to the membership and then to the officers of particular unions.

1. The scope of a union's political constituency varied with its economic position.

    a. Members of industrial and service unions, who had fewer skills than craft unionists, were usually less well paid and did more repetitive, physically exhausting, and less interesting work. They thus tended to be less satisfied and consequently more receptive to supporting substantial changes in government welfare policies.

    b. The scope of a union's political constituency varied with the need for political allies to offset a disadvantageous economic position, notably the industrial and service unions' lack of a monopoly of economic skills in their job markets. Similarly, industrial unions sought political allies to reduce their vulnerability to economic fluctuations and competition in a national market from low-wage, antiunion areas.

2. The scope of the labor movement's political constituency increased as its antiunion opposition became more intense and the political success of that opposition became more likely.

3. Measured directly in terms of acknowledged policy objectives, the scope of a union's constituency varied with the receptiveness of the political system to demands for collective policy outputs. Thus such collectivist demands increased with the decline of laissez-faire values in national politics and with the decline of the predominantly private-regarding values of local political machines.

4. As the interest diversity–cohesion ratio indicates, the more diverse a union's constituent interests, the broader the programs it favors in order to unite its membership.

a. The stronger welfare-state orientation of most industrial unions in part reflects their relatively greater heterogeneity in member job skills and ethnicity.

b. The broader policy goals of the national AFL (before the CIO merger) as compared with those of many of its non-industrial affiliates and its constituent state and local federations, reflected the more diverse constituency of a national multiunion federation.

5. As the interest diversity–cohesion ratio indicates, the greater the interest-group cohesion within the labor movement, and between it and other interests, the broader the unions' goals.

a. Interest cohesion was greater in partisan (particularly two-party) elections than in nonpartisan elections in which ethnic, racial, and economic divisions emerged among Democratic partisans.

b. Interest cohesion was greater in (partisan) elections than in legislative lobbying, so that party pressure on the labor movement was more frequent in the electoral process, whereas union pressure on the party occurred more frequently in the legislative process.

c. Interest cohesion on a given issue decreased with the degree to which a government policy output could be divided among particular individuals or groups.

d. Interest cohesion declined with high community growth and residential mobility, except in such highly structured aspects of the political process as Presidential elections.

D. Aggregation. The variation in labor's partisan role in national politics directly affected its propensity to aggregate constituent interests of the Democratic party.

1. Aggregating activities were more prominent among industrial than among nonfactory (especially craft) unions.

2. Aggregating activities were more prominent in national rather than in local union groups.

3. Aggregating activities were more prominent in partisan electoral politics than in nonpartisan campaigns or in the legislative process.

4. In national partisan elections aggregating activities were more prominent among unions in good-government cities than among those in machine cities.

5. Aggregating activities were more prominent on welfare-state issues, which have most frequently emerged since the coming of the New Deal, than on pluralist issues.

American Unions and Class Politics

This set of descriptive and explanatory propositions has summarized those findings strongly supported by the available evidence. But the data in this book also bears, perhaps more indirectly, upon the more general question of the broad political cleavages in industrial society. In order to analyze this larger issue, we shall now consider the relevance of several social and political traditions of analysis. Throughout, the focus will remain that of this entire volume, a comparison of political, social, and economic explanations of the political behavior of American unions in the early and mid-1960s.

Chapter X concluded that the presence of many nonworkers in the Democratic party's diverse constituency supported an interpretation of the unions' welfare-state oriented activities in partisan rather than in pressure-group or working-class terms. But the analysis that follows suggests that the partisan activity of the labor movement is, in fact, consistent with their members' class interests once the concept of class is properly redefined. In turn, this redefinition leads to a convergence of two analytic traditions often thought contradictory. One tradition, which derives from Marx, has explained class conflict in the polity as the product of economic structures and processes. The other tradition, which includes many distinguished American political analysts, explains such conflict in terms of variations in political structures and processes. Despite his own emphasis on economic interests in politics, this approach can be traced back to the discussion of size of constituency in James Madison's *Federalist* No. 10. We begin with an introductory summary which indicates the major assertions and some of the key terms (in italics) that this new definition of class politics entails.

To show that the welfare-state oriented activities of the American labor movement are consistent with class politics requires a reformulation of Marx's original concept of class. Following Ralf Dahrendorf, this chapter will conceive of *class* as referring to two, and only two, groups whose conflict in any given system is sufficiently important to produce substantial social change. In other words, class and class conflict are not descriptive or explanatory propositions, to be evaluated in terms of their verifiability, but *heuristic* concepts to be used for ordering our data and for suggesting verifiable propositions that specify causal relationships. Dahrendorf explicitly distinguishes this heuristic purpose of explaining change through group conflict from Talcott Parsons' integrationist synthesis of sociological theory, which seeks to explain why and how societies have maintained themselves over time.

Dahrendorf suggests that class conflict is not determined by individual preferences, but by socially defined *roles*—the patterns of behavior that other members of society expect from individuals in particular positions. For example, in Marx's analysis of capitalism, both workers, (the *proletariat*) and employers (the *bourgeoisie*), are expected to react to each other and to outsiders in terms of their *role interests*. Worker conflict with employers—the Marxist formulation of working-class conflict—grows out of the workers' interest in maximizing wages as their primary source of income and the employers' role-interest in minimizing wages as a cost of production. In Dahrendorf's terms, interests are *manifest* if the incumbents of a particular role are aware of their interests and act accordingly. Interests remain *latent*—Marx called this situation "false consciousness"—if the role incumbents are not aware of them.

Persuasively arguing that Marx's bourgeoisie-versus-proletariat concept of class conflict was too narrow to encompass twentieth-century politics, Dahrendorf advances a more general formulation which posits conflict between those in positions of authority and those outside of it. Nevertheless, this emphasis on "the exercise of or exclusion from"[1] authority not only fails to account for conflict in democratic political systems, but also removes the dynamic component that Marx himself used to explain much basic social change in his own time. For example, whatever conflict existed between ordinary citizens in America and the national political authorities between 1933 and 1938—which Dahrendorf would stress—hardly accounts for the substantial economic and political changes introduced during the New Deal. Accordingly, we shall propose in the pages that follow an alternative formulation that retains the economic component by defining the two classes in industrial society as the *economic authorities* and the *economic nonauthorities*. The former group includes all those incumbents in management positions with responsibility for and decision-making authority over the process of economic production. (It excludes leaders—formal and informal—such as union officials who do not have this direct responsibility for production.) Economic nonauthorities include both wage earners and those with no role at all in economic production. These two classes come into conflict over *rationalization* of production; that is, because there is a continuous change in productive methods in order to maximize total output, profit, or efficiency. Rationalization creates conflicting roles primarily because it is instrumental. In other words, those individuals who occupy the roles of economic authorities, if successful, must be concerned with the improvement of productive methods as a good in itself, without any special concern for the adverse consequences that changes in production impose on the economic nonauthorities. Even stated in this general way, this concept of class has a strictly limited heuristic purpose. It does not purport to explain, whatever its source: (1) integrative behavior that furthers social stability; (2) noneconomic conflict based on race, ethnicity, language, or religion; (3) economic conflicts in nonindustrial societies; and (4) contemporary conflicts between numerous social strata that are separated from each other by gradations of money and status.[2]

Since this concept is too broad to explain a particular pattern of conflict, the discussion that follows will specify more precisely the role interests of the economic authorities and nonauthorities in each historical situation. Marx's conceptualization of the struggle of bourgeoisie versus proletariat provided this kind of specification for the Western Europe of his time. But the European proletariat of that period was united by sentiments that Emile Durkheim termed *mechanical solidarity;* that is, by a mutual affinity based on the similarity of their economic position as wage earners vis-à-vis management. This sentiment has been subsequently undermined by an increasingly complex functional specialization or division of labor. In consequence, at least since World War II united *working*-class political action has become more and more difficult. As a result, the political unity of the economic authorities has more recently grown out of what Durkheim called "organic solidarity"; that is, out of the mutual interdependence of specialists for their well-being and survival. Of course, innovations in production introduced by the industrial economic authorities have long meant dislocation for ordinary workers—which is one of Marx's central points. But the current unprecedented level of economic interdependence has increased the economic nonauthorities' vulnerability, quite apart from their role as workers, to the social, economic, and ecological dislocations produced by industrial innovation.

The discussion that follows will, accordingly, specify contemporary class conflict as a cleavage between economic authorities in their role as *producers* and economic nonauthorities in their role as *consumers.* We must emphasize that "producers" designates only members of those households whose primary source of income is provided by the exercise of economic authority, although this group is also important in economic consumption. Accordingly, "consumers" will not include all those who engage in consumption—that would involve the entire society—but only members of those households whose heads are excluded from the exercise of economic authority in production. Some of these consumers may not be part of the labor force at all. Each class is therefore defined by the origin rather than by the size of an individual's income. Equally important, class cleavage in contemporary politics takes place *across* the market transactions between consumers and producers rather than between workers and employers within the productive process.

With the decline of working-class unity, unions can be relevant for united class activity in politics only by pursuing their members' role interests as consumers rather than as workers. Yet the threat to consumer role interests is rarely as direct and personal a threat as the possible loss of income or the worsening of working conditions that has concerned the working class. Consumer-class unity is thus more fragile and less easily achieved than the proletarian unity of, say, Britain or the United States in the 1930s. Indeed, cohesion among consumers depends on such political conditions as issues, party systems and organizational incentives, and size of the relevant constituencies. Consequently, American unions in the mid-1960s were most likely to pursue their members' class interests on consumer issues, raised in national politics through the Democratic party's organized consumer constituency.

The concluding part of the chapter, therefore, will interpret class conflict in democratic industrialized societies as the product of two distinct sets of attitudes: (1) recognition of shared interests in policy outputs that affect economic rationalization and (2) recognition of an interest in uniting to control the exercise of political authority. As we will show, both the character of economic production and the structure of the political system directly affect the extent of each type of recognition in different but complementary ways. This joint impact of political and economic factors suggests that a primarily political or economic explanation of class conflict has limited heuristic value in explaining contemporary American politics. Rather, contemporary politics may come to focus on the content of change—that is, on the quality of social life. In such circumstances, class itself, that is, the prevailing configuration of conflict, becomes more important as an independent explanatory concept than the equally heuristic concepts of economic or political causation.

Economic Causation Versus Political Autonomy

The conclusion of Chapter II conceptualized the union–Democratic party alliance formed during the New Deal as a flow channel for the welfare-state demands of American workers, which resembled but had a lower capacity than comparable union-party formations of Western Europe. Revisionist Marxists who recognize the independent effect of political and social factors could plausibly interpret this development as the emergence of American "proletarian class politics" in which the workers' discontent with industrial capitalism dominated the national political agenda.

Such a view, however, has considerable difficulty in explaining American labor politics in the 1960s. For one thing, union organizations, even when their members wavered, have become more and more intimately involved with a party that has always sought supporters outside the working class. Still more important, despite continuing concern with their particularistic organizational goals, the unions themselves have come to embrace the national party's occupationally diverse constituency as their own.

As Morris Janowitz has pointed out, several of Max Weber's observations, taken together, suggest the increasing independence or autonomy of the modern polity.[3] This autonomy can be operationalized as the discretion of political leaders in responding to the interests and demands generated by socioeconomic structures. Weber himself suggested that this autonomy extended in the course of political development from the state to political parties.[4] Paradoxical as it may seem, our analysis suggests that in national politics this same autonomy now extends to overtly economic union organizations or at least to their political specialists and top officials. For example, as factional leaders in the Democratic party, union officials joined in the discretionary decision to raise some issues, for example, Medicare, but gave less emphasis to others, like the problem of migrant labor. In each case, these priorities in part reflected political calculations of partisan advantage. Similar calculations determined when the unions raised narrower economic issues like repeal of state right-to-work laws.

This picture of political autonomy extending first to the state, then to the parties and finally to the unions recognizes an intertwining of political and economic roles that neither Samuel Gompers nor his socialist opponents in the AFL fully anticipated. But recognition of complexity does not by itself constitute political analysis. Indeed this particular complexity appears to vitiate the value of class conflict between workers and employers as an explanatory concept, by making it difficult to indicate those organizations that represent particular classes. In order to develop a concept of class that better accounts for the partisan activities of American unions, we must re-formulate it in terms appropriate to the post-proletarian politics that has followed the New Deal.

Dahrendorf's Revision of the
Marxist Concept of Class

In a landmark contribution to political sociology, Dahrendorf has provided us both with a definitive scholarly critique and an il-luminating substantive revision of Marx's concept of class. Following the approach of Theodore Geiger, Dahrendorf emphasized Marx's fundamentally "heuristic purpose."

> . . . for Marx the theory of class was not a theory of a cross section of society arrested in time, in particular not a theory of social strati-fication, but a tool for the explanation of changes in total societies. . . . Marx was not guided by the question "How does a given society in fact look at a given point of time," but the question, "How does the structure of a society change?"[5]

In particular, class conflict had grown out of the conflicting goals or interests generated by the basic structure of society, rather than out of "sociologically random" conflicts produced by the more transitory psychological preferences of particular individuals. Class conflicts can thus be numbered among dichotomous cleavages, in which would-be participants are forced to choose one side or the other, a point we shall find of considerable importance in our analysis of the political sources of class cleavage.[6]

Dahrendorf, however, goes on to identify systematically the fea-tures of contemporary industrial society that have invalidated Marx's specific proletariat-bourgeoisie concept. He cites, for example, the split between corporate managers and stockholders ("the decompo-sition of capital"), the fissuring of the proletariat into functionally differentiated subgroups ("the decomposition of labor"), the de-clining intensity of class conflict, and the decreasing importance of work itself in many individuals' total life.[7] Rather than attack Marx's formulation of Western European conflict in the third quarter of the nineteenth century, Dahrendorf cites this evidence to demonstrate the inapplicability of this formulation, as a broad-range theory, to other types of industrial society. Accordingly, he devotes considerable attention to the theoretical source of Marx's difficulties; that is, to Marx's "trick of definition" that equated the authority relation of superordination and subordination with the ownership of productive capital. As he points out, "power and authority are not tied to the legal title of property"; witness executives who operate but do not own large corporations.[8]

In order to formulate a more tenable broad-range concept of class, Dahrendorf replaces "the possession, or nonpossession, of effective private property by the exercise of, or exclusion from, authority as the criterion of class formation."[9] It follows that class conflict takes place between the authorities and the nonauthorities over governmental policies and personnel.[10] This formulation does indeed appear to be a broad-range concept because it accounts for the persisting if moderated struggle between workers and managers in the contemporary factory as well as for the proletariat-bourgeoisie conflict in Marx's time. In addition, it illuminates phenomena Marx's concept cannot explain, like the opposition to bureaucratic authority that animated many American student protests in the mid-1960s and Milovan Djilas' analysis of contemporary Communist parties as a new ruling class.[11] Most important of all, this approach enables Dahrendorf to examine systematically a vital but largely covert theme that Marx's materialism often obscured: the political determinants of class conflict and basic social change.

This reliance on authority relations rather than property relations as the basis for class conflict creates certain problems for Dahrendorf's analysis that stem from the complexity of authority as a concept and the variety of behaviors it designates. Specifically, the relationships between authorities and nonauthorities do not have the same meaning to the participants and the same implications for the polity in every contemporary industrial society. It is one thing, for example, for an employer to order a change in a method of production, which may or may not be prohibited by a union contract. In this instance he has operated within the generally accepted scope of his authority, whatever the substantive merit of his order. It is altogether another matter if the employer attempts either subtle or overt control of the workers' political behavior outside the factory. Indeed, he might well be thought to have acted entirely outside the scope of his legitimate authority. In such diverse cases, the conflict between the authorities and nonauthorities is likely to differ markedly.

This failure to take into account the wide diversity of possible authority relations may explain his difficulty in analyzing class conflict in democratic systems where class conflict takes place between the political authorities and the " 'mere' citizens." "The citizens of a democratic state are not a suppressed class, but they are a subjected class . . ."[12] If Marx made politics the reflex of property relations, this analysis converts class conflict into a function of political (i.e., authority) relations. This argument comes surprisingly close to the pre-Marxist antistate liberals' concern for legal structures and rules that Marxism scornfully dismissed as bourgeois formalism.

In any case, Dahrendorf ultimately alternates between two equally unpersuasive interpretations. One retains a structurally determined understanding of dichotomous class conflict, but fails to explain the data. The other accounts for the data but no longer conceives of class conflict as structurally determined or else fails to provide a clear definition of the two classes. His first alternative, the idea of class conflict between the political authorities and the mere citizens, only obscures the process of social change in the New Deal. In that case, as in the tenure of the Labour government in Britain after World War II, it seems far more heuristically useful to conceive of class conflict between the workers and many top political authorities on one side, and a procapitalist coalition on the other. More generally, democratic regimes differ from factories and contemporary communist states because their elite strata sometimes institute distinctively different policies in the course of competing for formal power. In such regimes, the possession or lack of the highest authority roles by itself indicates little about an actor's substantive orientation toward changing the basic norms and institutions of society. At different times resistance to authorities may indicate very different policy goals depending on the party in power.

At several points Dahrendorf explicitly recognizes this objection. In his own words, "authority is from the point of view of sociological analysis [that is, apart from individual psychological gratifications derived from its mere exercise] an instrumental value. In class theory, the possession of authority does not figure as a value sought for its own sake but as an opportunity to realize specific interests."[13] Political authorities, he adds,

> rule on behalf of somebody . . . the exercise of authority always involves both the chance to issue authoritative commands and certain interests which constitute the substance of these commands . . . In abstract, therefore, the ruling political class of post-capitalist society consists of the [administrative bureaucracy] . . . the governmental elites at its head, and those interested parties which are represented by the governmental elites.[14]

The latter include the party in power and its interest-group allies.[15] But by including the parties' interest-group allies, like organized labor, among the political authorities, Dahrendorf no longer makes the exercise of or exclusion from political authority the defining criterion of class membership. As a result, authority is no longer the structural determinant of the conflicting role interests that set the two classes against each other. If we say that these groups seek power or authority as goods in themselves (a view that Dahrendorf appears to reject), class alignments may change from election to election depending on the existing tactical situation. The resulting transitory alliance thus verges on the "sociologically random," since political loyalties and preferences are distributed without a strong systematic relationship to basic social categories. If, on the other hand, we stress authority as an instrumental value that enables such groups to achieve their policy goals, such alliances are bound together by the content of what Dahrendorf calls the "specific interests" that form a political coalition. But, in this latter case an unstable set of highly individualistic policy preferences replaces authority relations as the "criterion of class formation." As a result, we no longer have a structurally determined relationship between classes (that was the case between authorities and nonauthorities) that can account for both cohesion within each political coalition and for the policy differences that divide the two coalitions from each other.

In sum, Dahrendorf's reformulated concept of class is broad enough to encompass much of the data Marx could not explain. But, in part because of its overly restricted view of authority, it is still too narrow to account for the pattern of conflict in postproletarian democracies. Clearly, we need a concept of class that avoids an overly simple view of authority relations and simultaneously explains class conflict in contemporary industrial democracies. This requirement suggests the utility of a two-level concept of class. First, we should frame a broad-range theory that explains the underlying pattern of conflict in all industrial societies. We could then apply that broader theory to specific cases through a series of middle-range concepts, each designed to account for a specific set of political and economic conditions. As it happens, a single additional explanatory concept can resolve both of these difficulties, both by reducing our dependence on authority as the primary explanatory factor, and then by generating different middle-range theories for different socioeconomic contexts. This concept, in fact, was the dynamic component in class conflict that Marx made central to his economic explanation of social change.

A Revised Concept of Class and Class Conflict

Marx linked the phenomenon of social change with the explanatory concept of class conflict through his analysis of the economic goals that animated the bourgeoisie. As early as the *Communist Manifesto,* Marx and Engels characterized these activities in terms that later sociologists labeled functional, formal, or instrumental rationalization.

> The bourgeoisie, where it has got the upper hand, has put an end to all feudal, patriarchal, idyllic relations. It has pitilessly torn asunder the motley feudal ties that bound man to his "natural superiors," and has left remaining no other nexus between man and man than naked self-interest, than callous "cash payment." It has drowned the most heavenly ecstacy of religious fervor, of chivalrous enthusiasm, of Philistine sentimentalism in the icy water of egotistical calculation. . . .

The bourgeoise has subjected the country to the rule of the towns. It has created enormous cities, has greatly increased the urban population as compared with the rural, and has thus rescued a considerable part of the population from the idiocy of rural life.[16]

Apart from their genuine emotional ambivalence (rather than outright hostility) to the bourgeoisie as a class, these observations are striking for their emphasis on rationalization as the primary source of basic social change and conflict. On the one hand, the bourgeoisie's pursuit of profit led to class conflict by impoverishing the workers and alienating them from their own labor by making work itself repetitive, routine, and thus uncreative. On the other hand, rationalization made possible such high levels of production that men could contemplate a realm of freedom where eventually all could pursue the Greek ideal of cultivating whatever faculties they wished. They could "hunt in the morning, fish in the afternoon, rear cattle in the evening, criticize after dinner, just as . . . [they] have a mind, without ever becoming hunter, fisherman, shepherd, or critic."[17]

Because the heuristic purpose of the concept of class is to explain basic social change, Marx's concern with instrumental rationalization seems clearly relevant. But just as Marx confused the ownership of industrial capital with the more general phenomenon of superordination and subordination in authority relations, he also confused the specific case of the workers' alienation and exploitation with the much more general dislocation imposed by economic rationalization. Accordingly, our reformulated concept asserts that the two classes are divided—and divided singularly—by their conflicting latent role interests with respect to instrumental economic rationalization, whatever its source. Like Dahrendorf's concept, our revision holds that two classes are in turn differentiated from each other by their exercise of, or exclusion from, authority. This difference creates a dichotomous and structurally determined conflict rather than one based on a diverse set of conflicting attitudes randomly distributed in terms of social categories. But unlike Dahrendorf, we refer only to authority relations in the process of economic production. On the one side, the role interests of the economic authorities defines success in that role as the continuous, systematic improvement of the methods of production *without particular refer-ence to the consequences for the economic nonauthorities*. It is this lack of concern for consequences that, according to our concept of class, generates conflict. In this view, however, the latent role inter-ests of these economic nonauthorities, do not oppose all rationali-zation as such. According to Marx, economic progress through rationalization would reduce the length and exertion of work and increase real income. Similarly, we assume that the economic non-authorities' latent interest is to curb and channel, but not necessarily to end, such rationalization in order to minimize its disruptive social effects.

As these interests become manifest, our formulation assumes that the bulk of each group is likely to seek governmental assistance. Thus their conflict is often not over whether the government should interfere in economic life but over which class government policies should favor. The concept thus retains Dahrendorf's distinction be-tween class and social strata. As he argues, gradations of income, specific occupation, and social status may either reinforce or cut across and reduce the intensity of class conflict. But the latent class interests of the economic authorities and nonauthorities, with respect to instrumental rationalization, are not themselves affected by these factors. Consequently, this approach also follows Dahrendorf in treating those members of either class who do not act on their latent role interests as role deviants.

This formulation contrasts markedly with Dahrendorf's view that the possession or nonpossession of authority is the source and origin of the conflict between the two classes in industrial society. Certainly conflict over authority is a vital element in many political struggles, but we have seen that equating it with class conflict in-volved Dahrendorf in serious difficulties. In the present analysis, therefore, it is solely the instrumental rationalization of production that generates the issues about which class conflict centers. Exercise of or exclusion from authority roles—and then only authority roles in the economic process of production—merely indicates which individuals, or more precisely, the incumbents of which roles, will fight to advance or seek to curb this rationalization. As a result, the origins of class conflict and the basic issues between the classes are not affected by differences, for example in the acknowledged legitimacy or constitutional character of prevailing political-authority relations. (This is the case even though, as the last part of this chapter will argue, these political variables do affect the likelihood, extensiveness, and intensity of class conflict in any particular system.) Rather the real variations in class conflict, as it is defined here, are better accounted for in terms of the different consequences that instrumental rationalization has for the members of different societies.

It is clear, to begin with, that a broad-range concept that emphasizes instrumental rationalization is general enough to incorporate very diverse types of conflict in industrial society. It is obviously applicable to worker-employer conflict in industry and to the struggle between the proletarian economic nonauthorities and bourgeois economic authorities that Marx knew. In addition, it incorporates the at least latent—and sometimes manifest—conflict between the " 'mere' citizens" in communist states, who have not had economic authority and the elite of mainly party members that exercises economic as well as political authority. As suggested earlier, this revision also avoids many of the difficulties in both Dahrendorf's and Marx's concepts. Because we are not concerned with formal ownership of property, the concept has little difficulty handling the decomposition of labor into many skill groups and the decomposition of capital into owners and managers. The category of economic authorities comprises both owners of business enterprises and the growing and diverse group of executives who exercise authority in publicly owned corporations. For the purposes of political analysis, we assume that this class also includes the immediate families of these two groups; that is, all those members of a household who depend for their income—without respect to the size of that income—on the activities of persons in positions of economic authority. The class does not include trade-union leaders as they lack direct responsibility and authority over the productive process. The economic nonauthorities include not only the unskilled wage earners, but all other workers—and as we shall see, nonworkers—no matter what their skills, who are excluded from the exercise of economic authority.

Because this concept does not divide the classes in terms of formal exercise of political authority, we can use it to determine the class commitments of the elected governmental leaders—as Dahrendorf's concept cannot—by their policy positions toward economic rationalization. For example, President Roosevelt could be considered an ally of the economic nonauthorities on many issues, at least during much of the 1930s. This same focus on policy orientations also changes our approach to the problem of which class rules politically. Our question becomes not simply who exercises formal political authority, but which class' latent interests with respect to economic rationalization are most nearly realized by prevailing public policies. From this point of view, allies of the economic nonauthorities exercised very considerable although not complete political authority during much of the New Deal. Nevertheless, these questions with respect to economic authorities and nonauthorities could be asked about industrial societies in any historical period. As a result, they do not help us understand the substantial *change* in class relations since the time of Marx. In order to consider the class position of the American labor movement in different periods we must now provide greater economic and political specification to our revised concept of class.

Durkheim: Solidarity, The Division of Labor, and Class Conflict

The integrationist theory of social stability that Dahrendorf contrasts with the conflict or coercion explanation of social change put forward by Marx treats authority as a central source of cohesion. Nevertheless, Dahrendorf employs Weber's analysis of authority in tracing out the dichotomous and—as we shall see—essentially political side of Marx's concept of class. In order to apply our reformulated concept of class to American labor politics, we shall expand upon the economic side of Marx's concept by drawing upon another prominent integrationist theorist, Emile Durkheim.[18] Durkheim makes a fundamental distinction between the mechanical solidarity produced by a primitive division of labor and the organic solidarity that accompanies a complex functional specialization. But as Marx himself saw, this same division of labor can generate both conflict between the two classes and unity within each of them.[19] In our case, Durkheim's two types of solidarity illuminate the transition from proletarian to postproletarian class conflict.

In Durkheim's terms, the solidarity of the proletariat was essentially mechanical. In groups where men do very much the same work, they are bound together by a consciousness of their similarity that "comes from a certain number of states of conscience which are common to all the members of the same society." This feeling "reduces individuality" and grows "only in inverse ratio to [individual] personality."[20] In Marx's time, the division of labor had differentiated workers from the early industrial entrepreneurs. But this relatively primitive specialization left most workers in essentially the same predicament—without tools of production, valued job skills, or economic bargaining power. These similarities produced proletarian mechanical solidarity, which continued to characterize European socialism and unionism until after World War II.[21]

As Dahrendorf points out, however, several mutually reinforcing trends have eroded this consciousness of kind. First of all, the economic basis for worker militancy has receded. Increased productivity has diminished physical exertion in industry and the length of the average work week. Trade unions reduced, although, as Dahrendorf rightly stresses, they did not eliminate, management's authority over working conditions in the factory. Second and probably more important, an increasingly complex division of labor provided some workers with more interesting work and increasingly subdivided the working class in terms of skills, training, and pay. At least among industrial workers, specialization has thus reduced uniformity. Particularly because of this latter development, it has become increasingly difficult, as Theodore Lowi has pointed out to me, for American workers to unite on the issues that affect them as an occupational group. In Britain, a decline in proletarian mechanical solidarity encouraged a powerful group of Labourites to reassert the market and self-interest rather than fellowship and altruism as the basis of socialist planning.[22]

Evidently, significant class conflict over economic rationalization is possible only if the economic nonauthorities are united by new cohesion compatible with a complex division of labor. It is just this paradox of cohesion and individuality that Durkheim resolves through his concept of organic solidarity. Durkheim asked, "Why does the individual, while becoming more autonomous, depend more upon society? How can he be at once more individual [more differentiated] and more solidary?"[23] He answered by pointing out that extensive functional specialization of work directly encourages both individualism and the individual's dependence for his survival and well-being on the cooperative efforts of other equally specialized workers.[24] In turn, this mutual interdependence means that each member of a society becomes increasingly vulnerable to the changes initiated by others. It is this growth of mutual interdependence and the vulnerability of the economic nonauthorities that sets in motion the process by which worker-employer class conflict was substantially supplanted by a new form of class conflict in industrialized society. This new cleavage between economic authorities as producers and economic nonauthorities as consumers began to achieve a dominant place in national domestic politics in the 1960s.

Contemporary Class Conflict:
Consumer-Producer Politics

At two points Dahrendorf refers to Theodor Geiger's assertion that with respect to class politics a struggle between producers and consumers has superseded the bourgeois-proletarian conflict. Dahrendorf objects, however, that Geiger treats consumers as a stratum rather than a class.[25] We can avoid this difficulty if we assume a latent conflict of role interests between those who exercise authority in production and the economic nonauthorities *in their consumer roles.* By thus making producer-consumer conflict an historical specification of the economic authority-nonauthority cleavage, we retain the structurally determined character essential to a concept of class. For one thing, the producer-consumer distinction does not conform to either the differences of money or of status that separate economic and social strata. The consumer class includes those highly skilled and well-paid workers whose productive roles do not include the significant exercise of economic authority, so that producer-consumer divisions may occur in otherwise similar occupational groups.[26] At the same time, exercise of (or exclusion from) economic authority directly affects the conflict. Under condition of increasing interdependence, the instrumental character of economic rationalization (i.e., a concern for improving productive methods for their own sake) means that the activities of the economic authorities continuously disturb the physical, social, and economic environment. In turn, this disturbance produces a substantial dislocation of the economic nonauthorities' individual and collective patterns of consumption. It is useful to observe once again that we are concerned with economic authority and nonauthority roles only as a way of designating the members of the producer and consumer classes who are divided by their conflicting interests over instrumental rationalization. Our heuristic assumption is that those who hold economic authority positions have an interest in advancing the instrumental rationalization of production in highly developed economies in order to successfully perform their entreprenurial and managerial roles. Conversely, those who do not occupy authority roles have an interest in curbing such instrumental rationalization in order to reduce the adverse impact of economic change on their consumption patterns.

But even if this distinction between economic authorities and nonauthorities provides a structurally determined criterion for the formation of producer and consumer classes, our revised concept is heuristically useful only if it can account for many of the most important issues in contemporary political systems. Of course, contemporary economic rationalization may reduce social conflict in the long run by increasing total economic output; in any case, it may be less disruptive currently than it was during the period of capital accumulation a century ago. The cleavage will still be a useful concept if present political issues do involve the producer-consumer conflict we have specified. It is therefore relevant to note that many observers of communist regimes have begun to speak of citizen pressure on the party's political-economic elite for more consumer goods. Still more relevant, Beer concludes his analysis of democratic politics in Britain in terms similar to (if not identical with) ours, by including a broad definition of consumption. On the one side, British pressure groups represent many functionally differentiated producer interests in the administrative process, and the political parties in Parliament represent the interests of consumers, rather broadly defined, who are vulnerable to economic change.[27] In the United States, Lowi persuasively distinguishes between the redistributive or class issues that often benefit large groups, usually though not exclusively consumers, and the regulatory (and distributive) issues that primarily benefit various producer units.[28]

Certainly by the 1960s a congeries of such consumer issues had emerged in American politics. Some reflected the individual consumer's specific market interests in issues like the purity and safety of products, the accuracy of advertising and labeling, and rates of interest. Another set of issues reflected the severe deprivation imposed on some groups by the pace and direction of economic rationalization. Often, especially among poorly educated blacks and retirees, members of these groups were only consumers and were entirely excluded from the labor force. Perhaps the most general consumer-producer clash turned on the choice between sales taxes on consumption and progressive income taxes that tend to fall most heavily on economic authorities. A final set of issues included the creation, preservation, and restoration of public, collectively consumed goods, both tangible and intangible. *Creation* of such values includes the development of cultural and recreational opportunities by taxing economic activities and thus reducing profits or output. *Preservation* of such values usually involves such conservation issues as the development of the Indiana Dunes National Lakeshore park or protection of the Grand Canyon National Monument against flooding, both at the expense of industrial development. The *restoration* of public values designates the remedying of such deleterious effects of industrial production as air and water pollution.

Consistent with this volume's focus on the labor movement, we have stated each of these issues from the perspective of the economic nonauthorities' latent interests. Of course, it is true that, particularly on such issues as conservation and pollution, contemporary economic authorities are disadvantaged in their consumer roles by rationalization as much as, in Marx's view, the capitalists were alienated from their own creative efforts by their enslavement to the profit motive. For analytic purposes, our concept assumes that an economic authority's solidarity with others in similar roles will typically override his more diffuse latent interests as a consumer. Thus the concept would lose heuristic value to the extent this assumption proves unfounded. The devotion of American economic authorities to the rationalization of production at least in their own firms is obvious. Indeed, these activities have stimulated the economic growth of industrialized nations generally and the United States in particular. Of course, Marx himself anticipated such growth under capitalism and expected that, after a socialist revolution, heavy industrialization would free the workers from the constraints of physical labor. But contrary to Marx's own expectation, the steady rise in worker productivity and decline in yearly hours worked has made just this liberation possible, although in partial, piecemeal, and less than egalitarian fashion.[29]

At the same time, such economic gains have reduced the commitment of workers and unions to consumer-class politics by reinforcing their desire to maximize their role interests as workers, that is, economic nonauthorities in production. These feelings may well account for much of the rank and file opposition that union leaders encounter when they participate in partisan electoral politics, and their fear of criticism if they focus exclusively on consumer issues in lobbying. Indeed, the continuing economic differentiation of workers into specialized skill groups has reinforced American labor's pluralist politics, which remains a primary characteristic of many nonfactory unions and important for all AFL-CIO affiliates. Significantly, many workers and unions in particular industries have increasingly recognized certain common interests which they share with their employers, despite the continuing conflict over wages. In some geographical areas and industries, unions and management have united frequently to secure such common goals as a greater share of defense contracts.[30]

On the other hand, functional specialization has so differentiated the workers' producer interests that united action on *working*-class issues becomes increasingly difficult—except possibly on such issues as right to work that threaten the unions themselves. Indeed, these fissures have increasingly divided groups within the same industry and union. As a result, unions can act politically on behalf of their members' class—rather than narrower group—interests only on consumer issues, despite the continuing importance of some traditional labor matters. Without a consumer orientation there would be embarrassingly few political causes on which the top officials of many state labor federations, as well as the AFL-CIO itself, could speak for a united labor movement.

These conflicting forces produced a carefully balanced policy in the mid-1960s according to which the AFL-CIO divided its resources in national politics between mainly pluralist issues vital to specific unions and other, largely consumer-class issues that affected the interests of its entire membership. From this point of view, the union activities on behalf of Democratic party candidates who appealed to many nonworkers were consistent with the consumer-class interests of union members, but as consumers rather than producers. This orientation is particularly clear in congressional lobbying when we speak of the Democrats' organized welfare-state (in our terms, consumer) constituency rather than its more cautious and conservative formal leadership.

As Chapter X indicates, the AFL-CIO has thus come, by the mid-1960s, to represent consumer interests on such issues as reapportionment, aid to education, truth in packaging, and tax policies. This conclusion is supported by COPE's official choice of congressional roll calls in 1965 and 1966 with which to evaluate members of the Eighty-Ninth Congress. Of course, it is not always easy to distinguish between pluaralist issues, working-class issues which affect economic nonauthorities as producers, and those which affect them in their consumer role. But once the various issues are assigned categories, as in Table 9, the importance for COPE of consumer- rather than working-class issues in the Eighty-Ninth Congress becomes clear. Together with the fact that the unions' resources in congressional lobbying dwarf those of other consumer groups, this set of choices makes organized labor potentially—*but as of the mid-1960s far from certainly*—a major long-term force in consumer-class politics.

TABLE 9   Issues Used by COPE To Evaluate Members of the Eighty-Ninth Congress

	Consumer Issues	Working-Class Issues	Pluralist Issues	Mixed Issues
Senate	1. Reapportionment 2. Aid to education 3. Medicare 4. Department of Housing and Urban Development 5. Fair packaging 6. Rent subsidies	1. Right to work 2. Manpower training 3. Farm labor	1. Davis-Bacon construction pay provisions	1. War on Poverty 2. Voting rights
House	1. Aid to education 2. Medicare 3. Department of Housing and Urban Development 4. Rent subsidies 5. Public power	1. Right to work (three roll calls) 2. Minimum wage	1. Public works	1. War on Poverty 2. Voting rights 3. House Rules Committee

Source: "How Your Senators and Representatives Voted, 1965–1966" (Washington, D.C.: AFL-CIO Committee on Political Education, n. d.).

Political and Economic Sources of
Consumer-Class Politics

The heuristic value of the middle-range concept of consumer-class politics depends not only on its illuminating important cases of political conflict, but also on its specifying the conditions under which such conflict is likely to emerge. The testable, refutable propositions that such specification entails will also indicate the relative impact of economic and political conditions on contemporary democratic politics.

In this connection it is interesting to note a shift from economic to political explanations in Beer's discussion of British politics. Before World War II, working-class feelings were so strong that they directly reshaped the party system by enabling Labour to supplant the Liberals as the second party.[31] But in his study of collectivist politics after the war, Beer found more consumer politics in some political structures than in others. "Party does not merely aggregate the opinions of a large number of groups in the electorate, it goes a long way toward creating these opinions." Indeed, "the parties . . . have themselves in great part framed and elicited the very demands to which they then respond."[32]

This greater independent importance of the political system can be traced to the consumers' much weaker unity based on ties of shared interests typical of organic solidarity, which are much less intense than the sometimes quasi-religious sentiments of mechanical solidarity that united European workers.[33] American parties were also an important source of intergroup unity, and even of some political demands, in American politics before the New Deal. In that situation, regional, economic, and ethnic cleavages had much the same effect as the functional differentiation Beer observed in post-World War II Britain in reducing consciousness of kind as the basis for intergroup affinity within party coalitions. Even the sharply increased working-class consciousness during the New Deal never reached Western European levels. Given this more limited class feeling, the Democrats did not simply respond to existing proletarian demands, but powerfully stimulated the growth of unions, the workers' archetypal economic organization, by symbolic endorsements and the substantial legal assistance of the Wagner Act.

On the basis of the British case, we might explain this capacity of political parties to unite diverse groups by citing the role of the formal party leaders. Beer reports that, in competing for consumer support and framing consumer demands, the leaders of the major British parties could count upon "massive organizations" and a "Prussian discipline" among their followers unknown in American politics.[34] Yet as we observed in Chapter X, the Democrats played a comparable role in consumer politics largely through the party's organized interests rather than through its more cautious formal leadership. These arguments confirm Dahrendorf's view of political parties as key elements in contemporary class conflict.[35] Yet, as Chapter X indicates, the constraints of office inhibited the formal party leaders' support of some consumer issues—a finding that contradicts Dahrendorf's explanation based on the party's effort to control formal political authority. Rather, the chief similarity between the two groups most interested in consumer issues (the British party leaders and the Democrats' organized constituencies, including labor) was a common concern with uniting a broad electoral coalition.

It is this concern for electoral coalition building that also primarily differentiates party politics from the administrative process. In Britain many administrative decisions apply to only one or a few clients, which encourages groups to operate independently and, Beer reports, favors the interests of British producers. By contrast, vigorous party competition encourages combinations with other, preferably partisan allies, because individual interests are unlikely to assemble the requisite electoral majority.[36]

As organized labor's political behavior demonstrates, the difference between competitive partisan and nonpartisan or administrative politics is only one political variable that affects consumer-class unity. American unions are more prone to participate in these broad partisan coalitions in national (that is, large constituency) rather than in local politics. In any particular arena such participation on behalf of consumer interests is more likely to take place on redistributive issues than on more pluralist ones. Finally, such activity is likely to be much larger if, in defining the reward for political participation, the unions themselves have stressed collective public policy incentives rather than such divisible incentives as patronage or other individual material benefits.

In sum, conflict between the consumer and producer classes is built upon the organic solidarity and in turn a complex division of *economic* labor. Yet consumer-class unity—itself a prerequisite for class conflict—depends on the variation of key *political* structures best examined by the size-of-political-unit analysis. This intertwining of political and economic causal factors can be stated more systematically if we specify two component attitudinal variables as the most immediate determinants of the configuration of political conflict. One (derived from the interest homogeneity dimension in Chapter V) which we have just considered is *recognition of an interest in uniting to control the exercise of political authority.* The other (derived from the interest-cohesion dimension in Chapter V) is *recognition of shared interests in public policy.* Both of these attitudes are at least implicitly present in Marx's concept of class and class consciousness, and each is affected, but in a different way, by both political and economic structures. The first dimension explains the size (and often the heterogeneity) of the relevant coalitions that seek political power; that is, the degree to which overt political conflict approaches a *dichotomous* pattern. This dimension reflects Dahrendorf's concern with the control of authority as a primary focus of conflict. The second dimension measures the size of the groups that recognize a common interest in policy outputs, particularly with respect to economic rationalization. It thus indicates the extent to which the conflict revolves around the process of economic rationalization which, Marx thought, produces basic social change.

The joint effect of the two recognition dimensions is set forth in Table 10, which, it should be stressed, indicates the pattern or alignment of political conflict rather than its intensity or violence. As Table 10 indicates, class politics results (in democratic regimes) when the recognition of shared policy interests and of the interest in uniting for power are high, as in the upper-right quadrant of the table. Examples of class orientations include the AFL-CIO's behavior on redistributive issues in Congress, the behavior of Detroit COPE generally, and Los Angeles COPE in national, but not local, elections.

TABLE 10 **A Typology of Conflict in (Democratic) Industrial Societies**

	Recognition of Common Policy Output Interests with Respect to Economic Rationalization	
	LOW	HIGH
Recognition of an Interest in Uniting to Control the Exercise of Political Authority, Without Regard to Particular Outputs — HIGH	Machine politics, politics as the mastery of technique: Chicago Federation of Labor	Consumer-class or proletarian politics: Detroit COPE; Los Angeles COPE in national elections
LOW	Pluralism: Los Angeles local politics; pre-New Deal AFL on regulative or distributive issues	Sectarian ideological politics: French fourth Republic; New York City labor politics

In the opposite pluralist case (the lower-left quadrant) the two dimensions have low values as in union activity in Los Angeles local elections, in the AFL's position before the New Deal on almost all issues, and in the contemporary AFL-CIO's position on specifically trade-union issues in Congress.

The other two basic configurations of conflict indicated in Table 10 are mixed cases. A machine political style prevails when high recognition of the interest in uniting for power is combined with a low recognition of common policy interests. In this case, the mastery of political technique takes precedence over concern with class issues as exemplified by the Chicago Federation of Labor. Conversely, sectarian politics emerges when the interest in uniting to gain power is recognized far less than a common interest in policy outputs. In this case, workers are divided between two or more parties as in France and Italy in the 1950s and politics may tend to become an expression of goals rather than a mastery of technique.

Since Table 10 categorizes types of conflict rather than explains them, we now need to know under what conditions these recognition dimensions have high or low values. In other words, we want to know under what conditions a latent interest, in Dahrendorf's terms, is recognized and thus becomes manifest. In one case, such recognition depends on the size of the advantage (or latent interest) in uniting politically and the degree to which the advantage is perceived. In the other case, recognition of common policy interests depends both on how widely the policy interests are in fact shared and then the degree to which this sharing is perceived. To illustrate, the sharing of common policy interests is likely to vary with changes in the *common* vulnerability to economic rationalization. As indicated in Table 11, this common vulnerability decreases for workers as the division of labor advances; but the same functional specialization increases social and economic interdependence and, as a result, the common vulnerability of consumers. Thus the vertical dimension in Table 11 indicates an opposite development over time (that is, up the table) in the shared vulnerability of workers and consumers.

To merge Dahrendorf's and Easton's terminology, the conversion of latent interests into manifest ones, and then into demands and issues, depends on a *perception* that these common policy interests

TABLE 11 **Recognition of Common Policy Output Interests**

Degree of Common Vulnerability to Economic Rationalization on Consumers or Workers; Varies with Extent of Division of Labor		Perception of Shared Policy Interests	
		LOW	HIGH
	HIGH	"False consciousness": American *workers* in late nineteen century	High recognition: class consciousness; American New Deal; European socialism before World War II; possibly, American consumers, 1960s
	LOW	Low recognition: All consumers, 1860s; American *workers*, 1960s	Vestigial working-class consciousness; contemporary Europe

are shared by the economic nonauthorities. This perception or consciousness is the product of several factors, two of which are indicated in Table 12. One factor that increases perception is the extent to which the political system provides appropriate cues, like redistributive issues in which outputs tend to be collective and indivisible. Similarly, a class orientation is more likely among members of those organizations, like Detroit COPE, that rely on collective organizational incentives. It seems clear, however, that so complex an attitude as the perception of common policy interests is also affected by other attitudes. Earlier we attributed the weak class consciousness of American workers to the lack of inherited feudal status distinctions. To generalize, the perception of a common social situation, and thus common latent policy interests, varies with the size of the status differential between most economic authorities and the bulk of the economic nonauthorities.

A parallel analysis can be applied to the dimension indicating recognition of an advantage; that is, a *political* latent interest, in uniting to achieve power. As Table 13 indicates, recognition of such an interest varies with both the level of the latent interest (the extent of the advantages to be derived from uniting) and the degree to which any given advantage is manifest, that is, perceived by the members of a particular class. In turn, this advantage in uniting is determined by a variety of size of political-unit variables. They include: first, the degree to which an electoral system discriminates severely against minor (third, fourth, fifth, and still smaller) parties; second, the size of constituency; and third, the scope of conflict or percentage of participants out of the whole population that become involved in a constituency. In general, large constituencies, discrimination against minor parties, and wide conflict increase the advantages of uniting with others as measured against the costs of achieving unity.

Once again, however, the perception of this latent interest in uniting for political power is a complex variable depending on a variety of factors, two of which are indicated in Table 14 (where perception is greater as one moves up the table and to the right). On one side, the relatively simple division of labor in nineteenth-century British industry fostered powerful class feeling among the

TABLE 12 **Perception of Shared Policy Interests**

		Type of Policy Outputs and Organization Incentives	
		DIVISIBLE AND DISTRIBUTIVE	COLLECTIVE AND REDISTRIBUTIVE
Status Gap Between Economic Authorities and Nonauthorities	HIGH	Mixed perception: European workers before socialism; British unions in early period	High perception: Support for welfare-state programs in Europe
	LOW	Low perception: Machine politics' acceptance of laissez faire; AFL's voluntarism	Mixed perception: Support for American welfare-state programs and New Deal

TABLE 13   Recognition of an Interest in Uniting to Control the Exercise of Political Authority

		Perception of Advantage	
		LOW	HIGH
Advantage in Uniting to Control the Exercise of Political Authority (Depends on size of several political units)	HIGH	Moderate recognition: American national politics especially before World War II; decentralized parties	High recognition: Strong parties, often competitive two-party system
	LOW	Low recognition: Highly individualist politics, entrepreneurial style, e.g., Los Angeles	Moderate recognition: Detroit nonpartisan politics, organized politics in local nonpartisan systems

TABLE 14 Perception of an Interest in Uniting Politically

	Extent of Dichotomous Economic Division (produced by simple division of labor in early industrialism)	
Extent of Political Status Differences	LOW	HIGH
HIGH	Mixed perception: European systems with limited industrialization and exclusion from citizenship; Italy before national unity	High perception: Fully-developed political tensions; dichotomous economic cleavage and grievances over suffrage; nineteenth-century Europe
LOW	Low perception: Enfranchised peasants; France in 1800s; American freeholders (c. 1800)	Mixed perception: Dichotomous conflict but limited sense of political grievance; United States 1870 to 1896

proletariat, which in turn helped the workers to unite politically in support of the Labour party. In Detroit the acute grievances of the automobile workers, especially those who did very similar work on the assembly line, helped the UAW organize a sometimes dichotomous conflict in local politics, despite the obstacles to disorganization in the city's nonpartisan system. Over time, this economically generated mechanical solidarity has been undermined by the increasing division of labor. On the other side, a gap in political status also contributes to the perception of a common interest in uniting. For example, in Chapter II we considered the exclusion of the European lower classes from formal citizenship throughout much of the nineteenth century and the informal exclusion of many Americans from effective suffrage.

These tables make clear that no one set of variables accounts for either of the recognition dimensions that shape political conflict. But by considering economic and political variables together, we are better able to understand the complex character of their interaction. As we observed in Chapter V: *under conditions of either very strong or very weak socially and economically based affinity within a class, the size-of-political-unit variables have relatively limited impact on the configuration of conflict.* This proletarian-bourgeois conflict in Europe, where social and economic antagonisms were strong, appears to have varied less between local and national politics and on different types of issues than in the United States. Again, within American politics, dichotomous class cleavage appeared at all levels of Detroit politics and in all types of Detroit elections, reflecting the unusual strength of class feeling among the Autoworkers in the 1930s and 1940s. By contrast, Los Angeles politics—where class feelings were present but more diffuse—revealed considerably more variation by type of election and political arena. Conversely, in American politics before the New Deal, ethnic feeling vitiated much of the workers' mechanical solidarity, and the degree of class conflict thus varied only moderately on these size-of-political-unit dimensions.

Our present discussion enables us to formulate these observations more fully than in Chapter V. Size-of-political-unit variables are largely *cross-sectional.* They designate dimensions of internal variation within a system rather than changes in the system as a whole.

Taken by themselves, the differences in type of issue, organizational incentive, size of constituency, scope of conflict, and type of electoral system are most conveniently used to explain variations between arenas or processes within a single political system at a particular point in time. By contrast, changes in the division of labor and in social- and political-status relations are essentially *longitudinal* factors whose variation over time transforms all social and political life. Thus, to restate the argument of the preceding paragraph, the cross-sectional size-of-political-unit variables have the greatest importance when the longitudinal variables produce only intermediate levels of recognition of common policy interests and/or recognition of an interest in uniting for power. (The size-of-political-unit variables thus have the greatest impact in any one system when these recognition levels have, statistically, intermediate expected values.) In contrast with much of Europe, a moderate recognition of common policy interests in the American working class could be attributed to the combination of heavy industrialization and a relatively small gap in social status. Similarly, we can assume that because exclusion from suffrage of the American lower classes after 1896 was quite informal—as opposed to the legal and symbolic exclusion of European workers discussed in Chapter II—it led to an only moderate recognition of the advantage of uniting politically. By contrast, when we turn to contemporary, postproletarian politics, we expect only moderate consumer-class feelings in *both* Europe and America. First, recognition of shared policy interests is limited because the dislocations imposed on economic nonauthorities as consumers are less obviously disruptive to any one individual than the adverse impact that early industrialization imposed on the workers. Second, by comparison with the pre-World War II period, the process of functional specialization has reduced the similarities in work and life styles among the contemporary economic nonauthorities; in the case of European workers, these similarities had facilitated recognition of an interest in uniting for power.

Class, Economy, and Polity:
The Explanation of Social Change

This complex interrelationship among social and, especially, economic and political variables substantially complicates our problem of locating the determinants of class politics. Longitudinal variables, such as changes in the division of labor and in differences in political and social status, frequently affect the configuration of conflict through the development of the party system. In much of Europe, traditional proletarian, mechanical solidarity bolstered the political parties' capacity to emphasize common policy interests and maintain interparty unity. In the subsequent period, with its complex division of labor and its consumer politics, this party discipline has helped British parties as they bid against each other in Parliament for the consumer vote and cater to consumer interests. In America, small differences in political and social status have produced more pluralist and less centralized party organizations. But, as the case of organized labor and the Democratic party illustrates, the weakness of the party organization has increased organized labor's influence as a party faction. In particular, the unions have had the organizational resources—ample funds and skilled political specialists—to assume a position of party leadership because of their peculiar character as the only large group that has supported consumers and, yet, has recruited members on the basis of producer rather than consumer-role interests. On the other hand, the unions' status as organizations of wage earners has meant a commitment to pluralist producer issues that have limited their ability to unite a diverse consumer class. This consideration has encouraged them to depend upon and operate within the political party's coalition rather than independently. Indeed, the ability of the party to attract allies that the unions cannot attract by themselves, together with the substantial resources that Democratic leaders command by virtue of their public offices, has meant that unions and party leaders make different and distinct contributions to their partnership. For this reason, the union-party alliance has exemplified the cooperative functional specialization between partners with very different skills and resources typical of a consumer-class coalition based on organic solidarity.

It is just this cooperation between a political party and a primarily economic organization of wage earners that makes us doubt the analytic usefulness of the entire Marxian question of economic versus political causation. *Like the concept of class itself,* the notions of comprehensive economic and political explanations are heuristic concepts—ways of grouping variables or roles—designed to facilitate analysis. They are thus subject to evaluation in terms of their fruitfulness in generating specific propositions. This means, however, that economic and political explanations are not only alternatives to each other but to class explanations as well. Specifically, if an economic or political explanation is accepted, the concept of class has a limited explanatory power of its own. For example, class for Dahrendorf primarily designates a group of actors defined politically in terms of authority, and for Marx class designates a group of actors defined economically in terms of ownership of capital. In each case, the class concept primarily specifies the ways in which the more fundamental economic or political factors operate.

The concept of class expounded here turns out to be an analysis of those configurations of social conflict likely to alter basic social patterns. And given the importance of political, economic, and, indeed, social variables in shaping contemporary class politics in the complex ways we have just described, an overconcentration on either political or economic factors would lead to a cumbersome and unwieldly analysis. Of course, as these pages have shown, economic and political categories remain important for, among other purposes, understanding the origins of different patterns of class conflict. But, in accounting for basic social change, it may be most fruitful to focus instead on the policy output and uniting for power dimensions that affect the likelihood of class, as distinct from pluralist, machine, or sectarian politics.

These conclusions indicate that the heuristic function of the concept of class may vary with the specific character of the social change—that is, alterations in the basic patterns of allocating important values—that the analyst seeks to explain. To focus on either political or economic factors directly, and to treat class as simply an intervening variable through which the dominant economic or political factors operate, may be most useful in those cases where continuous rapid change is accepted much more completely in some sectors of society than in others. Marx's assertion of the decisive role of economic factors seems persuasive, for example, in those cases such as the Western Europe of his time, where the most vigorous advocates and agents of change were incumbents of economic authority roles. Economic influence on political life meant the successful effort of the bourgeoisie to have the political system assist rather than hinder the institutionalization of change. Conversely, the emphasis on political causal factors in the analysis of certain communist regimes asserts, in effect, that the most important advocates and agents of change are the political authorities in the party.

In these cases, class designates those roles or social positions that are responsible for instituting rapid social change. But once the working class obtains enough political influence to seek changes of its own through social-welfare policies, political leaders in democratic regimes can assume an at least partly autonomous mediating role. This political autonomy becomes even greater, as in contemporary consumer politics, when change is so widely accepted, that it takes place simultaneously throughout society. As noted earlier in this chapter, such autonomy characterizes not only party leaders but trade-union leaders active in the Democratic party coalition. Indeed, with organic solidarity and mutual interdependence, a change in one sector affects many others. It is the rapidity and complexity of these interactions that gives the configuration of conflict, that is, the extent of class as opposed to pluralist politics, such great importance in explaining ultimate political system policy outputs. By contrast, the more remote economic, social, or political origins of a given pattern of conflict may be so intertwined with each other that the heuristic distinction among economic, political, and social factors loses its explanatory power.

These considerations point to perhaps the primary challenge that confronts the American labor movement in the late 1960s, a challenge made all the more severe by the unions' relatively conservative and vitally influential role within the Democratic party in 1968. Because of the widespread acceptance of rapid social change, the political issues of the proletarian period in class politics have receded in importance. Our primary concern is no longer with the efforts of employers as economic authorities to impose their demands on the government over the opposition of their workers. Nor is it with the state's attempt to curb these employers on behalf of the workers or to mediate labor-management conflict. Rather, since so many groups in America have accepted a rapid rate of change, debate over the policy outputs of the political system has become increasingly concerned with the impact of instrumental rationalization on the quality of social life. Consumer issues largely concern the purposes hitherto instrumental economic activities should be made to serve, that is, the proper use we should make of material production. Since these problems touch upon major issues in Western political philosophy, it is by no means clear that contemporary consumer-producer class politics will prove any less important than proletarian-bourgeois conflict a century ago. It may be no exaggeration to conclude that the political importance of the American labor movement in the coming decades will be measured by its impact on these qualitative issues of consumer-class politics.

Notes

INTRODUCTION

1. The phrase is David Truman's in *The Governmental Process* (New York: Knopf, 1960), p. 139.
2. Samuel J. Eldersveld, *Political Parties: A Behavioral Analysis* (Chicago: Rand McNally, 1964), p. 480.
3. Harry M. Scoble, "Organized Labor in Electoral Politics: Some Questions for the Discipline," *Western Political Quarterly,* 16 (September 1963), 666–685.
4. A detailed analysis of such activity in Los Angeles may be found in Richard Baisden, "Labor Unions in Los Angeles Politics" (unpublished Ph.D. dissertation, University of Chicago, 1958). An analysis of the broad institutional factors affecting the Chicago situation may be found in Henry Pelling, "Labor in Politics in Chicago," *Political Studies,* 5 (February 1957), 21–35.
5. For a statement of how the ideal labor precinct worker should operate, see George Wartenberg, "Political Action in a Congressional District," in J. B. S. Hardman and Maurice Neufeld (eds.), *The House of Labor* (Englewood Cliffs, N.J.: Prentice-Hall, 1951), pp. 123–133.
6. Nicholas Masters, "The Organized Labor Bureaucracy as a Base of Support for the Democratic Party," *Law and Contemporary Problems,* 27, (1962), 255. (Masters' emphasis.)

CHAPTER I   THE PLURALIST PERIOD: THE AFL
UNTIL THE NEW DEAL

1. See Seymour Martin Lipset, *Political Man* (Garden City, N.Y.: Doubleday, 1960), p. 303.
2. V. O. Key, Jr., *The Responsible Electorate* (Cambridge, Mass.: Harvard University Press, 1966), chap. 3, esp. p. 55.
3. Angus Campbell, *et al., The American Voter* (New York: Wiley, 1960), p. 312. In 1956, a Republican year, members of the most politically committed unions were 67 percent Democratic, but this figure "fell to 55%, then to 51% [in still less political oriented unions] and finally to 44% where standards were least clear." P. 315. Equally important, almost the entire variation could be ac-

counted for by differences among the most loyal union members. P. 316.

4. Marc Karson, *American Labor Unions and Politics* (Carbondale: Southern Illinois University Press, 1958), p. 305.

5. Paul Jacobs, *The State of the Unions* (New York: Atheneum, 1963), p. 293.

6. C. Wright Mills, *The New Men of Power: America's Labor Leaders* (New York: Harcourt, Brace & World, 1948), pp. 184, 209.

7. *Ibid.,* p. 163.

8. Donald Blaisdell, *American Democracy Under Pressure* (New York: Ronald Press, 1957), p. 63. He also points out, "Pressure groups do practically everything in political campaigns that the parties do except the nominating of candidates. . . . They endorse candidates . . . raise money and spend it on behalf of particular candidates . . . ring door bells, make telephone calls . . . and use all the devices of propaganda." But on the next page he makes clear that "Both experience and observation reinforce the truth of the rule that success in pressure politics turns on neutrality as between the parties." Pp. 115–116.

9. Harmon Zeigler, *Interest Groups in American Society* (Englewood Cliffs, N.J.: Prentice-Hall, 1964), p. 246. Abraham Holtzman, *Interest Groups and Lobbying* (New York: Macmillan, 1966), p. 57.

10. Mary Zon, "Labor in Politics," *Law and Contemporary Problems,* 27 (Spring 1962), 241. For a similar statement of a decade earlier see Jack Kroll, "Labor's Political Role," *The Annals of the American Academy of Political and Social Science,* 274 (March 1951), 120.

11. V. O. Key, Jr., *Politics, Parties, and Pressure Groups* (New York: Crowell, 1964), p. 63.

12. Richard Rovere, "Labor's Political Machine," *Harpers Magazine,* 190 (June 1945), 601.

13. *Ibid.,* p. 593.

14. Max M. Kampelman, "Labor in Politics," in George W. Brooks, *et al.* (eds.), *Interpreting the Labor Movement* (Madison, Wisc.: Industrial Relations Research Association, 1952), pp. 171, 172.

15. A labor spokesman, for example, was able to quote Republican leaders, who told both *The New York Times* and the Washington *Daily News* that labor's role in the 1960 election was the single most important factor in Richard Nixon's defeat. Zon, *op. cit.,* p. 246.

16. Ralph M. Goldman, *The Democratic Party in American Politics* (New York: Macmillan, 1966), p. 21.

17. Clinton Rossiter, *Parties and Politics in America* (Ithaca, N.Y.: Cornell University Press, 1960), p. 95. In *Politics in Wisconsin*, Leon Epstein found that almost as many Democratic state legislators had been helped in political campaigns by labor (37.1 percent) as by the party organization (40.0 percent). (Madison: University of Wisconsin Press, 1958), p. 207. See also John Hutchinson, "Labour in Politics in America," *Political Quarterly*, 32 (April–June 1962), 140.

18. E. E. Schattschneider, "The United States: The Functional Approach to Party Government," in Sigmund Neuman (ed.), *Modern Political Parties* (Chicago: University of Chicago Press, 1956), p. 213. For his references to labor see pp. 209–214. As Harry Scoble has pointed out, even Schattschneider resorted to a pluralist, empirical interpretation of labor in national politics when he specifically addressed himself to pressure politics. He calculated that labor could deliver relatively few of its members' votes so that *"it is nearly impossible to translate pressure politics into party politics."* E. E. Schattschneider, *The Semi-Sovereign People* (New York: Holt, Rinehart and Winston, 1960), p. 53. (Schattschneider's emphasis.) See Harry M. Scoble, "Organized Labor in Electoral Politics: Some Questions for the Discipline," *Western Political Quarterly*, 16 (September 1963), 674. See also Hugh Bone's comments on pressure group activities as a party campaign organization. "Political Parties and Pressure Group Politics," *The Annals*, 319 (September 1958), 77. He subsequently flatly asserted that "Labor bargains with both major parties, often striking an identity with the Democrats." *American Politics and the Party System*, 3rd ed. (New York: McGraw-Hill, 1965), p. 566.

19. Nicholas Masters, "The Organized Labor Bureaucracy as a Base of Support for the Democratic Party," *Law and Contemporary Problems*, 27 (Spring 1962), 258.

20. Fay Calkins, *The CIO and the Democratic Party* (Chicago: University of Chicago Press, 1952), p. 147.

21. Scoble, *op. cit.*, p. 666. Scoble reviews many of the sources on labor politics, pp. 669ff.

22. *Ibid.*, p. 674. Scoble argues that Schattschneider based his estimate on too low a turnout rate and too small an estimate of differentials in the percentages of union and nonunion Democratic votes.

23. *Ibid.*, p. 684.

24. *Ibid.*, p. 685.

25. See, for example, Maurice Duverger, *Political Parties* (New York: Wiley, 1963), pp. 21ff.

26. *Ibid.*, pp. 24ff.

27. Samuel Beer, *British Politics in the Collectivist Age* (New York: Knopf, 1965), esp. part 2.
28. Schattschneider, *The Semi-Sovereign People, op. cit.,* pp. 21–22.
29. Compare *ibid.,* pp. 42–43.
30. For discussions of the emergence of such organizations earlier in the century and in the late nineteenth century, see Grant McConnell, *Private Power and American Democracy* (New York: Knopf, 1966), chap. 3; Blaisdell, *op. cit.,* p. 61, who identifies the term "pressure group" as coming into general use after 1924; and Theodore J. Lowi, "Toward Functionalism in Political Science," *American Political Science Review,* 57 (September 1963), 579–580.
31. See in particular, David Easton, *A Systems Analysis of Political Life* (New York: Wiley, 1965).
32. Gabriel Almond, "Introduction," *The Politics of the Developing Areas.* (Princeton: Princeton University Press, 1960.)
33. The analysis in these pages follows the observations of Morris Janowitz in "Political Sociology," in *The International Encyclopedia of the Social Sciences* (New York Macmillan, 1968).
34. For a discussion of constituency, see McConnell, *op. cit.,* chap. 4. On scope of conflict, see Schattschneider, *The Semi-Sovereign People, op. cit.,* chaps. 1, 2. On types of issues, see Theodore J. Lowi, "American Business, Public Policy, Case Studies and Political Theory," *World Politics,* 16 (July 1964), 677–693. On incentive systems, see Peter B. Clark and James Q. Wilson, "Incentive Systems: A Theory of Organizations," *Administrative Science Quarterly,* 6 (September 1961), 129–166 and Edward C. Banfield and James Q. Wilson, *City Politics* (Cambridge, Mass.: Harvard University Press, 1963), chaps. 9–11. McConnell refers to the relationship between constituency and other units of political analysis like ideology, tactics, and policy, *op. cit.,* pp. 113 ff.
35. Louis Hartz, *The Liberal Tradition in America* (New York: Harcourt, Brace & World, 1955).
36. See, for example, McConnell, *op. cit.,* chap. 9.
37. Gabriel Kolko, *Wealth and Power in America* (New York: Praeger, 1962), chap. 2.
38. Easton, *op. cit.,* p. 256–257.
39. See Hartz, *op. cit.,* esp. chaps. 1, 2.
40. John R. Commons, *et. al., History of Labour in the United States* (New York: Macmillan, 1936), II, pp. 6–7; and Leon Wolfe, *Lockout* (New York: Harper & Row, 1965), p. 18.
41. In addition to the sources already cited, a number of other authors may be consulted on this general topic. See, for example, David Shannon, *The Socialist Party of America* (New York: Macmillan,

1955), pp. 262ff., esp. 262–268; and Lewis Lorwin, *The American Federation of Labor* (Washington, D.C.: The Brookings Institution, 1933), pp. 354, 444–448. See also Philip Taft, *The A.F. of L. in the Time of Gompers* (New York: Harper & Row, 1957), pp. xvii–xviii; Selig Perlman, *A Theory of the Labor Movement* (New York: Kelley, 1949), p. 291; and Marc Karson, *op. cit.*, pp. 286f. who stresses the role of the Roman Catholic Church and certain psychological factors.

42. Lorwin, *op. cit.*, p. 355. See also Taft, *op. cit.*, pp. xvii–xviii.
43. Stanley Elkins, *Slavery* (Chicago: University of Chicago Press, 1959), chap. 2.
44. Wolfe, *op. cit.*, p. 229. See also Commons *et al.*, II, p. 495.
45. See Robert Littell, "Undercover Men," in Heber Blankenhorn (ed.), *Public Opinion and the Steel Strike* (New York: Harcourt, Brace & World, 1921).
46. Heber Blankenhorn, "Introduction," *Public Opinion and the Steel Strike* (New York: Harcourt, Brace & World, 1921), p. 4.
47. See M. K. Wisehart, "The Pittsburgh Newspapers and the Strike," in Heber Blankenhorn (ed.), *Public Opinion and the Steel Strike* (New York: Harcourt, Brace & World, 1921), pp. 87–155.
48. Commons *et al.*, *op. cit.*, II, 497. See also Norman J. Ware, *The Labor Movement in the United States: 1860–1895* (New York: Appleton-Century-Crofts, 1929), p. 45. Conditions were particularly bad in the West where both sides were less restrained. The National Guard, for example, killed eleven children and two women in the infamous Ludlow (Colorado) massacre of 1914. See Phillip Taft, *op. cit.*, p. 257.
49. Commons *et al.*, *op. cit.*, II, 504–508.
50. See *ibid.*, p. 181; Karson, *op cit.*, chap. 8; and J. Raymond Walsh, *CIO: Industrial Unionism In Action* (New York: Norton, 1937), p. 25.
51. Karson, *op. cit.*, p. 12 and Commons *et al.*, *op. cit.*, II, 374. Over 1,200 strikes per year took place in the 1890s. Wolfe, *op. cit.*, p. 2.
52. Ware, *op. cit.*, p. 135. The same pattern occurred in the case of the Frick Coke Company, where the union won a strike in 1887. By 1890, Frick and Carnegie were better prepared and triumphed. Wolfe, *op. cit.*, pp. 63–64.
53. Commons *et al.*, *op. cit.*, II, 5–6, 161.
54. Ware, *op. cit.*, p. xvi.
55. Karson, *op. cit.*, p. 13.
56. Ware, *op. cit.*, p. xv.
57. *Ibid.*, p. 320.
58. *Ibid.*, pp. xiii, 356.
59. See Commons *et al.*, *op. cit.*, II, 421 and Ware, *op. cit.*, chaps.

8, 9. The controversy with the AFL was started by a division within the skilled Cigar Makers and then exacerbated by both Samuel Gompers and the Knights' leadership in New York.

60. Ware, *op. cit.,* p. 204.

61. *Ibid.,* pp. 137–138.

62. *Ibid.,* pp. 121–122, 135, 145, 149, 153.

63. Lorwin, *op. cit.,* p. 32.

64. See Ware, *op. cit.,* p. 91 and Lorwin, *op. cit.,* p. 27.

65. Lorwin, *op. cit.,* p. 75 and Taft, *op. cit.,* pp. 191, 202. For another view, see James O. Morris, *Conflict in the AFL* (Ithaca, N.Y.: Cornell University Press, 1958).

66. Lorwin, *op. cit.,* p. 484. These figures are based on a report of the AFL Convention *Proceedings* for 1932.

67. Commons *et al., op. cit.,* II, 524. The unions in these two exceptional industries were strengthened by unique factors—the miners' isolation and the unusual social and political awareness of East European Jews.

68. Michael Rogin, "Voluntarism as an Organizational Ideology in the American Federation of Labor: 1886–1932" (Unpublished MA thesis, University of Chicago, 1959), p. 39.

69. In the 1920s, an Autoworkers organizing campaign was partly undermined by craft-union leaders interested in their right of jurisdiction over a small number of skilled craftsmen, even though General Motors agreed to experiment with a union if there were no jurisdictional conflicts. See Lorwin, *op. cit.,* 245–246.

70. Rogin, *op. cit.,* p. 45.

71. Karson, *op. cit.,* p. 136. See pp. 221ff. for the ethnic composition of the federation.

72. See Irving Bernstein, *The Lean Years* (Boston: Houghton Mifflin, 1960), pp. 87–88 and Taft, *op. cit.,* pp. 308ff.

73. Quoted by Karson, *op. cit.,* pp. 117–118.

74. See Commons *et al., op. cit.,* 509ff. The socialists retaliated at this convention by helping inflict on Gompers his one defeat in an election for AFL president. In 1890 Gompers successfully refused to seat the Central Federated Union of New York because it had admitted the Socialist Labor party, which Gompers denied was a labor union. Lorwin, *op. cit.,* pp. 30–31.

75. Taft, *op. cit.,* p. xiv. One example Taft describes (pp. 179ff.) involved a split among men's garment workers that led to the formation of the Amalgamated Clothing Workers of America.

76. Rogin, *op. cit.,* p. 52.

77. Quoted by Rogin, *op. cit.,* p. 160. See also McConnell, *op. cit.,* pp. 300ff.

78. This philosophy was also favored by Roman Catholics who actually

supported welfare-state measures but rallied to voluntarism as a bulwark against socialism. See Karson, *op. cit.*, chap. 9. Similarly, it won support among many rank and file members who, as one acute contemporary observer put it, kept their "politics and . . . every day affairs in separate thought tight compartments" like "the ordinary person's religion and science." Robert F. Hoxie, "President Gompers and the Labor Vote," *Journal of Political Economy*, 16 (December 1908), 700.

79. See Lorwin, *op. cit.*, pp. 58–59 and Rogin, *op. cit.*, p. 56.

80. Lorwin, *op. cit.*, p. 84. See also Taft, *op. cit.*, p. 230.

81. Rogin, *op. cit.*, p. 169. The AFL withdrew its opposition to unemployment insurance in 1932 only over the objections of a significant minority. Lorwin, *op. cit.*, p. 293. In theory, AFL unions attempted to provide some of the benefits that it believed the government should not offer. But the programs were extremely limited. As in the case of organizing industrial workers, the federation's affiliates claimed a jurisdiction that "was not exercised, but in the name of which the jurisdiction of other organizations, in particular the state, was denied." Rogin, *op. cit.*, pp. 181, 188.

82. Lorwin, *op. cit.*, pp. 88–89; Rogin, *op. cit.*, p. 104.

83. Lorwin, *op. cit.*, p. 127. See also Rogin, *op cit.*, pp. 122–123.

84. Lorwin, *op. cit.*, p. 191; Rogin, *op. cit.*, pp. 137–139.

85. Lorwin, *op. cit.*, p. 484.

86. The open-shop campaigns even succeeded in temporarily defeating the powerful San Francisco labor movement. *Ibid.*, p. 203.

87. Quoted by Rogin, *op cit.*, p. 145. *AFL Proceedings* (1926), p. 51.

88. *Ibid.*

89. Lorwin, *op. cit.*, p. 229. Compare McConnell, *op. cit.*, p. 301.

90. Juanita M. Kreps, "Developments in the Political and Legislative Policies of Organized Labor: 1920–1947" (unpublished Ph.D. dissertation, Duke University, 1947), p. 1.

91. *The American Federationist*, 13 (May 1906), 293. Quoted by Karson, *op. cit.*, p. 44. (My emphasis.)

92. Gompers himself urged AFL officials not to stump for Democratic candidate Bryan in either 1896 or 1900. But this attitude proved short lived. Taft, *op. cit.*, pp. 140, 293 and Karson, *op. cit.*, p. 30.

93. Karson, *op. cit.*, p. 34.

94. Avril E. Harris, "Organized Labor in Party Politics; 1906–1932" (unpublished Ph.D. dissertation, University of Iowa, 1937), p. 150. Gompers, for example, undertook two speaking tours that cost $1,200. And the federation spent $4,000 for other speakers plus $3,000 for printing and mailing. *Ibid.*, p. 156.

95. Karson, *op. cit.*, p. 48.

96. Hoxie, *op. cit.*, p. 694.

97. *Ibid.,* p. 696.
98. Karson, *op. cit.,* p. 55.
99. Harris, *op. cit.,* p. 188. In September and October *The American Federationist* featured a long series of statements by union officials attacking the Republicans and supporting the executive council's action as consistent with federation traditions because it was only advisory.
100. *Ibid.,* pp. 206, 215; Karson, *op. cit.,* pp. 61, 62.
101. See J. A. Cable, "Labor's Political Duty," *The American Federationist,* 15 (1908), 839. Two executive council members opposed the endorsement and one, Daniel J. Keefe, president of the Longshoremen, resigned. Keefe issued a statement that was publicized by the Taft forces. He was appointed commissioner of immigration after the election.
102. See *Charities and the Commons,* 21 (1908), pp. 149–150; Karson, *op. cit.,* p. 67; and Samuel Gompers, "The Campaign and Labor's Future," *The American Federationist* (December 1908), 1065.
103. Vaughan Davis Bornet, *Labor Politics in a Democratic Republic* (Washington, D.C.: Spartan Books, 1964), p. 33. See also Hoxie, *op. cit.,* p. 693.
104. See Karson, *op. cit.,* p. 70.
105. Harris, *op. cit.,* p. 256.
106. *Ibid.,* p. 260.
107. Other measures included workmen's compensation, legislative restrictions on child labor, convict labor, and immigration, and establishment of a Bureau of Safety in the Department of Labor. See Harris, *op. cit.,* p. 264 and "Labor's Influence Over Congress," *The Literary Digest* 48 (June 13, 1914), 1423–1424.
108. Bornet, *op. cit.,* pp. 38–39; Wilfred E. Binkley, *American Political Parties* (New York: Knopf, 1964), pp. 368–369.
109. Kreps, *op. cit.,* pp. 16, 44; Harris, *op. cit.,* p. 346.
110. See Harris, *op. cit.,* p. 346.
111. *Ibid.,* p. 380.
112. T. Wilbain Goodman, "The Presidential Campaign of 1920" (unpublished Ph.D. dissertation, Ohio University, 1951), pp. 295, 396.
113. Gompers urged workers to vote for the Democratic rather than farm or labor candidate in Washington state in order to defeat a conservative Republican. Taft, *op. cit.,* pp. 480–481.
114. See Rogin, *op. cit.,* pp. 82–83.
115. "Labor's Neutral Strategy," *The Literary Digest,* 98 (August 25, 1928), 15.
116. Bornet, *op. cit.,* p. 247.
117. *Ibid.,* p. 303.

118. *Ibid.,* pp. 161, 238.
119. Schattschneider, *The Semi-Sovereign People, op. cit.,* p. 10.
120. Bornet, *op. cit.,* p. 299.
121. Goodman, *op. cit.,* pp. 218, 370ff.
122. See V. O. Key, Jr., "A Theory of Critical Elections," *Journal of Politics,* 17 (February 1955), 3–18 and Samuel Lubell, *The Future of American Politics* (Garden City, N.Y.: Doubleday, 1955), chap. 3.
123. See Duncan MacRae, Jr., and James A. Meldrum, "Critical Elections in Illinois," *American Political Science Review,* 54 (1960), 669–683. Similar findings have been made for New Hampshire by Alon Jeffrey, "Electoral Reorientation in New Hampshire 1916–1964" (unpublished M.A. Thesis, University of Chicago, 1966); and for Michigan by J. David Greenstone (research in progress).
124. This gradual realignment was also paralleled by a fall in the assurance and determination of the business community, which opposed both labor and the Democrats. By the late 1920s, management hostility to the organization of its workers was much less certain. The typical employer "was not sure whether to crush organized labor under the American Plan or to woo the workers with welfare capitalism. More than anything else, he preferred not to think about the worker at all." Bernstein, *op. cit.,* p. 188.

CHAPTER II   LABOR AS A PARTY ORGANIZATION:
THE NEW DEAL AND AFTER

1. V. O. Key, Jr., *Politics, Parties, and Pressure Groups* (New York: Crowell, 1964), p. 543.
2. V. O. Key, Jr., "A Theory of Critical Elections," *Journal of Politics,* 17 (February 1955), 3–18.
3. See Fred I. Greenstein, *The American Party System and the American People* (Englewood Cliffs, N.J.: Prentice-Hall, 1963), pp. 31–32 and Samuel Lubell, *The Future of American Politics* (Garden City, N.Y.: Doubleday, 1955), pp. 48–51.
4. Milton Derber, "Growth and Expansion," in Milton Derber and Edwin Young (eds.), *Labor and the New Deal* (Madison: University of Wisconsin Press, 1957), pp. 3, 40.
5. Arthur Schlesinger, Jr., *The Coming of the New Deal* (Boston: Houghton Mifflin, 1958), p. 410. By 1946, C. Wright Mills found that the fathers of 23 percent of CIO union leaders in his sample belonged to this new immigrant stock as opposed to only 14 percent of AFL leaders, whereas 25 percent of the AFL leaders' fathers were

from old immigrant stock versus only 15 percent of the CIO leaders. *New Men of Power* (New York: Harcourt, Brace & World, 1948), p. 87.

Karson, reviewing the role of Catholic unionists, notes that "the Irish were not as powerful [in the CIO] as they were in the AF of L, but Italian and Polish Catholics made up for much of this loss." Marc Karson, *American Labor Unions and Politics* (Cardondale: Southern Illinois University Press, 1958), pp. 301–302. See also Samuel Lubell, *The Future of American Politics, op. cit.*, p. 49.

6. Milton Derber, *op. cit.*, pp. 28–31. See also, Philip Taft, *The A.F. of L. from the Death of Gompers to the Merger* (New York: Harper & Row, 1959), p. 202.

7. Leon Epstein, *Politics in Wisconsin* (Madison: University of Wisconsin Press, 1958), p. 204.

8. Taft, *The A.F. of L. from the Death of Gompers, op. cit.*, p. 74, and Mary Heaton Vorse, *Labor's New Millions* (New York: Modern Age Books, 1938), p. 9.

9. Taft, *The A.F. of L. from the Death of Gompers, op. cit.*, pp. 155, 166.

10. Schlesinger, Jr., *The Crisis of the Old Order* (Boston: Houghton Mifflin, 1957), p. 3; J. Raymond Walsh, *CIO: Industrial Unionism in Action* (New York: Norton, 1937), p. 60.

11. Schlesinger, *The Crisis of the Old Order, op. cit.*, p. 3, chap. 24.

12. *Ibid.*, chap. 26, and Bernard Karsh and Philip L. Garman, "The Impact of the Political Left," in Milton Derber and Edwin Young (eds.), *Labor and the New Deal* (Madison: University of Wisconsin Press, 1957), pp. 98–99.

13. Irving Bernstein, *The Lean Years* (Boston: Houghton Mifflin, 1960), chap. 13.

14. Karsh and Garman, *op. cit.*, pp. 96–97.

15. Schlesinger, *The Coming of the New Deal, op. cit.*, p. 567, and *The Politics of Upheaval* (Boston: Houghton Mifflin, 1960), pp. 634, 641.

16. Taft, *The A.F. of L. from the Death of Gompers, op. cit.*, p. 45. On the bonus army, see Bernstein, *Lean Years, op. cit.*, chap 13.

17. Walsh, *op. cit.*, pp. 108–111.

18. See Vorse, *op. cit.*, p. 104.

19. See Walsh, *op. cit.*, p. 112.

20. Vorse, *op. cit.*, pp. 64–65, 93.

21. Quoted by Walsh, *op. cit.*, p. 123.

22. Vorse, *op. cit.*, p. 13.

23. See, for example, Schlesinger, *The Coming of the New Deal, op. cit.*, pp. 137–142.

24. Walsh, *op. cit.*, pp. 268–269.

25. Vorse, *op. cit.*, p. 292.
26. Walsh, *op. cit.*, p. 179.
27. See *ibid.*, p. 122.
28. Vorse, *op. cit.*, pp. 232–234.
29. Quoted by Walsh, *op. cit.*, pp. 68–69.
30. E. E. Schattschneider, *The Semi-Sovereign People* (New York: Holt, Rinehart and Winston, 1960), p. 68. (Schattschneider's emphasis.)
31. Walsh, *op. cit.*, p. 29.
32. Murray Edelman, "Sensitivity to Labor," in Milton Derber and Edwin Young (eds.). *Labor and the New Deal* (Madison: University of Wisconsin Press, 1957), p. 171. The board initially pursued a policy highly favorable to the CIO against AFL craft unions, although eventually AFL complaints subsided when Roosevelt changed the compositioin of the board. *Ibid.*, p. 172.
33. See Philip Taft, "Labor's Changing Political Line," *Journal of Political Economy*, 45 (October 1937), 637.
34. Vorse, *op. cit.*, p. 58.
35. Edelman, *op. cit.*, p. 181.
36. *Ibid.*, p. 177.
37. See Elizabeth Brandeis, "Organized Labor and Protective Labor Legislation," in Milton Derber and Edwin Young (eds.), *Labor and the New Deal* (Madison: University of Wisconsin Press, 1957, pp. 210, 229–230.
38. Edelman, *op. cit.*, p. 188. He cites, for example, the Railroad Act of 1934, the Wagner Act, and very possibly the labor provisions of the National Industrial Recovery Act, as well as (later) the La Folette Committee's civil liberties investigation of antiunion behavior by corporations and local officials.
39. Louise Overacker, "Labor's Political Contributions," *Political Science Quarterly*, 14 (March 1939), 61.
40. Schlesinger, *The Politics of Upheaval, op. cit.* In fact, the UMW contributed $469,870, of which a $50,000 loan was repaid later. See Overacker, *op. cit.*, p. 58.
41. See Taft, *The A.F. of L. from the Death of Gompers, op. cit.*, p. 305 and Juanita Kreps, "Developments in the Political and Legislative Policies of Organized Labor: 1920–1947" (unpublished Ph.D. dissertation, Duke University, 1947).
42. See Schlesinger, *The Politics of Upheaval, op. cit.*, p. 590 and Edelman, *op. cit.*, pp. 181–182.
43. See Kreps, *op. cit.*, p. 156.
44. Joel Seidman, "Organized Labor in Political Campaigns," *Public Opinion Quarterly*, 3 (October 1939), 654.
45. See Kreps, *op. cit.*, pp. 76, 77.

46. See Taft, *The A.F. of L. from the Death of Gompers, op. cit.*, p. 307.

47. Quoted by Kreps, *op. cit.*, p. 137.

48. *Ibid.*, pp. 140–141.

49. See Kreps, *op. cit.*, pp. 161, 250–251, and Irving Bernstein. "John L. Lewis and the Voting Behavior of the CIO," *Public Opinion Quarterly* 5 (June 1941), 233–249.

50. Samuel Lubell, "Who Elected Roosevelt?" *Saturday Evening Post*, 213, No. 30 (January 25, 1941), 93.

51. Bernstein, "John L. Lewis," *op. cit.*, pp. 241ff.

52. See Kreps, *op. cit.*, pp. 135–136 and Joseph Rosenfarb, "Labor's Role in the Election," *Public Opinion Quarterly*, 8 (Fall 1944), 378.

53. Kreps, *op. cit.*, pp. 140–141 and Joseph Gaer, *The First Round* (New York: Duell, Sloan and Pearce, 1944), p. 255. See also Matthew Josephson, *Sidney Hillman: Statesman of American Labor* (Garden City, N.Y.: Doubleday, 1952), p. 592.

54. Quoted by Josephson, *op. cit.*, p. 630. See Richard Rovere, "Labor's Political Machine," *Harpers Magazine*, 110 (June 1945).

55. Rosenfarb, *op. cit.*, p. 377; see also Rovere, *op. cit.*, 594.

56. Samuel P. Huntington, "A Revised Theory of American Politics," *American Political Science Review*, 44 (September 1950) and Josephson, *op. cit.*, p. 677.

57. See Josephson, *op. cit.*, chap. 25.

58. Lubell, "Who Elected Roosevelt?" *op. cit.*, 9. See also his *The Future of American Politics, op. cit.*

59. Gaer, *op. cit.*, p. 93.

60. See Grant McConnell, *Private Power and American Democracy* (New York: Knopf, 1966), chap. 9, for a discussion of this indictment. In particular, consider the symposium, "The Crisis in the American Trade-Union Movement," in *The Annals of the American Academy of Political and Social Science* (November 1963). See also A. H. Raskin, "Making Strikes Obsolete," *The Atlantic*, 217 (June 1966), 47–52.

61. Lubell, *The Future of American Politics, op. cit.*, p. 191.

62. Paul Jacobs, *The State of the Unions* (New York: Atheneum, 1963), pp. 48–49, 56, 295. The CIO's main achievement, according to C. Wright Mills, was to make industrial workers, along with skilled tradesmen, the aristocrats of labor. (*Op. cit.*, p. 116.) As Mills put it, "each reform achieved [by American unions] gives the reformer one more stake in the existing system." P. 153.

63. Robert Hoxie, "Trade Unionism in the United States," *Journal of Political Economy*, 20 (July 1914), 203.

64. Walsh, *op. cit.*, p. 161. Philip Taft had a similar point of view in

1939 when he noted, apparently with approval, the lack of theorizing in the new industrial unions. "Labor's Changing Political Line," *op. cit.*, 640. This was obviously true of John L. Lewis; see Schlesinger, *The Coming of the New Deal, op. cit.*, p. 418. And, despite his socialist background, Sidney Hillman was "a pragmatist to the core." Josephson, *op. cit.*, p. 439.

65. *CIO Proceedings* (1943), p. 243; quoted by Kreps, *op. cit.*, p. 169.
66. See Taft, *The A.F. of L. from the Death of Gompers, op. cit.*, p. 202.
67. See Edwin E. Witte, "Organized Labor and Social Security," in Milton Derber and Edwin Young (eds.), *Labor and the New Deal* (Madison: University of Wisconsin Press, 1957), pp. 252–257; Elizabeth Brandeis, *op. cit.*, pp. 217ff.; and Taft, *The A.F. of L. from the Death of Gompers, op. cit.*, chap. 10.
68. See Taft, *The A.F. of L. from the Death of Gompers, op. cit.*, pp. 258, 262 and Brandeis, *op. cit.*, p. 232.
69. Kreps, *op. cit.*, p. 252 and George C. Higgins, "Union Attitudes toward Economic and Social Roles of the Modern State," in George Brooks *et al.* (eds.), *Interpreting the Labor Movement* (Madison, Wisc.: Industrial Relations Research Association, 1952), p. 150.
70. Kreps, *op. cit.*, pp. 142–143.
71. Morton Leeds, "The AFL in the 1948 Elections," *Social Research*, 17, No. 1 (June 1950), 207. As Leeds points out, the formation of LLPE as a separate political organization was also a funding device to enable the federation to finance political activities in the face of Taft-Hartley restrictions on the use of dues money. P. 208.
72. Leeds, *op. cit.*, p. 212; Mary Zon, "Labor in Politics," *Law and Contemporary Problems*, 27 (Spring 1962), 235.
73. Leeds, *op. cit.*, p. 218.
74. Taft, *The A.F. of L. from the Death of Gompers, op. cit.*, p. 322.
75. *Time*, 80 (November 13, 1964), 40. Compare Lubell, *The Future of American Politics, op. cit.*, pp. 201–207 and Fay Calkins, *The CIO and the Democratic Party* (Chicago: University of Chicago Press, 1952), chap. 2.
76. *Congressional Quarterly*, 20 (October 26, 1962), 2022–2023.
77. Karl Marx, *Capital*, "Preface to the Second Edition," in Lewis S. Feuer (ed.), *Basic Writings on Politics and Philosophy* (Garden City, N.Y.: Doubleday, 1959), p. 141.
78. Robert Michels, *Political Parties* (New York: Free Press, 1949), p. 56.
79. *Ibid.*, pp. 320–321.
80. Robert K. Merton, "Social Structure and Anomie," *The American Sociological Review*, 3 (October 1936), 673.

81. See Jacobs *op. cit.;* Richard A. Lester, *As Unions Mature* (Princeton, N.J.: Princeton University Press, 1958); and the "crisis literature" reviewed by McConnell, *op. cit.,* chap. 9.

82. Michels, *op. cit.,* p. 386.

83. V. I. Lenin, *The Struggle for the Bolshevik Party,* Vol. II, in J. Fineberg (ed.), *Selected Works* (New York: International Publishers, n.d.), p. 31.

84. *Ibid.,* p. 126 (my emphasis). See also p. 62 for a rejection of the notion of any compromise between these two approaches.

85. *Ibid.,* p. 132.

86. *Ibid.,* p. 52.

87. *Ibid.,* p. 53.

88. Nathan Leites, *A Study of Bolshevism* (New York: Free Press, 1953), p. 186.

89. Max Weber, *The Protestant Ethic and the Spirit of Capitalism* (New York: Scribner, 1958), p. 166.

90. Lenin, *op. cit.,* p. 59; Weber, *op. cit.,* pp. 156–157. Lenin's attack on mere economic gain as a motive was matched by a similar rejection of the equally spontaneous use of terror rather than rational calculation. Pp. 94–97.

91. Lenin, *op. cit.,* p. 139 (emphasis mine); Weber, *op. cit.,* chap. 3.

92. Lenin, *op. cit.,* p. 147.

93. Max Weber, *The Theory of Social and Economic Organization* (New York: Free Press, 1964), p. 331. Lenin, *op. cit.,* pp. 56, 105, 141, 143, 156.

94. *Ibid.,* pp. 30ff., 144.

95. See, for example, Peter Blau, *Dynamics of Bureaucracy* (Chicago: University of Chicago Press, 1955).

96. Richard Baisden, "Labor Unions in Los Angeles Politics" (unpublished Ph.D. dissertation, University of Chicago, 1958), pp. 309ff.

97. Joseph Schumpeter, *Capitalism, Socialism and Democracy* (New York: Harper & Row, 1962), chap. 12.

98. Helen Fuller, "Labor and Politics," *The New Republic,* 110 (January 1944), 111–113.

99. Lubell, *The Future of American Politics, op. cit.,* pp. 200–201.

100. Max Weber, "Bureaucracy," in H. H. Gerth and C. Wright Mills (eds.), *From Max Weber* (New York: Oxford University Press, 1958), p. 231.

101. On Franklin, see Weber, *The Protestant Ethic, op. cit.,* pp. 48ff.

102. Compare Taft, "Labor's Changing Political Line," *op. cit.*

103. This is also the view of Raymond Moley, "The AFL-CIO in 1962," *Newsweek,* 60, No. 18 (October 22, 1962), 112.

104. Compare Edward C. Banfield and James Q. Wilson, *City Politics*

(Cambridge, Mass.: Harvard University Press and the MIT Press, 1963), p. 279.

105. *AFL-CIO News* (May 5, 1962). Quoted by Zon, *op. cit.*, p. 235.
106. Reinhard Bendix, *Nation Building and Citizenship* (New York: Wiley, 1964).
107. *Ibid.*, pp. 72, 73 (Bendix's emphasis).
108. *Ibid.*, p. 65.
109. Walter Dean Burnham, "The Changing Shape of the American Political Universe," *American Political Science Review*, 59 (March 1965), 7–28.
110. Compare E. E. Schattschneider, "The United States: The Functional Approach to Party Government," in Sigmund Neuman (ed.), *Modern Political Parties* (Chicago: University of Chicago Press, 1956), p. 204. Burnham cites and refers to Schattschneider extensively throughout his analysis.
111. Burnham, *op. cit.*, p. 10.
112. See also Schattschneider, "The United States," *op. cit.*, p. 203. Compare T. Wilbain Goodman, "The Presidential Campaign of 1920" (unpublished Ph.D. dissertation, Ohio University, 1951): "another characteristic of the [1920] campaign was the general apathy of the voters," p. 363. As William Alan White observed in his autobiography, "the whole liberal movement of the 20th century . . . was tired. The spirits of the liberals . . . were bewildered." Quoted by Goodman, *op. cit.*, p. 396.
113. The upper-class character of the Republicans has been discussed by Seymour Lipset in *Political Man* (Garden City, N.Y.: Doubleday, 1963), pp. 303–307, 329, esp. *n* 45.
114. V. O. Key, Jr., *Southern Politics* (New York: Vintage Books, 1949), pp. 542ff; Burnham, *op. cit.*, pp. 24–27; Schattschneider, "The United States," *op. cit.*, pp. 198–206.
115. Bendix, *op. cit.*, pp. 73–74.
116. Karl Marx and Friedrich Engels, *The Communist Manifesto*, in Lewis S. Feuer (ed.), *Basic Writings on Politics and Philosophy* (Garden City, N.Y.: Doubleday, 1959), p. 16.
117. Burnham, *op. cit.*, p. 23. Schattschneider associates the decline in voter turnout after 1896 with "the marriage of the Republican party and big business" in the late nineteenth and early twentieth centuries "in which business was the senior partner." ("The United States," *op. cit.*, p. 200.)
118. Burnham, *op. cit.*, p. 24.
119. *Ibid.*, p. 26.
120. Burnham, *op. cit.*, p. 10.
121. *Ibid.*, p. 28. Here again we find a disjunction between Burnham's

specific comments on Michigan, where he alludes to the branch structure that labor, in effect, furnishes for the Michigan Democrats, and the more general reflections just quoted.

122. Bendix observes that nationalism is associated with the protests he studies, and rightly suggests that a Marxian stress on economic alienation cannot provide a persuasive explanation for it. Bendix, *op. cit.,* pp. 71, 72. The similarities that Schlesinger noted between this period and the New Deal may therefore reflect precisely this political aspect rather than a common bond of economic protest. See Arthur Schlesinger, Jr., *The Age of Jackson* (Boston: Little, Brown, 1946).

123. Burnham, *op. cit.,* p. 22.

124. Compare Schattschneider, *The Semi-Sovereign People, op. cit.,* pp. 71, 86, on the changes in "the mobilization of bias" produced by the Roosevelt revolution in American politics.

125. David Easton, *A Systems Analysis of Political Life* (New York: Wiley, 1965), esp. chap. 8.

126. Compare *ibid.,* chap. 9.

CHAPTER III   THE DILEMMAS OF PATRONAGE POLITICS

1. See Edward C. Banfield and James Q. Wilson, *City Politics* (Cambridge, Mass.: Harvard University Press, 1963), p. 116.

2. Mary Heaton Vorse, *Labor's New Millions* (New York: Modern Age Books, 1938), p. 121.

3. Barbara Warne Newell, *Chicago and the Labor Movement* (Urbana: University of Illinois Press, 1961), p. 147.

4. Fay Calkins, *The CIO and the Democratic Party* (Chicago: University of Chicago Press, 1952), chap. 4.

5. Banfield and Wilson, *op. cit.,* p. 115.

6. Compare Grant McConnell, *The Decline of Agrarian Democracy* (Berkeley: University of California Press, 1953), pp. 162, 173–174.

7. See in this connection, Banfield and Wilson, *op. cit.,* p. 116 and Leo M. Snowiss, "Chicago and Congress: A Study of Metropolitan Representation" (unpublished Ph.D. dissertation, University of Chicago, 1965), p. 423.

8. This is also the judgment of James Q. Wilson, who cites the relevant sources in *The Amateur Democrat* (Chicago: University of Chicago Press, 1962), p. 67. See, for example, Harold Gosnell, *Machine Politics: Chicago Model* (Chicago: University of Chicago Press, 1939); Martin Meyerson and Edward C. Banfield, *Politics, Planning and the Public Interest* (New York: Free Press, 1955); and Edward C. Banfield, *Political Influence* (New York: Free Press,

1961). See also Wilson, *The Amateur Democrat, op. cit.,* chap. 3 and James Q. Wilson, *Negro Politics* (New York: Free Press, 1960), especially chaps. 3 and 4, for a description of the black party organization and its relation to the rest of the party and to other black groups. See also David McCoy, "Patronage in Suburbia" (unpublished Ph.D. dissertation, University of Chicago, 1963).

9. See Donald S. Bradley and Mayer N. Zald, "From Commercial Elite to Political Administrator: The Recruitment of the Mayors of Chicago," *American Journal of Sociology,* 71, No. 2 (September 19, 1965), 164.

10. See Banfield and Wilson, *op. cit.,* p. 116.

11. See McCoy, *op. cit.,* chap. 2, on the difficulties of township organizations.

12. Sawyer and MacRae observe that job security considerations among state legislators and their supporters lend a similar conservative bias against maximizing party success in the legislature in order to assure the seats of those already elected. See Jack Sawyer and Duncan MacRae, Jr., "Game Theory and Cumulative Voting in Illinois: 1902–1954," *American Political Science Review,* 56 (December 1962), 945. Their conclusions seem validated by the situation described here.

13. Not every precinct worker has a job, but all, except those unusual spirits who love the interpersonal contact involved, are tied to the party by some material favor. Wilson reports that as many as 30,000 jobs may be available when the Democrats control the state government as well as local units (Wilson, *The Amateur Democrat, op. cit.,* p. 69). The number of patronage jobs remained roughly the same during the 1960s although it was somewhat reduced by reforms in the sanitary district and by Republican control of several county offices. See *The Chicago Daily News* (February 6, 1967), p. 1.

14. Banfield and Wilson, *op. cit.,* p. 118.

15. Compare Robert K. Merton, *Social Theory and Social Structure* (New York: Free Press, 1957), pp. 76–78. One expression of the leaders' lower-class background may be that politics is seen as almost exclusively the male's province. Not only has the party no women leaders, but, much more remarkably, it nominated very few women for any elective offices. Compare Meyerson and Banfield, *op. cit.,* p. 264. Indeed, the organization has recently been led by a group of Irish Catholics who have usually risen from working-class backgrounds. In the 1960s, the growing black (and Protestant) block of voters did not supply any major leaders for the entire party. On the dominance of Irish leadership see Banfield, *op. cit.,* p. 249.

16. *Newsweek* (January 7, 1963), 7.

17. Banfield and Wilson, *op. cit.,* p. 116.

18. See Wilson, *The Amateur Democrat, op. cit.,* chap. 10.

19. On the radical period see Eugene Staley, *History of the Illinois State Federation of Labor* (Chicago: University of Chicago Press, 1930), chap. 22.

20. The major unions who support this leadership were concentrated in the building trades and other allied unions like the Teamsters and the Building Service unions. In Chicago these three groups, as elsewhere, have been held together by their interdependence in strikes, particularly the dependence of the first two upon the Teamsters, although the Teamsters' help is usually reciprocated. The resulting triumvirate is described in Newell, *op. cit.,* chap. 10, esp. pp. 209–219.

21. Michael Rogin, "Voluntarism: The Political Functions of an Anti-Political Doctrine," *Industrial and Labor Relations Review,* 15 (July 1962), 534–535.

22. *The Federation News* (October 9, 1954).

23. Meyerson and Banfield themselves point out that such labor leaders can communicate with the party. One Housing Authority commissioner in their study, Henry A. Kruse of McFetridge's Building Service Union, "had the vocabulary—the vocabulary of words, intonation, gesture, dress, ethnicity—which made him understood by the alderman." But Kruse, consistent with McFetridge's conservatism, "was not a strong believer in public housing." Meyerson and Banfield, *op. cit.,* p. 265.

24. See Snowiss, *op. cit.,* p. 339.

25. Richard Rovere, "Labor's Political Machine," *Harpers,* 110 (June 1945), 598.

26. *The Federation News* (September 20, 1958).

27. Compare Banfield, *op. cit.,* p. 246.

28. *Ibid.,* p. 246.

29. The clearest example of the convergence of these various "good-government" goals appears in community conservationist elites in American local politics, which emerged in the 1950s. The term "conservationist" and the behavior of these politicians, including their capacity to ally with trade-union and liberal groups, as well as with central-business-district conservatives, are discussed by Robert E. Agger, Daniel Goldrich and Bert E. Swanson, *The Rulers and the Ruled* (New York: Wiley, 1964), pp. 23ff. and 648–650.

30. Compare Wilson, *The Amateur Democrat, op. cit.,* pp. 71–72.

31. Peter Rossi and Richard Dentler, *The Politics of Urban Renewal* (New York: Free Press, 1961), pp. 225–239.

32. See J. David Greenstone and Paul E. Peterson, "Big City Politics and the War on Poverty," in James Q. Wilson (ed.), *City Politics*

and Public Policy (New York: Wiley, 1968), p. 267. See the relevant passages in Walter Dean Burnham, "The Changing Shape of the American Political Universe," *American Political Science Review*, 59 (March 1965), 7–28.

33. Compare Daniel Bell, *The End of Ideology* (New York: Free Press, 1962), pp. 254–255.

CHAPTER IV   DETROIT: THE DILEMMAS OF POLITICAL POWER

1. The entry of the CIO into the party is recounted by Fay Calkins, *The CIO and the Democratic Party* (Chicago: University of Chicago Press, 1955), pp. 112–146 and Stephen B. and Vera H. Sarasohn, *Political Party Patterns in Michigan* (Detroit: Wayne State University Press, 1957), pp. 45–68.

2. See V. I. Lenin, *The Struggle for the Bolshevik Party*, Vol. II, in J. Fineberg (ed.), *Selected Works* (New York: International Publishers, n.d.), pp. 76–85.

3. Samuel J. Eldersveld, *Political Parties: A Behavioral Analysis* (Chicago: Rand McNally, 1964), pp. 78–79.

4. *Ibid.*, pp. 84, 480.

5. *Ibid.*, p. 328.

6. Anonymous author, quoted in David Greenstone, "A Report on Politics in Detroit" (Cambridge, Mass.: Joint Center for Urban Studies, 1961, pp. V-1 and V-2 (mimeo).

7. See Irving Howe and B. J. Widdick, *The UAW and Walter Reuther* (New York: Random House, 1949), pp. 47–65, 83–106.

8. See anonymous author, in Greenstone, *op. cit.*, p. V-5. By the mid-1960s both conflicts, especially that between skilled and unskilled workers, had reemerged.

9. For reflections on the distinctive character of the UAW as compared with the Steelworkers, see Seymour M. Lipset, *Political Man* (Garden City, N.Y.: Doubleday, 1960), pp. 378–379. For reflections on the continuing liberal character of the UAW into the 1940s, see Howe and Widdick, *op. cit.*, chap. 9, esp. pp. 195–199. The UAW has retained much of its pioneering concern for welfare issues. In 1960, it sponsored Detroit's Community Health Association, by now the area's largest group health plan. The association was designed to lower health costs not only for UAW members but anyone in the community willing to join.

10. These frustrations are discussed by Howe and Widdick, *op. cit.*, pp. 20–24. They are compared with those in other industries in a statistical analysis of survey data by Robert Blauner, *Alienation and*

Freedom (Chicago: University of Chicago Press, 1964), pp. 89–123.

11. Sarasohn and Sarasohn, *op. cit.*, pp. 33ff.

12. On the influence of ex-radicals in American labor, see Murray Seidler, "The Socialist Party and American Unionism," *Midwest Journal of Political Science,* 5 (August 1961), 207–236.

13. Much has been written about the impact of nonpartisan politics on electoral behavior. For a careful study of its impact in four Michigan cities, see Oliver P. William and Charles R. Adrian, *Four Cities* (Philadelphia: University of Pennsylvania Press, 1963), chap. 4.

14. This information comes from C. O. Smith and S. B. Sarasohn, "Hate Propaganda in Detroit," *Public Opinion Quarterly,* 10 (Spring 1946), 24–52. The endorsements of the Communist party and of Gerald L. K. Smith, a racist, were unsolicited.

15. Calkins, *op. cit.*, pp. 134–135.

16. Compare Arthur Kornhauser, Harold L. Sheppard, and Albert J. Mayer, *When Labor Votes: A Study of the Auto Workers* (New York: University Books, 1956), pp. 262ff.

17. Calkins, *op. cit.*, p. 128.

18. See James Q. Wilson, *Negro Politics* (New York: Free Press, 1960), pp. 42–44.

19. Fred I. Greenstein, *The American Party System and the American People* (Englewood Cliffs, N.J.: Prentice-Hall, 1963), p. 73.

20. Howe and Widdick, *op. cit.*, p. 175.

21. See, in particular, Calkins, *op. cit.*, pp. 114–115.

22. Compare the persuasive interpretation of the anonymous author in Greenstone, *op. cit.*, pp. V-18–V-19.

CHAPTER V   LOS ANGELES: THE POLITICS
OF DISORGANIZATION

1. More precisely, the city grew only 33.1 percent in the 1940s and 27.1 percent in the 1950s; the outlying areas (excluding Long Beach) grew 72.05 percent and 82.6 percent respectively. U.S. Bureau of the Census, *Eighteenth Census of the United States: 1960 Population,* I (Washington, D.C.: U.S. Government Printing Office, 1961), pp. 16, 66, 108.

2. See Wilson, *The Amateur Democrat* (Chicago: University of Chicago Press, 1962), p. 104 and U.S. Bureau of the Census, *Eighteenth Census of the United States: 1960, General Social and Economic Characteristics,* I, Part 6, California (Washington, D.C.: U.S. Government Printing Office, 1961), pp. 6–265.

3. Dean R. Cresap, *Party Politics in the Golden State* (Los Angeles: The Haynes Foundation, 1954), pp. 7–11. Cresap offers an excellent introduction to California parties.

4. Wilson, *The Amateur Democrat, op. cit.,* pp. 96, 98.
5. For a careful estimate of the few jobs available for patronage purposes, see *ibid.,* pp. 203–205.
6. *Ibid.,* pp. 104–105, lists a few of the many examples in the Democratic party.
7. Carey McWilliams. *California: The Great Exception* (New York: Wyn, 1949), chaps. 1, 13. James Q. Wilson, *A Report on Politics in Los Angeles* (Cambridge, Mass.: Joint Center for Urban Studies, 1959), pp. 1–10.
8. Carey McWilliams, *Southern California Country* (New York: Duell, Sloan and Pearce, 1946), pp. 238–239, 166, 171.
9. On the importance of the suffrage to lower-class citizens see Robert A. Dahl, *Who Governs?* (New Haven, Conn.: Yale University Press, 1961), pp. 84–85, 284.
10. California Department of Industrial Relations, *Union Labor in California: 1955* (San Francisco: State of California Printing Office, 1956), p. 9. In 1960, the biggest CIO unions in the state were the UAW, which ranked eighth, and the Steelworkers and the Communications Workers, which ranked thirteenth and fifteenth among all California unions. *Ibid.,* p. 21.
11. Irving Bernstein, "Trade Union Characteristics, Membership, and Influence," *Monthly Labor Review,* 83 (May 1959), 534.
12. See Richard Baisden, "Labor Unions in Los Angeles Politics" (unpublished Ph.D. dissertation, University of Chicago, 1958), pp. 31–128.
13. The full account of this issue is in *ibid.,* pp. 303–382.
14. Compare Cresap, *op. cit.,* chap. 1, esp. p. 5.
15. Wilson, *The Amateur Democrat, op. cit.,* p. 108.
16. *Ibid.,* p. 101.
17. Cresap, *op. cit.,* p. 103. McWilliams adds that as a result of the initiative and referendum introduced by the progressives, special interests have available another channel for seeking special legislation, the voting booth. Public relations firms have become major political agents for these interests. See McWilliams, *California: The Great Exception, op. cit.,* pp. 205–207. The most extensive discussion of the leading firm, Whitaker and Baxter, is in Stanley Kelley, Jr., *Professional Public Relations and Political Power* (Baltimore: Johns Hopkins Press, 1956), chaps. 2, 3.
18. *Los Angeles Citizen* (February 17, 1961).
19. See Bernstein, *op. cit.,* p. 535.
20. Buzzell has been described as "basically a conservative in politics, favoring as little government as possible. He even had doubts about the value of laws that assisted organized labor since, 'what a friendly administration gives, an unfriendly one can take away.' " See Baisden's description of those traditional concerns, pp. 138–302, 383–461.

21. See, for example, Wilson, *The Amateur Democrat, op. cit.,* chap. 12 and Cresap, *op. cit.,* chap. 1.
22. McWilliams, *California, The Great Exception, op. cit.,* p. 182. Even Johnson's progressive movement, he points out, made its reforms in about six years. Progressivism was then largely confined to Johnson's own success in winning reelection to the U.S. Senate.
23. Baisden, *op. cit.,* p. 313. See pp. 309ff. for a full account of the league.
24. McWilliams, *California: The Great Exception, op. cit.,* p. 139. See also pp. 128, 140.
25. See McWilliams, *Southern California Country, op. cit.,* pp. 273ff., esp. pp. 290–291. Even by 1960, Los Angeles unions had organized only 32.4 percent of the area's work force compared to 46.6 percent in the Bay Area. See California Department of Industrial Relations, *op. cit.,* pp. 24, 26.
26. For a careful but critical assessment of the effect of the club movement, see Wilson, *The Amateur Democrat, op. cit.,* chap. 4.
27. J. Totton Anderson, "The 1958 Election in California," *Western Political Quarterly,* 12 (March 1959), 289.
28. *Ibid.,* p. 291.
29. *Ibid.,* pp. 285–289, 291. Indeed, Los Angeles labor evidently withheld its opposition to the school exemption proposition until the politically conservative Cardinal McIntyre allowed a diocesan spokesman to oppose right-to-work publicly. See, on this general point, *Los Angeles Citizen* (October 24, 1958).
30. Anderson, *op. cit.,* p. 292.
31. On this general point see *ibid.,* p. 292.
32. See, for example, Baisden, *op. cit.,* chaps. 5, 6.
33. See E. E. Schattschneider, *Party Government* (New York: Holt, Rinehart and Winston, 1942), chap. 6.
34. "The Los Angeles County Committee is probably the most active in the California Democratic party. . . . In comparison with a county party organization in a large eastern city, however, it is feeble and inconsequential." Wilson, *The Amateur Democrat, op. cit.,* p. 101.
35. See V. O. Key, Jr., *Politics, Parties and Pressure Groups* (New York: Crowell, 1964), chap. 9.
36. For a discussion of shop societies as agencies of opinion formation and solidarity, see H. J. Lahne and Joseph Kovner, "Local Union Structure, Formality and Reality," *Industrial and Labor Relations Review,* 9 (October 1955), 24–31; Joseph Kovner and H. J. Lahne, "Shop Society and the Union," *Industrial and Labor Relations Review,* 7 (October 1953), 3–14; Joel Seidman *et al., The Worker Views His Union* (Chicago: University of Chicago Press, 1958), pp. 203ff.; and J. David Greenstone, "Political Norms and Group Proc-

ess in Private Government: The Case of a Local Union," *Midwest Journal of Political Science,* Vol. 9, No. 4 (November 1965).

37. See Theodore J. Lowi, "American Business, Public Policy, Case Studies and Political Theory," *World Politics,* XVI (July 1964), 677–715.

CHAPTER VI   LABOR'S CAMPAIGN APPARATUS: THE POLITICAL
INCENTIVES OF AN ECONOMIC ORGANIZATION

1. Among other works on incentive theory consult the following: Chester I. Barnard, *The Functions of the Executive* (Cambridge, Mass.: Harvard University Press, 1938), chaps. 6, 7, 9; Peter B. Clark and James Q. Wilson, "Incentive Systems: A Theory of Organizations," *Administrative Science Quarterly,* 6 (September 1961), pp. 129–166; James Q. Wilson, *The Amateur Democrat* (Chicago: University of Chicago Press, 1962), esp. chap. 6; Edward C. Banfield and James Q. Wilson, *City Politics* (Cambridge, Mass.: Harvard University Press, 1963), pp. 27–28, chap. 9; Robert A. Dahl, *Who Governs?* (New Haven, Conn.: Yale University Press, 1961), p. 52.
2. See Joseph Kovner and H. J. Lahne, "Shop Society and the Union," *Industrial and Labor Relations Review,* 7 (October 1953), 24–31.
3. Elihu Katz and Paul Lazarsfeld, *Personal Influence* (New York: Free Press, 1955), chaps. 2, 14.
4. Samuel J. Eldersveld, *Political Parties: A Behavioral Analysis* (Chicago: Rand McNally, 1964), p. 156.
5. *Ibid.,* p. 157.
6. *Ibid.,* p. 105.
7. *Ibid.,* pp. 504–505.
8. *Ibid.,* p. 265.
9. *Ibid.,* p. 104.
10. *Ibid.,* p. 480.
11. Fay Calkins perceived that labor had this problem at the beginning of the CIO's entry into the Democratic party. See *The CIO and the Democratic Party* (Chicago: University of Chicago Press, 1955), p. 136.
12. For a description of Abner's 1950 campaign for state senator against the wishes of the party organization, see *ibid.,* chap. 4.
13. The craft union's formal organization also operates as a substitute for the shop society in relation to securing member control of their local's government. See Joel Seidman *et al., op. cit.,* p. 189.

CHAPTER VII POLITICAL ACTION IN THE
CONGRESSIONAL DISTRICTS

1. *Chicago Daily News* (November 9, 1966).
2. Stimson notes that the harbor unions formed their own central body in 1902 when San Pedro was "described by the *Times* as the only 'union town' in southern California." Grace Stimson, *Rise of the Labor Movement in Los Angeles* (Berkeley: University of California Press, 1955), p. 215.

CHAPTER VIII THE LABOR-PARTY ALLIANCE

1. E. E. Schattschneider, *Party Government* (New York: Holt, Rinehart and Winston, 1942), p. 187.
2. David B. Truman, *The Governmental Process: Political Interests and Public Opinion* (New York: Knopf, 1960), p. 270. But see *ibid.*, pp. 280–281 for some qualifications to this view. Also see Clinton Rossiter, *Parties and Politics in America* (Ithaca, N.Y.: Cornell University Press, 1960), pp. 20–27, for a general statement of the power of interest groups to pressure the government and parties.
3. Rossiter, *op. cit.*, pp. 20–24, 95.
4. Robert K. Carr *et al.*, *American Democracy in Theory and Practice* (New York: Holt, Rinehart and Winston, 1955), p. 367. For a sophisticated statement of this overlap in function and of the possibilities of collaboration between parties and interest groups, see V. O. Key, Jr., *Politics, Parties, and Pressure Groups* (New York: Crowell, 1958), pp. 170–177.
5. See Almond, "Introduction" in Gabriel Almond and James S. Coleman (eds.), *The Politics of the Developing Areas* (Princeton, N.J.: Princeton University Press, 1960), pp. 26–45, esp. 39–40. Almond, of course, views these categories as two of the seven functions of the political system. In this book, however, aggregation and articulation will simply refer to some of the activities of parties and groups.
6. This language is David Easton's in *A Systems Analysis of Political Life* (New York: Wiley, 1965), chap. 9.
7. See Fay Calkins, *The CIO and the Democratic Party* (Chicago: University of Chicago Press, 1955), pp. 83–84 and James Q. Wilson, *Negro Politics* (New York: Free Press, 1960), pp. 125–126. In 1951, the Abner insurgents did help elect an independent black alderman, Archibald Carey, to a second council term. But Carey was defeated in 1955 when he supported the incumbent mayor, Martin Kennelly, who was not popular with blacks.

8. On the disorganization of Los Angeles blacks before the riots see Wilson, *Negro Politics, op. cit.,* pp. 24, 27–28, 37–38, and *The Amateur Democrat* (Chicago: University of Chicago Press, 1962), pp. 283–285.
9. In officially designated conservation areas they helped their members take advantage of credit advanced by the federal government. See J. David Greenstone, *A Report on Politics in Detroit* (Cambridge, Mass.: Joint Center for Urban Studies, 1961), p. V–69 (mimeo).
10. See Irving Howe and B. J. Widdick, *The UAW and Walter Reuther* (New York: Random House, 1949), pp. 223–225.
11. Almond, *op. cit.,* p. 39.
12. As one Detroit observer put it, "in the old days we had many caucuses in the party before each convention, Irish, Italian, Negro and what not . . . the district was balkanized into many separate groups and everyone felt free to break the agreements each group reached. Today everyone is welcome to caucus with labor, but they're honor bound to follow the agreement they reach. Labor just won't permit its people to be in any secret agreements. This is why you find so few old guard left . . . labor has taken the sport out of the party. It's not a game anymore." Compare Calkins, *op. cit.,* pp. 124–125.
13. Wilson, *Amateur Democrat, op. cit.,* pp. 269–270. For Wilson's analysis of this organizational conflict see pp. 273–275; on differences in political style see p. 269; on policy differences see pp. 274–275, 288.
14. See Wilson, *Amatuer Democrat, op. cit.,* p. 5, where he indicates that the amateurs, for example, are in fact a mixed empirical case.
15. *Ibid.,* pp. 3–4.
16. See Theodore J. Lowi, "American Business, Public Policy, Case Studies and Political Theory," *World Politics,* 16 (July 1964), 687, 692–694.
17. Compare the remarks of Grant McConnell, *Private Power and American Democracy* (New York: Knopf, 1966), pp. 111–112.
18. Compare Edward C. Banfield and James Q. Wilson, *City Politics* (Cambridge, Mass.: Harvard University Press, 1963), p. 279.
19. See Wilson, *The Amateur Democrat, op. cit.,* chap. 3.
20. The Cook County organization also controlled the party endorsements for statewide office. See *ibid.,* p. 75.
21. Carl J. Friedrich, *Constitutional Government and Democracy* (Boston: Ginn, 1946), pp. 589ff.
22. Wilson, *The Amateur Democrat, op. cit.,* p. 99.
23. For data on these districts see U. S. Bureau of the Census, *Congres-*

sional Disrtict Data Book (*Districts of the 88th Congress*) (Washington: U.S. Government Printing Office, 1963) pp. 228, 229, 236, 237.

24. For an excellent discussion of the fifteenth district party see Robert Francis Stout, "The Young Democratic Club of the Michigan Fifteenth Congressional District" (unpublished MA thesis, University of Detroit, 1956).

25. Compare the availability of office in the Canadian Cooperative Commonwealth Federation as a factor in maintaining wide membership involvement. Seymour M. Lipset, *Agrarian Socialism* (Berkeley: University of California Press, 1950), pp. 200ff.

26. See Stephen B. and Vera H. Sarasohn, *Political Party Patterns in Michigan* (Detroit: Wayne State University Press, 1957), p. 63.

27. Compare Calkins, *op. cit.*, pp. 134–135.

28. This process verifies at the intraparty level E. E. Schattschneider's observation that even the largest interests are subject to major parties. See *The Semi-Sovereign People* (New York: Holt, Rinehart and Winston, 1960), pp. 42ff.

CHAPTER IX   PARTY PRESSURE ON LABOR

1. This observation has been forcefully made by E. E. Schattschneider. See the *Semi-Sovereign People* (New York: Holt, Rinehart and Winston, 1960), pp. 58–59.

2. Leo M. Snowiss, "Chicago and Congress: A Study of Metropolitan Representation" (unpublished Ph.D. dissertation, University of Chicago, 1965), pp. 335ff.

3. Compare V. O. Key, Jr., *Politics, Parties and Pressure Groups* (New York: Crowell, 1958), chap. 13.

4. Snowiss, *op. cit.*

CHAPTER X   LABOR AND CONGRESS: UNIONS AS A CONSTITUENT PARTY INTEREST

1. See Angus Campbell *et al.*, *The American Voter* (New York: Wiley, 1960), pp. 244–247.

2. *Ibid.*, p. 249.

3. Fay Calkins, *The CIO and the Democratic Party* (Chicago: University of Chicago Press, 1952), pp. 100, 136.

4. See *The Wall Street Journal* (July 6, 1967), p. 14.

5. Harry T. Scoble, "Organized Labor in Electoral Politics: Some Questions for the Discipline," *Western Political Quarterly*, 16 (September 1963), 674.

6. See Cornelius P. Cotter and Bernard C. Hennessy, *Politics without Power* (New York: Atherton, 1964), pp. 24–65, and V. O. Key, Jr., *Politics, Parties and Pressure Groups* (New York: Crowell, 1961), chap. 12, esp. p. 315.

7. Rowland Evans and Robert Novak, "Labor and Politics," *Chicago Sun-Times* (December 10, 1966), p. 32.

8. Cotter and Hennessy, *op. cit.*

9. E. E. Schattschneider, *Party Government* (New York: Holt, Rinehart and Winston, 1942), p. 187. Compare Chapter VIII of this book.

10. For the data in this discussion see two AFL-CIO Committee on Political Education pamphlets, *"How Your Senators and Representatives Voted, 1963–1964,"* and *"How Your Senators and Representatives Voted, 1965–1966."*

11. V. O. Key, Jr., *Southern Politics* (New York: Vintage Books, 1949), pp. 395ff.

12. Compare the survey findings reported, in rather general terms, in *The Wall Street Journal* (July 6, 1967), pp. 1, 14.

13. Alan K. McAdams, *Power and Politics in Labor Legislation* (New York: Columbia University Press, 1964), p. 270.

14. *Ibid.*, p. 277. On AFL-CIO splits see pp. 270, 356.

15. *Ibid.*, p. 277.

16. Theodore J. Lowi, "American Business, Public Policy, Case Studies and Political Theory," *World Politics*, 16 (July 1964).

17. Campbell, *et al.*, *op. cit.*, p. 162.

18. On the power of the AMA see Stanley Kelley, Jr., *Professional Public Relations and Political Power* (Baltimore: Johns Hopkins Press, 1956), chap. 3 and Oliver Garceau, *The Political Life of the American Medical Association* (Cambridge, Mass.: Harvard University Press, 1941).

19. See Samuel Lubell, *The Future of American Politics* (Garden City, N.Y.: Doubleday, 1955), chap. 9 and *The Wall Street Journal* (July 6, 1967), p. 14.

20. David Easton, *A Systems Analysis of Political Life* (New York: Wiley, 1965), chap. 9.

21. E. E. Schattschneider, *The Semi-Sovereign People* (New York: Holt, Rinehart and Winston, 1960), p. 57.

22. Randall B. Ripley, "The Party Whip Organizations in the United States House of Representatives," *The American Political Science Review*, 58, No. 3 (September 1964), 561–577, esp. 575–576. See also Randall B. Ripley, *Party Leaders in the House of Representatives* (Washington, D.C.: Brookings, 1967).

23. Edward C. Banfield, *Political Influence* (New York: Free Press, 1961), p. 237.

24. See Leo M. Snowiss, "Chicago and Congress: A Study of Metropolitan Representation" (unpublished Ph.D. dissertation, University of Chicago, 1965).

25. V. O. Key, Jr. and Frank Munger, "Social Determinism and Electoral Decision: The Case of Indiana," in Eugene Burdick and Arthur J. Brodbeck (eds.), *American Voting Behavior* (New York: Free Press, 1959), pp. 296ff.

CHAPTER XI   CONCLUSION: LABOR POLITICS IN A FULLY
INDUSTRIALIZED SOCIETY

1. Ralf Dahrendorf, *Class and Class Conflict in Industrial Society* (Stanford, California: Stanford University Press, 1959), p. 136. For his discussion of manifest and latent interest see pp. 144–154, 173–179, 242.

2. Compare these observations with Dahrendorf's similar comment, *op. cit.,* p. 129.

3. Morris Janowitz and Dwaine Marvick, "Political Sociology," in *The International Encyclopedia of the Social Sciences* (New York: Macmillan, 1968); see Max Weber, "Politics as a Vocation" and "Class, Status, Party," in H. H. Gerth and C. Wright Mills (eds.), *From Max Weber* (New York: Oxford University Press, 1958).

4. Weber, "Class, Status, Party," *op cit.,* p. 194.

5. Dahrendorf, *op. cit.,* p. 19.

6. See *ibid.,* pp. 19–20, 129.

7. *Ibid.,* chap. 2.

8. *Ibid.,* pp. 30–31.

9. *Ibid.,* p. 136.

10. *Ibid.,* pp. 172–173.

11. Milovan Djilas, *The New Class: An Analysis of the Communist System* (New York: Praeger, 1957).

12. Dahrendorf, *op. cit.,* pp. 292–293. See also p. 232 where he designates change in the personnel occupying authority roles as the operational indicator of structure changes produced by class conflict.

13. *Ibid.,* p. 232.

14. *Ibid.,* p. 303.

15. *Ibid.,* p. 306.

16. Karl Marx and Friedrich Engels, "Manifesto of the Communist Party," in Lewis S. Feuer (ed.), *Basic Writings on Politics and Philosophy* (Garden City, N.Y.: Doubleday, 1959), pp. 9, 11.

17. Karl Marx and Friedrich Engels, "The German Ideology," in Lewis S. Feuer (ed.), *Basic Writings on Politics and Philosophy* (Garden City, N.Y.: Doubleday, 1959), p. 254.

18. Durkheim himself explicitly links one of his major concepts, the division of labor, to a stable integrationist view of society, observing that "great political societies can maintain themselves *in equilibrium* only thanks to the specialization of tasks." Indeed, he agrees with Spencer that "social harmony" and "unity" must be attributed to the division of labor. Emile Durkheim, *The Division of Labor in Society* (New York: Free Press, 1960), pp. 62, 200, and 203 (my emphasis).

19. Marx and Engels, "The German Ideology," *op. cit.,* pp. 252ff. Durkheim explicitly noted that solidarity could occur in social subgroups as well as within the whole society. Durkheim, *op. cit.,* p. 14.

20. Durkheim, *op. cit.,* pp. 109, 129.

21. One of Durkheim's chief indicators of mechanical solidarity was the presence of religious sentiment, defined not as a creed but in terms of feelings that were common to a certain number of people living together and that, besides, "are of an average intensity that is quite elevated." (*Ibid.,* p. 169). European socialism had just this character in its time of greatest rank and file loyalty. See for example Samuel H. Beer, *British Politics in the Collectivist Age* (New York: Knopf, 1966), pp. 128–129.

22. Beer, *op. cit.,* pp. 237–238.

23. Durkheim, *op. cit.,* p. 37.

24. See *ibid.,* pp. 129–131.

25. Dahrendorf, *op. cit.,* pp. 99, 275.

26. Compare Harold Wilensky, "Mass Society and Mass Culture," in Bernard Berelson and Morris Janowitz (eds.), *Reader in Public Opinion and Communication* (New York: Free Press, 1966), pp. 317–318.

27. Beer, *op. cit.,* p. 345.

28. Theodore J. Lowi, "American Business, Public Policy, Case Studies and Political Theory," *World Politics,* 16 (July 1964).

29. For a perceptive statement of this view, see Bert Hoselitz, "Karl Marx on Secular and Social Development: A Study in the Sociology of Nineteenth Century Social Science," *Comparative Studies in Society and History,* 6, No. 2 (1964), 161–162.

30. In Britain the socialists' failure to establish comprehensive physical planning in the 1940s must apparently be attributed to the functional economic specialization among trade unions as well as to that of the public and private economic authorities, all of whom valued their accustomed autonomy in their specialized sphere of competence. The Labour party's stress on consumer issues in the 1950s can therefore be seen as an attempt to exploit the remaining basis of similarity among economic non-authorities—their common consumer class interests. See Beer, *op. cit.,* pp. 200ff., esp. p. 211.

31. *Ibid.,* pp. 146–147 and 346–347. This is the case even though, as Beer makes clear, the emergence of the Labour party as a major electoral contender in part reflected tensions between its leaders and those of the Liberal party.
32. *Ibid.,* p. 347.
33. See Durkheim, *op. cit.,* p. 200.
34. Beer, *op. cit.,* pp. 348–351.
35. Dahrendorf, *op. cit.,* pp. 305–306.
36. Compare for example, V. O. Key's analysis of Arkansas or Florida with his discussion of Louisiana in *Southern Politics* (New York: Vintage Books, 1949), chaps. 5, 8, 9.

Bibliography

BOOKS

Agger, Robert E., Daniel Goldrich, and Bert E. Swanson. *The Rulers and the Ruled.* New York: Wiley, 1964.

Banfield, Edward C. *Political Influence.* New York: Free Press, 1961.

Banfield, Edward C., and James Q. Wilson. *City Politics.* Cambridge, Mass.: Harvard Univ. and M.I.T. Press, 1963.

Beer, Samuel. *British Politics in the Collectivist Age.* New York: Knopf, 1966.

Bell, Daniel. *The End of Ideology.* New York: Free Press, 1962.

Bendix, Reinhard. *Nation Building and Citizenship.* New York: Wiley, 1964.

Bernstein, Irving. *The Lean Years.* Boston: Houghton Mifflin, 1960.

Binkley, Wilfred E. *American Political Parties.* New York: Knopf, 1964.

Blaisdell, Donald. *American Democracy Under Pressure.* New York: Ronald Press, 1957.

Blau, Peter. *Dynamics of Bureaucracy.* Chicago: Univ. of Chicago Press, 1955.

Blauner, Robert. *Alienation and Freedom.* Chicago: Univ. of Chicago Press, 1964.

Bone, Hugh A. *American Politics and the Party System,* 3d ed. New York: McGraw-Hill, 1965.

Bornet, Vaughan Davis. *Labor Politics in a Democratic Republic.* Washington: Spartan Books, 1964.

California, State of. Department of Industrial Relations, Division of Labor Statistics and Research. *Union Labor in California, 1955.*

———. *Union Labor in California, 1960.*

Calkins, Fay. *The CIO and the Democratic Party.* Chicago: Univ. of Chicago Press, 1955.

Campbell, Angus, *et al. The American Voter.* New York: Wiley, 1960.

Carr, Robert K., *et al. American Democracy in Theory and Practice.* New York: Rinehart, 1955.

Cochran, Bert., ed. *American Labor in Mid-Passage.* New York: Monthly Review Press, 1959.

Commons, John R., *et al. History of Labour in the United States.* New York: Macmillan, 1936.

Cotter, Cornelius P., and Bernard C. Hennessy. *Politics without Power.* New York: Atherton Press, 1964.

Cresap, Dean R. *Party Politics in the Golden State.* Los Angeles: Haynes Foundation, 1954.

Dahl, Robert A. *Who Governs?* New Haven, Conn.: Yale Univ. Press, 1961.

Dahrendorf, Ralf. *Class and Class Conflict in Industrial Society.* Stanford, Calif.: Stanford Univ. Press, 1959.

Durkheim, Emile. *The Division of Labor in Society.* New York: Free Press, 1960.

Duverger, Maurice. *Political Parties.* New York: Wiley, 1954.

Easton, David. *The Political System.* New York: Knopf, 1953.

———. *A Systems Analysis of Political Life.* New York: Wiley, 1965.

Eldersveld, Samuel J. *Political Parties: A Behavioral Analysis.* Chicago: Rand McNally, 1964.

Elkins, Stanley. *Slavery.* Chicago: Univ. of Chicago Press, 1959.

Epstein, Leon. *Politics in Wisconsin.* Madison: Univ. of Wisconsin Press, 1958.

Feuer, Lewis S. ed. *Basic Writings on Politics and Philosophy: Karl Marx and Friedrich Engles.* Garden City, N. Y.: Doubleday, 1959.

Friedrich, Carl J. *Constitutional Government and Democracy.* Boston: Ginn, 1946.

Gaer, Joseph. *The First Round.* New York: Duell, Sloan & Pearce, 1944.

Goldman, Ralph M. *The Democratic Party in American Politics.* New York: Macmillan, 1966.

Gosnell, Harold. *Machine Politics Chicago Model.* Chicago: Univ. of Chicago Press, 1939.

Greenstein, Fred I. *The American Party System and the American People.* Englewood Cliffs, N. J.: Prentice-Hall, 1963.

Greenstone, J. David. *A Report on Politics in Detroit.* Cambridge, Mass.: Joint Center for Urban Studies of MIT and Harvard University, 1961. (Mimeograph.)

Hartz, Louis. *The Liberal Tradition in America.* New York: Harcourt, Brace & World, 1955.

Holcombe, Arthur N. *The Political Parties of Today.* New York: Harper & Row, 1924.

Holtzman, Abraham. *Interest Groups and Lobbying.* New York: Macmillan, 1966.

Howe, Irving, and B. J. Widdick. *The UAW and Walter Reuther.* New York: Random House, 1949.

Hudson, Ruth A., and Hajlmar Rosen. *The Union Member Speaks.* Englewood Cliffs, N. J.: Prentice-Hall, 1955.

Jacobs, Paul. *The State of the Unions.* New York: Atheneum, 1963.

Janowitz, Morris, and Dwaine Marvick. *Competitive Pressures and*

Democratic Consent. Ann Arbor: Bureau of Government, Institute of Public Administration, Univ. of Michigan, 1956.

Josephson, Matthew. *Sidney Hillman: Statesman of American Labor.* Garden City, N. Y.: Doubleday, 1952.

Kariel, Henry S. *The Decline of American Pluralism.* Stanford, Calif.: Stanford Univ. Press, 1961.

Karson, Marc. *American Labor Unions and Politics, 1900–1918.* Carbondale, Ill.: Southern Illinois Univ. Press, 1958.

Katz, Elihu, and Paul Lazarsfeld. *Personal Influence.* New York: Free Press, 1955.

Kelley, Stanley, Jr. *Professional Public Relations and Political Power.* Baltimore, Johns Hopkins Press, 1956.

Kennedy, Van Dusen. *Nonfactory Unionism and Labor Relations.* Berkeley: Institute of Industrial Relations, University of California, 1955.

Key, V. O., Jr. *American State Politics: An Introduction.* New York: Knopf, 1956.

———. *Politics, Parties, and Pressure Groups.* New York: Crowell, 1964.

———. *The Responsible Electorate.* Cambridge, Mass.: Harvard Univ. Press, 1966.

———. *Southern Politics.* New York: Knopf, Vintage edition, 1949.

Kolko, Gabriel. *Wealth and Power in America.* New York: Praeger, 1962.

Kornhauser, Arthur, Harold L. Sheppard, and Albert J. Mayer. *When Labor Votes: A Study of the Auto Workers.* New York: University Books, 1956.

Leiserson, William. *American Trade Union Democracy.* New York: Columbia Univ. Press, 1959.

Leites, Nathan. *A Study of Bolshevism.* New York: Free Press, 1953.

Lenin, V. I. "What is to be Done?" in J. Fineberg, ed., *Selected Works,* Vol. II, *The Struggle for the Bolshevik Party.* New York: International Publishers, n.d.

Lens, Sidney. *The Crisis in American Labor.* New York: A. S. Barnes, 1959.

Lester, Richard. *As Unions Mature.* Princeton, N. J.: Princeton Univ. Press, 1958.

Lipset, Seymour M. *Agrarian Socialism.* Berkeley: Univ. of California Press, 1959.

———. *Political Man.* Garden City, N. Y.: Doubleday, 1963.

Lorwin, Lewis. *The American Federation of Labor.* Washington, D. C.: Brookings, 1933.

Lubell, Samuel. *The Future of American Politics.* Garden City, N. Y.: Doubleday, 1956.

McAdams, Alan K. *Power and Politics in Labor Legislation*. New York: Columbia Univ. Press, 1964.

McConnell, Grant. *The Decline of Agrarian Democracy*. Berkeley: Univ. of Calif. Press, 1953.

————. *Private Power and American Democracy*. New York: Knopf, 1966.

McWilliams, Carey. *Southern California Country*. New York: Duell, Sloan and Pearce, 1946.

————. *California: The Great Exception*. New York: A. A. Wyn, 1949.

Merton, Robert K. *Social Theory and Social Structure*. New York: Free Press, 1957.

Meyerson, Martin, and Edward C. Banfield. *Politics, Planning and the Public Interest*. New York: Free Press, 1955.

Michels, Robert. *Political Parties*. New York: Free Press, 1958.

Mills, C. Wright. *The New Men of Power: America's Labor Leaders*. New York: Harcourt, Brace & World, 1948.

Newell, Barbara Warne. *Chicago and the Labor Movement*. Urbana: Univ. of Illinois Press, 1961.

Perlman, Selig. *A Theory of the Labor Movement*. New York: Kelley, 1949.

Rogin, Michael Paul. *The Intellectuals and McCarthy: The Radical Specter*. Cambridge, Mass.: M.I.T. Press, 1967.

Rossi, Peter H., and Richard Dentler. *The Politics of Urban Renewal*. New York: Free Press, 1961.

Rossiter, Clinton. *Parties and Politics in America*. Ithaca, N. Y.: Cornell Univ. Press, 1960.

Sarasohn, Stephen B., and Vera H. Sarasohn. *Political Party Patterns in Michigan*. Detroit: Wayne State Univ. Press, 1957.

Schattschneider, E. E. *Party Government*. New York: Holt, Rinehart and Winston, 1942.

————. *The Semi-Sovereign People*. New York: Holt, Rinehart and Winston, 1960.

Schlesinger, Arthur, Jr., *The Age of Jackson*. Boston: Little, Brown, 1946.

————. *The Coming of the New Deal*. Boston: Houghton-Mifflin, 1958.

————. *The Crisis of the Old Order*. Boston: Houghton-Mifflin, 1957.

————. *The Politics of Upheaval*. Boston: Houghton-Mifflin, 1967.

Schumpeter, Joseph. *Capitalism, Socialism and Democracy*. New York: Harper & Row, 1962.

Seidman, Harold. *The Labor Czars*. New York: Liveright, 1938.

Seidman, Joel, *et al. The Worker Views His Union*. Chicago: Univ. of Chicago Press, 1958.

Sexton, Patricia. *Education and Income*. New York: Viking, 1961.

Shannon, David. *The Socialist Party of America.* New York: Macmillan, 1955.

Staley, Eugene. *History of the Illinois State Federation of Labor.* Chicago: Univ. of Chicago Press, 1930.

Stimson, Grace. *Rise of the Labor Movement in Los Angeles.* Berkeley: Univ. of Calif. Press, 1955.

Taft, Philip. *The A. F. of L. in the Time of Gompers.* New York: Harper & Row, 1957.

————. *The A. F. of L. from the Death of Gompers to the Merger.* New York: Harper & Row, 1959.

Tocqueville, Alexis de. *Democracy in America.* Phillips Bradley, ed. New York: Vintage Books, 1945.

Truman, David. *The Governmental Process: Political Interests and Public Opinion.* New York: Knopf, 1960.

Vorse, Mary Heaton. *Labor's New Millions.* New York: Modern Age Books, 1938.

Weber, Max. *From Max Weber: Essays in Sociology.* H. H. Gerth and C. Wright Mills, eds. New York: Oxford Univ. Press, 1958.

————. *The Protestant Ethic and the Spirit of Capitalism.* New York: Scribner, 1958.

————. *The Theory of Social and Economic Organization.* Talcott Parsons, ed. New York: Free Press, 1964.

William, Oliver P., and Charles R. Adrian. *Four Cities.* Philadelphia: Univ. of Pennsylvania Press, 1963.

Wilson, James Q. *A Report on Politics in Los Angeles.* Cambridge, Mass.: Joint Center for Urban Studies of M.I.T. and Harvard University, 1959. (Mimeograph.)

————. *Negro Politics.* New York: Free Press, 1960.

————. *The Amateur Democrat.* Chicago: Univ. of Chicago Press, 1962.

Wolfe, Leon. *Lockout.* New York: Harper & Row, 1965.

Zeigler, Harmond. *Interest Groups in American Society.* Englewood Cliffs, N. J.: Prentice-Hall, 1964.

ARTICLES

Almond, Gabriel. "Introduction: A Functional Approach to Comparative Politics," in Gabriel Almond and James S. Coleman, eds., *The Politics of the Developing Areas.* Princeton: Princeton Univ. Press, 1960.

Anderson, Totton James. "The 1958 Election in California," *Western Political Quarterly,* Vol. XII (March 1959).

Bendix, Reinhard. "The Lower Classes and the 'Democratic Revolution,'" *Industrial Relations,* Vol. I (October 1961).

Bernstein, Irving. "John L. Lewis and the Voting Behavior of the CIO," *Public Opinion Quarterly*, Vol. V (June 1941).

————. "Trade Union Characteristics, Membership, and Influence," *Monthly Labor Review*, Vol. LXXXII (May 1959).

Bone, Hugh A. "Political Parties and Pressure Group Politics," *The Annals of the American Academy of Political and Social Science*, Vol. CCCXIX, (September 1958).

————. "The 1958 Election in Washington," *Western Political Quarterly*, Vol. XII (March 1959).

Bradley, Donald S., and Mayer N. Zald. "From Commercial Elite to Political Administrator: The Recruitment of the Mayors of Chicago," *American Journal of Sociology*, Vol. LXXI (September 19, 1965).

Brandeis, Elizabeth. "Organized Labor and Protective Labor Legislation," in Milton Derber and Edwin Young, eds., *Labor and the New Deal*. Madison: Univ. of Wisconsin Press, 1957.

Braunthal, Alfred. "American Labor in Politics," *Social Research*, Vol. XII (February 1945).

Brown, Seyom. "Southern California's Precarious One-Crop Economy," *The Reporter*, January 7, 1960.

Bunzel, John H., and Eugene C. Lee. "The California Democratic Delegation of 1960," in Edwin A. Bock and Alan K. Campbell, eds., *Case Studies in American Government: The Inter-University Case Program*. Englewood Cliffs, N. J.: Prentice-Hall, 1962.

Burnham, Walter Dean. "The Changing Shape of the American Political Universe," *American Political Science Review*, Vol. LIX (1965),

Clark, Peter B., and James Q. Wilson. "Incentive Systems: A Theory of Organizations," *Administrative Science Quarterly*, Vol. VI (September 1961).

Cutright, Phillips, and Peter H. Rossi. "Grass Roots Politicians and the Vote," *American Sociological Review*, Vol. XXIII (April 1958).

————. "Party Organization in Primary Elections," *American Journal of Sociology*, Vol. XIV (November 1958).

David, Henry. "100 Years of Labor in Politics," in J. B. S. Hardman and Maurice Neufeld, eds., *The House of Labor*. Englewood Cliffs, N. J.: Prentice-Hall, 1951.

Derber, Milton. "Growth and Expansion," in Milton Derber and Edwin Young, eds., *Labor and the New Deal*. Madison: Univ. of Wisconsin Press, 1957.

Edelman, Murray. "Sensitivity to Labor," in Milton Derber and Edwin Young, *Labor and the New Deal*. Madison: Univ. of Wisconsin Press, 1957.

————. "Symbols and Political Quiescence," *American Political Science Review*, Vol. LIV (September 1960).

Fuller, Helen. "Labor and Politics," *The New Republic*, January 1944.

————. "The Man to See in California," *Harper's Magazine,* January 1963.

Greenstone, J. David. "Political Norms and Group Process in Private Government: The Case of a Local Union," *Midwest Journal of Political Science,* Vol. IX (November 1965).

————, and Paul E. Peterson. "Big City Politics and the War on Poverty," in James Q. Wilson, ed., *City Politics and Public Policy.* New York: Wiley, 1968.

Higgins, Father George C. "Union Attitudes Toward Economic and Social Roles of the Modern State," in George Brooks, *et al.,* eds., *Interpreting the Labor Movement.* Madison, Wisc., Industrial Relations Research Association, 1952.

Hoxie, Robert. "President Gompers and the Labor Vote," *Journal of Political Economy,* Vol. XVI (December 1908).

————. "Trade Unionism in the United States," *Journal of Political Economy,* Vol. XX (March 1914).

Hudson, Ruth Alice, and Hajlmar Rosen. "Union Political Action: The Union Member Speaks," *Industrial and Labor Relations Review,* Vol. VII (April 1954).

Huntington, Samuel P. "A Revised Theory of American Politics," *American Political Science Review,* Vol. XLIV (September 1950).

Hutchinson, John. "Labour in Politics in America," *Political Quarterly,* Vol. XXXII (April–June 1962).

Janowitz, Morris, and Dwaine Marvick. "Political Sociology," in *The International Encyclopedia of the Social Sciences.* New York: Macmillan, 1968.

Kampelman, Max M. "Labor in Politics in Industrial Relations Research Association," in *Interpreting the Labor Movement.* Madison, Wisconsin, 1952.

Karsh, Bernard, and Phillip L. Garman. "The Impact of the Political Left," in Milton Derber and Edwin Young, eds., *Labor and the New Deal,* Madison: Univ. of Wisconsin Press, 1957.

Keenan, Joseph. "The AFL-LLPE and How It Works," in J. B. S. Hardman and Maurice Neufeld, eds., *The House of Labor.* New York: Prentice-Hall, 1951.

Kennedy, Van Dusen. "Association Bargaining," *Monthly Labor Review,* Vol. LXXXII (May 1959).

Kent, Frank R. "How the Boss Runs the Organization," in Edward C. Banfield, ed., *Urban Government.* New York: Free Press, 1961.

Key, V. O., Jr. "A Theory of Critical Elections," *Journal of Politics,* Vol. 17 (February 1955).

Key, V. O., Jr., and Frank Munger. "Social Determinism and Electoral Decision: The Case of Indiana," in Eugene Burdick and Arthur J.

Brodbeck, eds., *American Voting Behavior*. New York: Free Press, 1959.

Kovner, J., and H. J. Lahne. "Shop Society and the Union," *Industrial and Labor Relations Review*, Vol. VIII (October 1953).

Kroll, Jack. "The CIO-PAC and How It Works," in J. B. S. Hardman and Maurice Neufeld, eds., *The House of Labor*. Englewood Cliffs, N. J.: Prentice-Hall, 1951.

————. "Labor's Political Role," *The Annals of the American Academy of Political and Social Science*, Vol. CCLXXIV (March 1951).

Lahne, H. J., and Joseph Kovner. "Local Union Structure, Formality and Reality," *Industrial and Labor Relations Review*, Vol. IX (October 1955).

Lee, Eugene C., and William Buchanan. "The 1960 Election in California," *Western Political Quarterly*, Vol. XIV (March 1961).

Leeds, Morton. "The AFL in the 1948 Elections," *Social Research*, Vol. XVII (June 1950).

Leiserson, Avery. "Organized Labor as a Pressure Group," *The Annals of the American Academy of Political and Social Science*, Vol. CCLXXIV (March 1951).

Littell, Robert. "Undercover Men," in Heber Blankenhorn, ed., *Public Opinion and the Steel Strike*. New York: Harcourt, Brace & World, 1921.

Lowi, Theodore J. "American Business, Public Policy, Case Studies and Political Theory," *World Politics*, Vol. XVI (July 1964).

————. "The Public Philosophy: Interest-Group Liberalism," *American Political Science Review*, Vol. LXI (March 1967).

————. "Toward Functionalism in Political Science: The Case of Innovation in Party Systems," *American Political Science Review*, Vol. LVII (September 1963).

Lubell, Samuel. "Post Mortem: Who Elected Roosevelt?" *Saturday Evening Post*, January 25, 1941.

MacRae, Duncan, Jr., and James A. Meldrum. "Critical Elections in Illinois," *American Political Science Review*, Vol. LIV (Sept. 1960).

Martin, Curtis. "The 1958 Election in Colorado," *Western Political Quarterly*, Vol. XII (March 1959).

Marvick, Dwaine, and Charles Nixon. "Recruitment Contrasts in Rival Campaign Groups," in Dwaine Marvick, ed., *Political Decision Makers*. New York: Free Press, 1961.

Masters, Nicholas A. "The Organized Labor Bureaucracy as a Base of Support for the Democratic Party," *Law and Contemporary Problems*, Vol. XXVII (Spring 1962).

————. "The Politics of Union Endorsement of Candidates in the Detroit Area," *Midwest Journal of Political Science*, Vol. I (August 1957).

Miller, Glenn W., and Stephen B. Ware. "Organized Labor in the Political Process: A Case Study of the Right-to-Work Campaign in Ohio," *Labor History*, Vol. IV (Winter 1963).

Neufeld, Maurice. "Unions and Political Activity," in J. B. S. Hardman and Maurice Neufeld, eds., *The House of Labor*. Englewood Cliffs, N. J.: Prentice-Hall, 1951.

Overacker, Louise. "Labor's Political Contributions," *Political Science Quarterly*, Vol. XIV (March 1939).

Pelling, Henry. "Labor in Politics in Chicago," *Political Studies*, Vol. V (February 1957).

Raskin, A. H. "Making Strikes Obsolete." *The Atlantic Monthly*, June 1966.

Rogin, Michael Paul. "Voluntarism: The Political Functions of an Anti-Political Doctrine," *Industrial and Labor Relations Review*, Vol. XV (July 1962).

Rosenfarb, Joseph. "Labor's Role in the Election," *Public Opinion Quarterly*, Vol. VIII (1944).

Rossi, Peter H., and Phillips Cutright. "The Impact of Party Organization in an Industrial Setting," in Morris Janowitz, ed., *Community Political Systems*. New York: Free Press, 1961.

Rovere, Richard. "Labor's Political Machine," *Harper's Magazine*, June 1945.

Sawyer, Jack, and Duncan MacRae, Jr. "Game Theory and Cumulative Voting in Illinois, 1902–1954," *American Political Science Review*, Vol. LVI (December 1962).

Schattschneider, E. E., "The United States: The Functional Approach to Party Government," in Sigmund Neuman, ed., *Modern Political Parties*. Chicago: Univ. of Chicago Press, 1956.

Scoble, Harry M. "Organized Labor in Electoral Politics: Some Questions for the Discipline," *Western Political Quarterly*, Vol. XVI (September 1963).

Seidler, Murray. "The Socialist Party and American Unionism," *Midwest Journal of Political Science*, Vol. V (August 1961).

Seidman, Joel. "Organized Labor in Political Campaigns," *Public Opinion Quarterly*, Vol. III (October 1939).

Seidman, Joel, Jack London, and Bernard Karsh. "Political Consciousness in a Local Union," *Public Opinion Quarterly*, Vol. XV (Winter 1951).

Sheppard, Harold L., and Nicholas A. Masters. "The Political Attitudes and Preferences of Union Members: The Case of the Detroit Auto Workers," *American Political Science Review*, Vol. LIII (June 1959).

Smith, C. O., and S. B. Sarasohn. "Hate Propaganda in Detroit," *Public Opinion Quarterly*, Vol. X (Spring 1946).

Snowiss, Leo M., "Congressional Recruitment and Representation," in *American Political Science Review*, Vol. LX (September 1966).

Strauss, George. "The Shifting Power Balance in the Plant," *Industrial Relations*, Vol. I (May 1962).

Taft, Philip. "Labor's Changing Political Line," *Journal of Political Economy*, Vol. XLV (October 1937).

Velie, Lester. "The Secret Boss of California," *Colliers*, August 13, 1949 and August 20, 1949.

Wartenberg, George. "Political Action in a Congressional District," in J. B. S. Hardman and Maurice Neufeld, eds., *The House of Labor*. Englewood Cliffs, N. J.: Prentice-Hall, 1951.

Wilensky, Harold L. "The Labor Vote: A Union's Impact on the Political Conduct of Its Members," *Social Forces*, Vol. XXXV (December 1956).

———. "Mass Society and Mass Culture," in Bernard Berelson and Morris Janowitz, eds., *Reader in Public Opinion and Communication*. New York: Free Press, 1966.

Wisehart, M. K. "The Pittsburgh Newspapers and the Strike," in Heber Blankenhorn, ed., *Public Opinion and the Steel Strike*. New York: Harcourt, Brace & World, 1921.

Witte, Edwin E. "Organized Labor and Social Security," in Milton Derber and Edwin Young, eds., *Labor and the New Deal*. Madison: Univ. of Wisconsin Press, 1957.

Zon, Henry. "Political Education in Labor Unions," *Journal of Social Issues*, Vol. XVI (1960).

Zon, Mary Goddard. "Labor in Politics," *Law and Contemporary Problems*, Vol. XXVII (Spring 1962).

UNPUBLISHED MATERIAL

Baisden, Richard. *Labor Unions in Los Angeles Politics*. Ph.D. dissertation, University of Chicago, 1958.

Goodman, T. Wilbain. *The Presidential Campaign of 1920*. Ph.D. dissertation, Ohio University, 1951.

Harris, Avril E. *Organized Labor in Party Politics, 1906–32*. Ph.D. dissertation, University of Iowa, 1937.

Jeffry, Alon. *Electoral Reorientation in New Hampshire, 1916–1964*. M.A. thesis, University of Chicago, 1966.

Kreps, Juanita M. *Developments in the Political and Legislative Policies of Organized Labor: 1920–1947*. Ph.D. dissertation. Duke University, 1947.

Marx, Sue A. *1952 Election Study: Republican Voters in the UAW Membership*. M.S. thesis, Wayne State University, 1956.

McCoy, David. *Patronage in Suburbia.* Ph.D. dissertation, University of Chicago, 1963.

Rogin, Michael Paul. *McCarthyism and Agrarian Radicalism.* Ph.D. dissertation, University of Chicago, 1962.

LABOR PERIODICALS

The following labor periodicals were of continuing interest for the periods given:

The American Federationist, 1906–1912

Detroit Labor News, 1950–1962

Federation News, 1950–1962

Los Angeles Citizen, 1950–1962

Michigan AFL-CIO News, 1950–1962

Index

A NOTE ON THE TYPE

The text of this book was set on the Linotype in a face called TIMES ROMAN, designed by Stanley Morison for The Times (London), and first introduced by that newspaper in 1932.

Among typographers and designers of the twentieth century, Stanley Morison has been a strong forming influence, as typographical advisor to the English Monotype Corporation, as a director of two distinguished English publishing houses, and as a writer of sensibility, erudition, and keen practical sense. Composed, printed, and bound by the Haddon Craftsmen, Inc., Scranton, Pa.